The Marketing Plan

Fifth Edition

William A. Cohen, Ph.D.
Touro University International
Cypress, California

WILEY

John Wiley & Sons, Inc.

ASSOCIATE PUBLISHER	Judith Joseph
SENIOR ACQUISITIONS EDITOR	Jayme Heffler
MARKETING MANAGER	Frank Lyman
SENIOR PRODUCTION EDITOR	William A. Murray
SENIOR EDITORIAL ASSISTANT	Ame Esterline
SENIOR DESIGNER	Maddy Lesure
SENIOR ILLUSTRATION EDITOR	Sandra Rigby
COVER IMAGE	©PhotoDisc/Getty Images

This book was set in Times Roman by Matrix Publishing and printed and bound by Malloy Lithographing. The cover was printed by Phoenix Color.

This book is printed on acid-free paper.∞

To order books or for customer service please, call 1-800-CALL WILEY (225-5945).

ISBN-13 978-0-471-75529-6
ISBN-10 0-471-75529-X

Printed in the United States of America

10 9 8 7 6 5 4 3 2 1

Preface

Some have called this the era of marketing. Major articles not only in *Business Week*, but also in *Time, Newsweek,* and other popular magazines attest to this fact. Every organization needs marketing in order to be successful, and the key to marketing is the marketing plan. Even on a personal level, high-performance experts tell us we must have a plan to be successful. A good marketing plan is the difference between dreams and ideas and organized, tough-minded, financially accurate, bottom-line success.

Sometime after I incorporated marketing plans into the marketing course that I was teaching, a former student, Robert Schwartz, stopped by to tell me that he was interviewed for an article in *Entrepreneur Magazine*.[1] Robert had started a chain of pizza restaurants. His business was based on a marketing plan he developed in my class. His cash flow was an amazing $48,000 per month. Robert was an undergraduate student. Leon Abjian, a graduate student I taught, sold his marketing plan for $5,000.

A professional consultant had occasion to examine some of the plans prepared by my students. His verdict? The plans were the equivalent of those prepared by himself and other professionals. In his opinion, they were worth $25,000 each! Yet they all were developed by undergraduate and graduate students. Based on this assessment, several former students have gone into the business of preparing marketing plans for businesspeople; some have used their marketing plans to get the funds to start their own businesses; others have used them in corporations where they were employed.

More than 20 years ago, I began to supervise marketing plans done for real businesses. Many were done under contract, and the businesses paid the university for the business plans the students developed. And why not? They were 100 percent professional, and were extremely valuable to the businesses that paid for their development. Yet, the businesses paid only a small fraction of the $25,000 that one professional consultant estimated they were worth.

The aim of this book is to give you the knowledge to be able to develop truly outstanding, professional marketing plans. Along with your professor's guidance, this book will explain marketing planning and give you step-by-step procedures to produce a professional plan. It also provides forms that can greatly assist you in your efforts. Actual student plans prepared in the classroom are included. You will see how students adapted the basic ideas in this book and translated them into marketing plans for particular products or services. When you complete the book, you will not only know what to do, but also how and why. You will be able to develop an excellent and professional marketing plan.

Developing a marketing plan is not theoretical. It requires you to work hard, use your imagination, and integrate your knowledge of marketing with other disciplines such as accounting, finance, and management. It is worth the time and effort required. The method described in this book for producing a marketing plan has been action-tested in the classroom and in the real world by thousands of marketing students and professionals. If you work at it steadily over the time allocated, not only will you be successful, you will have a lot of fun doing it. It works!

William A. Cohen, Ph.D.
Touro University International

---

[1] "Entrepreneurship on Campus, A Panel Discussion on Teaching Entrepreneurship," *Entrepreneur*, (November 1984), p. 49.

Acknowledgments

I want to acknowledge and thank the students who contributed sample marketing plans for this edition, as well as the hundreds of others who helped teach me to teach others while developing marketing plans in my classes.

About the Author

Dr. William A. Cohen is Professor of Business Administration, Touro University International, and past Chairman of the Marketing Department and Director of the Small Business Institute at California State University, Los Angeles. He has also taught at the University of Southern California and the Peter Drucker School of Management at Claremont Graduate University and was President of California American University.

Among his 52 books translated into 17 languages are *Winning on the Marketing Front, The Entrepreneur and Small Business Marketing Problem Solver 3rd ed., Building a Mail Order Business, How to Make It Big as a Consultant,* and *The New Art of the Leader.* When in print, his marketing textbook, *The Practice of Marketing Management,* was adopted by more than 177 universities. His books have been recommended by Mary Kay Ash; Barry Goldwater; Peter F. Drucker; Jagdeth Sheth; former Secretary of State Alexander Haig; Astronaut Frank Borman; General H. Norman Schwarzkopf; Barry Gordon, longest serving president of the Screen Actors Guild; numerous CEOs of major corporations; and marketing professors all over the world.

Professor Cohen has been a consultant to the U.S. government and Fortune 500 companies, as well as to numerous small businesses. He was series editor for the John Wiley Series on Business Strategy and has served on numerous boards of directors, government commissions, and editorial advisory boards. He has also served as spokesperson for AT&T, given more than one hundred TV, radio, and print interviews, and made hundreds of speeches. He has been quoted or reviewed in *Harvard Business Review, USA Today, Business Week, Fortune, Success, Changing Times, Venture, Chicago Tribune, The Los Angeles Times, The Encyclopedia Britannica,* and many other publications.

Professor Cohen received the Outstanding Professor's Award at California State University, Los Angeles, and the Freedoms Foundation at Valley Forge Honor Medal for Excellence in Economic Education. In 1996, he was named CSULA Statewide Professor, the first business professor from his university to be given this award. In 1999, the Academy of Marketing Science named him one of four "Great Teachers in Marketing." Professor Cohen has also received numerous awards for excellence in directing consulting activities from the U.S. Small Business Administration and has supervised the preparation of more than 1,000 student marketing plans which have won major awards in student competitions and have been successfully implemented by their authors. In 2002 he received an Honorary Doctorate in Humane Letters from the International Academy for Integration of Science and Business in Moscow, Russia.

Professor Cohen has a B.S. from the United States Military Academy at West Point, an M.B.A. from the University of Chicago, and an M.A. and Ph.D. in management from Claremont Graduate University. He is also a distinguished graduate of the Industrial College of the Armed Forces, National Defense University, and a retired major general in the U.S. Air Force Reserve.

Contents

CHAPTER 5
STEP 5: DEVELOPING MARKETING TACTICS /54

CHAPTER 6
STEP 6: FORECASTING FOR YOUR MARKETING PLAN /72

CHAPTER 7
STEP 7: CALCULATING IMPORTANT FINANCIAL RATIOS
FOR YOUR MARKETING PLAN /86

CHAPTER 8
STEP 8: PRESENTING THE MARKETING PLAN   /96

CHAPTER 9
STEP 9: IMPLEMENTATION   /107

APPENDIX A
SAMPLE MARKETING PLANS   /109

APPENDIX B
SOURCES OF SECONDARY RESEARCH   /269

APPENDIX C
EXAMPLES OF SIMPLE RESEARCH AND A MARKETING RESEARCH CHECKLIST   /288

Prologue

THE POWER AND MYSTIQUE OF THE MARKETING PLAN

Not long ago, a candidate for president of the United States was presented with a campaign plan developed by his staff. The plan helped get him elected. Meanwhile, two Harvard Business School students, Mike Wigley and Jerry De La Vega, planned how to promote audio recordings. Their idea was to enable people to order any recording they wanted—right from their homes. Twelve months later they started their company. David Ishag, another Harvard classmate, joined them. The three entrepreneurs advertised on a cable television network that aired rock 'n' roll videos twenty-four hours a day. They called their company Hot Rock, Inc. Hot Rock received 50,000 inquiries in the first seventeen days. Sales grew 10 to 14 percent a month. They expected sales of $6.7 million for the first year. Yet this was no surprise.

In another part of the country, Stouffers Lean Cuisine, a line of frozen food, suddenly boosted its market share by more than 30 percent in the $500 million frozen-entree food market. This caught the industry by surprise ... but not those at Stouffers.

The Clorox Company had reached $1 billion in sales but profits were unimpressive. Shortly after that, half of the $1 billion revenue disappeared when a key division was sold. Yet only six years later Clorox again hit $1 billion in sales. Moreover, this time profits were double ... and Clorox had predicted and fully expected these figures. Glenn R. Savage, Clorox's marketing director, noted: "There's power in giving people very clear objectives."[1]

Gordon Bethune is CEO of Continental Airlines, one of the largest U.S. airlines. In 1994, it was bankrupt. Then Bethune took over. Since then it has become one of America's most admired corporations, winning numerous prestigious awards.[2] A few of these are Best Transatlantic Airline; Top International Airline—*National Airline Quality Rating Study;* No. 1 in Customer Satisfaction by J. D. Power and Associates; No. 1 in On Time Performance by the U.S. Department of Transportation; and a listing in *Fortune* magazine's top 100 U.S. companies to work for. Before the September 11, 2001, attacks it made the highest profits in its history. Since 9/11 it has steadily moved toward profitability, continuing to win award after award, despite an industrywide recession that caused the demise of competitors.[3]

What do these four vastly different types of companies in totally different industries have in common other than their success? The answer is the marketing plan. In each case, a marketing plan played a major role in enabling the company to reach its goals and the success it planned. This surprised everyone else but not those who did it. They had a marketing plan.

THE MARKETING PLAN IS ESSENTIAL FOR EVERY BUSINESS OPERATION

A marketing plan is essential for every business operation and for efficient and effective marketing of any product or service. This is true for a brand-new business and even for marketing a product, service, or product line within a company. Seeking success for any project without the use of a marketing plan is like trying to navigate a ship in stormy weather, through rough waters, under torpedo attack, and with neither a compass nor a clear idea of where you are going. It does require time to develop a marketing plan. But this is time well spent. It will save you time overall. The marketing plan will allow you to visualize clearly both where you are going and what you want to accomplish along the way. At the same time, a marketing plan details the important steps required to get you from where you are to where you want to be. An added benefit is that in compiling and developing the marketing plan, you will have thought through how long it will take to accomplish each step and what resources in money, time, and effort you will need. Without a marketing plan, you will not even know when or whether you have reached your objectives.

WHAT A MARKETING PLAN WILL DO FOR YOU

A properly developed marketing plan can accomplish a lot for a relatively small amount of focused effort. A marketing plan will:

- Act as a road map.
- Assist in management control and implementation of strategy.
- Inform new participants of their roles in implementing the plan and reaching your objectives.
- Assist in helping to obtain resources for implementation.
- Stimulate thinking and the better use of limited resources.
- Help in the organization and assignment of responsibilities, tasks, and timing.
- Help you become aware of problems, opportunities, and threats in the future.

Let's look at each of these benefits in turn.

The Marketing Plan Acts as a Road Map

Perhaps the basic purpose of the marketing plan is to act as a road map and tell you how to get from the beginning of the plan to reach your objectives and goals. Like a road map, the plan describes the environment in which you are likely to find yourself along the way. A road map might describe the geographical terrain as well as the type and classification of the various road arteries, times, distances, and available stops for emergencies, gasoline, food, repairs, and lodging. In the same fashion, the marketing plan will describe the environment of the marketplace, including your competitors, politics, laws, regulations, economic and business conditions, state of technology, forecast demand, social and cultural factors, and demographics of the target market, as well as your company's available resources.

The Marketing Plan Assists with Management Control and Implementation of Strategy

If you're on a trip, your strategy is the route that you plan to take. Your road map shows the route along with the expected physical and geographical environment. As you proceed, various problems may interfere with your planned strategy. You may need to detour because of unplanned circumstances. Perhaps road maintenance or severe weather makes the most direct route or the planned route impossible to use. In fact, it is virtually certain that almost nothing will go exactly as originally planned. Yet, because your environmental road map anticipates changes that may require detours, you can continue toward your destination with ease. In the same way, the marketing plan will allow you to spot alternative paths and redirect your activities toward them in order to arrive at your objective with minimum difficulty. You will be able to see clearly the difference between what is happening during the implementation of your strategy and what you had planned to happen. This will give you control of the situation and allow you to take the corrective action necessary to put your project back on track and to keep it on track to reach your final objective.

The Marketing Plan Informs New Participants of Their Roles and Functions

Successful implementation of a strategy requires integration of many actions, usually by many people and departments both inside and outside the organization. Timing is frequently critical. And it is most important that all concerned individuals understand what their responsibilities are as well as how their tasks or actions fit into the overall strategy. Having a marketing plan enables you to describe "the big picture" in detail. It allows everyone to see how their actions fit in with the actions of others. New people may be assigned to activities involving your plan. They, too, can be brought immediately up to date regarding their responsibilities, what they must do, and how to adapt to the work of others. Thus, the marketing plan can be used to inform all participants of your objectives and how and why these objectives will be done: by whom, with what, and when.

The Marketing Plan Plots the Acquisition of Resources for Implementation

You will find that your resources to accomplish any project are far from unlimited. Resources are always limited. This is true whether you are an individual entrepreneur attempting to obtain money from a potential investor or you are working in a large corporation and seeking resources for your project within the firm. A marketing plan plays an important part in persuading those who have the authority to allocate limited resources— money, people, and other assets—to your project. And with resources scarce, you must convince these individuals that you are going to use capital, goods, and labor in the most effective and efficient manner. You must not only persuade them that your objectives are achievable, but also that, despite competition and other potential threats, you will ultimately reach your goals. So, your marketing plan is also a sales tool. Even more, the marketing plan helps prove your control over the project from start to finish. It shows not only that you can see the final objective, but also that you know what you must do at every point along the way. This includes actions, costs, and alternatives. When you master the project on paper, you're already halfway there. Those who have the resources you need will be more likely to see the potential and give them to you.

The Marketing Plan Stimulates Thinking and Makes Better Use of Resources

Since no matter what, your resources will be limited, you must get the maximum results from what you have. A good marketing plan will help you make the most of what you have … to make one dollar do the work of ten. It will help you build on your strengths and minimize your weaknesses. It will also help you obtain a differential advantage over your competition. You can always do this by economizing where it doesn't count and by concentrating superior resources where it does. This leads to success. As you do the research for your marketing plan and analyze your strategic alternatives, your thinking will be stimulated. As the plan unfolds, you will modify it as new ideas are generated. Eventually you will reach the optimum: a well-organized, well-integrated plan that will make efficient use of the resources available and will help you anticipate most opportunities that can help or obstacles that can hinder your progress.

The Marketing Plan Assigns Responsibilities, Tasks, and Timing

No strategy will ever be better than those who implement it. Therefore timing and the assignment of responsibilities are crucial. A marketing plan clearly outlines these responsibilities so there is no question where they lie. You also want to schedule all activities to maximize the impact of your strategy while taking full advantage of the environment that is expected to exist at the time of its execution. Hard thinking during development will preclude suboptimization. Suboptimization occurs when one small element of the plan is optimized to the detriment of the overall project. Let's say that you are working on a marketing plan for a new personal computer. If the technical details alone are optimized, you may put the bulk of the funds on product development. This allocation may allow you to develop the best computer on the market but give you insufficient funds to promote it. You may have a far superior product, but you will sell only a few because most customers won't know about it. Because of suboptimization, the product will fail. A less grandiose technical solution might have satisfied the market and been better than that of your competition at a lower development cost. Funds would then be available to promote it properly.

A good marketing plan will ensure that every task will be assigned to someone in the correct sequence, and that all elements and strategies will be coordinated synergistically to maximize their effect and ensure the completion of the project with the resources available. Is this important? Consider Zegna, an 85-year-old Italian company that sell men's suits for $1,000 and up. In a recent year, U.S. sales were $100 million, up 30 percent over the previous year. In Europe, Zegna's sales were $500 million. That made the company one of Europe's fastest growing fashion groups. With Zegna, avoiding subobtimization is a major challenge. There are plenty of opportunities to err. Unlike its competitors, Zegna not only puts together its own clothes, but also spins the yarn. Zegna weaves the cotton, cashmere, and wool fabrics, everything that goes into its expensive garments. Not only that, Zegna has its own retail outlets.[4] By the end of 2002, Zegna had 379 retail stores worldwide and more than 400 at year-end 2003 at new locations in Hong Kong, St. Petersburg, Portofino, Warsaw, Bangkok, Seoul, Shenzen, Hangkhou, and Chendu—in sixty-four countries in all. According to experts, Zegna is clobbering its competition.[5]

The Marketing Plan Predicts Problems, Opportunities, and Threats
You may intuitively recognize some of the problems, opportunities, and threats that can occur as you work toward your objectives. Your marketing plan not only will document those of which you are already aware, but also will help you identify others that you couldn't see until you started working on your plan. It will enable you to think strategically and to consider what must be done about opportunities, problems, and threats that lie in the future. The more analysis and thinking you do as you plan, the more pitfalls you will see. That's not necessarily bad. Better to note them on paper before you get started than later, when it's too late. These potential problems must never be ignored. Instead, construct your marketing plan to take maximum advantage of the opportunities, think up solutions to the problems you find, and consider how to avoid the threats.

Getting in a Competitive Position Before You Start   With a marketing plan
you will be ahead of your competition even before you begin to execute your plan. You will have systematically thought it through from start to finish. You will already know where the future may lead. On paper, you will have coordinated all efforts to attain a specific objective. You will have developed performance standards for controlling objectives and goals, and you will have sharpened your strategy and tactics to a much greater extent than would otherwise have been possible. You will be much better prepared than any of your competitors for sudden developments. You will have anticipated those that are potential problems and will know what to do when they occur. Finally, more than any competitor, you will have a vivid sense of what is going to happen and how to make it happen. Your competitors are going to react, but you will have already acted in anticipation.

Types of Marketing Plans

Marketing plans tend to fall into a number of categories for different purposes. The two basic types are the new product and annual marketing plans.

The New Product Plan   The new product plan is prepared for a product, service product line, or brand that has not yet been introduced by the firm. It is smart to develop a complete new product plan even before you start the project. Granted the information at this stage may be sketchy, but it is still far better to start your thinking as early as possible before any major resources have been committed. In this way alternatives can be compared and analyzed. Moreover, you will have a general idea of the overall costs and timing of competitive projects. Naturally the marketing plan for a new product will have many more unknowns than the annual marketing plan. This is because the product will have little or no feedback from the marketplace and no track record with your firm. This last point is an important one to consider. It is not unusual for products that have achieved successful sales performance with one firm to fall far short of these goals in another. This is frequently due to certain strengths of the first firm that the second firm cannot duplicate and may not even know about. With a new product plan it is sometimes necessary to make assumptions based on similar products or services that the company has marketed or that have been introduced by other companies. But don't forget: if you use information based on other companies' experiences, you must assess your ability to duplicate their performance. Other sources of information may be necessary if you intend to modify data from other companies' experiences. This will be discussed later in this book. A marketing plan for a new product or service may also include development of the product from scratch. Of course, if the product already exists, its technical development as a part of your plan is not needed.

Annual Marketing Plans   Annual marketing plans are for those products, services, and brands that are already in your company's product line. Periodically, preferably once a year, this planning must be formally reviewed. Of course, the plan may be adjusted and modified in the interim as changes occur in the environment or in the company. But the review and annual creation of a new marketing plan for the coming year may help identify emerging problems, opportunities, and threats that may be missed during day-to-day operations and the "fire fighting" associated with the management of an ongoing product or service. Again, however, notice that the plan is for the future; it's how you will get from your present position to some other position. Therefore, there will still be unknowns, for which information must be forecast, researched, or, in some cases, assumed. Although annual marketing plans are usually prepared for only one year, it is of course possible to plan for several years and to modify the plan annually. On the other hand, product plans generally cover the entire life of the project, from initiation to its establishment in the marketplace. Establishment in the marketplace implies that the product is beyond the introductory stage and is growing, one hopes, at a predicted rate.

SUMMARY

In this section, we have discussed the importance of the marketing plan in satisfying objectives in the most efficient manner possible. We have noted the main benefits of a marketing plan:

*   Acting as a road map.
*   Assisting in management control and implementing strategy.
*   Informing new participants in the plan of their roles and functions.
*   Obtaining resources for implementation.
*   Stimulating thinking and making better use of resources.

- Assigning responsibilities and tasks and setting time limits.
- Being aware of problems, opportunities, and threats.

Knowledge of the preparation of a marketing plan is not the option of a successful manager of marketing activities. It is a requirement. But beyond that, it is an effective and valuable tool that will enable you to work daily to accomplish your objectives for the particular project that you are going to market.

NOTES

1. Joan O. C. Hamilton, "Brighter Days at Clorox," *Business Week* (June 16, 1997), p. 62.

2. Sheila M. Puffer, interview with Gordon Bethune, "Continental Airlines' CEO Gordon Bethune on Teams and New Product Development," *The Academy of Management Executive* (August 1999), pp. 28, 32.

3. Continental Web site, http://www.continental.com, accessed November 11, 2003.

4. John Rossant, "Is That a Zegna You're Wearing?" *Business Week* (March 4, 1996), pp. 84–85.

5. Zegna Web site, http://www.zegna.com/website.htm?selez=0&crc=, accessed February 4, 2004.

CHAPTER 1

STEP 1

PLANNING THE DEVELOPMENT OF A MARKETING PLAN

A good marketing plan needs a great deal of information gathered from many sources. It is used to develop marketing strategy and tactics to reach a specific set of objectives and goals. The process is not necessarily difficult, but it does require organization. This is especially true if you are not developing this plan by yourself and are depending on others to assist you or to accomplish parts of the plan. This is frequently the case both in the classroom and in the business world. Therefore, it is important before you start to "plan for planning." The time spent will pay dividends later. You will get back more than the time you invest up front.

To prepare for planning, you must look first at the total job you are going to do and then organize the work so that everything is done in an efficient manner and nothing is left out. If you do this correctly, every element of your plan will come together in a timely fashion. This means that you won't be completing any task too early and then waiting for some other task to be finished before you can continue. It also means that no member of your planning team will be overworked or underworked. To accomplish this, you must consider the structure of the marketing plan and all of its elements. Next you must organize your major planning tasks by using a marketing plan action-development schedule. This will give an overview of the entire marketing planning process, including who is going to do what and when each task is scheduled for completion. Managing the process is also important. You'll find some help with that in Appendix D, How to Lead a Team.

THE STRUCTURE OF THE MARKETING PLAN

Every marketing plan should have a planned structure or outline before you start. This ensures that no important information is left out and that everything is presented in a logical manner. One outline I recommend is shown in the marketing plan outline in Figure 1-1. However, there are other ways to organize a marketing plan that are at least as good. You may be required to use a specific outline. Or you may be able to use any outline you'd like. What outline you use is unimportant at this point. What is important is that your plan be presented in a logical way with nothing omitted. So, whether you are given a specific outline to follow or are allowed to develop your own, keep these two goals in mind.

Let's examine each section of this marketing plan structure in Figure 1-1 in more detail. You will find many sections common to all marketing plans.

TABLE OF CONTENTS

Executive Summary (overview of entire plan, including a description of the product or service, the differential advantage, the required investment, and anticipated sales and profits).

I.   Introduction
     What is the product or service? Describe it in detail and explain how it fits into the market.

II. Situational Analysis
     A. The Situational Environs
        1. Demand and demand trends. (What is the forecast demand for the product: Is it growing or declining? Who is the decision maker? The purchase agent? How, when, where, what, and why do they buy?)
        2. Social and cultural factors.
        3. Demographics.
        4. Economic and business conditions for this product at this time and in the geographical area selected.
        5. State of technology for this class of product. Is it high-tech state-of-the-art? Are newer products succeeding older ones frequently (short life cycle)? In short, how is technology affecting this product or service?
        6. Politics. Are politics (current or otherwise) in any way affecting the situation for marketing this product?
        7. Laws and regulations. (What laws or regulations are applicable here?)
     B. The Neutral Environs
        1. Financial environment. (How does the availability or unavailability of funds affect the situation?)
        2. Government environment. (Is current legislative action in state, federal, or local government likely to affect marketing of this product or service?)
        3. Media environment. (What's happening in the media? Does current publicity favor this project?)
        4. Special interest environment. (Aside from direct competitors, are any influential groups likely to affect your plans?)
     C. The Competitor Environs
        1. Describe your main competitors, their products, plans, experience, know-how, financial, human, and capital resources, suppliers, and strategy. Do they enjoy favor with their customers? If so, why? What marketing channels do the competitors use? What are their strengths and weaknesses?
     D. The Company Environs
        1. Describe your products, experience, know-how, financial, human, and capital resources, and suppliers. Do you enjoy the favor of your customers? If so, why? What are your strengths and weaknesses?

III. The Target Market
     Describe your target market segment in detail by using demographics, psychographics, geography, lifestyle, or whatever segmentation is appropriate. Why is this your target market? How large is it?

IV. Problems and Opportunities
     State or restate each opportunity and indicate why it is, in fact, an opportunity.
     State or restate every problem. Indicate what you intend to do about each of them. Clearly state the competitive differential advantage.

V.   Marketing Objectives and Goals
     State precisely the marketing objectives and goals in terms of sales volume, market share, return on investment, or other objectives or goals for your marketing plan and the time needed to achieve each of them.

VI. Marketing Strategy
     Consider alternatives for the overall strategy; for example, for new market penetration a marketer can enter first, early, or late, penetrate vertically or horizontally, and exploit different niche strategies.
     If the marketing strategy is at the grand strategy or strategic marketing management level, a market attractiveness/business capability matrix and product life cycle analysis should also be constructed.

VII. Marketing Tactics*
     State how you will implement the marketing strategy(s) chosen in terms of the product, price, promotion, distribution, and other tactical or environmental variables.

VIII. Implementation and Control
     Calculate the breakeven point and make a breakeven chart for your project. Compute sales projections and cash flows on a monthly basis for a three-year period. Determine start-up costs and a monthly budget, along with the required tasks.

IX. Summary
     Summarize advantages, costs, and profits and restate the differential advantage that your plan offers over the competition and why the plan will succeed.

X.   Appendices
     Include all supporting information that you consider relevant.

* Note under the marketing strategy and tactics sections how your main competitors are likely to respond when you take the action planned and what you will then do to avoid the threats and take advantage of the opportunities.

FIGURE 1-1.   Marketing Plan Outline

THE EXECUTIVE SUMMARY

The first part of the marketing plan structure or outline is the executive summary. It is a synopsis or abstract of the entire plan. It includes a description of the product or service, the differential advantage of your product or service over that of your competitors, the investment needed, and the results you anticipate. These can be expressed as a return on investment, sales, profits, market share, or in other ways.

The executive summary is especially important if your marketing plan is going to be used to help you to obtain the resources for implementation. Corporate executives are busy. There may well be more than just your marketing plan on which they must make funding decisions. Sometimes several competing marketing plans are submitted simultaneously, and only one is given the green light to proceed. If you submit your marketing plan to a venture capitalist, there will be many competing plans. A venture capitalist receives hundreds of plans every year, yet funds only a few. Therefore, it is hard to overestimate the importance of your executive overview.

The executive summary is a summary of the entire plan. It may be as long as a single paragraph to a few pages in length. From it a busy executive can get a quick idea whether to spend time on the project without reading the entire plan. Therefore, no matter how good the main body of your plan, your executive summary must be well thought out and succinct. It must demonstrate that you know what you're talking about and that your proposal has potential and a reasonable likelihood of success. If not, the executive judging your plan will probably read no further.

Usually the executive summary is one of the last elements to be prepared. This is because it is impossible to summarize accurately until you complete every other part. But even though you save it for last, remember that it will come at the beginning of the plan's documentation and must persuade the reader to read further.

THE TABLE OF CONTENTS

A table of contents sounds rather mundane and you may feel that it is unnecessary. You might be especially inclined to discard the idea if your marketing plan is short. But, let me tell you, a table of contents is absolutely necessary. It makes no difference whether your marketing plan is only a few pages or a hundred pages in length. It is required, never optional, because of a psychological factor that affects those who will evaluate your marketing plan for approval or disapproval.

If you are using your plan to acquire money or other resources to implement your project, the table of contents is important because many individuals from many functional disciplines will be sitting on the review board. Some may be experts in the technical area; they will be interested primarily in the technical details of your product or service. Others will be financial experts; they will want to examine your breakeven analysis, the financial ratios you have calculated, and other financial information. In fact, every expert tends to look first at his or her own area. Now, if you submit a table of contents, this will be fairly easy to do. The reader will scan the list of subjects and turn in a few seconds to the correct page. But if you fail in this regard, the evaluator of your plan will have to search for the information. If you are lucky, he or she will be able to find it anyway. Unfortunately, you won't always be lucky. When many plans must be reviewed, the evaluator may spend only a few minutes or even a few seconds in the search. That's where the psychological factor comes in. If the information can't be found easily, the evaluator may assume it's not there. This not only raises questions of what you don't know, but it may also give the competitive edge to a marketing plan done by someone else who made the information easier to find.

The need for a table of contents is especially critical when your plan is being submitted to venture capitalists. Venture capitalists put up large sums of money to businesses that already have a track record and have a marketing plan for future growth.

By the way, you may have heard that venture capitalists look only at business plans. Marketing and business plans are identical, especially in smaller companies and with start-ups and new products. When you are trying to obtain resources from a venture capitalist, or any investor, the two plans are synonymous. Either the business plan must have a heavy marketing emphasis or the marketing plan must include complete financial, manufacturing, and technical data.

Typically, funds are available for investment in less than 1 percent of the plans that are submitted. One venture capitalist I know said that he receives more than 1,000 marketing plans every month, each of which contains a minimum of thirty pages. Some exceed one hundred pages. Under the circumstances, do you think that anyone could actually go over all of these plans in great detail? Of course not. Accordingly, this venture capitalist looks first at the executive summary, and, if it appears to be interesting, spot-checks the plan using the table of contents for items of particular interest. If he can't find the information he wants after a few seconds' search, he discards the plan. With so many plans to look at, he just doesn't have the time. In this initial screening most of the plans are dropped, leaving only a few for a more detailed reading and a final decision. So don't forget this mundane tool, and be certain that the contents table is an accurate list of all the important topics in your marketing plan.

INTRODUCTION

The introduction is the explanation of the details of your project. Unlike the executive summary, it is not an overview of the project. Its purpose is to give the background of the project and to describe your product or service so that any reader will understand exactly what it is you are proposing. The introduction can be a fairly large section. After reading it the evaluator should understand what the product or service is and what you propose to do with it.

SITUATIONAL ANALYSIS

The situational analysis contains a vast amount of information and, as the term indicates, analyzes the situation that you are facing with the proposed product or service. The situational analysis comes from taking a good hard look at your environment. Many marketing experts refer to the process as *environmental scanning.*

I like to approach the situational analysis by dividing the analysis into four categories. I call them the *environs of the marketplace.* The four categories are situational environs, neutral environs, competitor environs, and company environs. Let's look at each in turn.

Situational Environs

Situational environs include demand and demand trends for your product or service. Is this demand growing, is it declining, or has it leveled off? Are there certain groups in which the demand is growing and others in which demand is declining? Who are the decision makers regarding purchase of the product, and who are the purchase agents? Sometimes the decision maker and purchase agent are the same, but often they are not. For example, one member of a family may be the decision maker with regard to purchasing a certain product, say a brand of beer. But the individual who actually makes the purchase may be another family member. Who influences this decision? How, when, where, what, and why do these potential customers purchase? What are the social and cultural factors? Are demographics of consumers important? Then, maybe you need to discuss educational backgrounds, income, age and similar factors. What are the economic conditions during the period covered by the marketing plan? Is business good or is it bad? High demand can occur in both a good or bad business climate depending on the product or service offered. What is the state of technology for this class of product? Is your product high-tech state of the art? Are newer products frequently succeeding older ones, thus indicating a shorter product life cycle? In sum, how does technology affect the product or service and the marketing for this product or service? Are politics, current or otherwise, in any way affecting the marketing of this product? What potential dangers or threats do the politics in the situation portend? Or do the politics provide opportunities? What laws or regulations are relevant to the marketing of this product or service?

Neutral Environs

Neutral environs have to do with groups or organizations. Does government influence this project? Is legislation on the state, federal, or local level likely to affect the demand or marketing of the product or service? What's happening in the media? Does current publicity favor your project, or does it make any difference? Look at special interest groups. Might they have some impact? Are any influential groups (e.g., consumer organizations) likely to affect your plans for marketing this product or service?

Competitor Environs

Competitor environs are those competing against you. They are important because they are the only elements of the environment that will intentionally act against your interests. In this section of the situational analysis, describe in detail your main competitors, the products they offer, their plans, experience, know-how, financial, human and capital resources, and suppliers. Most important, discuss their current and future strategies. Note whether your competitors enjoy favor with their customers or not, and why. Describe and analyze your competitors' strengths and weaknesses, what marketing channels they use, and anything else that you feel is relevant to the marketing situation as it will exist when you implement your project.

Company Environs

Company environs describe your situation in your company or company-to-be and the resources that you have available. Describe your current products, experience, and know-how, financial, human, and capital resources, suppliers, and other factors as you did environs. Do you enjoy favor with your customers or potential customers and why? Summarize your strengths and weaknesses as they apply to your project. In many respects this section talks about the same items as the competitor environs section.

THE TARGET MARKET

The target market is the next major section in your plan. Describe exactly who your customers are and what, where, when, why, how, how much, and how frequently they buy.

You may think that everyone is a candidate for your product or your service. In a sense this may be true, but some segments of the total market are far more likely candidates than others. If you attempt to serve every single potential customer segment, you cannot satisfy those that are most likely to buy as well as you should. Furthermore, you will dissipate your resources by trying to reach them all. If you pick the most likely target market, or markets, you can devote the maximum amount of money to advertising your product or service in a message that your most likely customers can best understand.

Remember, the basic concept of strategy is to concentrate your scarce resources at the decisive points. Your target markets represent one application of this concept. You usually cannot be strong everywhere. You must be strong where it counts, in this case the markets you target.

You should also indicate why the target market you have selected is a better candidate for purchase than others. Of course, you will include the size of each market.

How will you define your target markets? First, in terms of (1) demographics (i.e., such vital statistics as age, income, and education); (2) geography (i.e., their location); (3) psychographics (i.e., how they think); and (4) lifestyle (i.e., their activities, interests, and opinions). There are of course other ways of describing, and perhaps segmenting your market.

Knowing your customers is as important as knowing yourself (the company environs), your competitors (the competitor environs), and the other environs that you have analyzed.

PROBLEMS AND OPPORTUNITIES

The problems and opportunities section is really a summary that emphasizes the main points you have already covered in preceding sections. As you put your plan together, developed your situational analysis, and described your target market, you probably implicitly covered many of the problems and opportunities inherent in your situation. Here you should restate them explicitly and list them one by one. Group them first by opportunities, then by problems. Indicate why each is an opportunity or a problem. Also indicate how you intend to take advantage of each opportunity and what you intend to do about each problem.

Many marketing planners do well in showing how they will take advantage of the opportunities, but they do not explain adequately what they will do about the problems. To get full benefit from your plan you must not only foresee the potential problems and opportunities, but also decide what actions you must take to overcome the problems.

This foresight will help you during implementation. It will also favorably impress those who will decide whether to allocate resources for your particular project. In most cases, those who evaluate your plans will know when you omit a problem. That instantly makes a bad impression. An evaluator will then get one of two perceptions: Maybe you are intentionally omitting a difficult problem because you didn't know what to do about it, or maybe you didn't even recognize that you had a problem! Stating your problems and how you will handle them will give you a decided edge over others who submitted plans but did not take the time or trouble to consider the solutions to potential problems they might face in implementation.

Note that in the strategy and tactics sections, you will find additional potential problems. For example, when you initiate a particular strategy, a competent competitor isn't going to sit there and let you take his or her market. Competitor counteractions constitute a potential problem. You'll discuss these counteractions in those sections. You do not have to add these new potential problems and/or opportunities to this section. This is a summary section for your initial scan of your environment.

MARKETING GOALS AND OBJECTIVES

Marketing goals and objectives are accomplishments you intend to achieve with the help of your marketing plan. You have already prepared your reader by your earlier analysis of the target market. In this section you must spell out in detail exactly what you intend to do.

What is the difference between a goal and an objective? An *objective* is an overall goal. It is more general and may not be quantified. "To establish a product in the marketplace" is an objective. So is "to become the market leader" or "to dominate the market." Goals are quantified. "To sell ten thousand units a year" is a goal. *Goals* are also quantified in terms of sales, profits, market share, return on investment, or other measurements. There is one major cautionary note here: Don't get trapped into setting objectives or goals that conflict. For example, your ability to capture a stated market share may require lower profits. Make sure that all your goals and objectives fit together. You can do this by adjusting and reconfirming your goals and objectives after you have completed the financial portions of your plan.

MARKETING STRATEGY

In this section you will describe what is to be done to reach your objectives and goals. Your strategy may be one of differentiating your product from that of its competitors, of segmenting your total market, of positioning it in relation to other products, of carving out and defending a certain niche, of timing in entering the market, and so forth. Marketing strategy is a what-to-do section.

One important part of the marketing strategy section that is frequently left out and that you shouldn't omit is what your main competitors are likely to do when you implement your planned strategy, and what you will do to take advantage of the opportunities created, solve potential problems, and avoid serious threats. Herein is another terrific opportunity for you to demonstrate what a terrific marketing strategist and planner you are.

MARKETING TACTICS

Just as strategy tells you what you must do to reach your objectives, tactics tell you how you will carry out your strategy. List every action required to implement each of the strategies described in the preceding section and the timing of these actions. These tactical actions are described in terms of what is called the "marketing mix," or the "4 Ps" of marketing: product, price, promotion, and place. Sometimes the 4 Ps are known as strategic variables. However, these variables are really tactical because they are actions taken to accomplish the strategy you developed in the preceding section.

IMPLEMENTATION AND CONTROL

In the implementation and control section you are going to calculate the breakeven point and forecast other important information to help control the project once it has been implemented. You are also going to compute sales projections and cash flow on a monthly basis for a three-year period and calculate start-up costs in a monthly budget. After implementation you can use this information to keep the project on track. Thus, if the budget is exceeded, you will know where to cut back or to reallocate resources. If sales aren't what they should be, you will know where to turn your attention to realize an improvement.

THE SUMMARY

In the summary you discuss advantages, costs, and profits and clearly state the differential advantage, once again, that your plan for this product or service offers the competition. The differential or competitive advantage is what you have that your competitors lack. Basically it says why your plan will succeed.

The summary completes your marketing plan outline. You now have a good idea of the information that you'll need for your marketing. As you go through this book, forms will be provided to assist in completing every section of the marketing plan that we've talked about. As you complete these forms, you will automatically be completing your marketing plan.

Figure 1-2 is a sample marketing plan action development schedule that will assist you in planning to plan. Your schedule should be adjusted to your particular situation. It lists the actions that must be taken and shows you where to start and how long each action should take to complete. The horizontal line begins when the action is to be initiated and continues until its scheduled completion. An adjusted date is provided by a dashed line; thus as you proceed, you can use the action schedule to adjust dates when a certain action was not completed on time and the schedule must be modified. In this way you can develop and coordinate a planning process that fits your situation and any deadlines you might have for completing your plan.

If you are completing the plan on a team, names can be written along within the spaces provided for the tasks to indicate who is responsible for every action. A blank development schedule (Figure 1-3) is provided for your use in planning to plan.

KEEP YOUR MATERIAL ORGANIZED

It is very important to keep your material together to guard against loss and for updating as new data are received. A loose-leaf notebook is a helpful tool. Each section can be marked: executive summary, introduction, situational analysis, target market, problems and opportunities, marketing goals and objectives, marketing strategy, marketing tactics, implementation and control, and summary. As additional information is received in its rough form, it can be added to the appropriate section.

SUMMARY

In this chapter you have prepared yourself by planning to plan. You have examined the structure of the outline that will be used for developing your marketing plan, the information required in each of its sections, and a planning form that can be used to help you get organized and work efficiently. Finally, you have seen how to keep your material organized in a simple way by using a loose-leaf notebook.

Task	Weeks After Initiation											
	1	2	3	4	5	6	7	8	9	10	11	12
Secondary research into demographics, situational factors	↑————————			→								
Market research regarding potential demand	↑————————————				→							
Audit of competitors' and company environs	↑————————————————					→						
Investigation of neutral environs	↑————————————————					→						
Establishment of objective, goals, and overall strategy	↑————————————————————						→					
Development and specification of tactics; additional marketing research as required	↑———————————————————————————									→		
Development and calculation of implementation and control information	↑————————————————————————————————										→	
Writing and development of marketing plan document	↑———————————————————————————————————											→

FIGURE 1-2.   Sample Marketing Plan Action Development Schedule

Task	1	2	3	4	5	6	7	8	9	10	11	12

FIGURE 1-3.   Blank Marketing Plan Action Development Schedule

CHAPTER 2

STEP 2

SCANNING YOUR ENVIRONMENT

In this chapter you are going to decide what information you need for the introduction and situational analysis sections of your marketing plan and where you can obtain this information.

THE INTRODUCTION

In the introduction you must state what the product or service is, describe it in detail, and note why there is demand for it in the marketplace. To do this accurately and completely you need information that goes beyond product or service attributes and benefits. You must analyze the life cycle for your product or service. You see, every product and service class passes through a life cycle just as if it were a living thing. The shape of the curve as the product passes through the different stages of its life is called "the product life cycle."

The classic product life cycle is shown in Figure 2-1. Note that its stages are introduction, growth, maturity, and decline. Note also that sales and profits are plotted as a curve that changes shape from stage to stage. Different strategies work better for different stages. This is because conditions in each stage are different. The shape of the curve will have important strategic implications that are needed when you go to develop a strategy. For now, notice that the sales and profit curves differ. For example, note that profits peak in the growth stage, whereas sales continue to rise and then peak in the maturity stage.

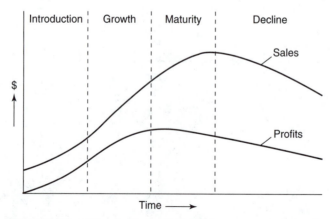

FIGURE 2-1. Classic Product Life Cycle

You must decide whether your product is in the introductory, growth, maturity, or decline stage. You may think that if you are introducing a new product, it is automatically in the introductory stage. If it is sufficiently different from other products or services of its class, maybe it is. When personal computers first came on the market, they were so radically different from the mainframe models used by large corporations that these products were in the introductory stage of their own life cycle.

So this raises an important question. Do you analyze a new product in its own life cycle, or in the life cycle of its class of products or services? The answer is that you can gain useful insights in looking at your new product both ways. Which is more important depends on how different your product is from what is already in the marketplace. Let's contrast a couple of new products so you can see what I'm talking about.

Take the common, garden-variety marketing textbook. Marketing textbooks have been around a long time. As a class, marketing textbooks are definitely not in the introductory stage. But what if the entire textbook were on a CD-ROM or the Internet? Both have already happened! Now you've got a class of new products that are in the introductory stage of their own product life cycle. That doesn't mean that the individual textbook in marketing, say, *The Marketing Plan,* fourth edition, doesn't have its own introductory stage also … only that it may make sense to consider where this product falls in the product class life cycle as well.

Perhaps your product is new, but its product class is in the growth stage of its life cycle. This could be confirmed if the product class had already been on the market for some time, but sales are still growing. A product that has been in the marketplace for some time and for which sales may still be increasing, but profits are not, is probably in the maturity stage. A typical product might be music recorded on a cassette tape. Finally, the product or service may be in the decline stage. A cigarette lighter might be toward the end of its product class life cycle and in the decline stage.

It may be unwise to introduce a new product that is approaching the end of its product class life, but not always. If your new product could immediately capture most of the declining market, it could still be very profitable.

You should also examine complementary products. These are products that do not directly compete with your product but in some way complement it or are used with it. If your new product is a computer, a complementary product could be a computer disk, peripheral equipment, or furniture built especially for computers. If your new product is a soft drink, complementary products could be the bottle, the bottle cap, or the package.

You should then investigate substitute products. These are products that are substitutes for the product you are introducing. These are not only direct substitutes through similar products made by a competitor, but substitutes in the sense that your target market can get similar benefits from them. If your new product is a video game, your direct substitutes for your product are other video games. But video games are actually a form of entertainment. What other entertainment might your potential customers buy with the money they could spend on your game? When the Wright brothers built the first airplane, no other airplanes existed. Therefore there was only indirect competition from substitute products. What were these substitute products? Some were other means of short-range transportation. Others were probably large luxury items used by the very wealthy. And for the military market, they might have been observation balloons or even horse cavalry.

Now you are ready to describe your product or service: its size, weight, color, shape, the material of which it is made, its function, what it does, and its benefits to potential users.

THE SITUATIONAL ANALYSIS

As we noted in Chapter 1, the situational analysis is an extensive and important part of the marketing plan. On the basis of the situational analysis, you will develop an optimal strategy that you can use to reach your goals and objectives. To make a situational analysis you must answer questions about the environment you are facing. To help you with this challenge, let's go over the questions in Figure 2-2 individually.

TARGET MARKET

Geographical location _____

Special climate or topography _____

_____

CONSUMER BUYERS

Cultural, ethnic, religious, or racial groups _____

_____

_____

Social class(es) _____

Reference group(s) _____

Basic demographics: Sex _____ Age range _____

Education _____ Income _____

Household size and description _____

_____

Stage of family life cycle _____

Family work status: Husband _____ Wife _____

Occupation (husband and wife) _____

Decision maker _____ Purchase agent _____

Risk perception: Functional _____ Psychological _____

Physical _____ Social _____ Financial _____

Income for each family member _____

Disposable income _____

Additional descriptions, classifications, and traits of target market _____

_____

_____

Target market wants and needs 1. _____

2. _____ 3. _____

4. _____ 5. _____

Product general description _____

_____

Frequency of usage _____ Traits _____

_____

Marketing factor sensitivity _____

_____

(Continues)

FIGURE 2-2.   Situational Analysis Questions for the Marketing Plan
Source: Copyright © 1985 by Dr. William A. Cohen. *Note:* This form is based on an earlier form designed by Dr. Benny Barak, then of Baruch College.

Size of target market _____

Growth trends _____

MEDIA HABITS

	Hours/Week	Category
Television	_____	_____
Radio	_____	_____
Magazines	_____	_____
Newspapers	_____	_____
The Internet	_____	_____

ORGANIZATIONAL BUYERS

Decision makers _____

_____

_____

_____

_____

Primary motivation of each decision maker _____

_____

_____

_____

_____

_____

Amount of money budgeted for purchase _____

_____

_____

Purchase history _____

_____

_____

_____

_____

_____

Additional descriptions, classifications, and traits of target market _____

_____

_____

Target market wants and needs 1. _____

2. _____ 3. _____

4. _____ 5. _____

Product general description _____

_____

(Continues)

FIGURE 2-2.   Situational Analysis Questions for the Marketing Plan *(Continued)*

Frequency of usage _____ Traits _____

Marketing factor sensitivity _____

_____

_____

Size of target market _____

Growth trends _____

MEDIA HABITS

	Hours/Week	Category
Television	_____	_____
Radio	_____	_____
Magazines	_____	_____
Newspapers	_____	_____
	Number/Year	
Trade shows	_____	_____
Conferences	_____	_____

COMPETITION

Competitor	Products	Market Share	Strategy

(Continues)

FIGURE 2-2. Situational Analysis Questions for the Marketing Plan *(Continued)*

RESOURCES OF THE FIRM

Strengths: 1. _____

                         2. _____

                         3. _____

                         4. _____

                         5. _____

Weaknesses: 1. _____

                         2. _____

                         3. _____

                         4. _____

                         5. _____

TECHNOLOGICAL ENVIRONMENT

_____

_____

_____

ECONOMIC ENVIRONMENT

_____

_____

_____

POLITICAL ENVIRONMENT

_____

_____

_____

LEGAL AND REGULATORY ENVIRONMENT

_____

_____

_____

SOCIAL AND CULTURAL ENVIRONMENT

_____

_____

_____

(Continues)

FIGURE 2-2.   Situational Analysis Questions for the Marketing Plan *(Continued)*

OTHER IMPORTANT ENVIRONMENTAL ASPECTS

_____

_____

_____

_____

_____

PROBLEMS/THREATS

1._____

2._____

3._____

4._____

5._____

OPPORTUNITIES

1._____

2._____

3._____

4._____

5._____

FIGURE 2-2.   Situational Analysis Questions for the Marketing Plan _(Continued)_

TARGET MARKET

The first environmental question under the target market section has to do with location. You will want to describe this location and its special climatic and geographical features. Is it a hot, humid environment? A cold, dry one? A desert? Mountainous area? Ocean-front? Suburban? Urban? Or what? Every climatic or topographical feature should be noted and described in detail.

Now the buyer can be categorized into consumers and organizational buyers. Organizational buyers buy for their organizations rather than for their own consumption. We'll look at consumer buyers first and at different ways of describing them.

Cultural, Ethnic, Religious, and Racial Groups

It is important to identify not only the groups that are potential targets for your product or service, but also the size and characteristics of each group.

Years ago, marketers thought that they could maximize their profits by mass marketing. Under this concept, they tried to sell the identical product to everyone. Extensive research and practical experience found this to be an error. It was far more profitable to segment the market according to certain common characteristics and to concentrate on marketing to the particular segments that could be served best. This is consistent with the marketing concept of focusing on the customer rather than on the product. By focusing on characteristics of your customer, you can satisfy his needs more easily. This is also consistent with the basic principle of strategy of concentrating superior resources at the decisive point.

Obviously it would be difficult to succeed by selling food products containing pork to Jewish or Muslim groups. Also, different groups prefer certain types of products. Have you ever heard of peanut butter soup? In West Africa it is a delicacy. East Asians eat tofu, or fermented soybean extract. You may drink only cow's milk, but others drink goat's milk. Many Chinese groups drink soybean milk. Among various nationalities insects, monkeys, and dogs are considered culinary delicacies. Some food we think of as "normal" would be shunned.

These preferences are crucial for the marketer as they can spell the difference between success or failure. Cultural, ethnic, religious, and racial segmentation of the market is only the tip of the iceberg. As you will see, there are many other ways to segment. All of them will help you satisfy your customers better and more easily.

Social Classes

The next environmental question has to do with social classes. The basic divisions are upper, middle, and lower, but you can categorize them more precisely as lower-lower (unskilled labor), upper-lower (basic wage earners and skilled workers), lower-middle (white-collar salaried), upper-middle (professionals and successful businesspeople), and upper class (the wealthy). Social classes are important as segments because people behave differently even though their income levels may be the same.

Some time ago, researchers surveyed three social groups that had identical incomes. One group consisted of young attorneys just graduating from law school. With their money they bought the best homes they could in prestigious neighborhoods. Naturally, these homes tended to be pretty small. They couldn't afford large homes in prestigious neighborhoods. Next, the researcher called on owners of small businesses whose income was the same as that of the young attorneys. Do you think they spent their money the same way? After all, they were making the same income. However, they didn't buy the same kind of homes at all. These small business owners bought the largest homes they could in average neighborhoods. Finally, the researcher looked at groups in yet another class. Certain workers had been employed for years by large companies and were making the same income as the small business owners and the young lawyers. This group didn't spend their money on homes in prestigious neighborhoods or on larger homes. Their homes were smaller and in less affluent neighborhoods. Where did their money go? They had better automobiles and household appliances, such as larger television sets, than the two other groups. Remember, all three groups had identical income.

If this research were conducted today, the findings might be different. Yet some kind of variation in buyer behavior among the social classes is still likely. Therefore this segmentation is important, and the identification of the segments, which may constitute your target market, is useful.

Reference Groups

Reference groups are those you turn to for information. They are especially important in the case of a general lack of information. Let's say that you are a member of a trade association that recommends a certain product. When other information is scarce or unavailable, this recommendation can be extremely influential in persuading you to use that product.

A reference group can also be a small number of trusted friends. Thus it is unimportant whether the reference group is large or small—only that you look to it for advice in making purchase decisions.

Demographics

The situational analysis question form now asks you to investigate certain fundamental attributes of your potential customers known as *demographics*. Of what sex is your target market? Are you trying to sell to both male and female or only male or only female? What is the primary age range? How well educated are your prospects? Most products appeal primarily to certain demographic segments that can be defined by answering these questions. If your product is an encyclopedia, would it appeal primarily to college graduates or to non-college graduates? In most cases the answer would probably be college graduates. Similarly, certain other types of product or service appeal to individuals with certain levels of education.

How much money is your prospect making? Can you sell a Rolls-Royce to someone whose annual income is less than $20,000 a year? Unless your prospect is independently wealthy, probably not.

How many people are in the household? Is it headed by a single parent? Male or female? Guardians? How many children are in the family, and what are their ages? All of these demographic facts may result in different purchasing behaviors.

Like a product, a family has also been described as having a life cycle, but the descriptive terms are different from those of the product life cycle. The family life cycle has been divided into nine stages:

1.   The unmarried not living with parents.

2.   A newly married couple; young with no children.

3.   A full nest; the youngest child under six.

4.   A full nest; the youngest child six or older.

5.   A full nest; an older married couple with dependent children.

6.   An empty nest; no children at home; head of family in the labor force.

7.   An empty nest; family head retired.

8.   A solitary survivor in the labor force.

9.   A solitary survivor retired.

Can you see where different products or services would appeal to each group?

Family Work Status and Occupations

If husband and wife are employed, both occupations should be listed. Or if one or both are retired or the family is on welfare, this is of interest to you as an astute marketer.

Decision Makers and Purchase Agents

Note the spaces on the form in Figure 2-2 for decision maker and purchase agent. The decision maker is the one who actually decides to buy the product; the purchase agent buys it. A wife may prefer a certain brand of dishwasher cleanser, but it may be her husband who actually buys the product if he happens to be doing the shopping. The implication is we may have to promote to both spouses for many products.

Consider also those who influence the decision maker and purchase agent. Children are subjected to a considerable amount of television advertising for many products, including toys and breakfast cereals. Children may not be decision makers or purchase agents, but their influence on other family members may be significant for your product. Many companies consider the millions of dollars invested in promoting to them as money well spent.

Risk Perception

Risk perception concerns the chance your customer takes in buying a product. Any new product has a certain amount of risk associated with it. There are other types of risk to the customer. Functional risk refers to its dependability; that is, whether it will work. Psychological risks concern the possibility that the buyer may be disappointed or feel cheated if the product proves to be less than expected. Physical risk has to do with damage to the user. Social risk is the one taken if the buyer feels open to ostracism or ridicule for using the product or service. Finally, there is financial risk. This is the risk of money lost in buying a product that turns out to be worthless.

Risk is calculated as perceived by the customer. It may or may not exist in reality. A totally reliable product may be perceived as risky by the potential buyer and a less reliable one as safe. In marketing, the perception is the reality. So if you have a low-risk product perceived as risky, you are going to have to plan for some kind of action.

Income for Each Family Member

In this section of the form, additional income that may come from other members of the family is documented. This income is of interest because the total may drastically alter what your prospect can afford and is likely to buy.

Disposable Income

Disposable income is the amount left over after the bills for basic necessities such as food and shelter have been paid. Money left over is disposable income. It can be used for entertainment, a vacation, or luxuries like expensive clothes. The amount of disposable income will vary depending on geographical, cultural, ethnic, religious, and racial considerations.

Additional Descriptions, Classifications, and Traits of the Target Market

This space in the form allows you to describe your potential buyers in any terms that have been omitted previously and that may be peculiar to the particular market you are targeting. For example, one segmentation system—VALS, which stands for value and lifestyles—that has become extremely popular was developed at the Stanford Research Institute (SRI) in California. SRI divided consumers into nine value and lifestyle groups. Other means of categorizing can also give you valuable insights into your target markets so that you are not trying to be everything to everybody and can concentrate on satisfying a well-defined target market.

More recently the firm of Roper Starch Worldwide looked into the problem of why one American brand succeeded globally while a comparable brand did not. Using answers from consumer surveys worldwide, the researchers divided consumers into three groups holding strong feelings and making up almost half the populations surveyed:

- *Nationalists,* comprising 26 percent of the survey, feel close to their own cultures but not to others.

- *Internationalists,* comprising 15 percent, feel somewhat close to three or more outside cultures.

- *Disengaged,* comprising 7 percent, consider themselves somewhat distant from their cultures.

These results can tell a company how to position its product in a foreign market, or even whether it should be there at all.[1]

Another firm developed Personicx, a household-level segmentation system that places each U.S. household into one of seventy life-stage segments, based on specific consumer and demographic characteristics. The large number of categories is said to allow for a greater precision of targeted marketing and accuracy of segmentation.[2]

Target Market Wants and Needs

Wants and needs are both important, but they are not identical. A *need* is a requirement for basic subsistence, such as ordinary food and shelter. *Wants* are desires for things that are nice to have but unnecessary for basic survival. You might want an expensive pair of shoes, but you don't really need them. Satisfying either represents opportunities for the marketer.

You've probably already heard about one of the most important theories of wants and needs. It originated with psychologist Abraham Maslow. Maslow's theory of human motivation involves a hierarchy of needs, beginning with basic physiological needs and progressing successively to the need for safety or security, the need for love, the need for esteem or self-respect, and self-actualization. Also at a high level, but not fitting on a direct hierarchy with the others, are two more classes: aesthetic needs and the need to know and understand.

Although there may be some overlap between needs, as one need is satisfied the next higher need becomes more motivating. The basic physiological need is breathing. If someone suddenly began to choke you and you could no longer breathe, I guarantee you would have no other immediate interest. No marketer offering an attractive product at a competitive price could gain your interest. Your immediate need would be for oxygen!

Once you had regained the ability to breathe, you might then have been interested in the next level. That's safety or security. Would you really be interested in buying an automobile at this point if you didn't know where your next meal was coming from?

You can see how needs affect customers' motivation to buy the products or services offered to them. No matter how good our product or service is, if some major lower level need has not been satisfied, your target customers may not be interested. In this section of the situational analysis form in Figure 2-2, identify specific target wants and needs that you intend to satisfy with the product or service you offer.

Product Description

The general description here is really an abbreviated version of the more detailed material given in the introduction to the marketing plan. Be certain to note frequency of use; that is, how frequently will the customer use your product or service? Also, write down product traits. What are the attributes of your product or service? These may include price, size, quality, packaging, and service. Finally, you will want to rank the market factor sensitivity; that is, how sensitive are your customers to the traits of your product or service, from the most sensitive to the least?

Size of the Target Market

State the total potential of each target market segment.

Growth Trends

Growth trends describe what is happening to your target market. Is it growing? Is it declining? Has it leveled off? Profits can be made under each of these conditions, but each level will call for different marketing actions. Therefore you want to know what the trends are for your target market.

MEDIA HABITS

Media habits is a major classification on the form shown in Figure 2-2. It is significant because if you know the habits of your prospects, you will understand how to reach them most efficiently. Consider the basic media, including television, radio, newspapers, and magazines. It would be helpful to know how many hours a week are devoted to each category. Many studies have been done on Internet buying habits. One study by the consulting firm Booz-Allen & Hamilton and by NetRatings, Inc., segmented those who use the Internet into seven categories from "Quickie" to "Loitering." The online-behavior studies concluded that some categories are quite likely to buy, while others are very unlikely, no matter how attractive the offer.[3]

ORGANIZATIONAL BUYERS

The basic information you need for organizational buyers is knowledge as to who are the decision makers. With organizations, you must frequently market to more than one individual. Sometimes these decision makers will include engineers and their supervisors, purchase agents, and test and quality assurance groups. Each decision maker may have different motivations. The primary motivation of each decision maker involved in a purchase should be determined and written down on the form.

The Amount of Money Available or Budgeted for the Purchase

Obtain an estimate of the amount of money available for the particular purchase for which the marketing plan is being developed. This is necessary because significant differences in the amount charged lessen the chances of success in marketing the product and at the very least must be explained.

If a group is accustomed to paying $25 per unit in quantities of 1,000 a year, $25,000 will have been budgeted. If a greater amount is to be charged, the decision makers are going to ask why, because this will require an increase in the budget. Even a lower price must be explained lest it be viewed as representing a change to lower quality.

Purchase History

The purchase history of the same or similar products will reveal buying patterns relating to the time of year in which the product was purchased and the quantities ordered.

Additional Industrial Buyer Information

Additional industrial buyer information, similar to what is needed about the consumer, is required. The exception is media information about trade-show and conference attendance.

COMPETITION

Competition is a critical element. It is an intelligent environmental factor that will act against your interests. Pay particular attention when you are targeting a stagnant or a declining market. If you are targeting the same market segment, your competitor can succeed only by taking sales from you. Therefore the more you know about your competition, the better. You should study your competitors, the products they are offering, the share of the market they control, and the strategies they are following. All of this information can be used as you plan your optimal strategy to help you succeed by giving your customers better service or a better product.

RESOURCES OF THE FIRM

Indicate resources of the firm in terms of strengths and weaknesses. Few organizations are strong in everything. Perhaps you have technical strength like the high-tech firms in Silicon Valley. Or perhaps marketing know-how is your forte. Maybe you are strong in financial resources. Just as you have strengths, you have weaknesses. Jot these down on the form as well. Weaknesses don't become strengths by pretending they don't exist.

TECHNOLOGICAL ENVIRONMENT

Sometimes technology changes and expands rapidly. In a single year in the early 1970s, handheld calculators declined in price by more than 50 percent. Simultaneously their performance increased. Computer technology is still growing by leaps and bounds. Computers equal to the best computers of a few years ago can now be carried around in the pocket. It can also work the other way around. The vinyl record industry, a $300 billion business, shrank to zero over a three-year period as CDs took over the entire market.

The Internet has revolutionized marketing in just a few years. Al Clemens, chief executive of Provident American, became successful as a medical insurer back in the 1970s by using television and celebrity endorsers to market directly to consumers. In this way, he bypassed insurance agents, a revolutionary idea at the time. In the late 1990s he formed a subsidiary with a new marketing plan, once again taking advantage of technology. His subsidiary, HealthAxis.com, became the first full-service online insurance agency.[4]

The technological environment may not be relevant to your particular situation. But if it is relevant, be sure to describe your situation completely.

ECONOMIC ENVIRONMENT

The economic environment involves the economy and business conditions that you will face as you enter the market. It is true that fortunes can be made in recessions and depressions, during inflation, and in periods of economic well-being. However, the products and services with which you are most likely to succeed in these different economic conditions are not the same. Therefore a description of the economic and business conditions that you are likely to encounter during implementation is necessary.

POLITICAL ENVIRONMENT

The political environment must be examined because of the effect that politics may have on your project. There are certain countries to which the U.S. government will not permit you to export, just as there are certain products from certain countries that cannot be imported. Japanese and Chinese imports are currently of major political interest. So is preventing the unrestricted export of sophisticated weaponry and the knowledge and skills of former Soviet nuclear scientists or of technology to certain countries including China, but especially those that may result in use by terrorists. Politics affect the marketing of products and services. It is a part of the environment that you cannot ignore.

LEGAL AND REGULATORY ENVIRONMENT

The legal and regulatory environment can cause major headaches. One small company invested more than $100,000 in its development of a bullet-resistant police helmet. Then it discovered that because of product liability, the product could not be sold at a profit. Another firm invested thousands of dollars in a new wine cooler on the assumption that the alcoholic beverage tax would be the same whether or not they used another firm's wine to mix with their fruit juice. It wasn't, and the difference in tax made the product unprofitable. Be forewarned: assess the legal and regulatory environment before you complete your marketing plan.

SOCIAL AND CULTURAL ENVIRONMENT

Sixty years ago wearing a bikini on a public beach would have been cause for arrest. Sushi, or raw fish, has been a popular product in Japan for hundreds of years, yet only twenty years ago sushi bars probably would have been unsuccessful in the United States. Today, sushi is extremely popular. Timing your entry into a market may be the dominant factor. So a smart marketer investigates the social and cultural environment for a product or service before developing the rest of his or her marketing plan.

OTHER IMPORTANT ENVIRONMENTAL ASPECTS

In this section other important environmental aspects that are peculiar to your product or service but that are not covered above should be listed and analyzed. An example might be a natural disaster such as a hurricane or an earthquake.

PROBLEMS AND OPPORTUNITIES

The problems and opportunities section of the form is really a summary of all that has gone before. You should review your entire environmental situation and restate every problem and opportunity that you can anticipate. Naturally there may be more or less than five problems and five opportunities, so don't be restricted simply because the form allows space only for that number.

Many marketing planners who have no trouble recognizing their opportunities hesitate to discuss their problems. This is a mistake. First, it is important to identify the problems clearly to give yourself the opportunity to avoid them once you have begun to develop your strategy. Second, if you have failed to include them and have listed only your opportunities, readers of your plan will suspect that you left them out intentionally or were not smart enough to acknowledge them. They would be more impressed if you described how you propose to overcome them.

SOURCES OF INFORMATION FOR COMPLETING THE ENVIRONMENTAL QUESTIONS FORM

To answer environmental questions you must do research. This research may be primary or secondary. Primary research entails interviews, business surveys, and a personal search for the answers. In secondary research you consult other sources. Secondary research is generally preferable because it is already available. It should be examined before you spend the time and money to do primary research. What are some secondary research sources?

1. *Chambers of commerce.* Chambers of commerce have all sorts of demographic information about geographical areas in which you may be interested, including income, education, businesses and their size, and sales volume.

2. *Trade associations.* Trade associations also have information regarding the background of their members and their industries.

3. *Trade magazines and journals.* Trade journals and magazines frequently survey their readership. They also contain articles of interest to you that describe competitive companies, products, strategies, and markets.

4. *The Small Business Administration.* The U.S. Small Business Administration was set up to help small business. Whether you own a small business or are a marketing planner in a large company, the studies sponsored can be extremely valuable to anyone doing research in the situational analysis of a marketing plan. The many printed aids supplied include statistics, maps, national market analyses, national directories for use in marketing, basic library reference sources, information on various types of business (including industry average investments and cost), and factors to consider in locating a shopping center.

5. *Databases.* Databases are electronic collections of relevant data from trade journals, newspapers, and many other public and private sources of information. They are accessed by computer, and companies sell access to their databases.

6. *Earlier studies.* Earlier marketing studies are sometimes made available to interested companies or individuals. These studies may have cost $40,000 or more when done as primary research. As a consequence, their results are not sold cheaply—although in effect you are sharing the cost with other companies that purchase the results with you. Several thousand dollars for a short report is not atypical. Nevertheless, if the alternative is to do the entire primary research project yourself, it may be far cheaper to pay the price.

7. *The "U.S. Industrial Outlook."* Every year the U.S. government publishes a document known as the "U.S. Industrial Outlook," which contains detailed information on the prospects of more than 350 manufacturing and service industries.

8. *The Statistical Abstract of the United States.* This abstract is also an annual publication of the U.S. government. It contains a wealth of detailed statistical data having to do with everything from health to food consumption, to population, public school finances, individual income tax returns, mortgage debt, science and engineering, student numbers, and motor vehicle travel. The *Statistical Abstract of the United States* is published by the U.S. Department of Commerce, Bureau of the Census.

9. *The U.S. Department of Commerce.* If you are interested in export, the U.S. Department of Commerce has numerous types of information, including amounts exported to countries in the preceding year, major consumers of certain items, and detailed information on doing business in countries around the world. You can find the local office of the Department of Commerce in the U.S. government listings in your telephone book.

10.   *The U.S. government.* The U.S. government has so many sources of information that it is impossible to list them all here. But so much information is available, and so much of it is free, that you would be well advised to see what can be obtained from federal sources. One recommended source that will give you access to this information is *Information U.S.A.* by Matthew Lesko (Viking Press). An additional listing of secondary-source information is contained in Appendix B of this book.

11.   *The Internet.* The Internet is a relatively new way to do research for your marketing plan, but it is very useful and important. Start with the search engines provided on your browser. There are many search engines. Some are specialized for certain areas of interest, and some search the whole Web. Even with a hundred million or more entries, what one search engine can't locate for you, another can. For an in-depth look, consult the following references:

- *Find It Online: The Complete Guide to Online Research, third edition,* by Alan M. Schlein, Michael Sankey and J. J. Newby (Facts on Demand Press, 2002).
- *Researching Online for Dummies (with CD-ROM)* by Reva Basch (Author), Mary Ellen Bates (Hungry Minds, Inc, 1998)
- *Searching and Researching on the Internet, 3rd ed.* by Ernest Ackermann and Karen Hartman (Franklin Beedle & Assoc, 2003).
- *The 10 Minute Guide to Business Research on the Net* by Thomas Pack (Que Education and Training, 1997).
- *The Internet Research Guide, revised edition,* by Timothy K. Maloy (Watson-Guptill, 1999).

PRIMARY RESEARCH

In some cases you must do primary research yourself. Minimize the cost by thorough planning. Time is also an important factor. Can you complete your primary research quickly enough to be of use in preparing your marketing plan?

Three basic methods of gathering primary data are face-to-face interviewing and mail and telephone surveying. Each has its advantages and disadvantages; for example, in face-to-face interviewing more detailed information can usually be obtained and the interviewer can use verbal feedback and read body language or facial expressions to probe for answers. But face-to-face interviewing can be costly in time and money. Mail surveys are perhaps the quickest but most impersonal method. Their disadvantages are low return rate and lack of feedback. The telephone is an excellent means of surveying the country in the shortest time. Telephone calls, however, can also be expensive and will provide no visual feedback to your questions. As this is written, new laws regarding telemarketing are being written. Will they affect research done over the telephone? They might. That's something you need to investigate before you implement telephone surveys.

SUMMARY

In this chapter we explored the environmental questions, the answers to which are necessary for completing the situational analysis of your marketing plan. We also recorded some of the sources of this information. If the information you need will not be available by the time the marketing planning must be done, then you must make the best assumptions possible, based on the information you have acquired. Don't forget to clearly state the assumptions you have made. You don't want anyone to mistake your assumptions for facts.

Having done the research and situational analysis and knowing what environment you will face in the marketplace, you are now ready to establish your goals and objectives. We will do so in the next chapter.

NOTES

1. Thomas A. W. Miller, "Cultural Affinity, Personal Values Factors in Marketing," *Marketing News* (August 16, 1999), p. H22.

2. Author unknown, "Acxiom Unveils Personicx as the Next Evolution in Consumer Segmentation," *Business Wire* (May 22, 2002).

3. Author unknown, "Study of Online Consumer Segmentation Uncovers 'Occasional-ization' as Next Step to Reviving Marketing and Retailing on the Web," *Business Wire* (April 2, 2001).

4. Marcia Stepanek, "Closed, Gone to the New," *Business Week* (June 7, 1999).

CHAPTER 3

STEP 3

ESTABLISHING GOALS AND OBJECTIVES

"Would you tell me, please, which way I ought to go from here?" asked Alice.

"That depends a good deal on where you want to get to," said the cat. "I don't much care where," said Alice.

"Then it doesn't matter which way you go," said the cat.

—Lewis Carroll, *Alice's Adventures in Wonderland*

You can't get *there* unless you know where *there* is. This chapter deals with establishing goals and objectives. They are the *there* of your marketing plan. Without them, you haven't got a marketing plan—you have a collection of facts and unrelated and partially related ideas. Moreover, research demonstrates that managers who make the need for action clear at the outset, set objectives, carry out an unrestricted search for solutions, and get key people to participate are more likely to be successful.[1] And a recent article on building effective teams states clearly that teams formed without clear goals are sure to fail.[2] So establishing goals and objectives are not an insignificant part of developing your marketing plan.

ESTABLISHING OBJECTIVES

Your objectives answer the question: What are you trying to achieve? The following objectives are typical:

- To establish a product, product line, or brand in the marketplace.
- To rejuvenate a failing product.
- To entrench and protect a market under attack by competitors.
- To introduce a new product.
- To harvest a product that is in the declining stage of its life cycle.
- To introduce a locally successful product nationally or overseas.
- To achieve maximum return on investment with a product or product line.

Normally, the statement of the objective should focus on a single task, but it is possible to have more than one objective or to specify additional conditions as long as they do not conflict with one another. If your objective is to introduce a product, you might add: "To dominate the market, while achieving maximum sales."

In the same vein your objective might be worded: "To rejuvenate a failing product while maintaining high profitability and with minimum investment."

But in establishing more than one objective, or a main objective with additional conditions, care must be taken that the objectives do not conflict. It may be desirable to maximize the market share that you have been able to capture for a new product and at the same time achieve maximum profitability, but the two may not be achievable simultaneously. Capturing the maximum market share may require a penetration pricing strategy, and the low price and lower margins may result in something far less than maximum profitability. In fact, you may be lucky to reach the breakeven point. Therefore, when you establish your objectives and you add conditions to them, be certain that there is no conflict and that achievement of one will not make it impossible to achieve another.

Spend the necessary time to make sure that your objective statement is worded the way you want it and that all important conditions have been incorporated. Even after you have finished with it, however, it will not be complete until you have specified a time by which the objective must be achieved. Ask yourself the question, "By what time?" for every objective that you establish. Let's say that you want to introduce a new product, dominate the market, and build maximum sales. "By what time?" Three months? Six months? Nine months? A year? Longer than that?

If one of your objectives is to harvest a product that is in the decline stage of its product life cycle, how much time will you have? If you are going to introduce a nationally successful product overseas, how long will it take before this introduction can be said to have been made?

Psychologists, time management experts, business researchers, and practitioners all tell us that specifying a time period is extremely important. Doing this will give you a target on which to focus and a guide that will tell you whether you're on schedule. It will also provide a date toward which everyone concerned with the marketing plan can coordinate their efforts.

In 1961 President John F. Kennedy set an objective for the United States. He said, "We're going to have a man on the moon by 1970." Note that he didn't just say, "We're going to put a man on the moon sometime." He said, "We're going to put a man on the moon by 1970." In actuality this goal was achieved in 1969. The fact that President Kennedy specified a date was of major significance. It not only helped us to achieve this national objective, but it also helped us achieve it before the target date set.

George A. Steiner, a man famed for his expertise in strategic planning, recommends ten criteria to help in developing objectives.[3] Use them as guidelines to ensure that your objectives, whatever they are, will benefit the firm's overall mission:

- *Suitability.* Your objectives must support the enterprise's basic purposes and help to move the company in that direction.

- *Measurability over time.* Objectives should state clearly what is expected to happen and when so that you can measure them as you proceed.

- *Feasibility.* Your objectives must be feasible. If they cannot be fulfilled, they motivate no one. Be certain that they are realistic and practical even if they are not easy and require considerable effort.

- *Acceptability.* The objectives you set must be acceptable to the people in your organization or to those who may allocate resources to implement your marketing plan. If your objectives are not acceptable, you will not receive the necessary funds. If someone besides yourself is working on the marketing plan and the objectives are not acceptable, you cannot expect to receive the same cooperation.

- *Flexibility.* Your objectives should be modifiable in the event of unforeseen contingencies and environmental changes. This does not mean that they should not be fixed, only that, if necessary, they can be adapted to environmental changes.

- *Motivating.* Objectives should motivate those who must work to reach them. If your objectives are either too easy or so difficult that they are impossible to achieve, they will not be motivating. If your objectives are difficult but achievable, they will challenge and motivate everyone to reach them.

- *Understandability.* Your objectives should be stated in clear, simple language that can be understood by all. If they are not clear, they may be misunderstood and some individuals may unintentionally be working against them. You may also alienate those who allocate resources and capital. Your plan may fail midway through execution simply because your objectives were not clear to everyone.

- *Commitment.* Make certain that everyone working on the development, planning, selling, and execution of the marketing plan is committed to your objectives. In the real-life business world, senior managers seek to do this by involving as many managers as possible in determining these objectives.

- *People participation.* Steiner points out that the best results are obtained when those who are responsible for achieving the objectives take some part in setting them. It is vitally important to consult with all who might participate in any way with the execution of the plan. If other staff members are committed to your objectives from the start, you will have much less trouble keeping them on track throughout the implementation of your plan. If you are working on your marketing plan as a team, you will find that ensuring everyone's participation and input will gain commitment to completing the plan. If one or two team members attempt to impose their ideas on the group, the opposite will occur. No matter how brilliant or "right" their ideas, they will be unable to gain the commitment of other team members.

- *Linkage.* Naturally the objectives should be linked with the basic purposes of your organization. They must also be linked with the objectives of other collateral organizations in your firm. They must be consistent with and meet top management objectives. It's no good setting objectives that involve high sales if this runs counter to top management's overall philosophy of serving an exclusive clientele. Ensure that the objectives you set are linked to other unique requirements of the environment of your firm.

After you have decided on the time frame for achieving your objectives, add it to the form in Figure 3-1.

GOALS

Goals are the specifics of the objectives. Let's look at one of the objectives we talked about: "Introduce a new product and dominate the market while achieving maximum sales. Time to achieve: one year."

Now the question is this: Does *introduce* mean to distribute it among 500 major retail outlets or at only one? Is *maximum sales* $100,000 in six months and then $1 million in one year? What are the figures that demonstrate introduction? What exactly do the words in your objectives mean? How about *dominating* the market? Is dominating the market having a market share of 100, 90, or 50 percent? When the market is fragmented, you may dominate the market by taking a 25 percent share (or less).

Objectives can also be broken down into smaller intermediate units within the specified overall period. These shorter-term objectives are also goals. Thus maximum sales may be defined at the end of the period indicated (one year) as well as at shorter intervals, say six months. The same can be done to define *dominating the market*.

Let's look at another example: "Rejuvenate a failing product with minimum investment while maintaining high profitability."

First, what does *rejuvenate* mean? In this case let's say that it means increasing sales by 30 percent over the preceding year. How about *minimum investment?* Let's say that the maximum amount that your company is ready to invest is $100,000. If you think this is the minimum amount that you can get the job done with, then your *minimum investment* may be $100,000. And *high profitability?* Well, profitability is related to the margin; that is, your costs compared with the selling price that was set. Let's say that the definition of high profitability is a margin of 60 percent. You can use this figure to define high profitability.

Again, you must consider the time for achieving these goals. You may want to indicate quarterly sales increases over the preceding year combined with a total sales increase of 30 percent at the end of the coming year. Both final and the intermediate figures are goals.

Objectives   Time to Achieve

1. _____   _____

2. _____   _____

3. _____   _____

4. _____   _____

5. _____   _____

Goals   Time to Achieve

1. _____   _____

2. _____   _____

3. _____   _____

4. _____   _____

5. _____   _____

Statement of Differential Advantage

_____

_____

_____

_____

_____

_____

_____

_____

_____

FIGURE 3-1.   Objectives, Goals, Differential Advantage Statement
Source: Copyright © 1985 by Dr. William A. Cohen.

You can now complete the goals section in Figure 3-1. Specifying your goals and writing them down makes sense. It allows you to concentrate your efforts on achieving what is really important in order to obtain the objectives that were set earlier.

Specificity also affects vision. Vision has to do with the future as the leader or manager sees the outcome of the project. One study of leaders discovered that groups were far more likely to follow leaders and were much more enthusiastic about doing so when the leaders set specific objectives and goals.[4]

In another study, more than 200 combat leaders who went on to very successful careers in civilian pursuits listed "declare your expectations," which included promoting vision, goals, and objectives, as one of the eight major principles of leadership.[5]

When goals and objectives are made specific, it is much easier to avoid conflict between individuals and groups that must carry out the tasks to reach them. Also, individuals will work together to coordinate their efforts in a synergistic way. This makes their efforts far more effective than if their actions were simply to achieve movement in a general direction toward a less specific goal.

THE CONCEPT OF COMPETITIVE OR DIFFERENTIAL ADVANTAGE

In all cases, you must direct your efforts toward satisfying the customer by achieving a competitive or differential advantage over your competitors. That's one reason organizations are always trying to improve their services. As they get better and better at what they do, the customer wins by getting better products at lower prices.

Some call this *competitive advantage,* others *differential advantage,* and yet others use all three words. This is unimportant. What is important is what the words stand for.

They mean not only that your product or service has one or more advantages, but that these are more important than the advantages that your competitors may have.

Also, do you seek one competitive advantage, or can there be more than one? There may be one overriding competitive advantage so significant that others are not as important. At other times, your statement of competitive advantage may encompass a number of advantages over your competitor. The number is less important than the total strength of your advantage or advantages over your competitors.

In addition, you should consider sustainability of your competitive advantage. That is, not only must you be able to attain a competitive advantage, but you also must be able to sustain it. But for how long? Certainly not indefinitely. The environment will change sooner or later and you will lose your competitive advantage, regardless of what you do. Rolles in England once held the monopoly on the self-sharpening razor for men, the sustainable competitive advantage being the patents on its unique self-contained sharpening system. Then in the 1960s, advanced steel manufacturing processes enabled the production of razor blades sharper than any manufactured previously. Rolles's advantage became irrelevant, and the Rolles Razor was withdrawn from the market. Your competitive advantage needs to be sustainable over the life of your planned strategy, not forever.

Include the concept of competitive advantage in your marketing plan. Once established, you must think about, develop, and find ways to promote your competitive advantage. If you have no competitive advantage, you will not succeed. Why should customers buy your product or service if it is identical to a competitor's product with which they are satisfied? Therefore the key question is, "Why should anyone buy from us as opposed to one or more of our competitors?"

Although your objectives and goals focus on what *you* want, the differential competitive advantage focuses on what your customer wants. What is the advantage of the customer buying your product or service? Think this through to determine how the two are linked. Your competitive advantage is derived from an eventual customer benefit.

Let's look at an example of this linkage. Why have so many Americans bought Japanese cars? Americans saw a benefit over American-made cars. It may be stated as "quality at an affordable price" or "value for the price."

This level of quality was made possible by a combination of factors. First was the notion that much higher quality than had previously been achieved was possible. Also, the Japanese automobile industry was automated to a far greater extent than its American competitors. This meant its labor force was more productive. Finally, the Japanese had a lower cost of labor. These factors were competitive advantages over American automobile manufacturers. Together they resulted in the benefit of "high quality at an affordable price."

This is not to say that American manufacturers may not also have competitive differential advantages that may exceed those offered by Japanese companies. As a matter of fact, American manufacturers in recent years have been capitalizing on their own differential advantages to achieve a link to customer benefits in addition to raising quality.

Competitive advantages can be derived from a number of widely varying factors. A competitive differential advantage could be the ability to buy in quantity from special sources not enjoyed by others. The resulting benefit to the customer: low price. You may have a great number of Ph.D.s in your research and development department. The resulting benefit to the customer: state-of-the-art technology. You may have a restaurant for which you have employed the best chef in your geographical area. The resulting benefit to the customer: the best gourmet food. Knowledge can also be a competitive differential advantage that will result in customer benefits; for example, marketing know-how translates into customer needs that are better satisfied.

You can even find competitive advantages in what you might think are disadvantages. When Mercedes-Benz introduced its diesel models, they didn't sell. Diesel fuel sold for almost the same price as gasoline then. Also, diesel fuel wasn't sold at many gasoline stations, so it was not as convenient to use. Finally, if you've ever heard a diesel engine, you know that it's much noisier than one burning gasoline.

Mercedes-Benz saved the product line by turning these disadvantages into competitive advantages. They promoted the fuel as exotic and exclusive, "not available at every gasoline station." As for the noisy engine? Mercedes-Benz said it was unique too. "It wasn't like gasoline burning engines that were so quiet you couldn't even tell if they were running or not. When you start up a diesel engine, you can hear its power." Mercedes-Benz knew that to the wealthy segments at which these products were targeted, uniqueness and exclusivity were major benefits.

Make sure that any competitive advantages have the following characteristics.

Advantages must be real. Wishes will not make it so. Some retail stores claim that their prices are lower than those of all their competitors. Sometimes even a cursory inspection will prove that this is untrue or that they are lower only in certain circumstances or with certain products. Thus the competitors' advantage will *not* be translated into a benefit for the customer. The benefits must be important to the customer. Note that I say *to the customer,* and not *to you.* Freeman Gosden Jr., who was once president of the largest direct response agency in the world, says, "It's not what you want to sell, but what your customer wants to buy." This principle is directly applicable to the competitive advantage. It's not the competitive advantage that you seek but rather the benefits as the customer sees them.

A major supplier of U.S. Air Force helmets once thought about getting into the motorcycle helmet market. As this company saw it, it could make a better protective motorcycle helmet than its competitors because of its experience with pilot helmets. This it did. These were more protective helmets. However, they were priced at approximately 30 percent more than the preceding top-of-the-line motorcycle helmets. This pricing was not arbitrary, merely based on higher manufacturing costs for a more protective product. If that was not enough, this expensive helmet was 15 percent heavier than competitive models. Despite all this, the company actually thought it had a competitive edge because of the greater protection. Within a year this manufacturer learned a hard lesson when the product failed. The customer did not want a more protective helmet. At least, not to the degree that the customer would pay 30 percent more and accept a 15 percent weight penalty. When the perception of competitive differential advantage differs between marketer and customer, the customer always wins.

Lee Iacocca says that in 1956, Ford decided that safety was of primary interest to the consumer and emphasized it in all the advertising of its 1956 models. Ford's sales plummeted, and the competition won on all fronts. Ford's claims were questionable. Quickly realizing that he lacked a competitive differential advantage, and needed one fast, Iacocca hit on what was really the main issue: ability to purchase the car. The year 1956 was one of mild recession, so Iacocca instituted a policy by which customers could purchase new cars for only $20 down and $56 a month. This made it easier to buy a Ford than competitive cars. Iacocca hit on the correct differential advantage, as perceived by his potential customers. His district went from last place to number one in sales.[6]

Advantages must be specific. Whatever your competitive differential advantages, they must be specific, just as objectives and goals must be specific. It is not enough to say, "We're the best." The question is, the best what? And why? To the customer nonspecificity translates into mere puffery and is not a competitive differential advantage.

Advantages must be promotable. Whatever your competitive differential advantages are, they must be promotable to the customer. The Edsel was a great failure in the marketplace and is frequently cited as a prime example of poor marketing. Yet Ford did extensive market research to determine what the customer wanted before introducing the Edsel line. This research indicated that power was an important competitive differential advantage. The Edsel was designed to be one of the most powerful cars ever built for its price range. Unfortunately, in the same year that the Edsel was introduced, a new government regulation limited automobile advertisers from promoting the high horsepower of engines. As a result this competitive differential advantage, although it existed and may have been desired by the customer, could not be promoted. If you are planning on a specific differential advantage, it is essential that your customer know it; otherwise it might as well not exist.

When you have thought through this challenge, return to Figure 3-1 and enter your statement of competitive differential advantage in the space provided on the form. What is it that you have that others haven't, and how does it translate into benefits to your potential customers?

SUMMARY

In this chapter we have examined objectives and goals: objectives being what you are trying to achieve, and goals being the specifics of your objectives. In both cases it is very important to indicate the time frame within which these objectives and goals should fall. Remember, there is a sound psychological basis for both specificity and time frame that will help you to organize your efforts. Although your objectives and goals are what *you* want, you must also be aware of what is wanted by your potential customers. Thus you must build and emphasize a concept of competitive differential advantage. This should be something unique that you will have but your competition will not. Otherwise there is no reason for your customers to buy from you, and they won't. And your competitive differential advantages must translate into benefits and satisfaction as perceived by your customers.

Develop strong objectives, goals, and competitive advantages and you will be well on your way to success. You will be in a position to develop strategy to reach your objectives and goals building on the competitive advantages you have formulated.

NOTES

1.   Paul C. Nutt, "Surprising but True: Half the Decisions in Organizations Fail," *The Academy of Management Executive* (November 1999), p. 75.

2.   *Darrel W. Ray*, "The Key to Building Productive Teams," *Nonprofit World 21,* 4 (July/August 2003), p. 21.

3.   George A. Steiner, *Strategic Planning* (New York: Free Press, 1979), pp. 164–168.

4.   Warren Bennis and Burt Nanus, *Leaders* (New York: Harper & Row, 1985).

5.   William A. Cohen, *The Stuff of Heroes: The Eight Universal Laws of Leadership* (Marietta, Ga.: Longstreet Press, 1998).

6.   Lee Iacocca, *Iacocca* (New York: Bantam, 1984), p. 39.

CHAPTER 4

STEP 4

DEVELOPING MARKETING STRATEGY

The word *strategy* stems from the Greek *strategos,* which means the art of the general. Many of the concepts that we use in marketing strategy evolved from early use in military strategy. The very top level of military strategy is sometimes called grand strategy. It entails many other elements besides that of military force, including economic power and diplomacy. At the next level down is military strategy itself. Military strategy involves all actions taken by military forces up to the point of reaching the battlefield. Finally, according to the military concept of strategy, we have tactics. Tactics are those actions taken on the battlefield. In all cases there are objectives: national objectives that are achieved by grand strategy, military objectives achieved by military strategy, and tactical objectives achieved by tactics. The basis of all strategy is the concentration of superior resources at the decisive point. For example, in the past decade, Procter & Gamble Company adopted a strategy of simplification. It trimmed its product line, slashing items in hair care alone by over half. It also standardized packaging and promotions worldwide. As one P&G executive said, "There is a real push in the company to do fewer, bigger things." By simplifying, P&G could concentrate resources where it counted. The results? P&G sales grew by a third in five years.[1]

THE STRATEGY PYRAMID

In marketing we have a similar concept. I call it the strategic pyramid (see Figure 4-1). At the very highest level of the pyramid is strategic marketing management (SMM). SMM seeks to achieve the mission of the firm. To do this, SMM decides on what businesses, product lines, and products to pursue. One level down is marketing strategy. This is the strategy you implement in support of the businesses, product lines, and products decided on in SMM.

Let's say that at the corporate or top organizational level a decision had been made to exploit the capability that your company has for manufacturing certain products. This would be an SMM decision. Moving one level down to the marketing strategy level, how might this be accomplished? Penetrating new markets might be one way. Expanding the share of the market that you already have for this product might be another. If you select the option for new market penetration, you might consider a niche strategy. That's a strategy whereby you market to a definable segment that you can dominate. If you have sufficient resources, you might consider a vertical marketing strategy. You would try to control more of the marketing functions between production and selling to the customer. You might also consider entry strategy, in which you would weigh the advantages against the disadvantages of being first, early, or late in the market with your new product.

FIGURE 4-1.   The Strategic Pyramid

If you decide on a strategy of market share expansion, you might choose product differentiation or market segmentation—that is, you could consider emphasizing a product that is considerably different from other products and go after the entire market. Or you could segment your market into smaller markets and enter each with a slightly different product. You might also consider a limited share expansion versus a general share expansion.

The lowest level in your strategic pyramid is marketing tactics. Tactics are the actions you take to support the marketing strategy decided on at the preceding level. To do this you manipulate certain marketing variables having to do with the product, price, promotion, or distribution. You can manipulate all of these variables, or only one, depending on your overall tactical plan.

Maybe the marketing strategy you decide on is market share expansion. One tactic for accomplishing this may involve modifying your product to increase its performance. It may involve a lower price to make your product more affordable. It may involve increased advertising, or advertising in new media or new media vehicles. Finally, your tactics may include different distribution channels, or more emphasis on the distribution channels you are currently using.

Because resources are always limited, you usually cannot do all of these; therefore you allocate your resources—your money, time, personnel, facilities, capital goods, and equipment—where they can have the most effect. The resulting tactical mix, known as a marketing mix, is what finally implements the decision that started at the very top of the corporate ladder with the mission of the firm.

Now let's look at the details of making these strategy decisions.

STRATEGIC MARKETING MANAGEMENT

To make the decisions that are necessary for developing strategy at the SMM level and then incorporating them into your marketing plan, you will need a method for deciding to what businesses, product lines, or products the firm should allocate its resources.

To do this, we will use a portfolio matrix and the product life-cycle curve. The portfolio matrix is a box with four cells. The vertical axis represents business strength. The horizontal axis represents market attractiveness. We will locate candidate businesses, product lines, or products in the matrix.

The product life cycle graphically shows what happens to product sales and profits as a new business, product line, or product passes through the phases of introduction, growth, maturity, and decline.

Let's look at the four-cell portfolio matrix first.

The Four-Cell Portfolio Matrix for Decision Making in SMM

The first step in using the four-cell matrix is to decide whether you are going to work with individual products, product lines, or even an entire business. If you have or are developing strategy for only a few products, you will plot their individual product positions in the matrix. If you have several product lines, you will plot them in the matrix. If you are doing SMM for a large corporation with many businesses, then you will plot businesses in the matrix.

If you are plotting products or product lines, what you plot are called strategic product units (SPUs). If you are working with businesses, you will plot strategic business units (SBUs). If you have many types of products, be sure to combine products into product lines, or even product line groupings, to form SPUs. Do the same if you have many businesses, to form SBUs. This will greatly simplify your work. It will also enable you to take advantage of economies of scale where possible. To establish SPUs or SBUs, look for similarities in customers served, product lines under a single manager, or products having identical competitors.

Once you have your SPUs established, you calculate the values of the SPUs for both business strength and market attractiveness. Now let's see how to do this.

Calculation of SPU Value for Business Strength   The first step in calculating the SPU value for business strength is to list the criteria important to the SPU being analyzed. Typical business strength criteria that may be relevant include:

Current market share	Raw materials cost
Growth rate	Image
Sales effectiveness	Product quality
The proprietary nature of the product	Technological advantages
Price competitiveness	Engineering know-how
Advertising or promotion effectiveness	Personnel resources
Facilities' location or newness	Product synergies
Productivity	Profitability
Experience curve effects	Distribution
Value added	

You may think of even more. The question is, which of these are relevant to you in your situation?

Once you've established which criteria of business strengths are relevant, you establish relative importance weightings. This isn't difficult to establish. All you need to remember is that all the weightings of the different relevant criteria together must total 100 percent.

Look at this simple example: Let's say that only four business strength criteria are considered important to you. We will assume that these are engineering know-how, size of your organization, organizational image, and productivity. Now, the question is, what is the relative importance of each of these four criteria to your business strength? After some thought, you decide that the most important is engineering know-how and that it is very important. You assign it a relative importance to the whole of 40 percent. You decide that the next most important criterion is organizational image. You give it 30 percent. Next you decide that the size of your organization and productivity are worth about 15 percent each. The addition of 40, 30, 15, and 15 percent equals 100 percent. If they didn't add up, you'd go back and adjust your weightings.

The weightings you establish will be used to rate all of your products, or SPUs against the same criteria. The only thing that will vary is how well each SPU does when measured against each. We'll use a point assignment to do this: 1 point means very weak; 2 points is weak; 3 points means fair. If the SPU looks good on this criterion, we'll give it 4 points if it's strong and 5 points if it's very strong.

Let's say for the specific SPU that you are analyzing you award a point rating of 5 for engineering know-how, 4 for organizational image, 2 for size of the organization, and 3 for productivity. You must now multiply the point rating for this particular SPU by the weightings you have established for the SPU (Figure 4-2) to arrive at a weighted rank for business strength of 3.95. Repeat this process for every SPU you are analyzing on the business strength computation sheet (Figure 4-3). Duplicate this figure and use a separate sheet for each SPU.

Market Attractiveness   Next you are going to calculate market attractiveness to plot along the horizontal axis of your matrix. Typical market attractiveness criteria include:

Size of the market segment	Ease of entry
Growth of the market segment	Life-cycle position
Market pricing	Competitive structure
Strength of demand	Product liability
Vulnerability to inflation and depression	Political considerations
Government regulation	Distribution structure
Availability of raw materials	

	Weight × Rating
Engineering know-how	0.40×5 pts = 2.00
Size of the organization	0.15×2 pts = 0.30
Organizational image	0.30×4 pts = 1.20
Productivity	0.15×3 pts = 0.45
	Total = 3.95

FIGURE 4-2.   Calculation of SPU Value for Business Strength

SPU #_____ Date_____

Business Strength Criteria	Weights	× Rankings	= Weighted Rank
	1.00	× Rank	=

FIGURE 4-3.   Business Strength Computation Sheet
Source: Copyright © 1983 by Dr. William A. Cohen.

Again, you may think of additional market attractiveness factors that are important to your company.

Let's assume that only four marketing attractiveness criteria are considered important. These are the size of the market, the growth rate of the market, the ease of entry, and the life-cycle position. You estimate that the relative importance of the size of the market is 40 percent, growth rate of the market is 30 percent, ease of entry is 25 percent, and life-cycle position, 15 percent.

Note that once again the relative importance of all the market attractiveness criteria must equal 100 percent. If it doesn't, we'll go back and reestimate our percentages until it does.

You must rate each market attractiveness criterion for the SPU being analyzed on a scale of 1 point for very unattractive, 2 points for unattractive, 3 points for fair, 4 points for attractive, and 5 points for very attractive.

Let's assume that you assign the following ratings: size of market, 4 points; growth of market, 4 points; ease of entry, 1 point; and life-cycle position, 5 points.

You then calculate the rating for each market attractiveness criterion by multiplying the weight times the point rating. Add it up it to find the total (Figure 4-4). Note that the total value is 3.40. Now we repeat the process for each of your SPUs. You can use Figure 4-5 and duplicate it to use a separate sheet for each SPU.

You are now able to plot the location of your SPU on the matrix (Figure 4-6). Note that in this matrix business strength increases from bottom to top and market attractiveness increases from right to left. The position of the SPU is located at the coordinates of business strength, 3.95, and market attractiveness, 3.40.

You can illustrate the amount of current sales for this SPU by the size of the circle illustrated and can indicate the percentage of the market share that this SPU represents with a shaded portion of the circle.

You can plot other SPUs in the same manner (see Figure 4-7). Each is calculated and compared against the criteria for business strength and market attractiveness, using the same relative importance percentages. Only the point ratings for each market attractiveness or business strength criterion differ. This causes the SPU to be located in different positions in the matrix.

The location of the SPU in the matrix suggests a number of strategic moves. Those in the upper left quadrant imply additional investment priority, which is logical since that quadrant contains SBUs that have attractive markets and for which the firm has considerable business strength. The names for the SPUs in each quadrant come from the names given to the original four-celled matrix designed by the Boston Consulting Group back in 1960. The measurements in that matrix were different, but the names still fit. The SPUs in the upper left-hand quadrant are known as *stars*.

SPUs that fall in the upper right-hand quadrant of the matrix imply selective investment. You have the business strength, but the market just isn't all that attractive. Still SPUs can be profitable in this quadrant. SPUs that fall in this quadrant in the matrix are called *question marks* or *problem children*.

The lower left quadrant of the matrix contains SPUs for which you must apply selective investment to move to star status or to manage for earnings. These SPUs can be moved by increasing your business strength and are known as *cash cows*. That's because if this SPU exists you are already in an attractive market even though your business strength is low. You don't have to use resources to get into the market, yet are benefiting from the market's attractiveness.

	Weight × Rating
Size of market	0.30 × 4 pts = 1.20
Growth of market	0.30 × 4 pts = 1.20
Ease of entry	0.25 × 1 pts = 0.25
Life-cycle position	0.15 × 5 pts = 0.75
	Total = 3.40

FIGURE 4-4.   Calculation of SPU Value for Market Attractiveness

SPU # _____ Date _____

Market Attractiveness Criteria	Weights	× Rankings	= Weighted Rank
	1.00	× Rank	=

FIGURE 4-5.   Market Attractiveness Computation Sheet
Source: Copyright © 1983 by Dr. William A. Cohen.

Finally you have *dog* SPUs located in the lower right-hand quadrant of the matrix. They can be moved; however, usually they are harvested or divested. You don't have the business strength, and why would you want to invest resources to move yourself into a less attractive market? In Figure 4-7, SPU 5 does indicate possible movement into the question mark quadrant. However, note that SPU 5 is a borderline SPU, already close to the star and the question mark quadrants.

If your SPUs are potential ones, it makes little sense to invest in them unless they are stars. The exceptions are if you have more opportunities than resources (rare) and they are close to the star quadrant.

Decisions as to which SPUs to invest in and possible SPU movements must be made considering other factors—such as sales, percentage of market share, and so on—after the graphic analysis using the four-celled portfolio matrix is complete. SMM is complete only when this has been accomplished.

PRODUCT LIFE-CYCLE ANALYSIS

Each product has a cycle of life that contains different stages: introduction, growth, maturity, and decline. This is called the product life cycle or PLC. During each stage of the PLC, the product exhibits characteristics and performances that favor the use of different marketing strategies.

There is also an overall trend for products to proceed more rapidly through the PLC. This can be important. The mechanical watch was invented hundreds of years ago and over the centuries proceeded very slowly through its life cycle. Yet over the past fifteen years

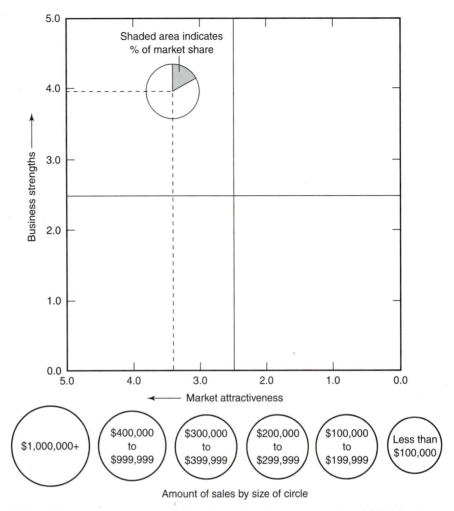

FIGURE 4-6.   Matrix Showing Sales, Size of Market, and Location of SPU: Business Strength versus Market Attractiveness

electronic watches have exhibited life cycles that are sometimes measured in months, not years. Electronic watches with features that once sold for several hundred dollars may sell today for less than fifty dollars.

Finally, if you can, it is best to maintain a portfolio of products in different stages. You don't want to get caught with all of your products in the maturity or decline stage. You can also have trouble with a large number of products in the introduction stage because of the considerable expense of introduction for each new product. With a number of new products in the introduction stage at once there is a heavy negative cash flow. The solution is to know in what stages your products are in the PLC.

THE INTRODUCTORY STAGE

In the introductory stage of the product life cycle, the organization experiences high costs due to marketing. Manufacturing is generally involved in short production runs of highly skilled labor content, and there is an overcapacity. These factors lead to high production costs. Furthermore, buyers have not yet been persuaded to purchase the product regularly. Many buyers may be altogether unaware of the product. Generally, the only good news in the introductory stage of a new product is that competitors are few or nonexistent. Profits, of course, are also nonexistent or negligible. The basic strategy during this stage is generally to establish market share and to persuade early adopters to buy the product.

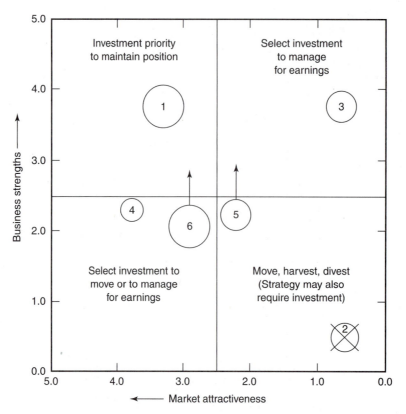

FIGURE 4-7.   Planning Strategic Moves of SPUs in the Four-Cell Matrix

GROWTH

In the growth stage the situation begins to change. The product has established itself and is successful. Sales are continuing to increase.

As a result, other companies are attracted and new competitors will probably be entering the market rapidly with their own version of the product. Marketing costs are still high, but manufacturing costs are reduced somewhat. An undercapacity develops because of a shift toward mass production. Distribution channels were probably limited in the introductory stage simply because of limited resources, but not any more. In the growth stage distribution tends to become intensive, and multiple channels may be used. All other things considered, profits tend to reach peak levels during this stage because of the increased demand and the fact that most companies take advantage of this demand with high pricing. Strategies followed during the growth stage are new market penetration and market share expansion. Tactical support of these strategies include product improvement, development of new channels of distribution, and a manipulation of price and quality.

MATURITY

The product in the maturity stage has changed its situation again. Although many competitors may remain from the growth stage, they are now competing for smaller and smaller market shares. As a result the competition heats up, and what is known as a shake-out begins to occur. Less efficient competitors go under or withdraw from the market. Buyers who have been purchasing the product exhibit repeat buying, and although sales continue to increase during this stage, profits begin to fall. Manufacturing costs are much lower during this stage, but the increased competition for a smaller market share ultimately forces prices down. This stage encourages a strategy of entrenchment, yet a search for new markets is still possible. Typical tactics include reducing some channels to improve profit margins, low-pricing tactics against weaker competitors, and increasing emphasis on promotion.

DECLINE

In the decline stage, as in the introductory stage, there are few competitors. Buyers who are purchasing the product are now sophisticated and much more selective. Production has problems again because there will be an overcapacity caused by reduced demand. Marketing expenditures will probably be reduced. In this stage both profits and sales are declining. At some point this will force a liquidation of inventory. The most logical strategy for the decline stage is some form of withdrawal, although entrenchment may also be followed in selective markets over the short term. Tactics in support of this strategy include reduction of distribution channels to those that are still profitable, low prices, and selective but quick spurts of promotion when rapid liquidation is needed. You've got to consider immediate liquidation versus a slow milking and harvesting of all possible benefits over a period of time. In any case, you must now be prepared for ultimate product removal.

LOCATING THE PRODUCT IN ITS PRODUCT LIFE CYCLE

Before you can analyze the PLC for strategy implications, you've got to locate the product in its life cycle. This requires considerable judgment. Although the general shape of the product life cycle shown in Figure 2-1 is true in many cases, it is not true in all. As a matter of fact many other shapes for product life cycle have been calculated, such as those shown in Figure 4-8. So before you can find out what position the product has taken in its life cycle, you must know what the life-cycle shape looks like. To do this, first look at what has happened to the product so far. Use Figure 4-9 to help you do this. Write down approximate sales, profits, margin, market share, and prices for varying periods over the product's life so far. You don't need exact figures, only whether your sales are high, low, or average or very high or very low. The same is true for profits, margins, and the other elements. You will also want to look at the trends and characterize them as declining steeply, declining, on a plateau, ascending, or ascending steeply.

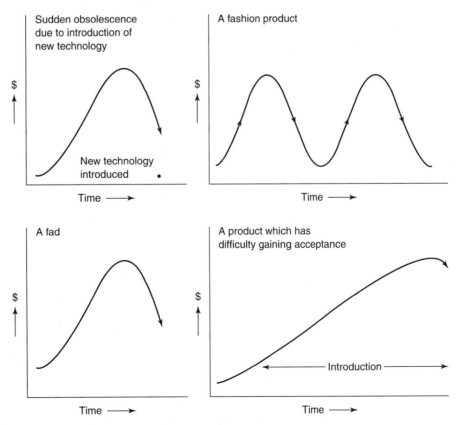

FIGURE 4-8.   Various Product Life-Cycle Shapes

Product _____ Date _____

	Period 1	Period 2	Period 3	Period 4	Trend
Sales					
Profits					
Margins					
Market share					
Prices					

Complete matrix with following information:

Very low or very small

Low or small

Average

High or large

Very high or very large

Characterize trends as:

Declining steeply ↓

Declining ↘

Plateau →

Ascending ↗

Ascending steeply ↑

FIGURE 4-9. Historical Trend Analysis Matrix
Source: Copyright © 1983 by Dr. William A. Cohen.

Next, you will use the form in Figure 4-10 to analyze the recent trends in competitors' product share and their strengths. These can be characterized as very weak, weak, medium, strong, or very strong.

Now you will take a closer look at recent trends in competitive product quality, performance characteristics, shifts in distribution channels, and their relative advantages. Write down this information on the form in Figure 4-11.

Finally you will accomplish an analysis of your competitors' short-term tactics using Figure 4-12. Be sure to note the probable meaning of each action.

Leave the analysis of the product and its competition and scan the historical information on product life cycles of similar or related products. What you want to do is take a

Your Product _____ Date _____

Strength code: VW = very weak   M = medium   VS = very strong
                  W = weak   S = strong

Competitor	Market Share	Strength	Products

FIGURE 4-10. Recent Trends of Competitors Products, Share, and Strength
Source: Copyright © 1983 by Dr. William A. Cohen.

Your Product _____ Date _____

Company	Product	Quality and Performance Characteristics	Shifts in Distribution Channels	Relative Advantages of Each Competitive Product

FIGURE 4-11.   Recent Trends in Competitive Products
Source: Copyright © 1983 by Dr. William A. Cohen.

Your Product _____ Date _____

Competitor	Action	Probable Meaning of Action	Check Most Likely

FIGURE 4-12.   Analysis of Competitors' Short-Term Tactics
Source: Copyright © 1983 by Dr. William A. Cohen.

product that is similar to the one you are analyzing and determine what happened to it during its introduction, growth, maturity, and decline. Get as much information as you can regarding the number and strength of competitors, profits, pricing, strategies used, and the length of time in each stage. Use the form in Figure 4-13 for this.

With this information turn to Figure 4-14, which is a matrix that contains sales and profits on the vertical axis and time in years or months on the horizontal axis. Use the other information to help determine the shape of the curve. Sketch a rough sales curve and a rough profit curve for the similar or related product you have just analyzed.

Your next step is to project sales of your current product over the next three to five years based on information from the first part of your analysis of your own and competing products. You can use the form in Figure 4-15 to estimate sales, total direct costs, indirect costs, pretax profits, and profit ratio, which is the estimate of total direct costs to pretax profits.

By comparing this information with the historical product information that you have already documented, you can estimate the profitable years that remain for your product. You can plot your product in its PLC using Figure 4-16.

DEVELOPING STRATEGIES FOR THE PRODUCTS IN EACH STAGE OF THE PRODUCT LIFE CYCLE

To develop strategies for products in each stage of the product life cycle, you must consider industry obsolescence trends, the pace of new product introduction, the average lengths of product life cycles of all the products that are in your product line, growth and profit objectives, and the general situation you are facing because of the present stage of the product's life cycle. You can use the alternative marketing strategies discussed in the next section. However, before you leave the PLC, you must understand that changes will sometimes occur that will alter the anticipated shape of the PLC. What can cause this to happen?

A need may disappear. Demand for the buggy whip is close to zero today not because the buggy whip itself was replaced but because the buggy was replaced by the automobile. Thus there was no longer a need for the product. In the same vein, demand for the iron lung, once essential to the breathing of many polio victims, is very low because the disease that most caused its use has been eradicated.

A better, cheaper, or more convenient product may be developed to fill a need. All engineers once carried a device known as a slide rule. This was a mechanical device used for making mathematical and other scientific calculations. When the electronic calculator was introduced in the early 1970s, it replaced hundreds of thousands of slide rules virtually overnight.

A competitive product may, by superior marketing strategy, suddenly gain an advantage. Adam Osbourne's second generation of computers failed and suddenly had its product life cycle terminated not because of technological inferiority but by IBM's superior marketing strategy when it introduced the famous PC.

Product _____ Similar or Related Product _____

Product stage	Introduction	Growth	Maturity	Decline
Competition				
Profits				
Sales (units)				
Pricing				
Strategy Used				
Length of Time in Each Stage				

FIGURE 4-13. Developing the Life Cycle of Similar or Related Product
Source: Copyright © 1983 by Dr. William A. Cohen.

Product DIET AD   Similar or related product "POUNDS-OFF"

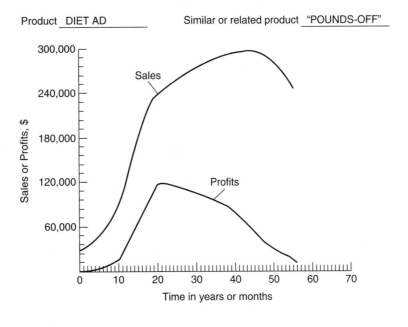

Product _____   Similar or related product _____

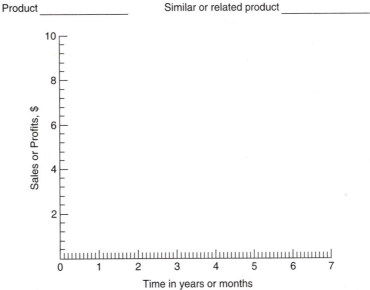

FIGURE 4-14.   Life-Cycle Curve of Similar or Related Product
Source: Copyright © 1983 by Dr. William A. Cohen.

Product _____ Date_____

Year	1	2	3	4	5
Estimated sales					
Estimated total direct costs					
Estimated indirect costs					
Estimated pretax profits					
Profit ratio (est. total direct costs to pretax profits)					

FIGURE 4-15.   Sales and Profit Projections
Source: Copyright © 1983 by Dr. William A. Cohen.

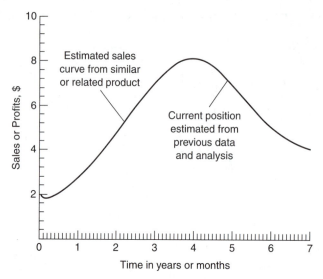

FIGURE 4-16.   Position in Product Life-Cycle Curve
Source: Copyright © 1983 by Dr. William A. Cohen.

There may be an intentional change in the shape of the curve by product repositioning, innovation, or extension. Arm and Hammer baking soda was once used only as an additive for home cooking. As the product went into the decline stage, its life was extended by its use as an odor absorbent in refrigerators. In the same way, the DC-10 became an advanced cargo tanker for the Air Force.

Any of these occurrences will cause the anticipated life-cycle curve to change. Under these circumstances, a new marketing plan and marketing strategy must be developed.

ALTERNATIVE STRATEGIES FOR THE MARKETING PLAN

As pointed out by marketing consultant Jay Abraham, there are really only three basic ways to increase business. You can increase the number of customers, you can increase the average size of the sale per customer, and you can increase the number of times customers return to purchase again.[2] The major alternative strategies that you might pursue are new market penetration, market share expansion, entrenchment, and withdrawal.

NEW MARKET PENETRATION

There are four classes of new market penetration strategy. They may be pursued simultaneously, although they need not be. They involve entry, niche, dimension, and positioning. Let's look at each in turn.

Entry

In new market penetration you can be first, early, or late. A company that chooses a strategy of being first is the first to benefit from its learning curve—that is, as it gains experience in manufacturing and marketing of the product it is using for new market penetration its cost goes down. This means that as competitors attempt to enter the market, the company that was there first has a cost advantage that can be passed on to the customer in the form of a lower price. Alternatively, the company can use this advantage against competitors by using their higher profits for additional promotion, to establish new channels of distribution, and so forth. Those customers who have been persuaded to buy the first product on the market and whose needs have been satisfied may be reluctant to switch because of inertia. Also, the firm that enters first picks up a certain momentum. Firms that enter later must catch up. Thus the first firm has an advantage. It can continue to innovate to maintain a lead over its competition. The first firm into a market also has an edge in dominating that market.

Yet, being first is not without its risks. As Peter F. Drucker said in his book *Innovation and Entrepreneurship,* to reap the benefits of being first requires an extreme concentration of effort on a clear-cut goal. Once a firm is successful in entering the marketplace first, it must expend considerable effort to maintain leadership, or everything that has been invested will be lost to one of the later-entering competitors. Being first does not automatically ensure victory. This firm must react and react strongly to later-entering competitors to maintain its lead.

A second possibility is that of entering the market early but not first. This early entry may be intentional or unintentional. Perhaps the firm intended to be first but was edged out by another firm. When this happens, the firm that is edged out may suffer all of the disadvantages of being first but reap none of the advantages. Early, rather than first, entry can be advantageous if the firm has sufficient resources to fight the firm ahead of it. It has somewhat reduced risk because risk in demand, technological obsolescence, and other areas of business have been absorbed by the first entry. Some knowledge will be gained of what works and what does not. This was all paid for by the firm that enters first. Finally, coincident with lower risk, much of the opportunity in the marketplace still exists. It is not a case of a product being in the mature stage of its life cycle, with many competitors fighting for reduced shares, or even of the later growth stages, with many competitors entering the market. This product is usually still in the very early stage of its introduction.

The major disadvantages of being early but not first are the barriers to entry set up by the first entry. Also, the market opportunity may be somewhat reduced. IBM overcame these disadvantages and captured a good share of the market for personal computers even though Apple got there first.

Finally, we have a late entry. Believe it or not, there are a number of advantages to entering the market after it is already established. For example, the fact that earlier entrants are usually committed to the previous direction of their products means that late entrants can include the latest technological improvements without penalty. The Japanese entered the American car market with brand new plants and manufacturing processes that competed against older, established American competitors who were tied to their obsolescent capital equipment and facilities. Late entrants may be able to achieve greater economies of scale because all entrants have a better idea of the actual size and demand of the market and can produce optimal facilities. Late-entry firms may also be able to get better terms from suppliers, employees, or even customers because earlier entrants may be locked into negotiations or fixed ways of doing business. Late entrants will enjoy reduced costs of research and development because they have been borne by earlier competitors. Finally, the late entrant can attack a perceived soft spot in the market, whereas a defending firm may have to defend everywhere.

Of course, a late entrant has some obvious disadvantages. At this stage several competitors have become established in the market and there are reduced opportunities.

Niche

A *niche* strategy simply means finding a distinguishable market segment, identifiable by size, need, and objective, and dominating it. You do this by concentrating all resources on fulfilling the needs of this particular niche and no other. This strategy can work because a niche may not be large enough to be worthwhile to larger competitors. This is a real advantage because the organization that practices a niching strategy may be smaller, yet be a king in its niche. It becomes a "big frog" in its chosen small pond. But even very large companies can employ a niche strategy. For example, the Canadian company Bombardier, Inc., is the world's number three builder of civilian aircraft and has captured 56 percent of the global market of aircraft for regional airlines. According to Bombardier's CEO, Robert Brown, Bombardier's strategy is to enter only select market niches in which it can be the number two or three player.[3] Drucker identified three separate niching strategies: the toll-gate, the specialty skill, and the specialty market.

A company attempting to dominate a particular niche with the toll-gate strategy seeks to establish itself so that potential buyers cannot do without its product. This means that the product must be essential, that the risk of not using it must be greater than the cost of the product, and that the market must be eliminated so that whoever controls the niche pre-empts others from entrance.

One maker of a small valve needed in all oxygen masks for fliers had strong patents protecting it. Though many companies manufactured oxygen masks, all had to use that particular valve. The niche was too small for other companies to pay the price to get in.

The specialty skill strategy can be used when a company has a particular skill that is lacking in other organizations. A management consultant who has acquired a particular skill in locating venture capital through contacts, knowledge, or other expertise usually has developed a particular niche that others cannot enter.

Then there is the specialty market strategy. This is somewhat akin to the specialty skill strategy, but rather than relying on a unique skill, it capitalizes on a unique market. One of my students was general manager of a mail order company selling unique products to physicians. The company followed this niche strategy, selling to this specialty market.

Drucker notes that the danger is that the specialty market will become a larger market and therefore more attractive to larger competitors. This is what happened to Osbourne and some of the early computer manufacturers. The market grew rapidly from a limited number of business and professional users. This encouraged larger manufacturers like IBM to develop strategies that overcame the nicher's leads.

Dimension

Another alternative for new market penetration is vertical versus horizontal expansion. Vertical penetration involves combining two or more stages of the production or marketing processes under a single ownership. Thus a farm that formerly sold its chickens to a food processor now buys a processor and sells prepared chickens to a retail store.

In a sense, vertical integration can be a type of niching. It also has the advantage of a narrow focus that can make marketing activities easier and more effective by the concentration of resources in a certain class of market. There may also be advantages in economies of scale of combined operations. One example might be lower transaction costs due to the purchase of a greater supply of raw materials. This could lead to bigger profits.

But vertical market penetration also has its disadvantages. There is a potential loss of specialization due to different management requirements for different types of operation in the vertical integration. Capital investment requirements and higher fixed costs will increase. Methods of management, marketing, and production may have little in common. Raising chickens doesn't require the same skills or equipment as processing them. Instead of an overall net reduced cost there may be an overall increase in costs.

Horizontal expansion means expansion into new markets. The risk here is that the new markets may not be well understood, even though the supplier has a good handle on the product and its marketing. Horizontal expansion may have an additional advantage in greater potential for sales than in vertical integration. It is a workable strategy in markets that are as yet untapped. It is more difficult when competitors are already established in markets in which penetration is sought.

Both vertical and horizontal new market penetration require an investment in resources. Therefore an assessment of the investment and the potential payoff, as well as the risks and uncertainties, must be considered before a decision can be made.

Positioning

Positioning refers to the position of the product in relation to those of competing products in the minds of the customers. The position of your product is always important. The position occupied by Rolls-Royce is different from Volkswagen's. A Brooks Brothers suit does not occupy the same position as a suit purchased at Kmart. But there are more subtle differences than these extremes. You should always have a particular position in mind and strive to achieve it with your other marketing strategy objectives.

Sometimes the positioning of the product can be the center of gravity in the whole situation, and it should receive emphasis equal to those of entry, niche, and dimension strategy.

MARKET SHARE EXPANSION

There are two basic market share expansion strategies. One is product differentiation versus market segmentation. The other has to do with a limited versus general expansion.

Product Differentiation versus Market Segmentation

Product differentiation and market segmentation are sometimes considered alternatives. Basically, product differentiation promotes product differences to the target market. Market segmentation is a strategy that emphasizes that subgroups of buyers may have common characteristics that can best be served individually.

Although product differentiation and market segmentation can be employed simultaneously, a company usually chooses one or the other. This is due in part to the fact that successful product differentiation results in giving the marketer a horizontal share of a broad and generalized market, whereas successful market segmentation tends to produce greater sales to the market segments that have been targeted. Both involve coordinating the market with the product offered.

The idea with product differentiation is to gain greater sales in a large market by differentiating the product so that it is superior to its competition. In market segmentation, a product is optimized for the target markets selected. Because the product is optimal for the market segments, it is superior to its competitors' products in these markets. The strategies may occur simultaneously when two or more competitors target the same segments. Then, both may pursue a product differentiation strategy in addition to market segmentation in the segments in which they are competing.

Varying conditions tend to call for one strategy or the other; for example, one marketing scientist, R. William Kotruba, developed the strategy selection chart shown in Figure 4-17 that illustrates the alternatives that must be considered.

Consider the size of the market. If the market segment served is already small, additional segmentation may not be possible because the financial potential is insufficiently attractive.

In some cases the consumer or buyer may be insensitive to product differences. This would also argue for a market segmentation strategy.

The stage of a product life cycle may also have an effect. As noted earlier, a new product priority is to become established in as large a market segment as possible. This would argue against a market segmentation strategy and for product differentiation.

The type of product may also be important. Oil, butter, salt, and gasoline are commodity products, which means that if these products are differentiated the variation will stand out and can be readily promoted to potential customers.

The number of competitors can affect which strategy is selected. With many competitors in the marketplace it is far more difficult to differentiate the product. Thus market segmentation strategy may be called for.

Of course, we must also consider competitive strategies. If many competitors are using the strategy of market segmentation, it will be difficult to counter with a product differentiation strategy because attempting to sell to all segments simultaneously means becoming all things to all people. That's a difficult proposition. Your best choice may be to do a little market segmenting of your own and to select your target market, along with your competitors, carefully. On the other hand, if many of your competitors are using a product differentiation strategy, you probably could counter with a market segmentation strategy.

Limited versus General Expansion

Depending on resources, objectives, and the competition, a firm can also initiate a limited or a general market share expansion. More than 140 years ago Confederate General Nathan Bedford Forrest said that his strategy was a matter of getting there "fustest with the mostest." Thus a new product intended for introduction on a national basis had better pursue a general market share expansion rather than alert its competitors to its intentions and give them the opportunity to preempt with a general market share expansion of their own.

Use product differentiation (left) Use market segmentation (right)

Emphasis on Promoting Product Differences	Strategy Selection Factors		Emphasis on Satisfying Market Variations
Narrow	Size of market		Broad
	A at 7, B at 9	1 2 3 4 5 6 7 8 9 10	
High	Consumer sensitivity to product differences		Low
	B at 2, A at 7	1 2 3 4 5 6 7 8 9 10	
Introduction	Stage of product life cycle		Saturation
	A at 7, B at 9	1 2 3 4 5 6 7 8 9 10	
Commodity	Type of product		Distinct
	B at 1, A at 8	1 2 3 4 5 6 7 8 9 10	
Few	Number of competitors		Many
	B at 2, A at 7	1 2 3 4 5 6 7 8 9 10	
Product differentiation	Typical competitor strategies		Market segmentation
	B at 3, A at 4	1 2 3 4 5 6 7 8 9 10	

(A) = Home computers   (B) = Salt

FIGURE 4-17.   Strategy Selection Chart
Source: Adapted from R. William Kotruba, "The Strategy Selection Chart," *Journal of Marketing* (July 1966), p. 25.

On the other hand, sometimes limited resources force a company to adopt a limited market share expansion strategy, or perhaps a limited market share expansion into certain areas or segments of the market. This may be because a general expansion is not possible due to the strength of the competition.

ENTRENCHMENT

Entrenchment means digging in. It is not a withdrawal strategy, nor is it one of new market penetration or market share expansion. Entrenchment may be necessary when a product is in its mature or even somewhat declining stage of the life cycle. In any case, the market is no longer expanding. Two different entrenchments are possible: repositioning and direct confrontation.

Repositioning

Repositioning means changing the position of your product in the mind of the buyer relative to competitive products. A repositioning strategy means that you will no longer position the product where it was before, but will position it somewhere else.

Some years ago a successful men's aftershave called Hai Karate was introduced. After several years of successful sales, the market contracted. There was a general shake-out, after which few competitors were left. Hai Karate was positioned first as a brand of after-shave that was more expensive than older brands like Old Spice, Aqua Velva, and Mennen, but less expensive than the prestige brands. When the market collapsed, marketing strategy options included withdrawal and entrenchment. One alternative for entrenchment was to reposition. The product could be repositioned as a cheap brand with a lower image than that of the old brands or as a prestige brand. In this case the brand survived by being repositioned against Old Spice and other similar brands.

Did you know that Marlboro, the macho man's cigarette, was once a woman's cigarette? The brand was introduced in 1926 as one of the first women's cigarettes with its positioning with the theme "Mild as May." It was ahead of its time and never caught on. In 1955, the Marlboro brand had less than 1 percent of the market. Then the Leo Burnett Company of Chicago got the advertising account and recommended repositioning. And so, the brand was repositioned, from a woman's cigarette to the most macho of male cigarettes. The product wasn't changed at all, but the advertising was. First the tattooed man was introduced, and later the well-known Marlboro Man. Within a year sales increased by 5,000 percent, and the brand became the leading filtered cigarette.[4] Cigarette smoking is not good for your health, but the Marlboro brand of cigarettes is unsurpassed as a lesson in repositioning.

The advantage of repositioning is finding a position in which competition is less or can be overcome more easily. Disadvantages include the cost of repositioning, promotion to make the consumer aware of the new position of the brand in relation to its competitors, and possibly repackaging and establishing new distribution channels.

Direct Confrontation

Direct confrontation means that you're going to fight it out toe-to-toe against the competition. Obviously this should never be attempted unless you are certain you are going to win. Usually it must mean that you have superior resources or the know-how to use your resources better than your competitors.

Reentrenchment by a direct confrontation is really a power strategy. If you lack power that exceeds that of your competition, then you shouldn't attempt it.

WITHDRAWAL

Withdrawal means that you are going to take this product out of the market. The only question is when and how. The mildest type of withdrawal is risk reduction, in which you don't withdraw the entire product or service from all geographical areas, but merely try to limit the risk of profit loss.

Going up the scale, you may consider harvesting. Harvesting implies an eventual total withdrawal but at a planned rate. You will harvest this particular product for maximum profits even as you are withdrawing from the marketplace.

Finally there is liquidation or sell-out. In liquidation you are leaving the marketplace now. This strategy is adopted when there are no advantages to harvesting over a period of time and an immediate use can be found for the resources that you gained by getting out of the marketplace at once. Repositioning can also be a part of this strategy. Certain alternative marketing strategies tend to be more effective at different stages of the product life cycle. This is shown in Figure 4-18. A summary of the alternative strategies is contained in Figure 4-19.

SUMMARY

In this chapter you've seen the three levels of strategy. These are strategic marketing management, marketing strategy, and marketing tactics. We examined ways of developing SMM strategies by the use of a four-cell portfolio matrix that measures factors having to do with business strengths and marketing attractiveness. We looked at developing marketing strategies using the product life cycle. We also considered other alternative marketing strategies. These included new market penetration, market share expansion, entrenchment,

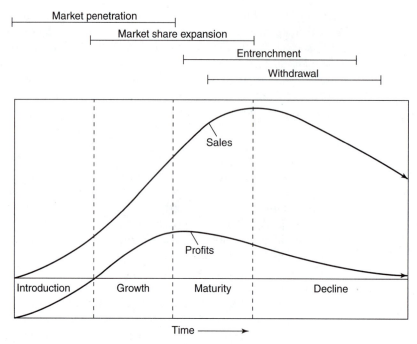

FIGURE 4-18.   The Product Life Cycle with Alternative Marketing Strategies
Implied at Each Stage

I. New Market Penetration
    A. Entry
        1. First
        2. Early
        3. Late
    B. Niche
        1. Toll gate
        2. Specialty skill
        3. Specialty market
    C. Dimension
        1. Vertical
        2. Horizontal
    D. Positioning

II. Market Share Expansion
    A. Product differentiation versus market segmentation
    B. Limited versus general expansion
    C. Repositioning

III. Entrenchment
    A. Direct confrontation
    B. Repositioning

IV. Withdrawal
    A. Harvesting
    B. Risk reduction
    C. Liquidation
    D. Repositioning

FIGURE 4-19.   A Summary of Alternative Strategies

and withdrawal. In preparing your market plan, it is helpful to indicate exactly what strategies you plan to use to meet the goals and objectives set. You will implement your strategies with the tactics that are discussed in Chapter 5.

NOTES

1.   Zachary Schiller, Greg Burns, and Karen L. Miller, "Make It Simple," *BusinessWeek* (September 9, 1996), pp. 96–104.

2.   Jay Abraham, *Getting Everything You Can Out of All You've Got* (New York: St. Martin's Press, 2000), p. 5.

3.   William H. Miller, "After 33 Years, a New Leader," *Industry Week* (July 5, 1999).

4.   Author unknown, "The Marlboro Man Meets the Surgeon General," http://xroads.virginia.edu/~CLASS/AM483_95/projects/marlboro/mman3.html, accessed November 7, 2003.

CHAPTER

STEP 5

DEVELOPING MARKETING TACTICS

Tactics tell you how to implement the strategy you have developed. There are two general classes of tactics. The first includes marketing variables that you can control fairly easily. The second involves manipulating marketplace environs. Let's look at each in turn.

MANIPULATING THE CONTROLLABLE VARIABLES

Professor E. Jerome McCarthy in Michigan conceptualized many controllable tactics under only four categories, each beginning with the letter "p": product, price, promotion, and place. These four categories of controllable marketing variables are known as "the four Ps."

PRODUCT

Three basic actions can be taken with any product. The product can be introduced into the marketplace, it can be modified or changed, and it can be withdrawn. Each alternative can be the best in different conditions.

A product may be introduced into the market to support a strategy of new market penetration. A tactic of product withdrawal may also support the same strategy. This is because the resources that were used to market the withdrawn product can be put to use elsewhere.

A product can also be changed or modified to alter the shape of the product's life cycle. When a product has been effectively rejuvenated in this fashion, there are a number of benefits. Goodwill toward the product and product awareness that is already established are retained. As a consequence, promotional costs for introducing and familiarizing consumers with a brand new product are unnecessary.

Other actions can be taken that will also affect your ability to implement a marketing strategy. These actions include decisions related to product quality, branding, and packaging.

Research has shown that product quality not only affects the image and the price that can be charged but also the product's profitability. This does not necessarily mean that the highest quality product is desired by customers in all instances. It is rather for a particular quality level of product or service that the customers want the best value, which translates to the highest quality they can get. This means you can sell, for example, an inexpensive automobile. But for the price, you must offer high quality with that price class.

That is where some marketers make a mistake. Within their class, they reduce quality to lower production costs. They think that this increases profitability. This is incorrect. The customer wants the best that he or she can get for the money and will reward marketers that provide it.

You must also analyze the situation carefully. During a depression or recession, when money is short, you generally expect less expensive products to be more successful. This isn't always true. When the United States sank into depression in 1929, cigar smokers proclaimed, "What this country needs is a good five-cent cigar." Yet a company selling premium cigars was started right in the middle of the depression. It grew into a multimillion-dollar company while many makers of five-cent cigars failed.

Branded products sell for much more than products that are not branded. You may have heard of Chiquita bananas and Sunkist oranges and Dole pineapples. But have you heard of TomAhtoes? TomAhtoes sell at about 30 percent per pound more than unbranded tomatoes. Clearly this is an exclusive brand.

Higher profit margins are only one reason for branding a product. Another is image and identification. Once a product's name has been planted in the mind of the consumer, it can be as important as any functional aspect of the product.

In general, there are four branding possibilities:

1. A company can use a new brand with a product or service in a category that is completely new to the company.

2. A company can introduce a new brand in a category in which the firm is already selling products.

3. A company can use a line-extension tactic in which the company's brand name is used to cover a new product as well as others already in the product line.

4. A firm can adopt a franchise extension in which a brand name familiar to the consumer is applied to products in a category that the firm has never marketed.

A new get-well card in Hallmark's line of greeting cards and a new ice cream flavor are examples of line extension, whereas franchise extension may include Ivory shampoo and conditioner developed from Ivory soap.

There are advantages and disadvantages to each of these tactics. A brand-line extension attempts to capitalize on some of the company's valuable assets in the form of goodwill, brand name, and brand awareness. The expectation is that a synergistic effect will help to promote the old and new products under the same label.

There are disadvantages to brand extension in some situations. An inexpensive Cadillac may increase sales over the short run for individuals who wish to own a prestige car but do not wish to pay a lot of money for it. Over the long run this tactic may cause the loss of buyers in Cadillac's traditional market segment of affluent consumers because Cadillac's high-priced, exclusive brand image would be less distinct. In the extreme, using a brand name for everything, such as Cadillac greeting cards or Cadillac gasoline, could destroy the old brand name with no gain to the new product.

Packaging is important to protect the product, to help promote it, and to make it stand out when displayed among many other products. In a recent year more than 5,000 new items appeared on grocery shelves. In this new product clutter, many experts have shown that simple repackaging can increase brand identification and awareness significantly.

PRICE

Three basic pricing tactics may be followed in introducing a new product: penetration pricing, meet-the-competition pricing, and price skimming.

Penetration pricing involves entering the market with a low price that will capture as large a share of the market as possible. The lower price is emphasized as a competitive differential advantage over the competition. Once the product is well established in the marketplace, the price may be raised to be level with or even higher than the competition.

When the Nissan was introduced to the United States as a sports car under the Datsun brand name in the early 1970s, it carried a low price compared with similar sports cars.

Then, as the market responded and the car became an established brand, the price was slowly raised. Now it is on the high end of the price scale for its product class.

Of course, low price tactics may always be introduced in support of an overall strategy. Some years ago Procter & Gamble reduced its supermarket specials and replaced these promotional tactics with lower list prices on all their products. Retailers didn't much like it. They lost income due to the loss of discounts and special deals. They responded by cutting back on purchases. However, customers bought more at the lower prices, and P&G held steady or increased volume market-share for thirty-eight months in a row.[1]

Meet-the-competition pricing involves introducing a product or service at about the same level as that of its competitors. If this tactic is used, you must differentiate your product in some other way. Some marketers who adopt this tactic offer higher quality or better service. Some bundle the product with several other products or benefits to increase the overall value. An entertainment system containing a TV, an AM-FM stereo, and a CD player may be priced at the price sum of the individual components. The bundling into a system provides a differential advantage. If you do not offer some competitive advantage, there is no reason for a consumer to switch from a competitive product or service.

Price skimming involves pricing a new product relatively high. Skimming is frequently done when the product or service is first in the marketplace. Computers, when first introduced, were frequently priced high. This was not only because of the cost of components and labor, but also because competition was almost nonexistent.

As competitors enter the market, the price is usually reduced to meet their lower prices or to make it more difficult for the competition to enter the market. Moreover, additional financial resources have been accumulated because of the higher profit margin. These resources can be used to fight the competition with other tactics. A company that uses the skimming tactic can spend more on promotion when competitors enter the market, and it can open additional channels of distribution.

However, the price can also be raised in the face of competition. Marketing genius Joe Cossman introduced a plastic-hose, lawn-sprinkling device. It consisted of a single flexible plastic tube with many holes in it. Although highly innovative, this product was easy to copy and manufacture and could not be protected by patent.

Even though the first season's market was all his, Cossman knew that competition would enter the following year at a lower price. Cossman's tactics were creative. He raised his recommended selling price and decreased the wholesale price to the retailer. Because of the larger margins offered to the retailers, Cossman shut his competitors out and maintained a market share through a second season with a higher retail price.

Other Tactical Pricing Tactics

You should also give consideration to other pricing tactics. There is always the alternative of promotional versus baseline pricing. P&G decided on lower baseline prices, as we saw earlier. The question is whether you should introduce a lower price to promote the product or maintain a standard price. Promotional pricing can increase sales. However, you've got to make certain that your customers don't get confused by the two prices. If your customers come to think of the promotional price as your standard price, you're in trouble. It will be difficult to sell at the baseline price once the promotional period has ended.

Various psychological pricing tactics are also useful and should be considered. Have you ever wondered why numbers such as $3.99 and $6.98 are used in selling products rather than $4.00 and $7.00? Psychologists have discovered that $3.99 is frequently seen as $3.00 rather than $4.00, and $6.98 as $6.00 rather than $7.00.

There are other important psychological considerations. At relatively low prices, a 10 percent difference may be perceived as significant by a potential buyer or prospect. So dropping your price 10 percent can make a real difference in sales. But if you've got a higher priced product, a 10 percent difference may not make any impact at all. So dropping a $1 product to 90 cents makes a difference. But knocking off $3 from a product selling for

$30.00 makes no difference. Yet the $3 is thirty times the ten-cent reduction! A 10 percent price difference is simply not perceived by the prospect as significant at higher prices.

Any markdowns must be examined from your customers viewpoint. The way to do this is to make certain that the pre-markdown price is perceived as a real value for the product. You might even explain why it is in your promotion before you reveal the mark-down price. Then a markdown will increase sales, and the baseline price can also be restored more easily if that is your plan.

You must also consider discount pricing. Most buyers expect that the greater the quantity purchased, the lower the price. This expectation is so pervasive that if you do not discount on larger quantities, you must have valid reasons that are acceptable to the buyer.

Finally, never forget the psychological aspect of pricing's effect on image. In 1999, the children's book market exploded over a British export with an eleven-year-old wizard who cast spells as the hero. The hero's name? Harry Potter. The books have been published in twenty-five languages in 130 countries. Warner Bros., which controls most of the merchandising rights, and Scholastic, Inc., which controls U.S. publishing rights, were faced with a marketing problem: how to turn this incredible popularity into sustainable long-term sales. The key, they felt, was a high-class image. So the books were released first only in hard cover, and they were priced at $18 a copy. And even at this price, books disappeared rapidly from bookstore shelves.[2] Before the fourth book in the series, *Harry Potter and the Goblet of Fire,* was released in 2002, again priced high and in hard cover, it immediately topped Amazon.com's unpublished best-seller list even though the title was a secret and no book review was available.[3]

A high price denotes an expensive image and a low price, a cheaper one. The same is true of quality. In many situations where buyers must make a choice among products, many will pick the product costing the most. They may feel that this increases the chances of their getting a higher quality product.

PLACE

Place has to do with channel and distribution tactics to support. There are six basic channel alternatives to consider:

1. Direct or indirect channels
2. Single or multiple channels
3. Length of channel
4. Type of intermediaries
5. Number of distributors at each level
6. Which intermediaries to use

A direct channel means selling directly to the consumer. Perishables may spoil if they must pass through many channels. Specialty products may require a great deal of explanation and demonstration that can best be done by the manufacturer.

Sometimes the limited resources of a smaller firm may prohibit the use of a direct channel, especially when a large number of customers are widely scattered. But getting to widely scattered customers or organizational buyers is such a benefit that larger firms may choose this alternative as well.

The use of indirect channels includes retailers, wholesalers, industrial supply houses, manufacturer's representatives, and agents. The fact that your profit margin on each item is far lower when sold through these intermediaries may be outweighed by the fact that you can reach many more customers than would otherwise be the case. Thus your overall profit could be much greater than if you attempted to sell direct.

The choice of multiple channels means working more than one simultaneously. Because an additional channel would seem to involve more outlets for sales and more chances for selling, you may wonder why multiple channels are not always selected.

There are several reasons. First, additional channels cost more money. This additional capital may not be available to you. Small companies with limited resources sometimes start with a single channel and expand to a greater number as more money becomes available. The same is true regarding where to distribute. A company may begin distribution locally and later expand to national distribution as more capital becomes available.

Interchannel rivalry is another reason for not always using multiple channels. Let's say you sell to retail outlets. These outlets will not be enthusiastic about your selling to other channels, particularly discount houses. Similarly, a mail-order catalog house won't want to see its product in retail stores and vice versa. So if you decide to operate with multiple channels anyway, you should recognize that one or more channels may not push your product aggressively. A channel could even boycott your product and refuse to handle it at all. Veterinarians did this to the Upjohn Company years ago when Upjohn refused to grant them exclusive use of a drug intended to cure an illness in cattle. Eventually, the company was forced to create a special product exclusively for veterinarians.

The length of the channel is based on the number of intermediaries along a single line of distribution. You don't have to sell to a retailer. You can sell to a wholesale distributor, who, in turn, sells to a retailer. But your channel could be even longer. You can employ an agent or sell to a jobber, who sells to a wholesaler. There is no single answer to the length of a channel. Factors to be considered include your strength as a manufacturer, the average order size, the concentration of customers geographically, seasonality of sales, geographical distance from producer to market, and the perishability of the product.

Types of intermediaries to use must also be considered. A wholesaler may be desirable when greater distribution is required over a larger area. When this is unnecessary, retailers may be preferred. A small company with limited resources may choose to work with manufacturer's representatives or agents who do not take title to the goods even though their profitability would be far greater with a sales force of their own. Why? To recruit, train, and maintain a sales force takes a lot of money and a lot of other resources. As noted earlier, many small companies lack them. Also, established manufacturers and agents who take a percentage of the sales price may also have the contacts and know-how to sell the product better than you could, at least in the near term.

You also need to decide on the number of distributors at each level of distribution. More distributors at each level are needed when the unit value of the product is low, the product is purchased frequently, the technical complexity of the product is high, service requirements and inventory investment are high, product differentiation is significant, the total market potential is high, geographic concentration is low, the manufacturer's current market share is high, competition is intense, and the effect on the customer's production process due to lack of availability is significant. When these factors are absent, you'll need fewer distributors at each level.

The selection of specific intermediaries does not depend only on their track records, although this certainly is a major consideration. You must also consider the market segment served, how well the intermediary knows and understands this market, how you and the intermediary fit together in policy, strategy, and image, and whether you and the distributor understand the roles each of you play in marketing the product.

Place tactics also require decisions in regard to physical distribution of the product. These include what physical distribution services are needed, how they should be provided, and what resources are required. Warehousing, packaging for transportation, the form of transportation, and distribution points must be considered. These all involve serious trade-offs among alternatives. Only in this way can you develop the best tactical "place" decisions.

PROMOTION

Most marketers divide promotion into additional categories of face-to-face selling, sales promotion, advertising, and publicity. Face-to-face selling requires decisions having to do with your own sales force or using the services of an agent to sell for you. We may have considered this decision previously under distribution. If so, you don't need to repeat your analysis. But if you haven't considered the alternatives, now is the time.

This decision can be especially important in the early stages of a firm's growth, when limited resources may argue against investing large sums to operate your own sales force.

Sometimes you must weigh this means of promotion against others. Never forget that you have limited resources for implementing your marketing plan. So you must weigh face-to-face selling against other ways of gaining sales.

The advantages of personal selling over other promotional methods include:

- More flexibility (your salesperson can tailor the sales presentation to fit a customer's needs, behavior, and motives in special situations)
- Immediate feedback from the customer (this will let you know when your appeal isn't working and must be adjusted)
- Instant receipts for sales
- Additional services to be rendered at the time of the sales call
- Flexible time to make the sale

In developing tactics for face-to-face selling, decisions must be made regarding recruitment, compensation, and training of your sales force, the allocation of exclusive or nonexclusive sales territories, and, perhaps most important, motivation of your salespeople to maximum performance.

Use of Sales Promotion Tactics

Sales promotion is one of the hottest areas of the promotional tactic variable. Companies spend more than $60 billion annually on this tactic. And no wonder … it can be extremely effective in boosting sales. A single display at the front of a store can increase a product's sales 600 percent.

Sales promotion techniques can involve sampling, coupons, trade allowances, price quantity promotion, premiums, contests and sweepstakes, refund offers, bonus packs, stamp and continuity plans, point-of-purchase displays, and participation in trade shows. Naturally, each of these options has a cost associated with it. Therefore testing is essential to determine which options work best in different situations. It is doubtful that any firm would be strong enough financially to employ all, or even most, of these techniques simultaneously. Therefore resources should be concentrated where they will have the greatest payback in implementing the mix of sales promotion tactics selected.

Sales promotion tactics are especially useful for new product introduction and during periods of high competition, when additional stimulation is necessary to increase sales.

Advertising and Publicity Tactics

Advertising and publicity tactics are usually required. Why? Because no matter how good the product or service, there will be no sales if the potential buyer or prospect has never heard of it and therefore cannot buy. So your main objective is to make the product or service known to the market and to present it in its most favorable light in comparison with competitive products.

Some marketers think that advertising and publicity works automatically and should be used in every marketing situation. This simply is not true. For one thing, it can be extremely expensive. No company has unlimited resources to spend on advertising everywhere simultaneously, just as no firm has unlimited resources to spend on many tactics. In some cases advertising may be only marginally beneficial. In others, it may not work at all.

Cigarette advertising on television and radio came to an end on January 2, 1971. Many cigarette manufacturers claimed that sales would drop drastically. Yet sales over the next few years actually increased without the television and radio advertising. The forced move from radio and television uncovered the amazing fact that other types of advertising were more effective. Some TV and radio advertising may have been hurting sales. Too much advertising by different manufacturers was probably canceling out the value of each other's promotion.

Publicity is sometimes touted as free advertising, with the added advantage of greater credibility because promotion seems to come from a third party. But publicity costs money. Even a simple release involves preparation and mailing costs.

Some years ago, the promotion of a science fiction book, *Battlefield Earth,* by L. Ron Hubbard, cost a staggering $750,000. Therefore, although it definitely makes sense to consider a publicity campaign in addition to advertising, it is not "free" in the true sense of the word.

One final point about advertising and publicity: Advertising can never force a consumer to buy products or services that are not really wanted or that are believed to have low value. Of course various governmental and nongovernmental regulatory agencies forbid misleading and inaccurate advertising. But also, the product or service must live up to its advertising or publicity claims or the customer will not buy it again. Even raising the expectations of the consumer by causing too much hype may cause products to be returned or ignored in the future, even though a product has technically met all the claims in its advertising.

Five key issues will determine whether your use of advertising and publicity is successful:

1.   Where to spend

2.   How much to spend

3.   When to spend

4.   What to say

5.   How to measure results

The answers to these questions depend on your overall advertising and publicity objectives, your target market, and certain broad alternatives for reaching the advertising objective.

The broad alternative objectives that you should consider are to stimulate primary demand for the product or service; to introduce unknown or new advantages or attributes; to alter the assessed importance of an existing product or service attribute; to alter the perception of a product or service; or to change the perception of competing products. Keep focused on what you are trying to accomplish.

In advertising, *media* refers to TV, radio, print, or whatever carries your message; *vehicle* is the particular TV channel and spot, magazine, or newspaper. In every case you must not only outline the cost of advertising in the media and vehicles chosen but also the expected benefits. These benefits should be quantified by sales or market share increases over a specific time period. In other words, an acceptable publicity or advertising objective would be to sell 500,000 units in three months or to capture 1 percent of the market in six months. Only in this way can you reconcile costs and benefits or determine whether results have met your expectations in your advertising and publicity tactical campaign.

Note the similarity in describing these benefits and objectives for your marketing plan.

PRIMARY INTERNET MARKETING TACTICS

The Internet has grown so much in recent years, especially as a marketing tool, that incorporating it into marketing tactics should always be considered. For example, in the summer of 1999 a movie that cost $50,000 to make was more successful than *Star Wars Episode I* in per screen average sales, with an average of $26,500 total per screen. The movie was *The Blair Witch Project.* Made by Hollywood "nobodies" with no-name actors and actresses, the movie became a blockbuster and grossed millions of dollars. What was the secret? The curious could find the movie at http://www.blairwitch.com, a Web site, and Internet marketing tactics were used extensively.

There are three main Internet marketing tactics. These are:

1. The World Wide Web
2. The Usenet
3. E-mail

Let's look at each in turn.

World Wide Web

The World Wide Web is a giant freeway of homepages, catalogues, electronic stores, and so forth. It is in color, has graphics and sound, and even video is a possibility.

Placing a color advertisement of multiple pages in a magazine and running it continuously, month after month, costs a significant amount of money. Never mind that a magazine does not have the flexibility of sound or video. On the World Wide Web, you can do this for a couple of hundred dollars a year.

Establishing a Web Site

Although some companies charge thousands of dollars or more to build a Web site, there is software with templates that allow anyone to establish a Web site. Many universities conduct courses in this subject. Some companies maintain templates on the Web to allow you to build your own site. (One that recently came across my desk was at http://freesitetemplates.com/. However, sites are always changing. Do a search of "web site templates" and see what you come up with.)

I have a Web site, http://www.stuffofheroes.com, which was developed to help promote my book *The Stuff of Heroes: The Eight Universal Laws of Leadership* (Longstreet Press, 1998). A student who was also an instructor in the subject at a community college developed the site. My plans are to convert the site to help promote my seminars and workshops.

Marketing at the Web Site

Once a Web site has been established, it can be used for many purposes:

- To sell a specific product or service directly
- To maintain a catalogue
- To open up a dialogue and communicate directly with customers
- To build an image as an expert in a certain field
- To conduct surveys and marketing research of your customers or prospects
- To build an e-mail list of prospects interested in certain products or services
- To announce monthly specials or sales promotions
- To provide new product information

Cybermalls

Cybermalls, or virtual malls, have been heavily promoted to potential marketers of products or services with full-page newspaper advertisements on weekends, free seminars, videotapes, and other methods. They promise the ability to cash in on the "Internet marketing bonanza." This promise is rarely met. Why not? The idea sounds good on the surface. Just like in regular shopping malls, you open a store on a cybermall. The cybermall develops your site and you pay yearly "rent" for it. Most offer some sort of "training," which is really consulting to help you with marketing questions. And most cybermalls bundle various services together: e-mail boxes, free virtual banners advertising your service, and so forth. Costs are high in comparison with a regular Internet service provider, or ISP, to put up a site which you can create yourself—the cybermalls may cost you as much as a thousand dollars or more a year, compared with $100 to $200 for an ISP to host the account.

Is a cybermall worth the additional costs? For most marketers, I would say "no." The mall theory supposes that (1) people come to visit the mall and stop in and buy your services just like a regular shopping mall, and (2) customers come for one thing and see your listing and go to visit your site, too. This is called "spillover."

However, the psychology of visiting a "brick and mortar" shopping mall is not the same as the virtual mall. People go to a regular mall partly for a good time. They go to see what's new, they socialize, they have lunch, and they may even go to a movie. For many it's a "day at the mall" and they "shop until they drop." People who visit a cybermall are usually looking for something specific. Few are interested in spending all day at a cybermall without the socialization with friends, spouse, or girlfriend/boyfriend that goes along with it. So even though the cybermall may be well promoted, and most are not, you're not going to get much "walk-in" business just because you are in "a mall." Spillover in most cybermalls is limited.

How to Market on the World Wide Web

The key to World Wide Web marketing is promotion, both online and offline. You've got to get prospects to your Web site. You can't rely on any search engine to do it for you. There is so much competition on the Web for any business or service that trying to build a business based on a search engine is ludicrous. So, offline publicity for your Web site is your primary ally.

Hot!Hot!Hot! was a Web Site that sold salsa hot sauce. The owners sold out a couple of years ago. They began in 1994, making Hot!Hot!Hot! one of the first businesses to attempt to sell anything online. It became hugely successful and is one of the folk heroes of the Internet. As it happens, the salsa business was located in Old Town in Pasadena, California, near my home, and I participated in some consulting for the owners of Hot!Hot!Hot! They told me that half of their salsa business came from their Web site, the other half from their storefront.

The key even back in 1994 was not a search engine. It was publicity. One of the owners had majored in public relations in college. She tirelessly promoted the business and the Web site through articles she wrote and interviews she gave to newspapers and magazines about the uniqueness of the business and what was then the uniqueness of Web site marketing. So any Web site marketing tactics must be in conjunction with other marketing efforts, and the Web site must be promoted heavily offline.

Using Banners

Banners are the color advertisements you can see on sites around all over the World Wide Web. You click on them, and they send you to an associated Web site. Spend advertising dollars for banners only where prospective clients hang out.

Amazon.com, an online bookseller, places banners all over the Web. But each banner is specific to the topic of the site in which it appears. Even so, probably much of Amazon's advertising dollar is wasted because frequenters of some Web sites are probably not readers or buyers of books.

Banner advertising can be free if you exchange banner advertising privileges with a noncompetitor. In fact, there are banner exchange services. Here are a couple:

- http://romconn.hypermart.net/exchange.html
- http://www.worldbannerexchange.com

Here are a few directories which list many such services:

- http://www.bxmegalist.com/
- http://www.positioned1.com/z-web-sites-91.htm

Banners can be created at http://www.worlddesignservices.com or by using programs at the sites listed above.

Cyberlinks

Cyberlinks are electronic links connecting one Web site to another. You "point" using your mouse at a particular link and "click" the button on the mouse. You are immediately taken to that Web site. Like much of marketing on the World Wide Web, this is a case of using proven marketing tactics in another environment. Links can be exchanged with noncompetitors.

Give Information Away

The concept of giving information away seems to confirm the law that whatever you give away comes back to you many times over. You can put articles you have published or even a newsletter on your Web site.

One interesting twist for articles and the like is not to put the article or newsletter on your Web site directly, but to put a link whereby your client or prospect can download this information to his or her computer.

By giving information away, you will attract prospects to return again and again, and many will become customers.

Usenet Marketing

The Usenet consists of interactive discussion groups, also called newsgroups. People participate by reading "postings" done by others, and maybe by adding their own in response. Some Usenets are screened for what is allowed to be posted and what is not. For others, it's a complete free-for-all. Each newsgroup has its own protocol and etiquette that you need to master before you market on them. A mass marketing of your services through postings would be ill advised. That's called "spamming." It can get you banned by some ISPs, and many ISPs won't do business with you once you do it. It's important to know the culture of the newsgroup you're dealing with before you begin to market through it.

You can reach the newsgroup through your browser. Here are a few lists of news groups:

- news.groups.reviews: http://www.gweep.ca/~drabble/
- Liszt's Usenet Newsgroup Directory: http://liszt.com/news/
- Borland USA: http://info.borland.com/newsgroups/

E-mail Marketing

E-mail is electronic mail. You type in a letter, press a button, and the message is instantly sent anywhere in the world. With the e-mail addresses of 1,000 or 10,000 potential customers, anyone can send a message to these potential customers instantly and it doesn't cost you a cent. However, there is one cautionary note. If the message is unwelcome, that's "spamming," just as with the newsgroups, and it can get the marketer in a lot of trouble.

So, it looks like Catch-22. There is this wonderful method of direct marketing that is instantaneous and costs nothing, but if you use it you're in trouble. There are several solutions to this problem. All depend on sending the advertisement only to someone who wants it. How can we know this?

1. Do research, offer something free, and make certain it is something the recipient is going to be interested in.
2. Ask visitors to the Web site if they would like to receive additional information about special offers periodically.

3. Rent e-mail lists of people who have specifically requested information about the kinds of products or services offered. These names are collected by others and rented to us.

4. Search programs are available that will search Usenets for keywords and construct a mailing list from the results. These lists must be used with care. In most cases, it is better to use the e-mail to invite them to a Web site where you can advertise the product or service.

If you use options two or three, you should note in your advertisement that this was information they specifically requested. That's just a little reminder to them and lets them know that you are not spamming.

Following are some sources and descriptions of e-mail lists you can look at:

*   http://www.catalog.com/
*   http://www.topica.com/
*   http://www.copywriter.com/lists
*   http://EmailUniverse.com/

Using E-mail for Publicity

You can get a lot of mileage through publicity to media using e-mail. However, again you must be careful to avoid spamming or your publicity will backfire. Paul Krupin publishes *The U.S. Media E-Mail Directory* and can be reached at http://www.imediafax.com/. He wrote a very useful article on getting news coverage, published on the Web by Hanson Marketing. Hanson Marketing's Web site carries a lot of useful information for consultants at http://www.hansonmarketing.com.

Krupin says that the Golden Rule for e-mail promotion to the media is to target and personalize. He gives ten commandments for sending e-mail to the media:

1. Think, think, think before you write. What are you trying to accomplish? Will a media professional publish it or toss it?

2. Target narrowly and carefully. Go for quality contacts, not quantity.

3. Keep it short—no more than three to four paragraphs filling one to three screens.

4. Keep the subject and content of your message relevant to your target.

5. If you are seeking publicity for a product or service or want to get reviews for a new book or software, use a two-step approach. Query with a "hook" and news angle before transmitting the entire news release or article.

6. Tailor the submittal to the media style or content.

7. Address each e-mail message separately to an individual media target.

8. Reread, reread, and reread and rewrite, rewrite, rewrite before you click to send.

9. Be brutally honest with yourself and your media contacts—don't exaggerate or make claims you can't prove.

10. Follow up in a timely manner with precision writing and professionalism.[4]

MANIPULATING MARKETPLACE ENVIRONS

For many years manipulating the environs for marketing tactics was largely ignored. Of course, it was recognized that demand, social and cultural factors, state of the technology, and politics and laws could be influenced. In general, however, marketing experts felt that it was far easier and less demanding for firms to attempt to manipulate the variables of product, price, promotion, and place. So environmental variables were assumed to be uncontrollable.

More recently the possibility of changing the context in which the organization operates, in terms of constraints on the marketing function and limits on the marketing organization, were investigated. Researchers found that these conditions can be used effectively and less expensively than was imagined.

The bottom line is that you should consider environmental marketing tactics as a possible alternative. Consider a company engaging in a private legal battle with a competitor on the grounds of deceptive advertising, or efforts to lobby Congress for a particular political action to ensure a more favorable business environment or to limit competition. Two marketing scientists, Carl P. Zeithaml and Valerie A. Zeithaml, did a great deal of work in this field and prepared a framework for environmental management tactics. Their division of these tactics into independent, cooperative, and strategic subcategories is shown in Figure 5-1.

TACTICAL QUESTIONS FOR THE MARKETING PLAN

The form contained in Figure 5-2 contains questions in each of the areas discussed in this chapter—product, price, promotion, and place—as well as in the use of the marketing environs to develop tactics. Completing this form will assist you in considering the trade-offs to develop powerful marketing tactics for your marketing plan.

SUMMARY

In this chapter you have learned how to develop marketing tactics to implement the strategies that you selected in Chapter 4. Marketing tactics have to do with your manipulation of product, price, promotion, and place and the marketing environs. In Chapter 6 you will learn how to determine the total potential available for any given market and how to forecast sales that will result from the strategy and tactics that you selected.

NOTES

1.   Zachary Schiller, Greg Burns, and Karen L. Miller, "Make It Simple," *BusinessWeek* (September 9, 1996), p. 96.

2.   Kerry Capell, Larry Light, and Ann Therese, "Just Wild about Harry Potter," *BusinessWeek* (August 9, 1999), p. 54.

3.   Brit Kjos, "New Harry Potter Book Shares Pre-Sale Frenzy with D&D," *Worthy News,* http://www.worthynews.com/news-features/harry-potter-2.html. Accessed November 7, 2003.

4.   Paul J. Krupin, "Ten Tips for Using E-Mail to Get News Coverage for Business," http://www.hansonmarketing.com/guest2-ahtml. Accessed January 13, 2000.

Environmental Management Tactic	Definition	Examples
Independent Tactics		
Competitive aggression	Focal organization exploits a distinctive competence or improves internal efficiency of resources for competitive advantage.	Product differentiation. Aggressive pricing. Comparative advertising.
Competitive pacification	Independent action to improve relations with competitors.	Helping competitors find raw materials. Advertising campaigns which promote entire industry. Price umbrellas.
Public relations	Establishing and maintaining favorable images in the minds of those making up the environment.	Corporate advertising campaigns.
Voluntary action	Voluntary management of and commitment to various interest groups, causes, and social problems.	McGraw-Hill efforts to prevent sexist stereotypes. 3M's energy conservation program.
Dependence development	Creating or modifying relationships such that external groups become dependent on the focal organization.	Raising switching costs for suppliers. Production of critical defense-related commodities. Providing vital information to regulators.
Legal action	Company engages in private legal battle with competitor on antitrust, deceptive advertising, or other grounds.	Private antitrust suits brought against competitors.
Political action	Efforts to influence elected representatives to create a more favorable business environment or limit competition.	Corporate constituency programs. Issue advertising. Direct lobbying.
Smoothing	Attempting to resolve irregular demand.	Telephone company's lower weekend rates. Inexpensive airline fares on off-peak times.
Demarketing	Attempts to discourage customers in general or a certain class of customers in particular, on either a temporary or a permanent basis.	Shorter hours of operation by gasoline service stations.
Cooperative Tactics		
Implicit cooperation	Patterned, predictable, and coordinated behaviors.	Price leadership.
Contracting	Negotiation of an agreement between the organization and another group to exchange goods, services, information, patterns, etc.	Contractual vertical and horizontal marketing systems.
Co-optation	Process of absorbing new elements into the leadership or policymaking structure of an organization as a means of averting threats to its stability of existence.	Consumer representatives, women, and bankers on boards of directors.
Coalition	Two or more groups coalesce and act jointly with respect to some set of issues for some period of time.	Industry association. Political initiatives of the Business Roundtable and the U.S. Chamber of Commerce.

(Continues)

FIGURE 5-1. A Framework of Environmental Management Strategies
Source: From "Environmental Management: Revising the Markets Perspective," by Carl P. Zeithaml and Valerie A. Zeithaml, *Journal of Marketing* (Spring 1984), pp. 50–57. Used with permission.

Environmental Management Tactic	Definition	Examples
	Strategic Maneuvering	
Domain selection	Entering industries or markets with limited competition or regulation coupled with ample suppliers and customers; entering high growth markets.	IBM's entry into the personal computer market. Miller Brewing Company's entry into the light beer market.
Diversification	Investing in different types of businesses, manufacturing different types of products, vertical integration, or geographic expansion to reduce dependence on single product, service, market, or technology.	Marriott's investment in different forms of restaurants. General Electric's wide product mix.
Merger and acquisition	Combining two or more firms into a single enterprise; gaining possession of an ongoing enterprise.	Merger between Pan American and National Airlines. Philip Morris's acquisition of Miller Beer.

FIGURE 5-1.   A Framework of Environmental Management Strategies *(Continued)*

PRODUCT

Product description _____

_____

_____

Life-cycle stage _____

Characteristics of stage _____

_____

_____

_____

Complementary products   1. _____ 2. _____

3. _____ 4. _____ 5. _____

Substitute products   1. _____ 2. _____

3. _____ 4. _____ 5. _____

Package: Message _____

Size _____ Shape _____ Color_____

Function _____ Material _____

Brand: Name _____

Type of branding _____

Forecast sales volume _____

Forecast production volume _____

_____

Basic product strategy _____

_____

_____

PRICE

Objectives 1. _____ 2. _____

3. _____ 4. _____

Basic per unit cost of acquisition _____

Other relevant costs _____

_____

_____

_____

_____

(Continues)

FIGURE 5-2.   Tactical Questions for the Marketing Plan
Source: Copyright © 1985 by Dr. William A. Cohen. *Note:* This form is based on an earlier form designed by Dr. Benny Barak, then of Baruch College.

Discount policy _____

_____

_____

Pricing strategy _____

_____

_____

Unit pricing _____

_____

_____

Forecast revenue _____

Forecast profit _____

DISTRIBUTION

Channels to be used and timing _____

_____

_____

_____

Alternative strategies: Push/pull _____

Intensive/selective/exclusive _____

PROMOTION

Positioning _____

_____

Advertising: Objectives   1. _____

2. _____   3. _____

Campaign theme _____

_____

Copy theme _____

_____

_____

_____

Graphics and layout _____

_____

_____

_____

(Continues)

FIGURE 5-2.   Tactical Questions for the Marketing Plan *(Continued)*

Media plan	Description	Length/size	Freq/dates	Cost
Newspapers	_____	_____	_____	_____
	_____	_____	_____	_____
	_____	_____	_____	_____
Magazines	_____	_____	_____	_____
	_____	_____	_____	_____
	_____	_____	_____	_____
Television	_____	_____	_____	_____
	_____	_____	_____	_____
	_____	_____	_____	_____
Radio	_____	_____	_____	_____
	_____	_____	_____	_____
	_____	_____	_____	_____
Other	_____	_____	_____	_____
	_____	_____	_____	_____
	_____	_____	_____	_____

Budget for advertising _____

Publicity: Objectives   1. _____   2. _____

3. _____   4. _____

Action/cost/timing

Description of action	Timing	Cost
_____	_____	_____
_____	_____	_____
_____	_____	_____
_____	_____	_____
_____	_____	_____
_____	_____	_____
_____	_____	_____
_____	_____	_____
_____	_____	_____
_____	_____	_____
_____	_____	_____

Budget for publicity _____

Personal selling: Objectives   1. _____

2. _____   3. _____

(Continues)

FIGURE 5-2.   Tactical Questions for the Marketing Plan *(Continued)*

Sales force size and type _____

_____

_____

Sales territories _____

_____

_____

Method of compensation _____

_____

_____

Budget for personal selling _____

Sales promotion: Objectives 1. _____

2. _____ 3. _____

Methods and costs

Method	Timing	Cost
_____	_____	_____
_____	_____	_____
_____	_____	_____
_____	_____	_____
_____	_____	_____
_____	_____	_____
_____	_____	_____

Budget for sales promotion _____

Summary of overall goals/costs/time to achieve of project _____

Goals 1. _____ 2. _____

3. _____ 4. _____

Overall cost _____ Timing _____

_____

_____

_____

_____

FIGURE 5-2. Tactical Questions for the Marketing Plan *(Continued)*

CHAPTER 6

STEP 6

FORECASTING FOR YOUR MARKETING PLAN

When you forecast, you attempt to predict the future. To a significant extent you will do this by analyzing the past. Of course, this does not necessarily mean that whatever happened in the past will continue to happen in the future, but it is here that the process of forecasting begins. By forecasting you will be able to establish more accurate goals and objectives for your marketing plan. But forecasting does even more for you. It will help you do all of the following:

- Determine markets for your products
- Plan corporate strategy
- Develop sales quotas
- Determine whether salespeople are needed and how many
- Decide on distribution channels
- Price products or services
- Analyze products and product potential in different markets
- Decide on product features
- Determine profit and sales potential for products
- Determine advertising and sales promotion budgets
- Determine the potential benefits of various elements of marketing tactics

So sales forecasting involves decisions made in all sections of your marketing plan. As you will see as you proceed, forecasting may involve some guesswork and a great deal of managerial judgment. Nevertheless, even guesswork becomes far more valuable when supported by facts and careful analysis.

If you simply pull facts out of thin air and construct your marketing plan based on them without a logical method of proceeding, many of your basic assumptions are as likely to be wrong as right. Succeeding under these conditions would be largely a matter of luck.

In this chapter you will learn how to optimize your hunches through forecasting techniques. This will make the figures in your marketing plan far more credible. It will also greatly increase your chance of success should you actually implement your plan.

THE DIFFERENCE BETWEEN MARKET POTENTIAL, SALES POTENTIAL, AND SALES FORECAST

Market potential, sales potential, and sales forecast all mean different things. *Market potential* refers to the total potential sales for a product or service or any group of products being considered for a certain geographical area or designated market, over a specific period. Market potential relates to the total capacity of that market to absorb everything that an entire industry may produce, whether airline travel, lightbulbs, or motorcycle helmets.

Let's say that there are one million new motorcyclists every year, and that one million old motorcycle helmets wear out every year and must be discarded. The market potential for motorcycle helmets in the United States is two million helmets every year. If helmets sell for $100 each, that would be a market potential of $200 million a year.

Sales potential refers to the ability of the market to absorb or purchase the output of a single company in that industry, presumably yours. Thus, if you are a motorcycle helmet manufacturer, the ability of the market to purchase that output might be only $50 million, even though the market potential is $200 million.

The term *sales forecast* refers to the actual sales you predict your firm will realize in this market in a single year. In using our motorcycle helmet example, perhaps your sales forecast will be only $20 million, even though the market potential is $200 million for the entire industry and the sales potential $50 million for your company.

Why the difference? Why can't you reach the full market potential in sales? Sales potential may not exceed market potential because of your production capacity. You can produce only $50 million in helmets, not $200 million.

There may be many reasons for not trying to achieve 100 percent of the sales potential of which you are capable. Perhaps to sell to the entire market would require more money than you have available for your marketing campaign.

Maybe the return on your investment to reach your full sales potential is insufficient to make this a worthwhile objective. To achieve 100 percent of anything requires consideration of the law of diminishing returns. This means that the marginal cost of each additional percentage point becomes greater and greater as you try to achieve the full sales potential. Therefore it may be wiser to stop at 90, 80, or even 70 percent of your sales potential because the significantly higher costs of achieving those final percentage points to get to 100 percent make the goal less desirable. There may be far better uses for your resources because the return on each dollar you invest elsewhere may be greater.

Finally, there may be some other reason that will discourage you from achieving 100 percent. Maybe competition is particularly strong. Perhaps there is an unfavorable factor in the marketing environment, such as the law that requires cyclists to wear helmets in your state being repealed.

Nevertheless, we must know the market potential and sales potential before we can calculate our sales forecast.

FINDING MARKET POTENTIAL

Sometimes it is possible to find the market potential for a specific product through research already done by someone else. Such research may have been previously accomplished by the U.S. government, a trade association, or an industry magazine. At other times it is necessary to derive the market potential for your products by using a chain of information. This latter method is called a chain ratio and involves connecting many related facts to arrive at the total market potential you are seeking.

For an export project some years ago, I wanted to explore the market potential for body armor used by foreign military forces. Because at that time only a few countries used this equipment, this number had to be determined by a chain ratio method.

First, I calculated the number of units of body armor used by U.S. military forces. I used a government publication called the *Commerce Business Daily*. It lists contracts awarded for most government purchases. An average number of body armor units per year was derived from a look at purchases over several years.

Next, I researched the size of the U.S. Army during that period. From the total annual sales of body armor to the U.S. Army and the average size of the ground forces during the same period, a ratio of body armor units per soldier could be developed.

Then, I consulted the *Almanac of World Military Power*. This book listed the strength of military forces for all countries. Because the body armor was a military item, the sale of it is controlled by the U.S. government. Therefore only those countries for which sales were likely to be approved by the U.S. government were included.

I added the figures for each country and calculated the total. Next, I took the ratio of body armor units per soldier developed earlier from U.S. data and applied it to this figure. The result was a total market potential of military body armor for export from the United States to foreign armies.

Note that this was not the sales potential for the sale of body armor by any single company for this market, nor was it a forecast of what body armor would be sold. It was the market potential for sales from the United States.

Let's look at another example. Let's say that a dance studio wishes to know the market potential for dance students in its geographical area. The first step would be to note the total population in the area served by the studio. If the area has a five-mile circumference, then you will want to know its population. These population figures can be obtained from the census surveys of the Department of Commerce. Sometimes your local Chamber of Commerce may have this information, or surveys may have been done by local or state governments.

Once you have the population, the next step is to arrive at the per capita expenditure for dancing lessons. Again, government statistics may be helpful. Industry associations of dance studios may be able to provide this information. You might also look for trade magazines having to do with professional dance and studio management. Naturally you must be sure that the geographical information furnished corresponds closely with the geographical area you are analyzing. Per capita expenditure can differ greatly, depending on the region of the country, its culture and climate, and the feelings and interests of its people.

If you multiply the population in the five-mile area by the per capita expenditure for dance lessons, you will end up with a total annual expenditure.

As you can see, the market potential for any product or class of product or service can be determined by doing a little detective work. Think about how you might get a market potential that is not available directly by linking other available information.

The Index Method of Calculating Market Potential

An alternate way of calculating market potential is by the use of indices that have already been constructed from surveys and basic economic data. One example is the survey published by *Sales and Marketing Magazine*. This magazine publishes a survey of buying power indices every year. It develops commercial indices by combining estimates of population, income, and retail sales. This results in a positive indicator of consumer data demand according to regions of the U.S. Bureau of Census by state, by its organized system of metro areas by counties, or even by cities with larger populations. You multiply the resulting buying power index (BPI) by national sales figures to obtain the market potential for any local area.

Let's say that you sell a certain national brand of television but only in the local area in your own city store. From the manufacturer you learn that ten million units are sold every year. Now you want to calculate the market potential for your city. You take the city's listed BPI and multiply it by ten million. The answer is the market potential for your city. The *Sales and Marketing Magazine*'s methodology also permits you to calculate the market potential with a custom BPI depending on demographics of your target market and your geographical area.

The BPI can also be used as a relative indicator to compare the potential buying power of the market you have targeted for your product. You can calculate a custom BPI for each market targeted.

Once you have the market potential, you can calculate sales potential by deciding how much of this market potential "belongs" to your firm. With no competition perhaps it's all yours. But, again, you must consider your capacity for satisfying the entire market. Once you have sales potential, you can turn to forecasting.

BOTTOM-UP AND TOP-DOWN SALES FORECASTING

There are two basic ways to forecast sales: the bottom-up and top-down methods. With the bottom-up method the sequence is to break up the market into segments and forecast each separately. You sum the sales forecast in each segment for the total sales forecast. Typical ways of doing this are by sales-force composites, industry surveys, and intention-to-buy surveys. We'll look at each of these later in the chapter.

To accomplish top-down forecasting, the sales potential for the entire market is estimated, sales quotas are developed, and a sales forecast is constructed. Typical methods used in top-down surveys are executive judgment, trend projections, a moving average, regression, exponential smoothing, and leading indicators. Let's look at each of these forecasting methods first.

Executive Judgment

Executive judgment is known by a variety of names like "jury of executive opinion," "managerial judgment," and even "gut feeling." With this method you just ask executives who have the expertise. This could be many individuals or one single person who may be responsible for the program. This method of forecasting is fairly easy to use, but it is not without its dangers. Experts on anything have differing biases and differing opinions.

To overcome individual bias, some unusual methods have evolved. Perhaps the best known is the Delphi Method. Experts are assembled and their opinions asked. Instead of stating these opinions orally, they are written down anonymously, along with the reasons behind them. A facilitator analyzes the results; calculates the range of answers, the frequency of each answer, and the average; and indicates the reasons given. This summary is returned to the group of experts. A second round is then conducted and the same questions are asked. This process may be repeated several times until a consensus emerges to result in the final forecast.

What makes this method work is that it enables expert opinion and reasoning to be shared without many of the psychological hang-ups of a public debate or alteration of opinion. It eliminates many psychological barriers, such as relative power, that are inherent in roundtable discussions and that might block legitimate input. The Delphi method has been a useful and accurate method of using executive judgment in forecasting.

Sales-Force Composite

A sales-force composite can be obtained by assigning each of your salespeople the duty of forecasting sales potential for a particular territory. These territorial estimates are then summed to arrive at an overall forecast. The dangers in obtaining a forecast this way are based on the possibility that customers may not be entirely truthful in giving information to the salesperson. Also, the salesperson may overstate or understate the area's potential.

Why would a salesperson do this? Perhaps fear of being assigned sales quotas that are difficult to reach may cause the potential to be understated. Or the salesperson may overstate the potential to prevent the area from being eliminated.

If you have a new business, you may not be able to use this method because you haven't got a sales force.

Trend Projections

A trend projection in its simplest form is an analysis of what has already happened, extended into the future. Your recorded observations of past sales may reveal that they have increased on an average of 10 percent every year. A simple trend projection would assume that sales will increase by 10 percent for the coming year as well.

If sales two years ago were $100,000 and last year were $300,000, and you projected the trend into the future by percentage, you would estimate $900,000 for next year. You might also estimate an increase in sales in absolute terms. If you did, you would estimate an increase of $200,000 each year. So next year's sales would be $500,000. Which type of linear project to use depends on your circumstances. You need to find out why you achieved the previous increase. If the reason can be related more to a percentage, then that's the way to do your trend analysis projection. If not, maybe an absolute dollar increase will provide a more accurate forecast.

A moving average is a more sophisticated trend projection. With this approach the assumption is made that the future will be an average of past performance rather than a linear projection. This minimizes the danger of a random event or element that could create a major impact on the forecast and cause it to be in error. Maybe a salesperson made a huge, unlikely sale.

I met a young real estate salesman once who sold an $18 million property three months after he started in the business. He was even written up in the local newspapers. It would have been unwise for his organization to create a sales forecast for the following year without some consideration that this type of event was unlikely to be repeated.

What can we do to take care of unusual events like this? Let's look at what would happen to our forecast using a moving average. The average of $100,000 and $300,000 for two years is $200,000—you would forecast $200,000 for the coming year. The moving average is simply summing up the sales in a number of periods and dividing by that number.

Which is the "correct" method of trend projection? Well, that's what makes marketing and forecasting so much fun. There isn't a correct method. You've got to consider other factors to help you decide which is correct for your situation.

Again, if you have no track record, you can't use this method.

Industry Survey

In the industry survey method, you survey companies that make up the industry for a particular product or service. The industry survey method has some of the characteristics of the bottom-up method, rather than the top-down, and some of the advantages and disadvantages of executive opinion and sales-force composites. Representatives of companies may answer inaccurately.

One thing you can do to minimize this is to make certain you talk to the right people. Some employees that want to help may not have access to accurate information, but try to give you some answer anyway. At other times, companies consider information highly proprietary. However, at times you can collect useful information, or you may find useful data from industry associations or trade magazines.

Naturally, no one is going to do your forecasting for you. What you may be able to obtain is information regarding the norm for salespeople in the industry and geographical area you're interested in. You then apply this or similar information to work out your forecast.

Regression Analyses

A regression analysis may be linear, or it may have to do with multiple regression. With linear regression, relationships between sales and a single independent variable are developed to forecast sales data. With multiple regression, relationships between sales and a number of independent variables are used. Computer programs can assist you in doing these calculations.

Sales predictions are made by estimating the values for independent variables and incorporating them into the multiple regression equation. Thus, if a relationship can be found among various independent variables—for example, units of computers sold, number of males between the ages of thirty-six and fifty-five, average family income, rate of inflation, and per capita years of education—a multiple regression equation based on this information can be developed to predict sales for the coming year.

Intention-to-Buy Survey

The intention-to-buy survey is done before the introduction of a new product or new service or for the purchase of any product or service for some period in the future. The main problem with these surveys is that individuals may not always give accurate information regarding their intention to buy products or services in the future. So what's new? you may ask. What is it this time?

Inaccurate responses may be due to an inadequate explanation, a misunderstanding on the part of the respondent, or to other psychological factors, such as the individual's unwillingness to offend or a desire to respond in a way that is socially acceptable.

Face-to-face surveys regarding sexually explicit reading matter frequently indicate almost no intent to purchase. Yet, if *Playboy* magazine can be used as an example, this is a multimillion-dollar business with a large number of readers and subscribers.

Also, there is something about actually making the purchase that distinguishes it from intending to do so. The respondent may have really believed he or she would buy if the product were available. However, when it comes to the moment of truth, there may be reasons that he or she never thought of to interfere with the sale.

Exponential Smoothing

Exponential smoothing is a timed series approach similar to the moving average method of trend analysis. Instead of a constant set of weights for the observations, however, an exponentially increasing set of weights is used to give the more recent values more weight than the older values.

This is exponential smoothing in its most basic form. More sophisticated models include adjustments for factors like trend and seasonal patterns. Forecasting techniques based on exponential smoothing are available on various computer programs. So you don't need to be a mathematical wizard. Just be able to put the disk in your computer and follow the directions.

Leading Indicators

Leading indicators to predict recessions and recoveries are used by the National Bureau of Economic Research. Typical leading indicators reported by this bureau include the prices of 500 common stocks, new orders for durable goods, an index of net business formation, corporate profits after taxes, industrial material prices, and changing consumer installment credit.

The problem of sales forecasting with these leading indicators is in relating them to specific products or services. When relationships are found, a multiregression model can be constructed. In fact, leading indicators are incorporated into some computer programs available for forecasting.

You can make rudimentary guesses based on leading economic indicators and apply them to your forecast. Many times this will have as good a chance of being correct as an expensive computer model.

WHICH METHOD TO USE

Some methods are more popular in forecasting than others. A survey of 175 firms conducted some time ago indicated that the jury of executive opinion and sales-force composite were the two most popular. This is shown in Figure 6-1. Another study, which confirms that the executive opinion method is still the most popular, found that the two quantitative methods, time series smoothing and regressional analysis, were in second and third place, respectively, with sales-force composite following.

Consideration of a sales forecasting method for your particular situation and for your marketing plan should not be based merely on popularity of the method, but on situational factors that affect you. These factors include the resources that you have available, the time available, accuracy required, your estimation of the accuracy that can be attained by

Method	Regular Use (%)	Occasional Use (%)	Never Used (%)
Jury of executive opinion	52	16	5
Sales-force composite	48	15	9
Trend projections	28	16	12
Moving average	24	15	15
Industry survey	22	20	16
Regression	17	13	24
Intention-to-buy survey	15	17	23
Exponential smoothing	13	13	26
Leading indicators	12	16	24

FIGURE 6-1.   Utilization of Sales Forecasting Methods by 175 Firms
Source: Adapted from Douglas J. Dalrymple, "Sales Forecasting Methods and Accuracy," *Business Horizons,* 18 (December 1975), p. 71.

different methods given to your sales force, your customers, the individuals surveyed, and the cost of the forecast. Thus your judgment in choosing a sales forecasting method, or a combination of methods, is of primary importance.

Alvin Toffler, author of *Future Shock* and *The Third Wave,* probably said it best: "You can use all the quantitative data you can get, but you still have to distrust it and use your own intelligence and judgment."

YOU NEED MORE INFORMATION FOR YOUR FORECAST

Forecasting sales alone is insufficient. You must also forecast the costs involved and when they occur. This is done with a project development schedule, a break-even analysis, a balance sheet, a projected profit and loss statement, and cash-flow projections. Let's look at each in turn.

The Project Development Schedule

The project development schedule, or PDS, is shown in Figure 6-2. It lists every task necessary to implement the project and the money spent during each period. These periods can be months or, in the case of the example indicated, weeks. Note that you don't need to know the exact date you will begin in order to develop an accurate PDS. All you need to do is describe the timing as "weeks or months after project initiation." If many departments or individuals are involved, you can include them all to see who is doing what. By incorporating the amount of money spent by each, you will see totals spent by each department, totals spent for each task, and when money is needed for each task.

The project development schedule shows your entire plan financially and graphically. It will reveal problems in timing, financing, and coordination before you start. Once you begin to implement the plan, it will help you to monitor and control the project.

The Break-Even Analysis

A break-even analysis is used for evaluating relationships among sales revenues, fixed costs, and variable costs. The break-even point is the point at which the sales from a number of units sold cover costs of developing, producing, and selling the product. Prior to this point, you will be losing money. Beyond it you will make money. It is an excellent means for helping you forecast both the success of the product and what you need to succeed before the project is actually initiated because it will tell you the following:

• How many units you must sell in order to start making money.

• How much profit you will make at any given level of sales.

Months After Project Initiation

Task	1	2	3	4	5	6	7	8	9	10	11	12
Manufacture of units for test manufacturing	$5,000											
Initial advertisement in test area	$10,000	$10,000	$10,000									
Shipment of units in test market area	$300	$200										
Analysis of test		$500	$700	$200								
Manufacture of units—1st year				$5,000	$10,000	$10,000	$10,000	$10,000				
Phase I advertising and publicity				$10,000	$30,000	$30,000	$15,000					
Shipment of units					$1,000	$1,000	$1,000	$1,000	$500			
Phase II advertising						$10,000	$10,000	$10,000	$10,000	$5,000	$5,000	$5,000

FIGURE 6-2.   Product Development Schedule

- How changing your price will affect profitability.
- How cost increases or reductions at different levels of sales will affect profitability.

Combining your sales forecasts with break-even analysis will tell you how long it will take you to reach break-even.

To accomplish a break-even analysis, separate the cost associated with your project into two categories: fixed costs and variable costs.

Fixed costs are those expenses associated with the project that you would have to pay whether you sold one unit or ten thousand units or, for that matter, whether you sold any units at all.

If you need to rent a building to implement your project and the owner of the building charges you $50,000, then this would be a fixed cost. You would have to pay the $50,000 whether you sold no units or millions of units. Research and development costs for a project or a product are also considered fixed costs. You have to spend this money whether you sell any of the product or not.

Variable costs are those that vary directly with the number of units you sell. If postage for mailing your product to a customer is $1, then $1 is a variable cost. If you sell ten units, then your postage is ten times $1, or $10. If you sell 100 units, your total variable costs for postage would be 100 times $1 or $100.

It is sometimes difficult to decide whether to consider costs as fixed or variable, and there may not be a single correct answer. Use judgment, along with the advice of financial or accounting experts if they are available. As a general guideline, if there is a direct relationship between cost and number of units sold, consider the cost as variable. If you cannot find such a relationship, consider the cost fixed. The total cost of your project will always equal the sum of the fixed costs plus the variable costs.

Here's an example of an item that you are going to sell for $10. How much profit would you make if you sold 1,000 units?

Fixed Costs

Utility expense at $100 per month for thirty-six months	$3,600
Telephone at $200 per year for three years	600
Product development costs	1,000
Rental expense	2,500
Total fixed costs	$7,700

Variable Costs

Cost of product	$1.00 per unit
Cost of postage and packaging	0.50 per unit
Cost of advertising	3.00 per unit
Total variable costs	$4.50 per unit

To calculate the break-even point, start with the equation for profit. Total profit equals the number of units sold times the price at which we are selling them, less the number of units sold multiplied by the total variable cost, less the total fixed cost.

If P stands for profit, p for price, U for the number of units sold, V for variable costs, and F for fixed costs, then our equation becomes

$$P = (U \times p) - (U \times V) - F$$

You can simplify this to

$$P = U\,(p - V) - F$$

Substituting the values given in your example, you have

$$P = \$1,000\,(\$10 - \$4.50) - \$7,700$$
$$= \$5,500 - \$7,700 = -\$2,200$$

The significance of the minus is that instead of making a profit at the particular number of units you have estimated, you have lost $2,200.

If you want to know how many units you must sell in order to reach the break-even point, you can again use the equation for profit:

$$P = U (p - V) - F$$

Since profit at the break-even point is by definition zero, you can transpose terms and let $P = 0$. Then the break-even point equals F divided by $p - V$.

Because you know that $F = \$7,700$, $p = \$10.00$, and $V = \$4.50$, the break-even point must equal $7,700 divided by $10.00–$4.50. That's $7,700/5.50 or 1,400 units.

This means that if you don't change price or reduce expenses, you must sell 1,400 units of the product before you can start making money.

You can calculate this graphically by using the chart in Figure 6-3. A break-even chart has an advantage over using the break-even equation. It shows you the relationship between profits and sales volume graphically. It is therefore easier for you to see how cost and other factors affect the results.

Even though there are advantages to break-even analysis, keep in mind that there are some limitations. First, break-even analysis shows profit at various levels of sales, but it does not show the return for our investment and other measures of financial efficiency. Because there are always alternative uses for a firm's financial resources, it is impossible to compare return on investment solely on the basis of break-even analysis. Also, break-even analysis does not allow you to examine the cash flow. One way to compare investment or capital budgeting alternatives is to consider the value of the cash flows over a period of time and to discount the cost of capital by an appropriate percentage. You can't do this with a break-even analysis alone because the time to reach the various levels of sales is not indicated.

Despite these shortcomings, break-even analysis is a useful technique and should always be included as a part of your marketing plan.

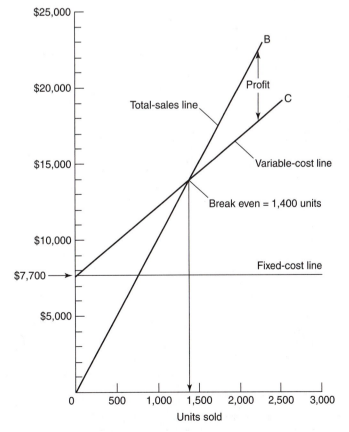

FIGURE 6-3. Break-Even Analysis Chart

The Balance Sheet, Projected Profit and Loss Statement, and Cash-Flow Projections

A balance sheet is usually calculated for businesses, but it can also be calculated for a project. Basically, it consists of financial snapshots of two or more points in your project. Most people select start-up and at least one other important milestone in the project.

In Figure 6-4, a balance sheet form is shown for Year 1 and Year 2. You calculate current assets, fixed assets, other assets, current liabilities, and long-term liabilities to arrive at a total net worth.

BALANCE SHEET

	Year 1	Year 2
Current Assets		
Cash		
Accounts receivable		
Inventory		
Fixed Assets		
Real estate		
Fixtures and equipment		
Vehicles		
Other Assets		
Licenses		
Goodwill		
Total Assets		
Current Liabilities		
Notes payable (due within 1 year)		
Accounts payable		
Accrued expenses		
Taxes owed		
Long-Term Liabilities		
Notes payable (due after 1 year)		
Other		
Total Liabilities		
Net Worth (Assets minus Liabilities)		

Total Liabilities plus Net Worth Should Equal Assets

FIGURE 6-4.   Balance Sheet

The projected profit and loss statement is shown in Figure 6-5. It is broken down on a monthly basis. Document total net sales, cost of sales, and gross profit. Also note controllable expenses and fixed expenses and develop a net profit or loss before taxes for every month. This may be done for only a single year, or it can be done for up to five years into the future, depending on the project.

The profit and loss statement along with the cash-flow projections in Figure 6-6 will show what happens between balance sheets. The latter displays cash, income, and expenses on a monthly basis from start-up. Do these for the same number of years that you did the profit and loss statement.

A cash-flow projection shows the availability of cash on a monthly basis. If you need additional cash to keep your project going, it will show when the money will be needed. Obviously this will be of great interest not only to you, but also to your potential investors or company finance officers. They will want to know not only how much is needed, but also when.

PROJECTED PROFIT AND LOSS STATEMENT

	Month 1	Month 2	Month 3	Month 4	Month 5	Month 6	Month 7	Month 8	Month 9	Month 10	Month 11	Month 12
Total Net Sales												
Cost of sales												
Gross profit												
Controllable expenses: salaries												
Payroll taxes												
Security												
Advertising												
Automobile												
Dues and subscriptions												
Legal and accounting												
Office supplies												
Telephone												
Utilities												
Miscellaneous												
Total Controllable Expenses												
Fixed expenses: depreciation												
Insurance												
Rent												
Taxes and licenses												
Loan payments												
Total Fixed Expenses												
Total Expenses												
Net profit (loss) (before taxes)												

FIGURE 6-5.   Projected Profit and Loss Statement

CASH-FLOW PROJECTIONS

	Start-up or prior to loan	Month 1	Month 2	Month 3	Month 4	Month 5	Month 6	Month 7	Month 8	Month 9	Month 10	Month 11	Month 12	TOTAL
Cash (beginning of month)														
Cash on hand														
Cash in bank														
Cash in investments														
Total Cash														
Income (during month): Cash sales														
Credit sales payments														
Investment income														
Loans														
Other cash income														
Total income														
Total Cash and Income														
Expenses (during month): Inventory or new material														
Wages (including owner's)														
Taxes														
Equipment expense														
Overhead														
Selling expense														
Transportation														
Loan repayment														
Other cash expenses														
Total Expenses														
Cash Flow Excess (end of month)														
Cash Flow Cumulative (monthly)														

FIGURE 6-6.   Cash Flow Projections

SUMMARY

In this chapter you have seen how to forecast everything you need for your marketing plan. You have seen how to calculate market potential, sales potential, and sales forecasts. You have seen how to forecast costs to develop a project development schedule with costs recorded periodically as needed, how to complete a break-even chart to determine how many units you need to sell to be profitable, how to determine how much money you made at any level of units sold, how to complete a balance sheet that indicates the status of your project at the end of various periods of time, and how to calculate a profit and loss statement and cash-flow projections on a monthly basis.

No marketing plan can be implemented without financial resources. The forecasts discussed in this chapter will enable you to know what financial resources are necessary, as well as the benefits that will accrue as a result of investing these resources.

You are now in a position to calculate important financial ratios and to use them to help determine how efficient your plan is and how beneficial it is to the firm compared with other alternatives. Knowledge of these financial ratios will help you to get resources from those in authority in your company or from outside lenders. They will add tremendous credibility to your plan. We will learn how to calculate them in the next chapter.

CHAPTER

7

STEP 7

CALCULATING IMPORTANT FINANCIAL RATIOS FOR YOUR MARKETING PLAN

The financial ratios in this chapter will help provide information so that you, or others, can compare your plan with competing plans on a financial basis. They will enable you to better understand the financial efficiency of your plan and will help you win support for your project. To do this you analyze your planned figures. If you implement your marketing plan, you can analyze what is actually happening partly by use of these financial ratios.

Some of these ratios are used primarily to measure the financial condition of an entire business, rather than a single project. However, with many marketing plans, especially start-ups, the project and the business are one and the same. You must decide which ratios are applicable to your situation and which are not.

MEASURES OF LIQUIDITY

Liquidity is the ability to use the money available. In general, the more liquid, the better the state of financial health. The ratios intended to measure liquidity will tell you whether you have enough cash on hand, plus assets that can be readily turned into cash, to pay debts that may fall due during any given period.

The Current Ratio

The current ratio is possibly the best-known measure of financial health. It answers this question: Does your business have sufficient current assets to meet current debts with a margin of safety for possible losses due to uncollectible accounts receivable and other factors?

The current ratio is computed by using information on your balance sheet. Divide current assets by current liabilities. Look at the sample balance sheet in Figure 7-1. Current assets are $155,000 and current liabilities are $90,000; $155,000 divided by $90,000 equals a current ratio of 1.7.

Is 1.7 a "good" current ratio? You cannot determine this from the numerical value of 1.7 by itself. A popular rule of thumb says that you want a current ratio of at least 2.0. However, a desirable current ratio very much depends on your business and the specific characteristics of your current assets and liabilities. That's why a comparison with other current ratios is a better indication. I'll give you sources for this information in the section "Sources of Ratio Analyses from All Industries" later in the chapter.

December 31, 20____

BALANCE SHEET

Current assets:

Cash	$ 35,000.00	
Accounts receivable	55,000.00	
Inventory	60,000.00	
Temporary investments	3,000.00	
Prepaid expenses	2,000.00	
Total current assets		$ 155,000.00

Fixed assets:

Machinery and equipment	$ 35,000.00	
Buildings	42,000.00	
Land	40,000.00	
Total fixed assets		$ 117,000.00

Other assets:

None		
Total other assets		0.00
Total assets		$ 272,000.00

Current liabilities

Accounts payable	$ 36,000.00	
Notes payable	44,000.00	
Current portion of long-term notes	4,000.00	
Interest payable	1,000.00	
Taxes payable	3,000.00	
Accrued payroll	2,000.00	
Total current liabilities		$ 90,000.00

Long-term liabilities:

Notes payable	$ 25,000.00	
Total long-term liabilities		$ 25,000.00

Equity:

Owner's equity	$115,000.00	
Total equity		$ 115,000.00
Total liabilities and equity		$ 272,000.00

FIGURE 7-1.   Sample Balance Sheet for XYZ Company

If after analysis and comparison you decide that your current ratio is too low, you may be able to raise it by the following actions:

1.   Increase your current assets by new equity contributions.

2.   Try converting noncurrent assets into current assets.

3.   Pay some of your debts.

4.   Increase your current assets from loans or other types of borrowing that have a maturity of at least a year in the future.

5.   Put some of the profits back into the business.

THE ACID TEST, OR "QUICK," RATIO

The acid test, or "quick," ratio is also a measurement of liquidity. You calculate this ratio as follows: cash plus government securities plus receivables divided by current liabilities.

The company shown in Figure 7-1 has no government securities. Therefore the numerator of this figure becomes $35,000 cash plus $55,000 in accounts receivable, or $90,000. This is divided by current liabilities on the same balance sheet of $90,000 to result in an acid test ratio of 1.0.

The quick ratio concentrates on very liquid assets whose values are definite and well known. So the quick ratio answers this question: If all your sales revenue disappears tomorrow, can you meet current obligations with your cash or quick funds on hand? Usually an acid test ratio of approximately 1.0 is considered satisfactory. However, you must also make this decision conditional on the following:

1. There should be nothing to slow up the collection of your accounts receivable.

2. The receipt of accounts receivable collections should not trail the due schedule for paying your current liabilities. In checking out this timing, you should consider payment of your creditors sufficiently early to take advantage of any discounts that are offered.

If these two conditions are not met, then you will need an acid test ratio higher than 1.0. It is a mistake to believe that the current or the acid test ratio should always be as high as possible. Only those from whom you have borrowed money would agree. Naturally, they are interested in the greatest possible safety of their loan. However, you do not want to have large sums of money lying idle and not earning you additional profits. If you do have idle cash balances and receivables and inventories that are out of proportion to your needs, you should reduce them.

Be conservative enough to keep a safety pad and yet bold enough to take advantage of the fact that you have these resources that can be used to earn additional profits. Before making the decision as to the right amount of liquidity, you should consider the next two ratios: average collection period and inventory turnover.

AVERAGE COLLECTION PERIOD

The average collection period is the number of days that sales are tied up in accounts receivable. This number can be calculated by using your profit and loss statement or income statement as shown in Figure 7-2. Divide net sales by the days in your accounting period.

In Figure 7-2 net sales are $1,035,000, and your accounting period is 365 days. This equals $2,836. This is the average sales per day in the accounting period.

Next, look at your accounts receivable, which you obtained from the balance sheet, Figure 7-1. Accounts receivable are $55,000. Divide $55,000 by the average sales per day in the accounting period. $55,000 divided by $2,836 equals 19.

The result, 19, is the average number of days sales are tied up in receivables. It is also your average collection period.

This tells you how promptly your accounts are being collected, considering whatever credit terms you are extending. It also gives you other important insights. First, the quality of your accounts and notes receivable—that is, whether you are really getting paid rapidly or not. It also shows you how good a job your credit department is doing in collecting these accounts.

Now the question is whether the figure of nineteen days is good or not good. A rule of thumb says the average collection period should not exceed one and one-third times the credit terms offered. Therefore, if you offer terms of thirty days to pay and the average collection period is only nineteen days, you are doing very well. On the other hand, anything in excess of forty days ($1\frac{1}{3} \times 30 = 40$) would indicate a problem.

INVENTORY TURNOVER

Inventory turnover will show you how rapidly your merchandise is moving. It will also show you how much capital you have tied up in inventory to support the level of your company's operations for the period that you are analyzing. For your marketing plan, you can analyze planned inventory turnover.

To calculate inventory turnover, simply divide the cost of goods sold, which you obtain from your income statement, by your average inventory.

From Figure 7-2, your income profit and loss statement, the cost of goods sold equals $525,000. You cannot calculate your average inventory from Figure 7-1. You only know

For the year ended December 31, 20____

INCOME STATEMENT

Sales or revenue	$ 1,040,000.00	
Less returns and allowances:	5,000.00	
Net sales		$ 1,035,000.00
Cost of sales:		
Beginning inventory, Jan. 1, 20____	250,000.00	
Merchandise purchases	500,000.00	
Cost of goods available for sale	750,000.00	
Less ending inventory, Dec. 31, 20____	225,000.00	
Total cost of goods sold		525,000.00
Gross profit		$ 510,000.00
Operating expenses:		
Selling and general and administrative		
Salaries and wages	180,000.00	
Advertising	200,000.00	
Rent	10,000.00	
Utilities	5,000.00	
Other expenses	10,000.00	
Total operating expenses		405,000.00
Total operating income		$ 105,000.00
Other revenue and expenses		0.00
Pretax income		$ 105,000.00
Taxes on income	50,000.00	
Income after taxes but before extraordinary gain or loss		$ 55,000.00
Extraordinary gain or loss		0.00
Net income (or loss)		$ 55,000.00

FIGURE 7-2.   Sample Income Statement for the XYZ Company

that for the period for which the inventory is stated, it equals $60,000. Let's assume that the previous balance sheet indicated that your inventory was $50,000. Then the average inventory for the two periods would be $60,000 plus $50,000 divided by 2, or $55,000.

Now, let's see what inventory turnover is: Cost of goods sold, $525,000, divided by average inventory, $55,000, equals 9.5.

This means that you turned your inventory 9.5 times during the year. Put another way, through your business operations you used up merchandise that totaled 9.5 times the average inventory investment. Under most circumstances, the higher the inventory turnover, the better, because it means that you are able to operate with a relatively small sum of money invested in this inventory.

Another implication is that your inventory is the right inventory. You know this because it is salable and has not been in stock too long. But even here you must consider that too high a figure may signify a problem. Very high inventory turnover may mean that you have inventory shortages. Inventory shortages soon lead to customer dissatisfaction. This, in turn, may mean a loss of customers to the competition in the long run.

Is 9.5 a satisfactory inventory turnover or not? Again, the desirable rate depends on your business, your industry, your method of valuing inventories, and numerous other factors that are unique to your situation. Once again, it is helpful to study and compare your turnover rate with that of similar businesses of your size in your industry. After you have been in operation for some time and have a track record, experiences with inventory turnover will indicate what is good and what is not with less reliance on industry comparisons.

Of course, you can analyze specific inventory turnover for different products or even groups of products or product lines in your marketing plan. This will show you which items are doing well and which are not.

You may also prepare turnover analyses for periods that are much more frequent than a year. Even monthly or weekly periods may be necessary or required for perishable items or items that become obsolete very quickly. You will know to reorder "hot" items early and in plenty of time and which items you should not order. You will also know which items you must order before their value goes down to a point at which you can no longer sell them.

PROFITABILITY MEASURES

Measures of profitability are essential if you are to know how much money you are making, whether you are making as much as you can, or whether you are making money at all. Several ratios will assist you in determining this. These are the asset earning power, return on owner's equity, net profit on sales, investment turnover, and, finally, return on investment (ROI).

Asset Earning Power

Asset earning power is determined by the ratio of earnings before interest and taxes to total assets. From the income statement in Figure 7-2 we can see that total operating profit or income is $105,000. Total assets from the balance sheet, Figure 7-1, are $272,000. $105,000 divided by $272,000 equals 0.39, or 39 percent.

Return on the Owner's Equity

Return on the owner's equity shows the return that you received in exchange for your investment in your business. To compute this ratio you will usually use the average equity for twelve months. If this isn't available, use the average of figures from two balance sheets, your latest and the one before.

Return on the owner's equity equals net profit divided by equity. Net profit from Figure 7-2 is $55,000. Equity from Figure 7-1 is $115,000. Assuming the equity from the period before is also $115,000, use this as an average. Therefore, return on the owner's equity equals $55,000 divided by $115,000. That equals 0.48, or 48 percent.

You can calculate a similar ratio by using tangible net worth in lieu of equity. Tangible net worth equals equity less any intangible assets, such as patents owned and goodwill. If no intangible assets exist, the two will be equal.

Net Profit on Sales

The net profit on sales ratio measures the difference between what you take in and what you spend in the process of doing business. Again, net profit was determined to be $55,000. Net sales from Figure 7-2 are $1,035,000. Therefore net profit on sales equals 0.053, or 5.3 percent. This means that for every dollar of sales the company has earned a profit of 5.3 cents.

The net profit on sales ratio depends mainly on operating costs and pricing policies. If this figure goes down, it could be because you have lowered prices, or it could be because costs have been increasing while prices have remained stable.

Compare this ratio with those from other similar businesses. Also consider trends over a period of time. By comparing net profit on sales ratios for individual products, you will know which products or product lines need additional emphasis and which should be eliminated.

Investment Turnover

The ratio of investment turnover is annual net sales to total assets. In this case net sales of $1,035,000 divided by total assets of $272,000, from Figure 7-1, equals 3.8.

Once again, compare with other similar businesses and watch for trends.

Return on Investment (ROI)

ROI is a great way of measuring profitability of your investment or proposed investment. There are several ways of calculating return on investment.

One simple way is to take net profit and divide it by total assets. In this case (Figure 7-1) the net profit equals $55,000. Total assets are $272,000. Therefore, $55,000 divided by $272,000 equals 0.20, or 20 percent.

You want the highest net profit for the smallest amount of total assets invested. You can use this rate of return on investment for intercompany and interindustry comparisons, as well as pricing costs, inventory, and investment decisions, and many other measurements of efficiency and profitability. However you use it, always be sure that you are consistent in making your comparisons—that is, be sure that you use the same definitions of net profit and assets invested.

Here are some additional measures of profitability using ROI:

1. Rate of earnings on total capital employed equals net income plus interest and taxes divided by total liabilities and capital. This ratio serves as an index of productivity of capital as well as a measure of earning power in operating efficiency.

2. Rate of earnings on invested capital equals net income plus income taxes divided by proprietary equity and fixed liabilities. This ratio is used as a measure of earning power of the borrowed invested capital.

3. Rate of earnings on proprietary equity equals net income divided by total capital including surplus reserves. This ratio is used as a measure of the yield on the owner's investment.

4. Rate of earnings on stock equity equals net income divided by total capital including surplus reserves. This ratio is used as a measure of the attractiveness of common stock as an investment.

5. Rate of dividends on common stock equity equals common stock dividends divided by common stock equity. This ratio is used to indicate the desirability of common stock as a source of income.

6. Rate of dividends on common stock equity equals common stock dividend per share divided by market value per share of common stock. This ratio is used as a measure of the current yield on investment in a particular stock.

SOURCES OF RATIO ANALYSES FROM ALL INDUSTRIES

To be able to compare your business with other businesses in your industry, it is necessary to obtain pertinent data on other businesses. The following are sources of this information:

1. Dun & Bradstreet publishes key business ratios in its monthly *Dun's Review* as well as in its annual "Cost of Doing Business" report. Contact Business Information Systems, 99 Church Street, New York, NY 10007.

2. Accounting Corporation of America, The Research Department, 1929 First Avenue, San Diego, CA 92101. This organization publishes *Parameter of Small Businesses,* which classifies its operating ratios for various industry groups on the basis of gross volume.

3.   National Cash Register Company, Marketing Services Department, Dayton, OH 45409. This firm publishes *Expenses in Retail Businesses,* which examines the cost of operations in more than fifty kinds of businesses; information is obtained from primary sources, most of which are trade associations.

4.   Robert Morris Associates, Philadelphia National Bank Building, Philadelphia, PA 19107. Robert Morris has developed and published ratio studies for more than 225 lines of business.

5.   The Small Business Administration. The SBA has a series of reports that provide expenses as a percentage of sales for many industries. Although the reports do not provide strict ratio information, a comparison of percentage expenses will be very useful for your financial management.

6.   Trade associations. Many national trade associations publish ratio studies, including the following:

Air Conditioning & Refrigeration Institute (ARI), 4301 North Fairfax Drive, Suite 425, Arlington, VA 22203; Phone: 703-524-8800; Fax: 703-528-3816; E-mail: ari@ari.org; Web site: http://www.ari.org.

Air Transport Association of America (ATA), 1301 Pennsylvania Avenue, Suite 1100, Washington, DC 20004-7017; Phone: 202-626-4000; Fax: 202-626-4166; e-mail: ata@air-transport.org; Web site: http://www.airlines.org.

American Bankers Association (ABA), 1120 Connecticut Avenue NW, Washington, DC 20036; Phone: 202-663-5000; Toll-free: 800-338-0626; Fax: 202-663-7543; Web site: http://www.aba.com.

American Booksellers Association (ABA), 828 South Broadway, Tarrytown, NY 10591; Phone: 914-591-2665; Toll-free: 800-637-0037; Fax: 914-591-2720; E-mail: info@bookweb.org; Web site: http://www.bookweb.org.

American Electronics Association (AEA), 5201 Great American Parkway, Suite 520, Santa Clara, CA 95054; Phone: 408-987-4200; Toll-free: 800-284-4232; Fax: 408-986-1247; E-mail: For contact list see http://www.aeanet.org /AboutAeA/AeAContactInfo.asp Web site: http://www.aeanet.org.

American Forest & Paper Association (AF&PA), 1111 19th Street NW, Washington, DC 20036; Phone: 202-463-2700; Fax: 202-463-2785; Web site: http://www.afandpa.org.

American Furniture Manufacturers Association (AFMA), PO Box HP-7, High Point, NC 27261; Phone: 336-884-5000; Fax: 336-884-5303; Web site: http://www.afma4u.org.

American Meat Institute (AMI), 1700 N. Monroe Street, Suite 1600, Arlington, VA 22209; Phone: 703-841-2400; Fax: 703-527-0938; Web site: http://www.meatami.com.

American Society of Association Executives (ASAE), 1575 I St. NW, Washington, DC 20005-1168; Phone: 202-626-2723; Fax: 202-371-8825; E-mail: asae@asaenet.org; Web site: http://www.asaenet.org.

American Supply Association (ASA), 222 Merchandise Mart, Suite 1360, Chicago, IL 60654; Phone: 312-464-0090; Fax: 312-464-0091; E-mail: asaemail@interserv.org; Web site: http://www.asa.net.

American Wholesale Marketers Association (AWMA), 1128 16th Street, Washington, DC 20036; Phone: 202-463-2124; Toll-free: 800-482-2962; Fax: 202-463-6456; E-mail: davids@awmaner.org; Web site: http://www.awmanet.org.

Association of American Publishers (AAP), 71 Fifth Avenue, New York, NY 10003-3004; Phone: 212-255-0200; Fax: 213-255-7007; Web site: http://www.publishers.org.

Automotive Aftermarket Industry Association (AAIA), 4600 East-West Highway, Suite 300, Bethesda, MD 20814-3415; Phone: 301-654-6664; Fax: 301-654-3299; E-mail: aaia@aftermarket.org; Web site: http://www.aftermarket.org.

Bowling Proprietors' Association of America, Inc. (BPAA), 5301 South 76th Street, Greendale, WI 53129; Phone: 1-800-514-BOWL (2695); Web site: http://www.bowl.com.

Building Owners & Managers Association International (BOMAI), 1201 New York Avenue NW, Suite 300, Washington, DC 20005; Phone: 202-408-2662; Fax, 202-371-0181; E-mail: info@boma.org; Web site: http://www.boma.org.

Carpet & Rug Institute (CRI), 310 Holiday Avenue, PO Box 2048, Dalton, GA 30722: Phone: 706-278-3176; Toll-free: 800-882-8846; Fax: 706-278-8835; Web site: http://www.carpet-rug.com.

Door & Hardware Institute (DHI), 14170 Newbrook Drive, Chantilly, VA 20151-2232; Phone: 703-222-2010; Fax: 703-222-2410; Web site: http://www.dhi.org.

Food Marketing Institute (FMI), 800 Connecticut Avenue NW, Washington, DC 20006; Phone: 202-452-8444; Fax: 202-429-4519; E-mail: fmi@fmi.org; Web site: http://www.fmi.org.

Food Service Equipment Distributors Association (FEDA), 223 West Jackson Boulevard, Suite 620, Chicago, IL 60606; Phone: 800-677-9605; Fax: 800-677-9607; E-mail: ray@feda.com; Web site: http://www.feda.com.

Healthcare Distribution Management Association, 1821 Michael Faraday Drive, Suite 400, Reston, VA 20190; Phone: 703-787-0000; Fax: 703-787-6930; Web site: http://www.healthcaredistribution.org.

Independent Insurance Agents and Brokers of America, 127 South Peyton, Alexandria, VA 22314; Phone: 703-683-4422; Toll-free: 800-221-7917; Fax: 703-683-7556; E-mail: info@iiaba.org; Web site: http://www.independentagent.com.

Independent Office Products and Furniture Dealers Association, 301 North Fairfax Street, Alexandria, VA 22314; Phone: 703-549-9040; Fax: 703-683-7552; E-mail: info@iopfda.org; Web site: http://www.iopfda.org/.

Institute of Management Accountants (IMA), 10 Paragon Drive, Montvale, NJ 07645-0000; Phone: 201-573-9000; Toll-free: 800-638-4427; Fax: 201-573-8483; E-mail: ima@imanet.org; Web site: http://www.imanet.org.

International Association of Plastics Distributors (IAPD), 4707 College Boulevard, Suite 105, Leawood, KS 66211; Phone: 913-345-1005; Fax: 913-345-1006; E-mail: iapd@iapd.org; Web site: http://www.iapd.org.

International Fabricare Institute (IFI), 12251 Tech Road, Silver Spring, MD, 20904; Phone: 301-622-1900; Toll-free: 800-638-2627; Fax: 301-236-9320; E-mail: wecare@ifi.org; Web site: http://www.ifi.org.

International Hardware Distributors Association (IHDA), 401 North Michigan Avenue, Suite 2200, Chicago, IL 60611-4267; Phone: 312-644-6610; Fax: 312-527-6640; E-mail: ihda@sba.com; Web site: http://www.arcat.com/arcatcos/cos40/arc40180.cfm.

Kitchen Cabinet Manufacturers Association (KCMA), 1899 Preston White Drive, Reston, VA 20191-5435; Phone: 703-264-1690; Fax: 703-620-6530; E-mail: dtitus@kcma.org; Web site: http://www.kcma.org.

Laboratory Products Association (LPA), 225 Reineker, Suite 625, Alexandria, VA 22314; Phone: 703-836-1360; Fax: 703-836-6644; Web site: http://www.lpanet.org.

Material Handling Equipment Distributors Association (MHEDA), 201 Route 45, Vernon Hills, IL 60061; Phone: 827-680-3500; Fax: 847-362-6989; E-mail: connect@mheda.org; Web site: http://www.mheda.org.

Mechanical Contractors Association of America (MCAA), 1385 Piccard Drive, Rockville, MD 20850-4329; Phone: 301-869-5800; Toll-free: 800-556-3653; Fax: 301-990-9690; E-mail: john@mcaa.org; Web site: http://www.mcaa.org.

Motor & Equipment Manufacturers Association (MEMA), 10 Laboratory Drive, PO Box 13966, Research Triangle Park, NC 27709-3966; Phone: 919-549-4800; Fax: 919-549-4824; Web site: http://www.mema.org.

National Association of Electrical Distributors (NAED), 1100 Corporate Square Drive, Suite 100, St. Louis, MO 63132; Phone: 314-991-9000; Fax: 314-991-3060; E-mail: info@naed.org; Web site: http://www.naed.org.

National Association of Music Merchants, Inc., 5790 Arnada Drive, Carlsbad, CA 92008; Phone: 760-438-8001; Toll-free: 800-767-6266; Fax: 760-438-7327; Web site: http://www.namm.com.

National Automatic Merchandising Association (NAMA), 20 North Wacker Drive, Suite 350, Chicago, IL 60606; Phone: 312-346-0370; Fax: 312-704-4140; Web site: http://www.vending.org.

National Beer Wholesalers Association (NBWA), 1100 King Street, Suite 600, Alexandria, VA 22314; Phone: 703-683-4300; Toll-free: 800-300-6417: Fax: 708-683-8965; E-mail: info@nbwa.org; Web site: http://www.nbwa.org.

National Electrical Contractors Association (NECA), 3 Bethesda Metro Center, Suite 1100, Bethesda, MD 20814; Phone: 301-657-3110; Fax: 301-215-4500; E-mail: neca@necanet.org; Web site: http://www.necanet.org.

National Electrical Manufacturers Association (NEMA), 1300 North 17th Street, Suite 1847, Arlington, VA 22209; Phone: 703-841-3200; Fax: 703-841-5900; Web site: http://www.nema.org.

National Grocers Association (NGA), 1005 North Glebe Road, Suite 250, Arlington, VA 22201-5758; Phone: 703-516-0700; Fax: 703-516-0115; E-mail: info@nationalgrocers.org; Web site: http://www.nationalgrocers.org.

National Home Furnishing Association (NHFA), PO Box 2396, High Point, NC 27261; Phone: 336-883-1650; Toll-free: 800-888-9590; Fax: 336-883-1195; E-mail: mail@nhfa.org; Web site: http://www.nhfa.org.

National Lumber & Building Material Dealers Association (NLBMDA), 40 Ivy Street SE, Washington, DC 20003; Phone: 202-547-2230; Toll-free: 800-634-8645; Fax: 202-547-8645; E-mail: shawn@dealer.org; Web site: http://www.dealer.org/.

National Paper Trade Association (NPTA), 500 Bi-County Boulevard, Suite 200E, Farmingdale, NY 11735; Phone: 631-777-2223; Toll-free: 800-355-NPTA (6782); Fax: 631-777-2224; Web site: http://www.gonpta.com.

National Paperbox Association (NPA), 113 South West Street, Third Floor, Alexandria, VA 22313; Phone: 703-684-2212; Fax: 703-683-6920; E-mail: boxmoore@paperbox.org; Web site: http://www.paperbox.org.

National Parking Association (NPA), 1112 16th Street NW, Suite 300, Washington, DC 20036; Phone: 202-296-4336; Toll-free: 800-647-PARK (7275); Fax: 202-331-8523; Web site: http://www.npapark.org.

National Restaurant Association (NRA), 1200 17th Street NW, Washington, DC 20036; Phone: 202-331-5900; Fax: 202-331-2429; E-mail: isal@restaurant.org; Web site: http://www.restaurant.org.

National Retail Federation (NRF), 325 Seventh Street NW, Suite 1000, Washington, DC 20004-2802; Phone: 202-783-7971; Toll-free: 800-NRF-HOW2 (800-673-4692); Fax; 202-737-2849; E-mail: nrf@nrf.com; Web site: http://www.nrf.com/

National Retail Hardware Association (NRHA), 5822 West 74th Street, Indianapolis, IN 46278; Phone: 317-290-0338; Toll-free: 800-772-4424; Fax: 317-328-4354; E-mail: nrha@iquest.net; Web site: http://www.nrha.org.

National Shoe Retailers Association (NSRA), 7150 Columbia Gateway Drive, Suite G, Columbia, MD 21046-1151; Phone: 410-381-8282; Toll-free: 800-673-8446; Fax: 410-381-1167; E-mail: ingfo@nsra.org; Web site: http://www.nsra.org.

National Sporting Goods Association (NSGA), 1601 Feehanville Drive, Suite 300, Mount Prospect, IL 60056; Phone: 847-296-6742; Fax: 847-391-9827; Web site: http://www.nsga.org.

National Tire Dealers & Retreaders Association (NTDRA), 11921 Freedom Drive, Suite 550, Reston, VA 20190-5608; Toll-free: 800-876-8372; Web site: http://www.tirestyres.com/assn/rs000149.html.

North American Equipment Dealers Association (NAEDA), 1195 Smizer Mill Road, Fenton, MO 63026-3480; Phone: 636-349-5000; Fax: 636-349-5443; E-mail: naeda@naeda.com; Web site: http://www.naeda.com.

North American Heating, Refrigeration, & Air-conditioning Wholesalers Association (NHRAW), PO Box 16790, 1389 Dublin Road, Columbus, OH 43216; Phone: 614-488-1835; Fax: 614-488-0482; E-mail: nhramail@nhraw.org; Web site: http://www.hardinet.org.

North American Wholesale Lumber Association, 3601 Algonquin Road, Suite 400, Rolling Meadows, IL 60008; Phone: 847-870-7470; Fax: 847-870-0201; Web site: http://www.lumber.org.

Optical Laboratories Association, 11096-B Lee Highway, Suite 102, Fairfax, VA 22030-5014; Phone: 703-359-2830; Toll-free: 800-477-5652; Fax: 703-359-2834; E-mail: ola@ola-labs.org; Web site: http://www.ola-labs.org.

Paint & Decorating Retailers Association, 403 Axminster Drive, Fenton, OH 63026; Phone: 636-326-2636; Fax: 636-326-1823; E-mail: info@pdra.org; Web site: http://www.pdra.org.

Petroleum Equipment Institute (PEI), PO Box 2380, Tulsa, OK 74101; Phone: 918-494-9696; Fax: 918-491-9895: E-mail: pei@peinet.org; Web site: http://www.pei.org.

Risk Management Association1 Liberty Place, 1650 Market Street, Suite 2300, Philadelphia, PA 19103-7398; Phone: 215-446-4000; Toll-free: 800-677-7621; Fax: 215-446-4101; E-mail: customers@rmahq.org, Web site: http://www.rmahq.org.

Shoe Service Institute of America (SSIA), 5024-R Campbell Road, Baltimore, MD 21236; Phone: 410-931-8100; Fax: 410-931-8111; Web site: http://www.ssia.info.

Textile Care Allied Trades Association (TCATA), 271 U.S. Highway 46, No. 203-D, Fairfield, NJ 07004-2458; Phone: 973-244-1790; Fax: 973-244-4455; E-mail: info@tcata.org; Web site: http://www.tcata.org.

United Fresh Fruit & Vegetables Association (UFFVA), 901 Pennsylvania Avenue NW, Suite 1100, Washington, DC 20006; Phone: 202-303-3400; Fax: 202-303-3433; E-mail: uffva@uffva.org; Web site: http://www.uffva.org.

Urban Land Institute (ULI), 1025 Thomas Jefferson Street NW, Suite 500W, Washington, DC 20007-5201; Phone: 202-624-7000; Toll-free: 800-321-5011; Fax: 202-624-7140; E-mail: joinuli@uli.org; Web site: http://www.uli.org.

Wine & Spirits Wholesalers of America (WSWA), 805 15th Street NW, Suite 430, Washington, DC 20005; Phone: 202-371-9792; Fax: 202-789-2405; E-mail: juanita.duggan@wswa.org; Web site: http://www.wswa.org.

Also recommended is the Small Business Network at http://www10.americanexpress.com/sif/cda/page/0,1641,15657,00.asp.

SUMMARY

In this chapter we've looked at many financial ratios that can be used to measure the financial efficiency of what we plan to do. These ratios can be used by comparing our planned figures with alternative approaches and also by comparing our planned ratios with others that are published for the same industry. If your marketing plan is implemented, you will want to return to this chapter to use actual rather than planned information. In this way the ratios enable us to monitor our implementation and to make adjustments as we proceed.

Now we have all the information needed to put together an outstanding presentation of your marketing plan. You'll see how to do that in the next chapter.

CHAPTER

8

STEP 8

PRESENTING THE MARKETING PLAN

By the time you have reached this chapter, you should have all the information necessary to put together a first-rate marketing plan. But now you have another hurdle. You've done all necessary research and assembled your material. You've completed the situational analysis and scanned your environment. You've established goals and objectives and developed marketing strategy and tactics. You've peered into the future and forecasted sales and costs. You've developed extensive financial information and measured its efficiency. Now it is important not to trip up. You must present your marketing plan to those who have the authority to approve it or give you the resources you need to implement it. You need to do this in the most professional manner possible. The purpose of this chapter is to show you how to do this.

THE MARKETING PLAN AS A PRODUCT

Your marketing plan is a sales document. But it is also a product representing your concept for the project or business. It must be as professional a product as you can make it. There is an old saying, "You can't judge a book by its cover." It may be true, but it is irrelevant. A professional-looking plan has a far better chance of success than one that is highly creative with accurate information, but that has been put together in a haphazard fashion with grammatical or spelling errors. So, your marketing plan must look as good as it is. If it does, the psychological advantage is yours. The reader will proceed from the premise that your plan is accurate and that you know what you are talking about.

On the other hand, if your marketing plan doesn't look professional, the contents must overcome a significant negative bias. Let's see what you can do to make your plan look more professional.

The first thing you can do is have your plan typed by a single person. That way the printing will have a consistent style and format throughout the document. It should be neat and free from typographical errors and obvious corrections. In this day of computerization, this shouldn't pose any problem.

A standardized method of typing and collating the different sections of the plan should be used. Which method you choose is usually not critical, unless specified by whoever has asked you to prepare the plan. Standardization also means a single way of doing footnotes, bibliography, and so forth. Several style manuals are available. Pick one and stick with it.

Sometimes, when several people work on a single marketing plan, different sections of the plan are assigned to each of the participants. Although there is nothing inherently wrong with this, one individual should be assigned the task of assembling the overall product to ensure that its writing, styling, typing, and formatting are consistent. If one coordinator is not assigned, it is not unusual to find sections that do not fit together.

It is sad to report, but I have seen a conclusion in one section nullified by a statement in another section. I have also seen terminology that is inconsistent among different sections.

If the typing or printing is done by different individuals, the marketing plan may have an inconsistent appearance due to different styles of type, darkness of imprint, margins, fonts, and paper. This guarantees a shoddy-looking product, so don't let this happen to you!

Illustrations and charts should be included as a part of your marketing plan. You must never, however, include illustrations or any unnecessary information merely to pad the marketing plan and make it appear more substantial. Information that may distract from the presentation can be added as an appendix. The survey form used to gather research might be an example. But even information in the appendix should be necessary and relevant and not added simply to increase the size of the document.

There is no minimum length for a marketing plan. Many venture capitalists prefer shorter plans, say fifty or fewer pages. This is because they review so many marketing and business plans that they prefer to have the essential facts in the plan and to request additional information only if needed. This is usually not the case if you are preparing the marketing plan in the classroom, someone else is paying you to prepare it, or you are preparing one as a member of a large corporation. Then, it is best to ensure that all the information is available right from the start. This will require at least fifty pages and maybe more.

Make your plan long enough to tell your entire story, always considering what your readers will want to know. If you need more pages to cover essential information, use them. On the other hand, if you have covered all the information you think is necessary for your reader, then stop. Don't pad.

The final point to consider is binding. Some excellent plans are typed neatly and compiled with correct and complete information, yet they still fail to give a professional appearance simply because a cheap binding is used. What amazes me is how easy and inexpensive it is to get a really top-of-the-line binding. Yet many fail to get it for their plans.

Hardcover binding, bound like a book, is available from many printers for less than $10. One cautionary note: In their enthusiasm, one of my student teams got their marketing plan bound in leather to the tune of $70! I don't recommend needless expense, even for a professional plan.

If you are unable to obtain hardcover binding, consider spiral binding. A mechanical means of doing rapid spiral binding is available at many printers. Check the yellow pages of your telephone book for additional sources. Again, the point here is to make your marketing plan look as professional as you can. Your marketing plan should be good, and it should look good.

THE FORMAL PRESENTATION

In most cases, simply preparing the marketing plan is insufficient. You must also make a formal presentation of your marketing plan to someone else. This may be to individuals who may be interested in funding your plan or to higher management in your company who must give the approval to implement it. Your professor may have you do a formal presentation of your plan in the classroom.

In all cases you must first consider the object of your presentation. Usually the object of a marketing plan is to persuade management or investors to allocate money to enable you to implement your project. Remember that no one is going to give you money for your plan unless they are convinced that it will succeed and will make money for them.

What will these people want to know? They'll want to know how much money can be made, how much money will be needed from them and when, how long it will be before they will get their money back, exactly what you will do with the money, and why you will succeed with your project. Therefore, although the outline of your marketing plan can be used as described in preceding chapters, some minor changes may be needed to maximize the impact of your presentation.

Here is one outline for a formal presentation:

I.   Introduction. In the introduction you cover the information in your executive summary, including the opportunity and why it exists, the money to be made, the money that's needed, and some brief financial information, such as return on investment, to support the extent of the opportunity as you see it.

II.   Why You Will Succeed. In this section you will cover your situational analysis and environmental scanning and the research you did to support it. You conclude the section with problems, opportunities, and threats, as well as the project's goals and objectives. Finally, you spell out your differential competitive advantage. The essential message in this part of the presentation is why you will succeed even though others may fail.

III. Strategy and Tactics. In this section you will cover the strategy you are going to follow as well as the tactics used to implement that strategy.

IV.   Forecast and Financial Information. In this section you will discuss your forecast, project development schedule, profit and loss statement, and financial ratios and data. This section will contain a detailed description of what you need and when you need it. Sometimes, because of the limited time available for the presentation, you may have to cut down on this section and present only the main points. The important financial information, however, should always be available so that in the question-and-answer session that follows you can provide the additional data, if required.

V.   Conclusion. In this final part of your formal presentation you will restate the opportunity and why you will succeed with it, the money that is required, and the expected return on the investment. You told 'em. Now tell 'em what you told 'em.

Preparing for Your Presentation

Your first step in preparing for your presentation is obtaining the answers to several important questions. These include the time and date of your presentation, where it is to be held, the time allowed, who the audience is, who is in the audience, and the purpose of your presentation. You should also think about the audience's attitude, their knowledge and preconceived notions, and anything that requires particular care. After getting this information, you can write down the main points to cover.

Probably ninety-nine times out of a hundred, the purpose of presenting your marketing plan will be to obtain resources. This holds true whether you are an entrepreneur presenting a marketing plan to the loan officer of a bank, a venture capitalist, or someone else who is going to lend you money, or whether you are a member of a company and have been asked to prepare a plan as a potential investment. The exception is a plan that you have prepared as a consultant to an entrepreneur or larger corporation interested in implementing it. In this case your main object is to demonstrate that you have done your job by preparing a plan that your client can use to get resources and eventually to implement.

Think through and write down the answers to these questions, because they can affect what you are going to cover and how you are going to do it.

Your next step is to make an outline of your main and supporting points. To develop this outline you need not follow the outline of the written marketing plan report. Remember that you may wish to change your order in presenting different elements depending on your audience and their backgrounds, interests, and concerns. With different audiences, different sections or topics must be emphasized. If the audience is primarily financial, don't leave out any financial information from your presentation. On the contrary, you should emphasize it.

On the other hand, an engineering audience will probably be more interested in the technical aspects of your product, its manufacture, and so forth. Some financial data can be excluded in order to have the time to include more technical information. Now, you are probably doing this for your marketing class at the direction of your marketing professor. Need I say what emphasis your plan should have?

Remember, the purpose of developing a special outline is to allow you to make the maximum. The following technique is sometimes useful in helping you prepare your outline and its supporting points. Obtain a number of 3 × 5-inch file cards and, without stopping to think, write down everything you think should be emphasized in your presentation, one item to a card. Don't try to coordinate or organize anything at this point. If you have statistics that you think you should include, or anecdotes, quotes, or even jokes, write each on a separate card.

Once you have written down as many ideas as you can, begin to organize the cards into your main points and supporting points. Statistics will be supporting points to some main points. So will anecdotes, jokes, and quotes. By using this system, you will soon have a stack of cards for each major element of your presentation. They will automatically be organized in a logical fashion.

After you complete your presentation by arranging your ideas using these cards, you can prepare a complete written outline. Notice that this is a flexible system. You can move cards around, as well as add cards and points to your presentation as new ideas occur.

Note that I have not said to write a speech. Your presentation should never be written out word for word. If you do, you will probably present it that way. Marketing plan speeches are dull and boring. You want your marketing plan presentation to reflect the work, the accuracy, and the potential it represents for whoever implements it. But above all, you want it to be exciting. This cannot be done with a written speech. So leave your presentation as an outline.

Once you have completed your outline you can begin planning for your visual aids.

Planning for Visual Aids

Visual aids can greatly enhance the impact of your presentation and should always be used in making a presentation of a marketing plan. Your basic options are the use of 35-mm slides, overhead transparencies, charts, handouts, videos, computer presentations, or chalkboards. All have their advantages and disadvantages. Let's look at each of them.

Slides (35-mm) A 35-mm projector and 35-mm slides are easy to carry around. Furthermore, the slides can be done in color, look quite professional, can be manipulated by the presenter, and yield an extremely professional experience. The disadvantages are the lead time to prepare the slides, the cost, and the difficulty of changing a particular slide once it has been developed. New systems are now available by which 35-mm slides are constructed by computer and then enhanced, in color or otherwise, rapidly and at relatively low cost per unit. However, the equipment costs several thousand dollars. This system will not be readily available to everyone.

Overhead Transparencies Overhead transparencies are as portable as 35-mm slides. Most of these projectors are heavier, more cumbersome, and less transportable, although some models available today are as portable and only slightly larger than slide projectors. There is a lead time associated with the preparation of overhead transparencies, if you have them done professionally. However, if camera-ready artwork is available, duplicating machines located at many printing shops can make instant overhead transparencies from your artwork. Also, desktop publishing programs available for many computers allow you to make professional-quality transparencies yourself. Another advantage of an overhead transparency is that you can write on it as you talk. As a result, you can also make changes in the transparency if required. This you cannot do with a 35-mm slide. Although you can talk and operate a projector with overhead transparencies at the same time, this is more difficult than with a 35-mm projector since the latter can be operated remotely.

Videos A videotape presentation allows a lot of flexibility and can add interest to your presentation. However, there are drawbacks. First, don't get so carried away with your presentation on film that you make the video your entire presentation, unless this has been requested. Practice with the tape to ensure the timing fits with the rest of your presentation. Of course, a television and videocassette player or other means to show your video must be available. Most presenters work with equipment furnished by someone else. Frequently, the first time they see the equipment is when they make their presentation. As a result, many times presenters struggle with getting unfamiliar equipment to work. This distracts from your presentation and can irritate your audience.

Computer Presentations   Computer technology has advanced to the point where some very sophisticated multimedia presentations can be easily developed and used with a portable computer and a device linking it to an overhead projector. *PowerPoint* is perhaps the most popular. Here again, there is a danger of getting carried away with sound effects and visuals. While entertaining, this can distract from your basic purpose in making the presentation. Again, be careful of equipment. Practice with the actual equipment you will use. I have seen presenters start their presentation and discover that the equipment available is not compatible with what they have put together and that no one can see the presentation except in complete darkness … under which conditions they cannot see their notes. Veteran presenters of multimedia always have standard overheads as backup.

Handouts   Handouts are easy to make. They can be reproduced in quantity, even in color if required. Handouts can be changed and new information substituted for the old. But handouts suffer from two major disadvantages. First, if the information is extensive and the audience large, a considerable amount of material must be carried around and distributed. Second, audiences may read ahead in your handout and miss the points you are covering. At the same time, a dramatic sequence of events that you've built into your presentation may be spoiled as the audience reads ahead to your "punch line." Handouts that are exact duplicates of transparencies or multimedia programs are great as backup should some electronic means fail. They are also useful when members of the audience ask for copies of your transparencies.

Charts   Charts can be the flip variety, or they can be large cardboard or plastic devices that are used in conjunction with your other visual aids. Charts are much less portable than 35-mm slides, transparencies, or handouts. One advantage of a chart, however, is that if you have an artistic bent you can prepare them on your own and thus need not allow as much lead time as with professionally prepared overhead transparencies or 35-mm slides. This places them in the same category as handouts as far as this particular attribute goes. However, if you do prepare your own charts, it is important that it *not* be done the night before. You need to allow enough time to check them for accuracy, typographical errors, and so forth. If you do them the night before, you are almost certain to make errors.

Chalkboards   Chalkboards, or plastic boards on which you can write with colored markers, can also be useful during presentations. The major disadvantage is that you cannot prepare your material ahead of time. In this case, the advantage is also the disadvantage, for there is much more drama and spontaneity in having your audience see the point you wish to get across as you write it. However, there are usually so many disadvantages with chalkboards that, at best, they can be used only as an adjunct to your other systems. These include the facts that they are not readily transportable, the material is not permanent, you cannot use the material to key your memory (an advantage with all four other visual systems), and chalkboards may not always be available where you give your presentation.

Whatever system of visual aids you plan on, you should prepare your visual aids immediately, even before you begin to practice for the first time, and not wait until the last moment. I recommend that you attempt a presentation in the time you have been allocated at least once. When you are reasonably confident that your presentation will not change in its major points, have your visual aids constructed. One reason is the long lead time. It is always a lot longer than you think it will be. Also, you want to allow yourself time to proofread the material that is done for you by someone else.

After having given hundreds of presentations using all of these methods, I have found that in 90 percent of the cases you will get typographical errors. If your visual aids are prepared at the last minute, you may find that insufficient time is available to correct the errors. So once you know what you want on your visual aids, have them made at once. You can practice with dummy visual aids while the real ones are being prepared.

Use of Products as Visual Aids   Sometimes the product that is the subject of your marketing plan is available. These products can be very useful for adding interest to your presentation. However, if you use products as part of your visual aids, make sure they are relevant. If your product is interesting and the particular twist or unique advantage you have in your product is worth seeing, then it's worth showing. On the other hand, if your marketing plan concerns a product that everyone is familiar with, don't use it as a visual aid unless there is some unique aspect that should be seen or demonstrated. Do something else with the time you have available.

To summarize our discussion on visual aids, I'd like you to think about the following points as you prepare for your presentation.

Make sure you use aids that contain material that is easy to read, without too much information on each. They must make an impact on the audience and reinforce what you say, or make what you say more easily understood. If there is too much information in a single view, your audience may get lost. If the type is too small, your audience will not be able to read what you have prepared.

Even your pointing techniques may be important. If you are going to use a pointer, be careful that when you use it you do not turn your body so as to cut off the view of some-one in your audience. The best way to avoid this is to follow this rule: If you are standing to the right of the view of your presentation, then have the pointer in your left hand. This will keep you from turning your back on the audience and cutting off the view of members of the audience who are to your right front. On the other hand, if you are standing to the left of the view, use the pointer in your right hand. In this way, you will not turn your back and cut off the view of individuals in the audience who are on your left front.

Keep your visual aids covered until you use them. Displaying many visual aids simultaneously only causes distractions. It may cause your audience to become more interested in your visuals than in you. So show one visual. Then, only when you're ready, show the next.

The Practice Sequence

I want to emphasize that you must never memorize anything. If you try to memorize your presentation, you may forget it. Memorization simply isn't necessary. Nor is it necessary to read your presentation. Believe me when I tell you, I learned this lesson the hard way.

As a young Air Force officer, I was once asked to make a presentation to 300 science and math teachers on space navigation, a topic in which I had great interest at the time. I prepared superb 35-mm full-color slides and spent considerable time writing and honing a one-hour speech. I wrote down every single word. I memorized this speech perfectly, word for word, and coordinated it with my very excellent multicolor slides.

When the day came I looked out at 300 science and math teachers, gulped once, and could barely remember my name. After several stumbling attempts to try to remember the speech I thought I had memorized perfectly, I reached in my pocket and read my speech word for word.

What a mistake! Hours of work wasted unnecessarily for a boring speech. After all, I knew the subject matter. By simply flipping through my slides, I could have talked to my audience and told them about each. That really was all that was required for an excellent presentation.

The same is true for you. To give an outstanding presentation of your marketing plan, you don't have to memorize anything. You don't have to bore your audience to death by reading a speech, either. You know your subject better than anyone else. Once you are prepared, just going through your presentation as you use your visuals to support what you say will enable you to communicate with your audience for maximum impact. In this way, you can give an outstanding presentation.

If your visual aids are complete while you practice, use them during your practice. If not, write the content of your visual aids on 8 x 10 ½-inch sheets of paper and practice with them. You can use the cards that you prepared earlier to help remember the main points. I recommend going through your presentation three times and making adjustments as necessary in order to complete the presentation and get your points across in the time you have been allotted.

If you use cards to supplement what you have displayed on your visual aids to help you remember the main points, do not write more than a few words on the cards. If you do, you will read them. And once you begin to read your cards, you will probably continue to read them. Then you are back to reading a speech. So write just a few words on each and only use them as cues. Of course, the same is true of the visual aids. They should be sparsely worded for maximum impact. You simply look at the visual aid and speak about it to your audience.

As I fine-tune my presentations, I may add statistics, I may take out a point here or add one there, and I may modify other parts of what I originally intended to discuss. One element is fixed: I concentrate on staying within whatever time constraints have been given me. Time is crucial.

The Importance of Controlling Your Time

You must always control your time, and practice within as well as give your presentation in the allotted time. This is true whether you are making a fifteen-minute presentation or one lasting several hours. Why is this so? The individuals in your audience, no matter how critical and important they feel your presentation will be to them, allot a certain amount of time for it in their schedules. If you exceed this time, even by a few minutes, you will make it more difficult, even impossible, to achieve the objective of your presentation. If you exceed your allotted time by only a few minutes, it may be annoying. If you go over by more than that, this could set up a negative reaction due to its impact on the schedules of those in the audience.

Let me give you a couple of examples to illustrate just how important controlling your time can be. A few years ago a large aerospace corporation was competing for a major government contract with the Air Force. Fifty representatives from the Air Force flew in to receive what was to be a full day's presentation to end no later than 4:00 P.M. The presentation, however, was not well planned by the presenters. By 3:30 P.M. it was clear their full presentation could not be completed as planned within the allotted time. The audience was not given a choice. The presenters plunged on, determined to cover every single one of their overhead transparencies. The presentation was completed more than an hour late. As a result, most of these government representatives had to reschedule their return flights. While the presentation was sufficiently important that these representatives listened to the full presentation, they were definitely unhappy with the poor planning on the part of the prospective contractor. Maybe this was only one factor among many, but this company did not win the contract.

Mistakes like this in time control are not limited to industry. One practice generally followed in hiring university professors is to require the candidate to make a presentation to the department. Typically this presentation is on the candidate's research. This presentation is critical because the membership of the department has a say in whether or not to hire the candidate.

Several years ago, a major university reviewed the credentials of a candidate who had graduated from a well-known university. This individual's background was so outstanding that the members of the department were in favor of hiring the candidate even before he made his face-to-face appearance.

They asked the candidate to limit his presentation to twenty-five minutes due to the prior commitments of his audience. All fourteen members of this department listened attentively as the candidate began. His presentation was interesting and relevant. However, twenty-five minutes after he started he was still speaking. At thirty minutes professors in the audience began to fidget; several had other meetings scheduled. A few had classes and excused themselves. Thirty-five minutes went by, then forty. The candidate finally concluded at forty-five minutes.

This candidate was still hired as a professor by the institution involved. However, the candidate had interviewed for a position leading to tenure and promotion and because of just twenty minutes, he was offered only a one-year appointment. After one year, he might be considered for the original position that was offered. Twenty minutes cost this professor one year in time toward a promotion to the next rank, including pay, allowances, and other fringe benefits.

The lesson is clear. Ask if there is a certain time allotted for your presentation. If there is, do not exceed this time. Practice to make sure that you stay within this time. Give yourself a slight cushion. And when you make your presentation, control your time.

Once you have practiced three times and have pretty good control over your presentation, I recommend that you do the presentation twice more, only this time in front of other people. This can mean a spouse, friend, brother, sister, or whomever. The important thing is that we are not looking for a pat on the back but for a real critique. This includes the answers to a number of questions:

- Should I talk louder or softer?

- Did I use eye contact?

- Did I talk in a conversational fashion, or did I simply start reading from my cards or visual aids?

- Did I have a good opener that grabbed the interest of my audience?

- Did I close my presentation with impact?

- Did I use supporting matter such as anecdotes or statistics?

- Was there something particular I said that was liked?

- Something not liked?

- If available, were my visual aids written large enough, and could they be read? Do they need to be changed or improved in some way?

- Was there anything in my presentation that could not be understood, and, if so, what could I do to make it understandable?

- Are there any other points or comments or advice that may be relevant?

Questions and Answers and How to Prepare for Them

Questions and answers are going to be a part of every marketing plan presentation you make. The first thing you must do is prepare ahead of time. Research has shown that approximately 85 percent of the questions asked can actually be anticipated. So once you have prepared your presentation, think about what questions might be asked by your audience, and prepare for them. You might also have your practice audience ask questions, both to test your preparation for answering them and your ability to think on your feet.

Next have your facts, figures, quotes—all of this information—available. Many astute presenters who cannot fit all the information they would like into their presentation due to time restrictions have other visual aids ready and waiting. That way when this information is requested, it can be immediately used to good advantage.

An example might be financial information such as cash flow on a monthly basis. You may not have the time to cover this in your formal presentation; however, it would not hurt to have an overhead transparency or some other visual aid available so that when you are asked a question about these details, you can immediately use it. This will demonstrate not only your knowledge, but also your preparation for any eventuality.

Remember to keep cool no matter how embarrassing the question or even whether you can answer it. I recommend a four-step procedure in answering questions. First, restate the question that has been asked. This ensures that the entire audience has heard the question and that you understand it. It also gives you additional time to think about your answer. Second, state your position or your answer to the question. Third, state the supporting reasons for your position. Finally restate your position to make it clear to everyone.

In general, keep your answers brief. If you know the individual who asked the question, use his or her name. If the individual is right and you are wrong about something, admit it. Or if you don't know something, admit that also. Simply say, "I don't know." Of course, if every other answer is, "I don't know," you can expect your audience to believe that you have not done a very good job of preparing or are not very much of an expert on the marketing plan or on your material.

Never get sidetracked or get in a quarrel with someone who has asked a question. Always be tactful, even with individuals who attack you or your position. Harshly correcting a questioner can turn others in your audience against you even if they agree with your point of view. This is because the audience may be members of the same firm or group. Also, they may resent the manner of your response to an innocent question, even if it is not tactfully asked.

Use of the Mental Visualization Technique

I've always worried about speeches before I made them. As I lay in bed thinking about what I was to do the next day, I would go over the entire speech in my mind. I rehearsed it again and again. I never thought much about this. Then, on January 13, 1982, *The Wall Street Journal* published an article entitled "Why Do Some People Out-Perform Others?" It talked about a psychologist by the name of Charles Garfield who had investigated top performance among business executives. Garfield said that he was most surprised by a trait that he called mental rehearsal, which had meanwhile caught on as a popular concept in sports. According to Garfield, top chief executives would imagine every aspect and feeling of a future presentation, including a successful ending, while less effective executives would prepare their facts and the presentation agendas, but not their psyches.

Now I teach this technique to others to help them prepare for presentations. They report outstanding success with it. All that is necessary is that you take a few minutes before falling asleep the night before your presentation. Visualize everything from greeting your host and your audience to going through your presentation to a successful conclusion. See your conclusion in detail, with smiles and vigorous applause. Repeat this again and again, each time with a favorable conclusion. You will find that you can go through an entire hour's presentation in a few seconds, and thus you can have as many as thirty or more repetitions of success even before you go before your audience to make your presentation for the first time.

I believe this technique has several benefits. First, because you visualize a success again and again, you come to expect that success and, more frequently than not, that is exactly what you will receive. Secondly, mental rehearsal seems to eliminate excessive nervousness. While all of us may be a little bit nervous when we make a presentation, this is probably good. If we weren't nervous at all, we probably would come across as rather dull and uninteresting. But too much nervousness can cause us to stumble, and it may make our audience nervous as well. With mental visualization, you have made your presentation so many times before that when you stand and look at your audience, the sting is gone. It is "old hat." After all, didn't you make the same presentation before the same audience thirty or more times the night before?

I highly recommend that you try this technique. From my own experience and the experience of so many others, I know that it will work wonders in helping you present your marketing plan in an interesting way, without nervousness.

The Keys to Success for Marketing Plan Presentations

The number-one key for making your marketing plan presentation a success is to be enthusiastic about your project. If you aren't enthusiastic, you certainly cannot expect anyone else to be. What happens when you really don't have a great deal of enthusiasm for a project? Perhaps it was not your idea at all. In the classroom, it is your professor who decides that you must make this presentation. At work, it is probably your boss who instructed you to prepare this marketing plan presentation for top management. It really doesn't make any difference. My recommendation is that if you really aren't interested in the project, then you must act; you must pretend that you are highly interested. This is crucial.

Whenever I discuss acting or pretending, I think about the movie *Patton*. George C. Scott played the famous World War II general. In one scene depicting an event during the Battle of the Bulge, things were not going very well for American forces. General Patton suddenly turned to an aide and exclaimed, "If any of our commanders retreat, shoot them!"

The aide was shocked. In disbelief, he asked, "You really don't mean that?" Patton answered, "It really is not important whether you know whether I really mean it or not. It's only important that I know." In other words, Patton was acting.

Now, in fact, Patton was a tremendous actor. I know this for a fact because Patton's diaries have been published. During World War I, Patton was twenty-nine years old and the commander of the first U.S. tank forces in France. He wrote to his wife, saying, "Every day I practice in front of a mirror looking mean." He called this his "war face." Patton felt that his mean-looking "war face" saved lives, because it meant his men were more afraid of him than they were of the enemy.

But Patton isn't the only one who recommends acting in order to achieve success. Mary Kay Ash developed a $100 million cosmetics company, and to her salespeople, she recommends, "Fake it 'til you make it." In other words, until you actually have a good day, pretend you're already having one. Or, until you have success, pretend that you are already achieving it. If you do this, if you pretend to be enthusiastic about your product and your project even though you are not, I promise you that this enthusiasm is contagious, and that your audience will be enthusiastic as well.

You must dress professionally. You represent your marketing plan. Appearance does count. As pointed out previously, although you may not be able to judge a book by its cover, psychologically people will do so. The same goes for your presentation. If you have any doubts about how to dress, the most famous book on this subject is called *Dress for Success* by John T. Molloy. Another important book is *Power Dressing* by Victoria Seitz, a professor at California State University San Bernardino. I highly recommend both of these books.

If you have any kind of test to do, or something that must work as a part of your presentation for your marketing plan, it is wise that you practice this test fully, and not just go through the motions.

Several years ago, a Navy project engineer made a presentation about an important Navy project. When Navy aviators must eject from aircraft over water, they have a serious problem in getting rid of their parachutes once in the water. The normal procedure is to climb into a small, one-person life raft. It is attached to a nylon line, attached to the parachute harness, that extends fifteen feet below the pilot. It opens automatically at ejection.

However, the pilot must climb into the raft while wearing heavy flight equipment, including boots, helmet, and survival gear. Obviously this is difficult. Worse, the parachute canopy can fill with water. But even if it doesn't, its water-soaked weight may drag the aviator straight down to the bottom.

So the Navy teaches its aviators to use an emergency release to get rid of the parachute canopy just as their feet splash the water. Naturally, most pilots cheat a little in case the quick release gets stuck. They actually start dumping their "chute" a few feet before they hit.

However, there is a serious problem. Because the ocean appears flat, it is very difficult to judge height. As a result, many aviators who think they are a few feet above the water release their parachutes while they are still several hundred feet in the air. This practice can be dangerous.

In order to overcome this problem, the Navy developed a special squib. This is a light explosive charge that automatically releases the canopy when a sensor attached to the life raft contacts water. Remember, it hangs fifteen feet below the pilot and so comes in contact with the water first. In this way, the parachute is jettisoned safely without endangering the pilot.

The Navy project manager did an outstanding job of presenting. His presentation included films of how the system worked, 35-mm slides, and handouts illustrating the project. For the grand finale, he donned a parachute himself and held up a jar of seawater. He told his audience of several hundred that he would introduce the sensor into the seawater. He told them that they would hear a loud crack as the squib exploded, and that the parachute canopy trailing behind the harness he had donned would immediately separate.

The audience prepared themselves, some holding their hands over their ears, and others waiting expectantly for the loud report of the exploding squib. The presenter inserted the probe into the seawater with high drama. There was a loud silence. Nothing happened. He extracted the sensor and inserted it again, and again, and again. Nothing happened.

Finally, red-faced as the audience began to snicker, he examined the harness. He discovered that someone had forgotten to replace a discharged battery. With no current there was nothing to ignite the squib.

Here was an important and outstanding presentation ruined by a demonstration that went awry. It was a mistake that need not have happened if a full demonstration had been done during the practice stage.

Throughout your presentation you should try to establish empathy with your audience. You can do this by being friendly. Remember, the audience is not your enemy. Enjoy yourself, and think of yourself as the host of your presentation.

The presentation and your written marketing plan report go together. They support one another, and they will support your achieving whatever objectives you have set.

SUMMARY

In this chapter we have seen that presenting the marketing plan has two main elements: the written report and the formal presentation. This is not the frosting on the cake. Both are necessary for success. You will be successful by focusing on preparation and ensuring that your plan is presented with a high degree of professionalism.

With professionalism, your excellent content will be supported by an excellent package. I hope that you have learned that professional is not accidental. Yet if you implement the techniques outlined, you cannot miss. In the classroom, your professionalism in presenting your plan will lead to a high grade. In the "real world" it will help to get you the resources to implement your marketing plan. You may not implement your plan in the classroom, but when you graduate and begin to use your marketing skills, you will. You are now ready to see, in the next chapter, how this is done.

CHAPTER 9

STEP 9
IMPLEMENTATION

Regardless of how good your marketing plan is or how well you have presented it, once you have received the go-ahead you must actually carry out the actions you have planned. Implementation is the final stage in the marketing planning process. During implementation, you can and should use your plan to help you. But the execution of your plan is not automatic. Your plan is not a light switch that, simply turned on, automatically completes every task, tactic, and strategy in exactly the manner you planned. To implement your marketing plan successfully, you must exercise control to ensure that you will reach your planned objectives and goals. To accomplish this you must monitor the implementation of your plan periodically. Use your project development schedule and measure planned resource allocations against those actually used, along with the time frame in which they were to be used. Measure expected results against actual results. Calculate your financial ratios.

Once implementation has been initiated, things never go exactly as planned. This may be because your planning was not perfect (and what planning ever is?), or it may be because of a change of one or more marketplace environs. Perhaps your competition responded in a way that you never expected. All of this is normal. It simply means that you must make adjustments to get back on track to achieve the objectives and goals you set.

Conceptually, certain actions are always required in implementation:

1. If you are the one responsible for implementing the plan, or some subsection of the plan, take complete responsibility for implementation. This does not only mean responsibility for initiating the actions contained in the plan but also responsibility for reaching the goals and objectives contained in the plan.

2. Track all tasks, tactics, and strategies and measure what is planned against what actually happens. Make adjustments as required and do not blindly continue any action simply because it is in your plan.

3. Track the changes in the environs as the implementation of your marketing plan progresses. Changes will sometimes tell you that actions planned for the future should not be taken or should be altered. And just as an ounce of prevention is worth a pound of cure, an ounce of change taken now may be well worth a pound of change at a later date, when a foreseeable or predictable threat grows and causes a major problem in implementation.

No marketing plan, regardless of how good it is, with brilliant strategies and clever tactics, can succeed without being implemented. You cannot win your objectives by implementing a poor marketing plan. But you cannot win your objectives by poorly implementing a good marketing plan either.

Therefore I wish you the development of an outstanding marketing plan. And if you implement it, I wish you an outstanding implementation as well.

APPENDIX

A

SAMPLE MARKETING PLANS

The marketing plans in this section were all done by students as a part of regular courses in marketing. They range from plans for entrepreneurial start-ups to plans for a division of a large corporation. They involve different products and varied services. They were accomplished by teams consisting solely of marketing majors, and mixed teams from other disciplines. They were done by students taking the entry-level undergraduate course in marketing and students at the graduate level. They were developed by native-born American students and mixed teams of American and foreign students. Moreover, in this edition, reflecting the international emphasis which is so important, foreign plans from Australia, Brazil, and Indonesia are also included. Also for the first time, two plans that were developed and graded over the Internet have been included.

These students sometimes used different approaches. They applied the concepts and techniques of marketing to develop the best plans they could. These plans are not perfect, but they are good.

My purpose in including them is to show you what can be done as well as to give you some new ideas. Sometimes the students used a different approach than you might want to use. They saw things differently than you might today. They came up with unique solutions to what might even be different problems than you may find. This is true even if you were to develop a plan for the identical product and industry. I hope their efforts will challenge and motivate you to develop the most professional marketing plan you can. Only by stretching to your limits can you grow to your potential for mastering this important marketing skill.

AI

PROMOTING HEALTHY FAMILIES

Developed by
ANNETTE R. DAVIDSON
SAIM KEFELI
JONATHAN RO
EMY YULIATY

Contents

EXECUTIVE SUMMARY

This marketing plan was constructed to promote a health plan called Healthy Families, which is underwritten by the state of California and designed for children of the working poor. Enrollees to this program must select a physician for primary care services, who is oftentimes affiliated with at least one Independent Physicians Association (IPA), such as Superior IPA. Superior IPA was established six years ago. Among its competitive advantages, Superior IPA is a physician-owned entity. It has a very strong infrastructure that prevents mistrust between the physicians and the IPA, which has historically plagued many IPAs. In the wake of folding IPAs, it became known as a reliable and stable entity in the health care business. Superior keeps the physicians involved in all the aspects of the IPA, including some management tasks and financial decision making. Another competitive advantage for Superior IPA is that it is launching an aggressive marketing effort to increase its member (patient) base, which is something its competitors have yet to do. Superior also has a contract with CAP Management Systems (CMS). CMS is responsible for helping Superior IPA market its services to the public.

The product CMS is marketing is the Healthy Families Program, which amounts to low-cost insurance that provides health, dental, and vision coverage to children one to eighteen years old. The cost of the care is low, but the quality of health care provided by Superior IPA is the same as the care provided for those individuals paying in full. Healthy Families is a state-funded health care program, and the state of California is eager to provide health care to all its children.

California's effort to provide health care insurance to more uninsured children was made possible last year when Congress passed and President Clinton signed the State Children's Health Insurance Program (CHIP). This is the largest expansion of children's health coverage since the adoption of Medicaid in 1965. CHIP is a $4 billion-per-year national initiative to help states provide health insurance for uninsured children in low-wage working families. California created the Healthy Families Program to use its share of these funds to cover low-income, uninsured children.

CMS, after reviewing extensive demographic and psychographic data, has chosen to market this program to a specific demographic sector in its surrounding geographic market. Specifically, the characteristics of our target market are as follows: one to eighteen years of age, primarily Hispanic, household of three to four members, household income level ranging from \$32,387 to \$35,524, no current health insurance coverage, and a U.S. citizen or legal immigrant.

According to the break-even analysis, CMS will have to enroll 264 new members in the Healthy Families Program at Superior IPA. The marketing budget after all expenses is \$320 per month for the first year. Since this program was started by the state, the majority of the printed material needed to promote, explain, and enroll in the program is provided by the state free of charge. Money allotted for marketing will be spent only on supplemental materials needed and/or the vehicle used to get the materials in the hands of the target market. The state of California will allocate additional funds to CMS, as it has been issued \$6 million from the federal government to promote this program, and the funds must be spent each year or the funds will be transferred to another state. CMS will apply each year for a portion of the allocated funds to supplement its marketing efforts. CMS will request a minimum of \$100,000 per year.

INTRODUCTION

A time traveler from three decades ago would not recognize the current health care industry. Up until approximately a decade ago, health insurance in the United States operated primarily under an "indemnity" or "fee-for-service" (FFS) model. Under that system, a holder of a health insurance policy was free to visit any physician of his or her choosing. In turn, the physician would bill the policyholder's insurance company for whatever services were provided.

In effect, the FFS model was a self-referral model to health care, and it had one major weakness in that it did not provide any incentives for the medical community to control costs. Although there are other contributing factors, lack of control was a primary contributing element that fueled extraordinary inflation in medical costs.

The managed care approach to health care delivery differs most significantly from the FFS model in that it provides strong incentives for the medical community to control costs. Under managed care, physicians and other providers of medical services generally enter into written agreements with health insurance companies, in which the physician agrees to accept a set dollar amount per member for primary care services. This system of prefunding a provider for a given number of patients who enroll with that provider is also called "capitation" in health care lingo.

As you can see, a capitated provider has strong incentive to carefully manage the utilization of services of his or her patients because that has a direct impact on the bottom line. Ultimately, the theory is that capitated providers will be less likely to prescribe unnecessary procedures and will instead try to instill "wellness" in the patient's health regimen. Wellness is generally used in the health care community to describe an overall approach to health care in which the focus is to keep members at a generally good level of health. Presumably, this helps to minimize severe episodes of illness that require more expensive and invasive medical intervention.

In the western United States, managed care plans have gained wide acceptance with the public, and many managed health care companies have become powerful regional businesses as a result of it. In response to this, physicians formed alliances among themselves, and these affiliations are commonly called "Independent Physicians Associations" or IPAs. By pooling their membership, physicians of an IPA are in a better position to negotiate with health care companies for more favorable terms than if each were to go it alone.

Superior IPA is one such affiliation of family practice and specialist physicians. There are approximately 163 physicians affiliated with Superior IPA, and their practices are located in various parts around west San Gabriel Valley. The physicians of Superior IPA treat Medicare, Medi-Cal, and Commercial patients who are members of most major health plans such as Blue Cross, UHP, and Universal Care.

Currently, Superior IPA has a very low number of Healthy Families enrollees, and it desires to grow that membership primarily through an informational and educational blitz in its service area. Healthy Families is a federal- and state-funded health care plan that is intended for children ages one to eighteen who come from families loosely defined as "working poor."

Our marketing plan studies demographic and other relevant data to determine whether Superior IPA's service area is suitable for the Healthy Families health plan and, if so, how that market can be reached.

SITUATIONAL ANALYSIS

Situational Environment

People, for many years, have had a vested interest in the health care industry. They use health services not only when they need urgent medical attention but also for preventive purposes such as regular checkups. The enormous width of the industry encompasses many specializations and services that range from tetanus vaccinations to artificial heart transplantation surgeries. Furthermore, the unpredictable manner of people's medical needs, along with the requirement of fast response for these needs, make health care a dynamic industry. The need for fast and accurate medical response for the numerous medical needs makes it imperative for the various components of the health care delivery system to work in concert. Since people's health is at stake, high-quality service is paramount. It is quite a challenge to provide quality service in today's environment of increasingly managed care.

As managed care plans gained wider popularity and acceptance with the public, physicians discovered it to be to their advantage to pool their resources and form affiliations. These affiliations are often called Independent Physicians Associations (IPA), and there are some advantages to forming this alliance. Perhaps the most notable one is that pooling their membership gives them greater bargaining strength when negotiating with health plans on rates.

Of course, not all IPAs are alike. They come in all shapes and sizes, in that some IPAs are actively managed by their affiliated physicians while others have delegated day-to-day management to outside management firms.

Unfortunately, some IPAs have encountered fiscal trouble despite the apparent merits of affiliation, primarily because "they lacked a solid financial base, a clear approach to governance and a strong infrastructure" (Finger, 1999). As a result, many IPAs throughout the country have filed for bankruptcy. These failures do not help engender trust between physicians and health plans. Even without failures, physicians sometimes complained about losing some autonomy and being told what types of treatments they can or cannot apply. Moreover, having no financial control over the IPA, many physicians felt like outcasts.

IPAs face many external and internal challenges, perhaps much more than they can handle. In fact, some experts do not expect many of them to continue as viable businesses. Industry observers think that most of them will file bankruptcy within the next eighteen to twenty-four months due to "the combination of poor management and inadequate payment from health plans" (Bernstein, 1999).

It is in the interest of the health plans, physicians, and patients that IPAs remain financially viable and solvent. Health plans need a stable network of contracted physicians to provide health care to their members in select service areas. Conversely, a member wants to have confidence that his or her primary care physician will be around when medical attention is needed. In the purest Darwinian sense, the current existence of some IPAs might signal the end of unfit IPAs and the start of a period of domination by a group of fewer, but better managed, IPAs.

Neutral Environment

Special agencies of the state and federal government normally regulate the health care industry, and their work has become more involved with the growth of managed care plans. The complexity of the issue, the number of parties involved, and the fact that all the parties have been hurt in some way renders the whole issue hard to solve with temporary or minor regulations that are applied by local or state governments. The solution seems to be a health care reform that is introduced by the federal government.

Fortunately, economic and political conditions enable the federal government to focus on health care. After decades of struggling with issues such as the Cold War, budget deficit, and nuclear threats, the U.S. government finally has the resources to deal with issues such as environmental protection, health care, and social security. Despite favorable conditions and the general expectation that the federal government will start health care reform, the elections that will be held next year reduce the chances for such reforms to take place over the next two years. However, with so many industry observers, it seems certain that everything will change, and will change dramatically.

Another strong influence on health care is the new health consciousness that started to affect lives for the last two decades. Increasing general welfare, favorable economic conditions along with stable political conditions help not only governments but also the public focus on different issues. Naturally, the health care industry benefits considerably from this trend. Increasing awareness will result in an increasing number of people covered by the managed care plans that provide health care at a low price. In particular, the number of children enrolled in managed care plans is expected to grow even higher due to the tendency of parents to seek better care for their children. Managed care plans for children are expected to benefit most from this trend of health consciousness, compared with other types of managed care plans.

In addition to all these, the California state government is placing a special emphasis on managed care plans for children, called the Healthy Families Program. The state promotes this managed care plan by publishing and distributing brochures and booklets. This actually provides free advertising for the IPAs. In addition, the government has passed laws in favor of the managed care program such as the one that makes legal immigrant children eligible for the program. The current changes are expected to be followed by some major changes that will increase the overall eligibility levels of families (Heath, 1999). The increase in market size along with an increase in the number of applications being filed will dramatically increase the number of people enrolled in Healthy Families, creating a promising future for the IPAs providing Healthy Families to their members.

Competitor Environment

The competitor environment of Superior IPA consists of IPAs and medical groups that accept the Healthy Families members and are located within the target market area.

When we consulted the Healthy Families Hot Line and Web sites and studied its geographic locations, we learned that two other IPAs in Superior IPA's service area were direct competitors. These two IPAs are considered competitors because of the overlap in service areas, the number of physicians in those IPAs currently serving the community, the variety of languages spoken by bilingual physicians, and the choice of contracted health plans they currently have that qualify for the Healthy Families Program. The two competitors are:

- *Allied Physician IPA,* which has a network of more than 600 physicians and has contracted health plans with Blue Shield, UHP Healthcare, Health Net, and LA Care Health Plan. Bilingual physicians can speak languages such as Chinese Mandarin, Tagalog, Cantonese, Fookien, Spanish, Taiwanese, Burmese, Vietnamese, Korean, Hindi, Urdu, Armenian, Arabic, Japanese, Farsi, French, German, and Italian.
- *Pacific IPA,* which has a network of 200 physicians, contracted health plans with Blue Cross, Blue Shield, and Health Net. The bilingual physicians can speak in languages such as Chinese Mandarin, Cantonese, Spanish, Taiwanese, Vietnamese, Korean, Hindi, and Japanese.

The competitors' strength is that they have more physicians than Superior IPA (which has a network of 163 physicians). In addition, they have many varieties of bilingual physicians, which will be more favorable for the large Asian population living in the San Gabriel Valley and neighboring cities. Convenient location and a beautiful building may attract more walk-in customers to the Allied Physicians IPA. Furthermore, the Allied Physicians IPA is affiliated with more hospitals than Superior IPA, giving its patients more alternatives for further treatments.

The major weakness of these competitors is their lack of promotions. Since the Healthy Families Program is considered a new managed care plan, promotional materials and further information will be helpful in building awareness within the community. Strategies used by competitors depend on interested customers, word of mouth, current patient lists, and promotion by the Healthy Families Program itself. Among other weaknesses are the lack of an established image and reputation, and market presence of the competitors.

To counteract the strength of the competitors, our marketing plan for Superior IPA will emphasize building customer awareness of the presence of the Healthy Families Program. By doing so, CMS will also emphasize the existence of Superior IPA as its image provider for this program, so that every prospective customer will be more likely to choose physicians associated with Superior IPA.

Company Environment

Superior IPA is an independent physician association with a network of 163 physicians. It is a nonprofit mutual benefit corporation that is owned by physicians. The physicians are scattered throughout the west San Gabriel Valley and neighboring cities. Superior IPA also has physicians at distant places such as Glendora, Santa Monica, and San Clemente.

Superior IPA was established six years ago. It has now become a corporation that is identified as reliable and stable in the health care industry. This success depends on two major elements. First, it has always had good business management. Since 1995, Superior IPA has been under contract with a professional management services organization, CAP Management Systems (CMS). Since then, CMS has been handling the management of Superior IPA, and this contract is expected to be kept valid for the oncoming years. Second, Superior IPA is a nonprofit corporation that is owned by the physicians themselves. Therefore, all physicians have unlimited access to the financial records, and they all participate in the decision-making processes. This establishes a feeling of trust within the organization, which is then reflected in the physician-member and health care company relationships.

With the physicians currently specializing in a total of thirty-eight areas, Superior IPA can provide a wide range of services. It has contracts with all major health care companies, and although it provides service for most managed care plans, most of the members are covered by Medi-Cal managed care plan. Currently, it has 3,486 members, 3,083 of whom are Medi-Cal members. But when these members' incomes increase they will be able to join the Healthy Families Program instead of Medi-Cal. Superior IPA also established a good relationship with a nearby hospital, Garfield Medical Center, and it provides Superior its facilities as needed. Overall, it has good contracts with all parties, and it established a superior network of health care providers to provide premium health care service.

Competitive Advantages

Probably the most important competitive advantage of the company is that unlike many IPAs, it is owned by the physicians themselves. It has a very strong infrastructure that prevents mistrust between the physicians and the IPA, and it keeps the physicians involved in all aspects of the IPA including management, providing a primary motivation for solving many problems that resulted in disasters for many IPAs such as staff layoffs or postponing payments.

A second advantage has been that the majority of the physicians are Asian. Considering that the immediate target market within the two-mile radius primarily consists of Asians (46 percent to be accurate), this has been a fairly important advantage over the other IPAs, because Asians feel more comfortable with Asian physicians and make their decisions on this issue accordingly. This issue was more important in cases where the patients are younger than eighteen and feel more comfortable communicating with the physician in his/her own language. Market expansion efforts will come from achieving this synergy from the Hispanic market too (see "Target Market").

Another important advantage is that Superior IPA has been in the market for six years, and during this time it has managed to establish a trustworthy name. Unlike many other IPAs, Superior IPA does not suffer from management problems and it has good relationships with the health care companies. The members and the health care companies are confident that Superior IPA will be in the market for a long time, and this provides a considerable advantage in a market full of uncertainty and discomfort.

In addition to all that, Superior IPA has a distinctive future that separates it from the rest: It provides high coordination among the members, the health care company, and physicians. It uses procedures that clearly state the actions to be taken in any given situation. This makes all the interactions easy and clear, eliminates the confusion, and makes the health care company–IPA-physician-member relationships comfortable. Since every party knows what it can expect and what it is expected to do, everything runs smoothly and problems become easy to detect and solve.

Finally, Superior IPA has a strong relationship with a nearby hospital, Garfield Medical Center. Because both parties know each other well and recognize what to expect from each other, they managed to establish specific procedures that help them work in harmony. The members of Superior IPA benefit from this relationship, since they can use facilities of the Garfield Medical Center. This increases the quality of the service and provides a major advantage over other IPAs.

Each of these points not only furnishes Superior IPA with necessary features to survive and stay in the market for an extended period of time, but also provides a distinctive advantage, making it unique among many other IPAs. It provides high-quality service and establishes strong relations with all other parties; Superior IPA ensures a healthy and stable future.

TARGET MARKET

Demographics

This is the most common basis for segmenting consumer markets because markets are strongly related to demand and are relatively easy to measure. The characteristics that are used in segmentation are age, gender, median income, and ethnicity of the population in each service area.

- **Age and gender:** In each service area, the segment markets are divided into three groups: population of females and males whose ages are below six, population of females and males whose ages are between six and thirteen, and population of females and males whose ages are between thirteen and eighteen years of age. This category is based on the eligibility age to apply for the Healthy Families Program, which is between one and eighteen years of age.
- **Median income:** Using the median income for each segment, we can determine the number of members in each household and determine if they fall between the federal poverty levels.
- **Ethnicity:** Market segmentation of the market based on ethnicity is used to determine the market behavior (which will be used in the "Psychographic Segmentation" section), and therefore it will be used to determine the best ways to approach this market.

Although CMS would prefer to target the entire population surrounding Superior IPA, a market segmentation strategy will be implemented. This will allow CMS to develop an optimal, cost- and time-efficient strategy to reach its goal to increase the number of patients using Superior IPA. CMS will accomplish this by promoting the Healthy Families Program at Superior IPA to the Hispanic population in the San Gabriel Valley and surrounding cities.

The characteristics of our target market were derived from a demographic analysis using population statistics provided by The MEDSTAT Group (MEDSTAT, 1999). The characteristics are as follows:

- One to eighteen years old
- Primarily Hispanic
- Household of three to four members
- Household income level ranging from $32,387 to $35,524
- No current health insurance coverage
- U.S. citizen or legal immigrant

The above target market is eligible for the Healthy Families Program at Superior IPA. We chose to promote Healthy Families to the Hispanic market for a multitude of reasons. First, when reviewing the previously stated population data, we found that approximately 64 percent of the population in the Combined Service Area is Hispanic (MEDSTAT, 1999).

Second, Healthy Families is a state-funded managed care program and the state of California is eager to provide health care to all children. California's effort to provide health care insurance to more uninsured children was made possible last year when Congress passed and President Clinton signed the State Children's Health Insurance Program (CHIP). This is the largest expansion of children's health coverage since the adoption of Medicaid in 1965. CHIP is a $4-billion-a-year national initiative to help states provide health insurance for uninsured children in low-wage working families (100% Campaign, Web site). California created the Healthy Families Program to use its share of these funds to cover low-income, uninsured children (*Healthy Families Handbook,* 1999).

Psychographics

Demographic data are used to segment markets because these data are related to behavior and are relatively easy to gather. However, demographics are not in themselves the cause of behavior. CMS realizes that it should go beyond demographic attributes in an effort to better understand why consumers behave the way they do, which involves examining attributes related to how a person thinks, feels, and acts.

The Hispanic community may have some apprehension about the health care system or no awareness of the benefits of preventive care (*La Opinion,* Interview). For this reason, *La Opinion,* a well-respected Hispanic newspaper, has published supplements to its newspaper focusing on health and well-being. These highly targeted supplements focus on the health issues that affect and interest Latinos most (*La Opinion,* Brochure). CMS may take advantage of this venue in the November issue. *La Opinion* also offers assistance in targeting the ad specifically to the audience needed. It will be important to focus on educating the Hispanic community that obtaining health services through the Healthy Families Program will in no way affect their status with Immigration and Naturalization Services (INS) and that the Healthy Families Program does not share any information with the INS. This topic will be reviewed in the "Marketing Tactics" section.

According to *La Opinion,* the following facts may be useful in selecting venues for advertising Superior IPA and the Healthy Families Program:

- Hispanic adults accounted for 42 percent of all adults who attended rock/Spanish rock concerts in Los Angeles and surrounding cities.
- 55 percent of Hispanic adults attended one or more movies in the past twelve months.
- 46 percent have purchased CDs in the past three months.
- Hispanic adults accounted for 39 percent of all adults attending dance/nightclubs in the past twelve months.
- Hispanic adults accounted for 84 percent of all adults who attended an international soccer game in the past twelve months.
- Hispanic adults accounted for 83 percent of all adults who attended a Galaxy soccer game in the past twelve months.
- Hispanic adults accounted for 40 percent of all adults who attended a Dodgers baseball game in the past twelve months.
- Hispanic adults accounted for 40 percent of all adults who attended a Lakers basketball game in the past twelve months.
- 2.2 million Hispanics travel on L.A. freeways every weekend.
- 72 percent of Hispanic adults in the Los Angeles area and surrounding cities are involved in community, church, and school events (*La Opinion,* Brochure).

Geographics

CMS divided its markets also based on the service area definitions. The service area definitions are based on actual facility discharges by zip code. To determine the areas, actual inpatient and outpatient cases for the most recent fiscal year were ranked by zip code in descending order. Once ranked, the areas were defined on a basic formula. These areas are:

- *Two-mile radius:* inpatients and outpatients residing within a two-mile radius.
- *Primary Service Area (PSA):* top 70 percent of combined inpatients and outpatients by zip code.
- *Secondary Service Area (SSA):* next 15 percent (71–85 percent) of combined inpatient and outpatients by zip code.
- *Combined Service Area (CSA):* combination of PSA and SSA equaling 85 percent of combined inpatient and outpatient cases by zip code.

Thus, the target market is the west San Gabriel Valley and neighboring cities (see Appendix A for map of service area). This includes, but is not limited to, the following cities: Alhambra, Montebello, Rosemead, San Gabriel, Monterey Park, West Covina, Baldwin Park, Los Angeles, Temple City, El Monte, Covina, Pasadena, La Puente, and Arcadia. Superior IPA provides a complete network of general practitioners and specialists in this service area. Approximately 488,847 people are eligible based on our analysis.

STRENGTHS, WEAKNESSES, OPPORTUNITIES, AND THREATS

Strengths

Nonprofit, Mutual Benefit Organization As previously stated, Superior IPA is a nonprofit, mutual benefit organization, which is dedicated to fully serving its physicians and members. Accordingly, financial statements are disclosed, and trust among physicians is established. This creates an environment that will enable physicians and their staff to work well and provide the best service for members of the community.

Bilingual Physicians Superior IPA provides the community with a variety of bilingual physicians who can communicate in numerous languages such as Chinese Mandarin, Cantonese, Vietnamese, Korean, Japanese, Tagalog, Spanish, Taiwanese, Arabic, Italian, French, Portuguese, Armenian, Turkish, and Cambodian. The majority of Superior IPA physicians can speak Chinese, which gives them an edge over the competition because there is a significant Chinese population living within its primary service area.

Trustworthy Physicians Most of the physicians associated with Superior IPA have been serving the Asian community in the San Gabriel Valley and neighboring cities for many years. They are among the most qualified physicians in the area to ensure the finest level of medical excellence. Each of them is affiliated with the most respected hospitals and medical centers, such as Garfield Medical Center, Alhambra Hospital, San Gabriel Valley Medical Center, Monterey Park Hospital, Whittier Hospital Medical Center, and Greater El Monte Community Hospital.

Private Practice Superior IPA provides health services to its patients through a variety of local and private practice offices, not in a clinic. This enables patients to choose and visit the closest one of the many offices that are scattered throughout many cities, including Monterey Park, Alhambra, Rosemead, San Gabriel, El Monte, West Covina, Montebello, Temple City, Pasadena, Arcadia, Covina, Baldwin Park, La Puente, and Los Angeles.

Partnership Superior IPA has partnered with Garfield Medical Center and Tenet Health Systems to better serve its community by enabling patients to receive further treatments easily. Furthermore, the partnership with CMS as its management services organization provides Superior IPA with the best management for smooth relations between its physicians and patients.

Direct Referral Program Superior IPA provides direct referral to specialists; this enables patients to get better treatment conveniently, while benefiting the specialists as well.

Weaknesses

Limited Number of Spanish-Speaking Physicians The demographic and ethnic analysis indicates that our target market is children who come from Hispanic families or communicate in Spanish as their first language. In fact, of all the primary care physicians in Superior IPA, only 36 percent speak Spanish. This number may be considered low since our target market consists of a large number of Hispanic families. Besides, one of the main competitors, Allied Physicians IPA, has a large number of Spanish-speaking physicians (60 percent of the primary care physicians speak Spanish). Our strategy will be to attract more Spanish-speaking physicians to join Superior IPA in the future in order to establish better communication channels between physicians and patients.

Limited Contracted Health Plan In the Los Angeles area, there are numerous health care companies offering the Healthy Families Program, such as Community Health Plan, Blue Cross HMO, Blue Shield HMO, Health Net, Kaiser Permanente, L.A. Care Health Plan, Molina, Dental Plan (Superior Dental Plan, Delta Dental, Denticare), and Vision Services Plan.

However, Superior IPA has limited contracts with health care companies such as Blue Cross, Molina, and UHP. Limiting the number of contracts with health care companies may hinder Superior IPA from attaining the market share it strives for since our consumers will not be able to choose from a wide variety of health care companies. To counteract this weakness, we will attract more health care companies to contract with in order to provide our potential members with a large variety of health plans.

Opportunities

Large Numbers of Prospective Customers Based on our analysis in the target market section, there is a large number of prospective customers who are potentially eligible (approximately 488,847 people are eligible based on our analysis in the "Target Market" section). This means that Superior IPA faces an important opportunity for growth. Therefore, our marketing strategy will be based on introductory and growth models (which will be explained in more detail in the "Marketing Strategy" section).

Future State Regulation Currently, children who are eligible for the Healthy Families Program are those whose family income level falls between 133 percent and 200 percent of the Federal Poverty Level (FPL) for ages one to six and between 100 percent and 200 percent for ages six to eighteen.

As of November 1999, children between 200 and 250 percent of the FPL (and more with income deductions) will be eligible. The budget expanded coverage for children by increasing eligibility from 200 percent to 250 percent of the Federal Poverty Level (see Table A1-1 below). For example, if a child comes from a family of two and the family's annual income is $27,000, then the child is qualified for the Healthy Families Program based on the new regulation. In the past, the child would not qualify for the program if the annual income falls at more than 200 percent of FPL. Therefore, prospective families for this program will increase if the new regulation is activated.

Table A1-1. Percent of Federal Poverty Levels

Percent of Federal Poverty Level	Number of Family Members				
	2	3	4	5	6
100	10,850	13,650	16,450	19,250	22,050
200	21,700	27,300	32,900	38,500	44,100
225	24,413	30,713	37,013	43,313	49,613
250	27,125	34,125	41,125	48,125	55,125
275	29,838	37,538	45,238	52,938	60,638
300	32,550	40,950	49,350	57,750	66,150

Source: The Federal Register.

The budget also allows the income deductions that are used in Medi-Cal to be applied to Healthy Families, such as child-care or work-related expenses. That means children with family incomes above 250 percent of poverty may also be eligible in the near future.

Threats

Strong Competitors   Two main competitors will be somewhat of a threat for Superior IPA in terms of their large numbers of physicians, the variety of languages spoken by physicians, and their contracted health plan, as we stated earlier in the competitor environment. However, Superior IPA is located in an area where the target market is quite large, so that there will be enough room for all the IPAs. Furthermore, these two main competitors do not promote Healthy Families; therefore, people are not fully aware of their market presence. Our strategy will be to provide prospective customers with the most updated information regarding Healthy Families, and through our marketing tactics, we will try to attract them to join the program with Superior IPA as their provider.

Limited Numbers of Physicians Associated with Superior IPA   As our marketing plan becomes more successful, a possible problem will be the limited number of physicians associated with Superior IPA. If the number of physicians remains the same and the number of members increases in the future, then the physician-to-member ratio will go up. This will be a problem for providing the best service to our patients/members. Therefore, in the future, we will be working on increasing our number of physicians, especially Spanish-speaking physicians, since our target market largely consists of Hispanic families.

MARKETING OBJECTIVES AND GOALS

Marketing Objectives

Because it was introduced in June 1998, the Healthy Families Program is considered a new health care program and many people are not fully aware of its existence. Therefore, our marketing objectives in this project are:

1.   Being the first to promote this concept, we will be able to penetrate the market and attract more patients to sign up with the Healthy Families Program with Superior IPA as their provider. Our objective is to increase the number of Healthy Families memberships within Superior IPA.

2.   By increasing the number of memberships, we will be able to increase the overall capitation revenue, which is our ultimate objective.

3.   To introduce Healthy Families to prospective audiences who have little or no awareness about health plans for children.

4.   Educate prospective members that Healthy Families has not collected information regarding immigration status. The program will not provide information on the immigration status of such parents to the INS or use immigration information to demand repayment information from recipients for services lawfully provided.

Marketing Goals

Our marketing goals are:

1.   To introduce the Healthy Families Program to at least 50 percent of all prospective customers within the west San Gabriel Valley area.

2. To increase the number of members in the Healthy Families Program by 81 percent from year 2000 to year 2002 (see Table A1-2 below).

3. To increase the capitation revenue by 196 percent from year 2000 to year 2002 (see Table A1-2 below).

The details regarding the number of target members and capitation revenue are as follows:

Table A1-2. Number of Members and Related Capitation Revenues per Year

	2000	*2001*	*2002*
Number of members	698	1,003	1,265
Capitation revenue	$116,226	$259,242	$343,956

MARKETING STRATEGY

For promoting Healthy Families, it is crucial to focus on the fact that the product is still in the introductory phase. Many of the potential members are still unaware of the Healthy Families Program and that Superior IPA offers it. It will be a focus of CMS to educate the local population about the existence of Healthy Families at Superior IPA and stimulate more demand for its services. Typically this phase, as it relates to the product life cycle (see Figure A1-1), is risky and plagued with expensive marketing dollars (Etzel et al., 1997).

CMS is at an advantage since the *Healthy Families Handbooks,* which are provided by the Department of Health Services, are free of charge and contain the majority of the information that CMS seeks to share with the local community. Since this handbook would be costly to print, this represents a considerable cost advantage for CMS.

Our marketing philosophy will be based on two basic strategies, information strategy and image strategy. Consumers purchase a product because it provides satisfaction. The thing that makes a product capable of satisfying wants is its utility, and it is through marketing that much of a product's utility is created. Healthy Families is considered a new program that was introduced by the state in June 1998, so most people are not fully aware of its presence. Unless you know a product exists and where you can get it, the product has no value. Therefore, informing the prospective buyers that a product exists needs information utility. Through information strategy, we are trying to build awareness that there is a new type of children's health plan in addition to Medi-Cal for Children. Normally, people only know about Medi-Cal for Children, which was designed for low-income families and

FIGURE A1-1. Product Life Cycle

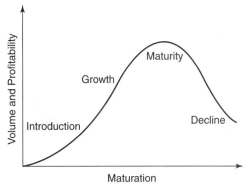

Source: Peter Kovacek; Pkovacek@flash.net.

provides no-cost medical service for their children under twenty-one. Healthy Families is a low-cost insurance that provides health, dental, and vision coverage to children who do not currently have insurance or whose family income is too high to qualify for no-cost Medi-Cal. As people are informed of the existence of the Healthy Families Program, we will, through image strategy, deliver the message that Superior IPA is their main provider. Image strategy is the emotional or psychological value that a person attaches to a product or brand because of its reputation or social standing. Superior IPA's brand image must be a gateway for all prospective customers as they decide to enroll in the program. The overall strategy can be summarized as follows:

- Information Strategy

1. CMS will deliver the message to the community and build or increase their awareness of the existence of the Healthy Families Program as low-cost health coverage besides no-cost Medi-Cal.

2. CMS will educate families of the importance of having health care coverage for their children and help them understand the benefits of regular and preventive health care.

3. CMS will motivate them to take the actions necessary to apply and obtain health coverage for their uninsured children.

4. CMS will inform families that information and free enrollment assistance is available in their neighborhood in seven languages.

5. CMS will add special services to differentiate its product. All new enrollees will be called to see if all of their needs are being met.

6. CMS will issue a newsletter to repeat customers informing them of important medical issues.

- Image Strategy:

1. CMS will continue delivering the message and build awareness in the community while introducing Superior IPA as a primary provider in Healthy Families Program.

2. CMS will create a brand identity for Superior IPA as "their local doctor's office who cares about its community."

3. CMS will emphasize the benefits of enrolling with Superior IPA. Benefits include bilingual physicians and service provided to all prospective customers.

4. CMS will stress the easy application process for the Healthy Families Program and that there is free assistance in filling out the application form. Healthy Families will help them choose the right plan and the right physician and drive the target population or all eligible customers to enroll. Superior IPA will also have a certified application assistant in each office so that they may help potential clients fill out the application in the office. This will dramatically increase the probability that patients will stay with Superior IPA for their medical needs.

- Promoting the Image:

1. CMS will use vehicles such as special events, partnerships, promotional opportunities, on-site marketing, local advertising, community marketing, grass-roots collateral materials, mass media, and media relations as well as both traditional and nontraditional forms of marketing simple in form and image. More detail will be provided in the "Marketing Tactics" section.

Another crucial focus for CMS will be to mitigate the fears of potential clients regarding the INS. Although federal guidelines were recently issued clarifying that the use of Healthy Families will not affect a family's immigration status, the fear by Hispanic families is so entrenched that it will be essential to educate families about the issue (100% Campaign, Web site). Materials provided by the state at no cost will be distributed by CMS to the potential members explaining that the use of the Healthy Families Program will in no way affect their status. The material is available in English and Spanish, and phone numbers are provided for those who have more questions. The state will also provide funding to assist CMS in this campaign. This is explained further in the following section on "Marketing Tactics."

MARKETING TACTICS

Product

Technically, the company to be promoted is Superior IPA. One vehicle to promote Superior IPA is to promote one of the products it offers, called Healthy Families. CMS's primary goal is to increase the number of patients who use Superior IPA when they join the Healthy Families Program. Superior IPA has 163 general practitioners and specialists in the previously stated service area.

Superior will be providing the Healthy Families services to clients who meet the criteria established by the state of California. The qualifications are as follows:

- Children ages one to eighteen
- Families with incomes at or below 250 percent (as of November 1, 1999) of the Federal Income Guidelines
- Children without employer-sponsored health insurance in the last three months
- Children not eligible for Medi-Cal
- Children who are U.S. citizens, nationals, or eligible immigrants
- Children who live in California

The Healthy Families Program amounts to low-cost insurance that provides health, dental, and vision coverage to children who meet the above-stated criteria. It is important to mention that even though the cost of the care is low, the quality of health care provided by Superior IPA is the same as the care provided for those individuals paying in full. This is a crucial point and will be stressed in our advertising campaign, since low-cost health care is typically thought of as a low-quality care.

Price

Family size, family income level, and the health care company chosen determine the monthly premium for Healthy Families. The monthly premiums range from $4 to $9 a month for each child up to a maximum of $27 for all children within the household. Incentives are provided to pay premiums in advance, to receive one month free. Specifically, for every three months paid in advance the fourth month is free. In addition to the monthly premiums, a co-payment of $5 is required at the time of service. However, this co-payment is not required if the service is of a preventive nature (such as immunization shots) rather than regular health care. The total expenditure per family is $250 per year. Once this limit is reached, all services provided thereafter are free to the family. (See Appendix B for a *Healthy Families Handbook.*)

Promotion and Place

There are numerous low-cost vehicles to promote Healthy Families and Superior IPA to our target market. If CMS dedicated one full-time, bilingual marketing person, CMS could

Table A1-3. Analysis of Advertising Costs

Description	Basic cost	Remark	Year			Total
			2000	2001	2002	
Movie Theaters	$20/screen/week	Minimum of 18-week commitment required. Average theater in Alhambra has 7 screens. $20 × 7 × 18 = $2,520. Run two times a year at 18 weeks each. $2,520 × 2 = $5,040.	$5,040	$5,040	$5,040	**$15,120**
10-Minute Promotional Video	$1,500	$1,500 is cost of producing the promotional video. It is free to run it on local cable.	$1,500	$0	$0	**$1,500**
Monterey Park, Bus Shelter Advertising	$300	$300 is cost of preparing and producing the poster to be placed in bus shelter advertising. The city of Monterey Park does not charge for advertising in bus shelters as long as it serves a clear public benefit.	$300	$0	$0	**$300**
Spanish Language Newspaper	$3,870	Cost of half-page ad per year in *La Ola*. Circulation is 100,000.	$3,870	$3,870	$3,870	**$11,610**
Newsletter Quarterly	$1,875/quarter	$1,875 × 4 = $7,500 per year	$7,500	$7,500	$7,500	**$22,500**
		Total Cost	**$18,210**	**$16,410**	**$16,410**	**$51,030**

accomplish the goal of increasing the number of patients for Superior IPA. This person would use a combination of marketing techniques, such as person-to-person selling, sales promotion, advertising, and publicity.

This marketing person could find out about all of the local trade shows and community events that are reaching similar audiences. A booth would be set up to distribute the *Healthy Families Handbooks* and Superior IPAs physician roster to individuals who fit the target market criteria. This method is extremely cost effective since the *Healthy Families Handbooks* are free and will have all of the information the potential member will need, including phone numbers to call if they have difficulty filling out the forms. The methods are as follows:

Establishing Key Alliances and Community Involvement Creating strategic alliances with other nonprofit organizations that are targeting the Hispanic community. This will help share and thereby lower the cost of promotions. CMS will request help from public and private organizations.

Current Members In an effort to keep existing customers, a newsletter could be sent out to promote Healthy Families and discuss medical issues related to the Hispanic market. If the newsletter were a folded 11 × 17, two-sided, two-color process, the cost to print 10,000 units would be $675 plus tax (Lambert Printing Company, Interview). Postage for this newsletter would cost $1,200, according to the U.S. Post Office (U.S. Post Office, Interview).

Private Sector In the private sector, small businesses can help promote Superior IPA by allowing us to provide materials for their employees that explain the Superior IPA and the Healthy Families Program. The focus of the promotion will be to explain that when your children have preventive health care, the parents decrease their absentee rates from work and their children will be happier and more productive in school. Also, those children will receive critical preventive care they need to prevent or detect illness before it becomes more serious.

Public Sector In the public sector, CMS will create allies with schools, child-care organizations, religious congregations, advocacy groups, grass-roots organizations, the local Chamber of Commerce, Community Based Outreach, the PTA, and many others.

Community Based Outreach (CBO), for instance, is sensitive to culture and language and intimately familiar with the populations it serves. It has the ability to work well directly with the low-income, hard-to-reach target audience. CBO conducts demographic research and assists in developing coalitions and networks. Its success is based on how well it connects various causes in an effort to share resources. CBO will have extensive public relations campaigns, which will help CMS reach as many prospective families as possible. CBO also maintains connections with corporations and will enlist their help as well as the media's help to portray the benefits of a healthy lifestyle.

According to Yahoo.com's Yellow Pages, there are five Catholic churches in our target area (Yahoo Yellow Pages, Web site). Most of these churches were willing to allow the information to be distributed to their parishioners. Many of the churches were also willing to make announcements during Spanish and English services informing the parishioners that the information was available and where to find it. There are also approximately fifteen junior high schools and approximately seventeen high schools to which CMS could target its effort of informing the public.

Ads will be displayed in theaters and on buses as well. When advertising in a theater, the cost is based on an eighteen-week minimum and a ten-screen theater. It costs $20 per screen, times eighteen weeks and ten screens for a total of $3,600 (Edwards Cinema

Corporate Office, Interview). Many of the cities in our target market vary in their approach to advertising on bus benches and city buses. All of the cities provide ways for CMS to advertise free of charge, since Superior IPA is a nonprofit organization.

Local Cable Another vehicle is the local cable channel, which allows nonprofit organizations to run ads for free. Information could be projected in English and in Spanish promoting the need for adequate health care for children. The ad could explain how Superior IPA has everything they need to keep their family healthy and that they have been serving the local community for many years. Superior IPA will provide the phone numbers and contacts of certified application assistants to help potential members in signing up for the Healthy Families Program. Ads for the local cable channel may be in two forms; they may be all text or in video form. A professional, eight-to-ten-minute video may be provided for $1,500 (Gary Center, Interview).

Spanish Media There are local Spanish newspapers and radio stations available for a fee. Wave Community Newspapers are geared for multicultural audiences. *La Ola* is a Spanish newspaper published by Wave Communications, which is doorstep delivered in our target region. The cost varies depending on the length of the ad and whether or not color is used. A full-page ad with 100,000 circulation is $7,740 per year. A half-page ad with the same circulation is $3,870 per year.

La Opinion is another newspaper in the area, but its circulation is beyond our geographic scope and the cost is much higher. *La Opinion* provides a large variety of services at varying prices. The cost will be determined by the breadth and depth of the proposed advertising campaign. However, due to our nonprofit status, we may advertise in its supplement Health section in the November issue free of charge. *La Opinion* will also provide assistance in writing and developing the material prior to printing.

State Financial Assistance As previously stated, there is a $4-billion-a-year national initiative to help states provide health insurance to uninsured children in low-wage working families. Of these funds, California has been allocated $6 million. CMS will file the proper paperwork in an effort to receive a portion of these funds to offset the advertising expenses. Grants may be written to receive funds in the amount of $100,000 or more depending on the remaining funds available. All funds allocated to the state of California must be designated by the end of the calendar year or the funds will become available for another state to use. CMS will apply for funds each year to supplement its campaign.

ORGANIZATION, EVALUATION, CONTROL, AND IMPLEMENTATION

1. Organization Chart for Project

In terms of the outreach initiative, the Marketing Coordinator must necessarily take a central role in ensuring that critical steps be executed at the appropriate time. Due to the newness of the Healthy Families program, our marketing plan calls for an approach to advertising that is educational and informational in nature. To help realize that vision, we have identified some important action items that need to be followed through on. Those action items, and related parties, are also summarized in the following chart.

Organization chart for Project

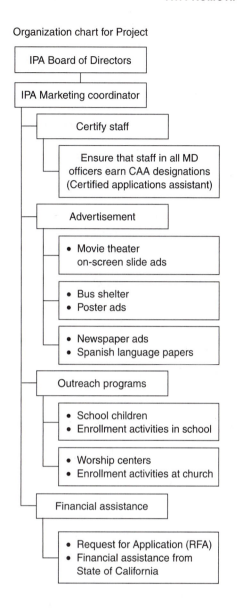

2. Project Development Schedules

The following schedule summarizes the timing of action steps that need to be taken as prescribed in this marketing plan.

Due Date	Action Step	Affected Party(ies)
2/2000	Meet with account executive of Spanish language newspapers, *La Ola,* to discuss costs and other issues related to running advertisement for Health Families and the IPA.	• Marketing Coordinator • *La Ola* account executive
2/2000	Initiate contact with leadership of local area churches (Protestant and Catholic) to discuss possibility of disseminating information and application forms about the Healthy Families program.	• Marketing Coordinator • Leadership of local area churches

Due Date	Action Step	Affected Party(ies)
3/2000	Get at least one front office staff person at every physician's clinic certified as Certified Application Assistance. (CAA)	• Marketing Coordinator • Front office manager at each physician's office.
3/2000	Meet with account executive at Edwards Theater Corporate office to discuss and plan pre-movie slide advertisement. Continue contact with account executive on as-needed basis until advertisement begins run in movie theaters.	• Marketing Coordinator • Edwards Theater account executive
5/2000	Initiate contact with council members of the city of Monterey Park and prepare presentation to convince city that Healthy Families presents a clear benefit to a significant number of city residents.	• Marketing Coordinator • City of Monterey Park council members
5/2000	Meet and discuss costs and other issues related to the preparation and production of poster suitable for bus shelter advertising. These posters will be used in the event that the city of Monterey Park votes to permit advertisement of Healthy Families in conjunction with the IPA's name in city bus shelters.	• Marketing Coordinator • Outdoor advertising account executive
6/2000	Make presentation to Monterey Park council members as planned.	• Marketing Coordinator • City of Monterey Park council members
7/2000	Meet and discuss costs and other issues related to the professional production of informational/promotional videos. These videos to be run on local cable television free of charge and will be designed to strongly associate Healthy Families with the IPA.	• Marketing Coordinator • Video production company
7/2000	Initiate contact with officials of local school districts to discuss possibility of conducting Healthy Families presentation in conjunction with back-to-school activities.	• Marketing Coordinator • School district officials
8/2000	Obtain and complete the Request for Application (RFA) forms from the state of California. These documents to be completed so that IPA considered when state awards funds for outreach programs.	• Marketing Coordinator • Upper management (CEO, COO, CFO, Director of IPA Operations)
9/2000	Meet with applicable representatives to discuss scheduling of IPA's professionally produced informational videos on local cable television. Continue communication as appropriate until videos begin airing on local cable.	• Marketing Coordinator • Representatives of local cable television
9/2000	Conduct presentation at local schools to teachers and students to identify and sign up eligible enrollees.	• Marketing Coordinator • School officials
11/2000	Contact state representative to follow up on status of the RFA that was submitted in consideration of possible financial assistance for outreach programs.	• Marketing Coordinator • State of California representatives
1/2001	Finalize written agreement with city of Monterey Park regarding the nature and duration of the advertisements to be placed in bus shelters.	• Marketing Coordinator • City of Monterey Park council members
1/2001	Finalize with the outdoor advertising company the poster to be used in Monterey Park bus shelters.	• Marketing Coordinator • Outdoor advertising account executive
3/2001	Meet with Edwards Theater account executive to extend on-screen advertising for 2001.	• Marketing Coordinator • Theater account executive
3/2001	Contact all physicians' offices to ensure that at least one person is a CAA and conduct followup procedures as necessary.	• Marketing Coordinator • Front office manager at each physician's office.
5/2001	Meet with Monterey Park council members to present report on effectiveness of advertisement campaign and express desire to continue in second half of the current year.	• Marketing Coordinator • City of Monterey Park council members

Due Date	Action Step	Affected Party(ies)
5/2001	Meet with outdoor advertising agency to discuss updating or adjusting the ad poster as necessary.	• Marketing Coordinator • Outdoor advertising account executive
7/2001	Contact school district officials to express desire to conduct back-to-school Healthy Families enrollment in similar fashion as last year.	• Marketing Coordinator • School officials
8/2001	Obtain and complete RFA for state assistance in financing outreach programs.	• Marketing Coordinator • Upper management (CEO, COO, CFO, Director of IPA Operations)
9/2001	Conduct presentation at local schools to teachers and students to identify and sign up eligible enrollees.	• Marketing Coordinator • School officials
10/2001	Meet with local cable representative to extend airing of informational video.	• Marketing Coordinator • Cable television representatives
11/2001	Contact state representative to follow up on status of the RFA that was submitted in consideration of possible financial assistance for outreach programs.	• Marketing Coordinator • State of California representatives
1/2002	Meet with Monterey Park council members to present report on the effectiveness of bus shelter advertising last year and express desire to continue some form of advertising in current year.	• Marketing Coordinator • City of Monterey Park council members
1/2002	As necessary, meet with outdoor advertising agency to discuss adjustments to poster or other issues related to bus shelter advertising.	• Marketing Coordinator • Outdoor advertising account executive
3/2002	Meet with Edwards Theater account executive to extend on-screen slide advertising for 2002.	• Marketing Coordinator • Theater account executive
5/2002	Conduct Healthy Families information and enrollment fairs at area churches.	• Marketing Coordinator • Church leadership
7/2002	Contact school officials to plan for back-to-school enrollment drive in September.	• Marketing Coordinator • School officials
8/2002	Complete and submit RFA to state for consideration of financial assistance in outreach efforts.	• Marketing Coordinator • Upper management (CEO, COO, CFO, Director of IPA Operations)
9/2002	Conduct back-to-school informational meeting at area schools and enroll eligible children.	• Marketing Coordinator • School officials

IPA
Breakeven Analysis

Number of Members	Per Member				Fixed Cost	Number of Members	Total Revenue	Total Costs
	Revenue	Fee to PCP	Fee to Specialist	Net Income (Before Fixed Costs)				
0	25.25	8.00	12.00	5.25	1,388.60	0	0.00	1,388.60
10	25.25	8.00	12.00	5.25	1,388.60	10	252.50	1,588.60
20	25.25	8.00	12.00	5.25	1,388.60	20	505.00	1,788.60
30	25.25	8.00	12.00	5.25	1,388.60	30	757.50	1,988.60
40	25.25	8.00	12.00	5.25	1,388.60	40	1,010.00	2,188.60
50	25.25	8.00	12.00	5.25	1,388.60	50	1,262.50	2,388.60
60	25.25	8.00	12.00	5.25	1,388.60	60	1,515.00	2,588.60
70	25.25	8.00	12.00	5.25	1,388.60	70	1,767.50	2,788.60
80	25.25	8.00	12.00	5.25	1,388.60	80	2,020.00	2,988.60
90	25.25	8.00	12.00	5.25	1,388.60	90	2,272.50	3,188.60
100	25.25	8.00	12.00	5.25	1,388.60	100	2,525.00	3,388.60
110	25.25	8.00	12.00	5.25	1,388.60	110	2,777.50	3,588.60
120	25.25	8.00	12.00	5.25	1,388.60	120	3,030.00	3,788.60
130	25.25	8.00	12.00	5.25	1,388.60	130	3,282.50	3,988.60
140	25.25	8.00	12.00	5.25	1,388.60	140	3,535.00	4,188.60
150	25.25	8.00	12.00	5.25	1,388.60	150	3,787.50	4,388.60
160	25.25	8.00	12.00	5.25	1,388.60	160	4,040.00	4,588.60
170	25.25	8.00	12.00	5.25	1,388.60	170	4,292.50	4,788.60
180	25.25	8.00	12.00	5.25	1,388.60	180	4,545.00	4,988.60
190	25.25	8.00	12.00	5.25	1,388.60	190	4,797.50	5,188.60
200	25.25	8.00	12.00	5.25	1,388.60	200	5,050.00	5,388.60
210	25.25	8.00	12.00	5.25	1,388.60	210	5,302.50	5,588.60
220	25.25	8.00	12.00	5.25	1,388.60	220	5,555.00	5,788.60
230	25.25	8.00	12.00	5.25	1,388.60	230	5,807.50	5,988.60
240	25.25	8.00	12.00	5.25	1,388.60	240	6,060.00	6,188.60
250	25.25	8.00	12.00	5.25	1,388.60	250	6,312.50	6,388.60
260	25.25	8.00	12.00	5.25	1,388.60	260	6,565.00	6,588.60
270	25.25	8.00	12.00	5.25	1,388.60	270	6,817.50	6,788.60
280	25.25	8.00	12.00	5.25	1,388.60	280	7,070.00	6,988.60
290	25.25	8.00	12.00	5.25	1,388.60	290	7,322.50	7,188.60
300	25.25	8.00	12.00	5.25	1,388.60	300	7,575.00	7,388.60
310	25.25	8.00	12.00	5.25	1,388.60	310	7,827.50	7,588.60
320	25.25	8.00	12.00	5.25	1,388.60	320	8,080.00	7,788.60
330	25.25	8.00	12.00	5.25	1,388.60	330	8,332.50	7,988.60
340	25.25	8.00	12.00	5.25	1,388.60	340	8,585.00	8,188.60
350	25.25	8.00	12.00	5.25	1,388.60	350	8,837.50	8,388.60
360	25.25	8.00	12.00	5.25	1,388.60	360	9,090.00	8,588.60
370	25.25	8.00	12.00	5.25	1,388.60	370	9,342.50	8,788.60

Breakeven point = 264 enrollees

IPA
Projected Statement of Cash Flows – 2000 to 2002

	FYE 12/31/2000	FYE 12/31/2001	FYE 12/31/2002
Net Income from Operations	7,503	144,496	167,193
Less:			
Capitation Receivable	116,226	259,242	343,956
Total Receivable	116,226	259,242	343,956
Plus:			
Accounts Payable	16,663	14,539	14,539
Accrued Expenses – IBNR	92,060	200,207	262,224
Total Payables and Accrued Expenses	108,723	214,746	276,763
Positive/(Negative) Cash Flow From Operations	0	100,000	100,000

IPA
Income Statement – 2000
Product Line – Healthy Families

	Jan	Feb	Mar	Apr	May	Jun	Jul	Aug	Sep	Oct	Nov	Dec	YTD	PMPM	% Gross
Member Months	174	201	225	240	279	325	375	423	498	553	612	698	4,603		
Capitation Revenue	$4,394	$5,075	$5,681	$6,060	$7,045	$8,206	$9,469	$10,681	$12,575	$13,963	$15,453	$17,625	$116,226	$25.25	100.00%
PMPM	25.25	25.25	25.25	25.25	25.25	25.25	25.25	25.25	25.25	25.25	25.25	25.25			
MEDICAL EXPENSES															
Capitated Fees – PCP	1,392.00	1,608.00	1,800.00	1,920.00	2,232.00	2,600.00	3,000.00	3,384.00	3,984.00	4,424.00	4,896.00	5,584.00	36,824.00	8	31.68%
Capitated Fees – Lab													0.00	0	0.00%
Capitated Fees – Other													0.00	0	0.00%
Specialist Fees	2,088.00	2,412.00	2,700.00	2,880.00	3,348.00	3,900.00	4,500.00	5,076.00	5,976.00	6,636.00	7,344.00	8,376.00	55,236.00	12	47.52%
Reinsurance Expense													0.00	0	0.00%
Total Medical Expenses	3,480.00	4,020.00	4,500.00	4,800.00	5,580.00	6,500.00	7,500.00	8,460.00	9,960.00	11,060.00	12,240.00	13,960.00	92,060.00	20	79.21%
Income Before Non-Medical Expenses and Other Revenue	913.50	1,055.25	1,181.25	1,260.00	1,464.75	1,706.25	1,968.75	2,220.75	2,614.50	2,903.25	3,213.00	3,664.50	24,165.75	5	20.79%
NON-MEDICAL EXPENSES															
Management Fees	600.00	600.00	600.00	600.00	600.00	600.00	600.00	600.00	600.00	600.00	600.00	600.00	7,200.00	2	6.19%
Insurance Expense	300.00	300.00	300.00	300.00	300.00	300.00	300.00	300.00	300.00	300.00	300.00	300.00	3,600.00	1	3.10%
Interest Expense													0.00	0	0.00%
Marketing Expense	320.00	320.00	320.00	320.00	320.00	320.00	320.00	320.00	320.00	320.00	320.00	320.00	3,840.00	1	3.30%
Purchases Services													0.00	0	0.00%
Legal & Accounting	166.00	166.00	166.00	166.00	166.00	166.00	166.00	166.00	166.00	166.00	166.00	166.00	1,992.00	0	1.71%
Dues & Subscriptions													0.00	0	0.00%
Taxes & Licenses													0.00	0	0.00%
Bank Charges	2.60	2.60	2.60	2.60	2.60	2.60	2.60	2.60	2.60	2.60	2.60	2.60	31.20	0	0.03%
Total Non-Medical Expenses	1,388.60	1,388.60	1,388.60	1,388.60	1,388.60	1,388.60	1,388.60	1,388.60	1,388.60	1,388.60	1,388.60	1,388.60	16,663.20	4	14.34%
Income (Loss) Before Other Revenue	(475.10)	(333.35)	(207.35)	(128.60)	76.15	317.65	580.15	832.15	1,225.90	1,514.65	1,824.40	2,275.90	7,502.55	2	6.46%
OTHER REVENUE															
Participation Fees													0.00	0	0.00%
Interest Revenue													0.00	0	0.00%
Other Revenue/Other Expense													0.00	0	0.00%
Total Other Revenue	0.00	0.00	0.00	0.00	0.00	0.00	0.00	0.00	0.00	0.00	0.00	0.00	0.00	0	0.00%
NET INCOME	(475.10)	(333.35)	(207.35)	(128.60)	76.15	317.65	580.15	832.15	1,225.90	1,514.65	1,824.40	2,275.90	7,502.55	2	6.46%

IPA
Income Statement – 2001
Product Line – Healthy Families

	Jan	Feb	Mar	Apr	May	Jun	Jul	Aug	Sep	Oct	Nov	Dec	YTD	PMPM	% Gross
Member Months	712	734	757	789	803	839	879	898	913	957	983	1,003	10,267		
Capitation Revenue	$17,978.00	$18,533.50	$19,114.25	$19,922.25	$20,275.75	$21,184.75	$22,194.75	$22,674.50	$23,053.25	$24,164.25	$24,820.75	$25,325.75	$259,241.75	$25.25	100.00%
PMPM	25.25	25.25	25.25	25.25	25.25	25.25	25.25	25.25	25.25	25.25	25.25	25.25			
MEDICAL EXPENSES															
Capitated Fees – PCP	5,696.00	5,872.00	6,056.00	6,312.00	6,424.00	6,712.00	7,032.00	7,184.00	7,304.00	7,656.00	7,864.00	8,024.00	82,136.00	8	31.68%
Capitated Fees – Lab													0.00	0	0.00%
Capitated Fees – Other													0.00	0	0.00%
Specialist Fees	8,188.00	8,441.00	8,705.50	9,073.50	9,234.50	9,648.50	10,108.50	10,327.00	10,499.50	11,005.50	11,304.50	11,534.50	118,070.50	12	45.54%
Reinsurance Expense													0.00	0	0.00%
Total Medical Expenses	13,884.00	14,313.00	14,761.50	15,385.50	15,658.50	16,360.50	17,140.50	17,511.00	17,803.50	18,661.50	19,168.50	19,558.50	200,206.50	20	77.23%
Income Before Non-Medical Expenses and Other Revenue	4,094.00	4,220.50	4,352.75	4,536.75	4,617.25	4,824.25	5,054.25	5,163.50	5,249.75	5,502.75	5,652.25	5,767.25	59,035.25	6	22.77%
NON-MEDICAL EXPENSES															
Management Fees	600.00	600.00	600.00	600.00	600.00	600.00	600.00	600.00	600.00	600.00	600.00	600.00	7,200.00	1	2.78%
Insurance Expense	300.00	300.00	300.00	300.00	300.00	300.00	300.00	300.00	300.00	300.00	300.00	300.00	1,511.00	0	0.58%
Interest Expense													0.00	0	0.00%
Marketing Expense	143.00	143.00	143.00	143.00	143.00	143.00	143.00	143.00	143.00	143.00	143.00	143.00	1,716.00	0	0.66%
Purchases Services													0.00	0	0.00%
Legal & Accounting	166.00	166.00	166.00	166.00	166.00	166.00	166.00	166.00	166.00	166.00	166.00	166.00	1,992.00	0	0.77%
Dues & Subscriptions													0.00	0	0.00%
Taxes & Licenses													0.00	0	0.00%
Bank Charges	2.60	2.60	2.60	2.60	2.60	2.60	2.60	2.60	2.60	2.60	2.60	2.60	31.20	0	0.01%
Total Non-Medical Expenses	1,211.60	1,211.60	1,211.60	1,211.60	1,211.60	1,211.60	1,211.60	1,211.60	1,211.60	1,211.60	1,211.60	1,211.60	14,539.20	1	5.61%
Income (Loss) Before Other Revenue	2,882.40	3,008.90	3,141.15	3,325.15	3,405.65	3,612.65	3,842.65	3,951.90	4,038.15	4,291.15	4,440.65	4,555.65	44,496.05	4	17.16%
OTHER REVENUE															
Participation Fees													0.00	0	0.00%
Interest Revenue													0.00	0	0.00%
Other Revenue/ Other Expense	100,000.00												100,000.00	10	38.57%
Total Other Revenue	100,000.00	0.00	0.00	0.00	0.00	0.00	0.00	0.00	0.00	0.00	0.00	0.00	100,000.00	10	38.57%
NET INCOME	102,882.40	3,008.90	3,141.15	3,325.15	3,405.65	3,612.65	3,842.65	3,951.90	4,038.15	4,291.15	4,440.65	4,555.65	144,496.05	14	55.74%

IPA
Income Statement – 2002
Product Line – Healthy Families

	Jan	Feb	Mar	Apr	May	Jun	Jul	Aug	Sep	Oct	Nov	Dec	YTD	PMPM	% Gross
Member Months	1,012	1,036	1,050	1,066	1,087	1,109	1,138	1,176	1,199	1,235	1,249	1,265	13,622		
Capitation Revenue	$25,553.00	$26,159.00	$26,512.50	$26,916.50	$27,446.75	$28,002.25	$28,734.50	$29,694.00	$30,274.75	$31,183.75	$31,537.25	$31,941.25	$343,955.50	$25.25	100.00%
PMPM	25.25	25.25	25.25	25.25	25.25	25.25	25.25	25.25	25.25	25.25	25.25	25.25			
MEDICAL EXPENSES															
Capitated Fees – PCP	8,096.00	8,288.00	8,400.00	8,528.00	8,696.00	8,872.00	9,104.00	9,408.00	9,592.00	9,880.00	9,992.00	10,120.00	108,976.00	8	31.68%
Capitated Fees – Lab													0.00	0	0.00%
Capitated Fees – Other													0.00	0	0.00%
Specialist Fees	11,385.00	11,655.00	11,812.50	11,992.50	12,228.75	12,476.25	12,802.50	13,230.00	13,488.75	13,893.75	14,051.25	14,231.25	153,247.50	11	44.55%
Reinsurance Expenses													0.00	0	0.00%
Total Medical Expenses	19,481.00	19,943.00	20,212.50	20,520.50	20,924.75	21,348.25	21,906.50	22,638.00	23,080.75	23,773.75	24,043.25	24,351.25	262,223.50	19	76.24%
Income Before Non-Medical Expenses and Other Revenue	6,072.00	6,216.00	6,300.00	6,396.00	6,522.00	6,654.00	6,828.00	7,056.00	7,194.00	7,410.00	7,494.00	7,590.00	81,732.00	6	23.76%
NON-MEDICAL EXPENSES															
Management Fees	600.00	600.00	600.00	600.00	600.00	600.00	600.00	600.00	600.00	600.00	600.00	600.00	7,200.00	1	2.09%
Insurance Expense	300.00	300.00	300.00	300.00	300.00	300.00	300.00	300.00	300.00	300.00	300.00	300.00	3,600.00	0	1.05%
Interest Expense													0.00	0	0.00%
Marketing Expense	143.00	143.00	143.00	143.00	143.00	143.00	143.00	143.00	143.00	143.00	143.00	143.00	1,716.00	0	0.50%
Purchases Services													0.00	0	0.00%
Legal & Accounting	166.00	166.00	166.00	166.00	166.00	166.00	166.00	166.00	166.00	166.00	166.00	166.00	1,992.00	0	0.58%
Dues & Subscriptions													0.00	0	0.00%
Taxes & Licenses													0.00	0	0.00%
Bank Charges	2.60	2.60	2.60	2.60	2.60	2.60	2.60	2.60	2.60	2.60	2.60	2.60	31.20	0	0.01%
Total Non-Medical Expenses	1,211.60	1,211.60	1,211.60	1,211.60	1,211.60	1,211.60	1,211.60	1,211.60	1,211.60	1,211.60	1,211.60	1,211.60	14,539.20	1	4.23%
Income (Loss) Before Other Revenue	4,860.40	5,004.40	5,088.40	5,184.40	5,310.40	5,442.40	5,616.40	5,844.40	5,982.40	6,198.40	6,282.40	6,378.40	67,192.80	5	19.54%
OTHER REVENUE															
Participation Fees													0.00	0	0.00%
Interest Revenue													0.00	0	0.00%
Other Revenue/ Other Expense	100,000.00												100,000.00	7	29.07%
Total Other Revenue	100,000.00	0.00	0.00	0.00	0.00	0.00	0.00	0.00	0.00	0.00	0.00	0.00	100,000.00	7	29.07%
NET INCOME	104,860.40	5,004.40	5,088.40	5,184.40	5,310.40	5,442.40	5,616.40	5,844.40	5,982.40	6,198.40	6,282.40	6,378.40	167,192.80	12	48.61%

IPA
Balance Sheet – Healthy Families
January 1 – December 31, 2000

	Jan	Feb	Mar	Apr	May	Jun	Jul	Aug	Sep	Oct	Nov	Dec
CURRENT ASSETS												
Cash In Bank	15,000.00	15,000.00	15,000.00	15,000.00	15,000.00	15,000.00	15,000.00	15,000.00	15,000.00	15,000.00	15,000.00	15,000.00
Capitation Receivable	4,393.50	9,468.75	15,150.00	21,210.00	28,254.75	36,461.00	45,929.75	56,610.50	69,185.00	83,148.25	98,601.25	116,225.75
Maxicare Withhold												
UHP Withhold												
Risk Pool Receivable												
Total Current Assets	19,393.50	24,468.75	30,150.00	36,210.00	43,254.75	51,461.00	60,929.75	71,610.50	84,185.00	98,148.25	113,601.25	131,225.75
OTHER ASSETS												
Prepaid Expenses												
TOTAL OTHER ASSETS	0.00	0.00	0.00	0.00	0.00	0.00	0.00	0.00	0.00	0.00	0.00	0.00
TOTAL ASSETS	19,393.50	24,468.75	30,150.00	36,210.00	43,254.75	51,461.00	60,929.75	71,610.50	84,185.00	98,148.25	113,601.25	131,225.75
CURRENT LIABILITIES												
Accounts Payable	1,388.60	2,777.20	4,165.80	5,554.40	6,943.00	8,331.60	9,720.20	11,108.80	12,497.40	13,886.00	15,274.60	16,663.20
Accrued Expenses												
Accrued Expenses – IBNR	3,480.00	7,500.00	12,000.00	16,800.00	22,380.00	28,880.00	36,380.00	44,840.00	54,800.00	65,860.00	78,100.00	92,060.00
TOTAL CURRENT LIABILITIES	4,868.60	10,277.20	16,165.80	22,354.40	29,323.00	37,211.60	46,100.20	55,948.80	67,297.40	79,746.00	93,374.60	108,723.20
LONG-TERM LIABILITIES												
TOTAL LONG-TERM LIABILITIES	0.00	0.00	0.00	0.00	0.00	0.00	0.00	0.00	0.00	0.00	0.00	0.00
TOTAL LIABILITIES	4,868.60	10,277.20	16,165.80	22,354.40	29,323.00	37,211.60	46,100.20	55,948.80	67,297.40	79,746.00	93,374.60	108,723.20
EQUITY												
Paid In Capital	15,000.00	15,000.00	15,000.00	15,000.00	15,000.00	15,000.00	15,000.00	15,000.00	15,000.00	15,000.00	15,000.00	15,000.00
Retained Earnings – Prior												
Retained Earnings – Curr Yr	(475.10)	(808.45)	(1,015.80)	(1,144.40)	(1,068.25)	(750.60)	(170.45)	661.70	1,887.60	3,402.25	5,226.65	7,502.55
TOTAL EQUITY	14,524.90	14,191.55	13,984.20	13,855.60	13,931.75	14,249.40	14,829.55	15,661.70	16,887.60	18,402.25	20,226.65	22,502.55
TOTAL LIABILITIES & EQUITY	19,393.50	24,468.75	30,150.00	36,210.00	43,254.75	51,461.00	60,929.75	71,610.50	84,185.00	98,148.25	113,601.25	131,225.75
	0.00	0.00	0.00	0.00	0.00	0.00	0.00	0.00	0.00	0.00	0.00	0.00

SUMMARY

Healthy Families is a terrific health plan because it is ultimately underwritten by the state. The state of California is throwing money at us to conduct outreach, and it has plenty of ready materials we can use for our outreach efforts. As previously stated, CMS's primary goal is to increase the number of members of Superior IPA by 81 percent. CMS can achieve this within the three-year time frame, because Superior IPA has a very large population of potentially eligible people in its service area. CMS will diligently inform the target market on the importance of health care for children, the value of the Healthy Families Program, and the exceptional service provided by Superior IPA.

BIBLIOGRAPHY

100% Campaign: Press Release. [Web site]. http://www.100percentcampaign.org/join.html [October 23–26, 1999].

Bernstein, S. (1999, September 12). News analysis; State reforms don't address problems of doctor groups. *The Los Angeles Times,* D4.

Edwards Cinema Corporate Office. [Interview].

Etzel, M. J., Walker, B. J., & Stanton, W. J. (1997) *Marketing,* 11th ed., Irwin McGraw-Hill.

Finger, A. L. (1999, April 12). "Could your IPA go under? Steer it to safety." *Medical Economics,* Oradell, 76 (7), 205–214.

Gary Center. [Phone Interview]. (562) 691–3263.

Healthy Families Handbook. (1999) [Brochure].

Heath, R., & Associates. (1999, September 13). *Healthy Families, Medi-Cal for Children*, Information Update, V. 5.

Lambert Printing Company. (1999, October 24). [Proposal] (562) 690–7372.

La Opinion. [Phone Interview].

La Opinion, Para Ti Health Care Supplements. [Brochure] P. 2–3.

La Opinion, Para Ti Health Care Supplements. [Brochure] P. 10–15.

The MEDSTAT Group Inforum Consulting Services—Population Profile. (1999). p. 1 [Brochure].

The MEDSTAT Group Inforum Consulting Services—Population Profile. (1999). p. 2 [Brochure].

U.S. Post Office. [Interview].

Yahoo Yellow Pages, Yahoo [Web site]. www.yahoo.com.

A2

LEGAL BEAGLE COFFEE SHOP

Developed by
DARRELL BAUM
VLADIMIR MENDOZA
UNDER THE SUPERVISION OF
DR. JENS BIERMEIER
CALIFORNIA STATE UNIVERSITY LOS ANGELES

Contents

EXECUTIVE SUMMARY

The Legal Beagle specialty coffee shop is a start-up company that will be privately held. The coffee shop will be at an exclusive location near the campus of Loyola Law School. This new location will create an optimal social gathering place for the students of Loyola and a new place for the residents in the neighborhood. The company's competitive advantage is that it will be the only coffee shop in the neighborhood and the closest coffee shop to the Loyola campus.

The proprietor will put up $10,000 in personal funds and request loans of up to $100,000. The majority of retail sales will come from sales of specialty coffee drinks. Snack and other beverage items will be available for retail sale. The margin for coffee sales is 86 percent, and the margin for snack and beverage items is 50 percent and less.

The specialty coffee industry has experienced tremendous growth over the past twenty years. A slight retrenchment in the number of stores is occurring at this time, but it is expected to turn around to a strong positive in 2005. At the same time as the retrenchment in the United States, coffee wholesale price is at its lowest in over 100 years. Aficionados of specialty coffee are very aware of this, and from this awareness a movement towards Fair Trade coffee and organically grown coffee has developed.

The business start-up costs are estimated to be $96,192. Eighty-three percent of the start-up cost is dedicated to the construction design and layout. Supplies, furnishings, and machinery are just under $16,000. The first year will show a net loss of $102,000, and by year four, the company will be out of the red.

INTRODUCTION

The specialty coffee industry was a $10.74 billion industry in 2001 with a growth rate of 38 percent (Reuters, 3/17/2002). The industry began over twenty years ago in America but its roots originated in Europe. The origin of espresso, espresso being the mainstay of the specialty coffee industry, dates back to turn of the century Italy 1903. Luigi Bezzera, the proprietor of a manufacturing company, sought to shorten the workers' coffee breaks by introducing pressure to the coffee brewing process, hence reducing the time to make coffee. He called his new machine the "fast coffee machine" in Italian (http://www.coffeefest.com/). In the late 70s and early 80s travelers to Italy and other parts of Europe were struck by the popularity of coffee bars. One of the travelers was Howard Schultz of Starbucks, a chain of five coffee retail stores in 1983. The first Starbucks coffee bar opened in 1984 in downtown Seattle. Today, Starbucks operates 5,900 coffee shops with aspirations of opening 20,000 soon (Factiva.Starbucks).

Los Angeles is the land of specialty coffee shops. Angelinos love their coffee. The proprietor of the Legal Beagle will be entering a market that is well educated on the numerous versions of coffee. Customers look for two very important qualities in a coffee shop, the service and good coffee. If the service is excellent and the coffee is average, one can still retain customers. And if the service is average and the coffee is average, there are a number of other shops that will satisfy customers' needs.

SITUATIONAL ANALYSIS

Situational Environs

Business Conditions   There were over 12,000 specialty coffee shops in the United States in 1999. This number increased from a total of 5,000 in 1995 (Russo). A number of chains are emerging to compete with Starbucks such as the Coffee Beanery with 190 shops, Seattle's Best Coffee with 120 stores, and Caribou Coffee with 150 doors. These chains have expectations of expanding into as many as 1,000 plus stores each over the next five years (Walkup). The consumer craving for flavor and places to socialize seems insatiable. This still allows room for the independent specialty coffee shop owners who can find parity with these chains but can marginally differentiate through product, service, and convenience.

State of Technology   The modern espresso machine was perfected in Italy in the late 1940s. A good cup of Italian espresso consists of 25 milliliters of water at 195 degrees Fahrenheit forced through ground coffee (finely ground powder). It is a talent to make a good cup of espresso with the right amount of beans and water. Baristas, or espresso machine operators, are typically trained to create the perfect espresso.

There are four types of machines, the manual, semiautomatic, automatic, and super-automatic. La Pavoni and Cimbali espresso manufacturers, who date back to the early 1900s, make the four different types. What is most common in specialty coffee shops is the automatic. The automatic machines have pumps and a volumetric control to ensure a consistent cup for each brew. A grinder is needed with an automatic machine. Espresso machines' size and capacity are defined by groupings. A double-grouping is the average size in a low- to medium-volume shop, and the machine produces approximately 150 shots per hour. It is important to choose a quality machine from a reliable distributor. If a machine breaks down and parts are not available, this can adversely affect business (Bendall).

Demand Trends   Americans love their coffee. According to the National Coffee Association in a 2001 survey, 52 percent of the adult U.S. population that is over 18 years of age drinks coffee every day, which translates to 107 million daily drinkers. Of this group, 29 million American adults drink gourmet coffee beverages every day, whether espresso-based beverages (latte, espresso, café mocha, cappuccino) or frozen and iced coffee beverages. Another 28 percent of the population, or 57 million adults, drink coffee occasionally. On a per capita basis, men drink as much coffee as women, which is 1.7 cups per day each. Coffee drinkers consume on average 3.3 cups of coffee per day. Sixty four percent of all coffee is consumed at breakfast: 28 percent between meals and 8 percent at all other meals. Women are more excited about coffee varieties currently available, and a higher proportion of women indicated that drinking coffee is a good way to relax. Women are more price conscious then men (http://www.coffeescience.org/, Trends).

An emerging trend is flavored coffees. Just as beverage industry giants (i.e., Coke, Pepsi-Co, and Cadbury Schwepps) are adding flavor to their brand portfolios, so are coffee retailers. The coffee and tea flavoring industry has responded with a profusion of flavors ranging from the widely known caramel and chocolate to seasonal pumpkin spice and the more recent fruit flavors of papaya and mango. This trend can be attributed to consumers' hunt for peak taste (*Tea & Coffee Trade Journal,* 11th Annual). Flavored syrups hold some leverage over the ready-to-drink market in the ability to customize drinks on an individual basis. Market needs can be met market by market (*Tea & Coffee Trade Journal,* New Flavors).

Social and Cultural Factors   One of the key factors in the success of specialty coffee houses is that they have become gathering places. People ages 18 to 24, who are the fastest growing group of customers, are attracted to this positioning (Walkup).

Demographics   A study by www.coffeescience.org found that people ages 20 to 29 are more likely to attest to the popularity of coffee, more likely to perceive coffee to be a good value, more likely to feel better about drinking coffee, less price conscious, more likely to drink more coffee in the coming year, and more accepting of espresso-based drinks. People ages 30 to 59 are more likely to attest to the popularity of coffee and to be less price conscious. And finally, people ages 60+ are more concerned about news/medial reports about caffeine, more price conscious, less excited about the variety of coffee available, and less interested in espresso-based beverages (http://www.coffee-science.org/, Perceptions).

Economic Conditions   Even though there were nearly 12,000 specialty coffee shops in 1999, with the current economic environment, there are expectations of this number decreasing to 10,000 and then rebounding by the end of this decade to 15,000 (Russo). The specialty coffee industry is especially attractive because of the high margins and the increased ability for vertical integration. The average cost to make a cup of an espresso coffee drink is $0.32. Given the average price of an espresso drink is $2.25, the margin of 86 percent far exceeds the average retail margin of 50 percent. Volume is key to maintaining profitability. Many shops expand beyond serving coffee drinks. Some will expand into selling coffee beans, coffee accessories, pastries, snack items, and meal items. Internet access provided at a fee or free is fast becoming popular. An attractive atmosphere, a high level of service, and an excellent quality product will create a loyal customer base.

Laws and Regulations   When starting a new business, there are certain permits required. Table A2-1 lists the types of permits, the section codes, and the associated costs.

Table A2-1   Permits, Section Codes, and Costs

Permit Type	Description	Section Code	Costs
Building	Construction permit for remodeling.	91.106	$680
Electrical	Electrical permit for rewiring and installation of equipment.	93.0201	Depends on estimated electrical usage and wiring.
Mechanical (HVAC)		95.0112	$1700
Plumbing	Pressure vessel permits (water heater).	94.103.1	$1275

Design and layout can be developed to minimize costs associated with building and health inspection violations. Issues related to city ordinances oftentimes surprise proprietors, such as the number of parking spaces required, the number and size of bathrooms, the number and positioning of fire exits, and the upgrading of electrical panels, among other things. Companies that are experienced on these matters can be employed for a fee.

The Los Angeles County Department of Health Services developed a series of discussions that addresses layout and design issues to minimize costs. These discussions are listed at the end of this appendix, in section A2-1, "Los Angeles County Department of Health Services," *Plan Check Construction Guide* and they cover the following topics listed in Table A2.2:

Table A2.2   Los Angeles County Department of Health Services, Plan Check Construction Guide Topics

Plan Check Program Service	Walls & Ceilings	Lavatories/Hand Washing Sinks	Food Storage Areas
The Importance of Planning	Lighting	Toilet Facilities	Installation of Equipment
Fee Schedule	Ventilation	Dressing Rooms	Plumbing
Floors	Flies, Rodents, and Vermin	Food Service Equipment	Special Requirements

Food safety in Los Angeles County and the eighty-five cities located within it is the responsibility of Environmental Health's Food Inspection Program in partnership with the food industry. Environmental Health has assembled a series of manuals to assist the food facility operator in understanding the inspection process, developing a clearer understanding of good food handling practices, identifying areas within their operation that have the greatest potential for the spread of food-borne illness, and enhancing safeguards that minimize the risk associated with the food supply (http://www.lapublichealth.org/eh). Environmental Health offers an online food handlers guide with self-exam. The Web site is http://www.lapublichealth.org/eh/fhgde/INDEX.HTM.

A self-inspection guide is also provided. Inspectors utilize a number of categories to develop the final grading system seen in restaurants. This information is listed at the end of this appendix, in section A2-2, "Environmental Health Self-Inspection Guide." Table A2.3 lists the categories from the guide.

Table A2.3 Environmental Health Self-Inspection Guide Categories

Food Preparation Area	Utensil Washing and Sanitizing	Delivery Transportation/Receiving
Employee Practices	Food Storage Area	Facilities
Refrigeration/Freezer Units	Utensil Storage Area	Exterior Premises
Physical Inspection of Food Preparation Area	Front Service Area	

Neutral Environs

Financial Environment The retail price for coffee has not changed for years, whether you drink a latte at $3.00 or buy a can of coffee in the grocery store. The wholesale price of coffee is at its lowest in 100 years. In country after country, coffee growers are struggling to stay in business (Bachman). This has created a myriad of problems, which includes poorer quality coffee beans, coffee farmers walking away from their land, massive unemployment, and regional economies being devastated (http://www.usaid.gov/).

Within the specialty coffee industry this issue is problematic when considering the target market's desire for high-quality coffee. Companies such as Wild Oats and Green Mountain Coffee have listened to the plight of the farmer and have taken steps to purchase "Fair Trade" beans only. When consumers see the Fair Trade Certified label, it provides assurance that the farmers received a fair minimum floor price for their harvest that covers the cost of sustainable production. The Fair Trade price is $1.41 per pound for organic coffee. This results in more income and improved health care, education, and housing for coffee farming families. Farmers are given direct access to U.S. markets under this program, thereby eliminating intermediaries (RR Newswire, Wildoats).

Environmental Issues Those coffee growers that are not abandoning their farms are uprooting the plants and cutting back forest growth to plant other crops. Cutting back forest growth is having a negative impact on the land and the environment. The remaining farmers practice poor husbandry techniques and little or no fertilizer is used, which results in reduced overall quality (http://www.usaid.gov/).

Special Interest Environment For the most part, the drinkers of specialty coffee are aware of the coffee farmer's plight. They look and ask for coffee that is Fair Trade, single-origin, estate grown, or certified organic. For certification of Fair Trade and organic coffee any of the following organizations can qualify the coffee:

- Quality Assurance International
- Skal
- Organic Crop Improvement

Media Environment A number of articles are widely available in trade journals, business journals, magazines, and newspapers. The public that drinks specialty coffee is informed on this issue as a result. The U.S. government, through its United States Agency for International Development, has developed a 17-page response to the issue of devalued coffee prices. Action is being taken at the government, business, and grassroots levels.

Competitor Environs

The main competitors of the coffee shop are the Loyola Law School coffee cart and cafeteria. Marriott Catering owns the franchise for both locations. The coffee cart offers a variety of convenient items besides the Seattle's Best brand of coffee and specialty coffee. Students regularly go to get a quick pick-me-up or snack. A number of chairs and tables are located throughout the campus with a higher concentration near the coffee cart. The area near the coffee cart is a gathering place. Hours are from 7 A.M. until 8 P.M. The coffee cart menu is shown in Table A2.4.

Table A2.4   Coffee Cart Menu

Menu	Retail Price	Sm	Lg
Hot Espresso Beverages			
Latte		$ 2.75	$ 3.25
Espresso		$ 1.50	$ 1.90
Cappuccino		$ 2.25	$ 3.25
Vanilla Latte		$ 3.00	$ 3.50
Café Mocha		$ 3.00	$ 3.50
Caramel Machiatto		$ 3.25	$ 3.75
Caramel Mocha		$ 3.25	$ 3.75
Café Ole		$ 1.75	$ 2.00
Café Americana		$ 1.75	$ 2.00
Add Shot	$ 0.50		
Extra Syrup	$ 0.25		
Extra Soy	$ 0.25		
Blended Frozen Espresso Beverages			
Mocha	$ 3.50		
Mocha Bianco	$ 3.50		
Vanilla Mocha	$ 3.50		
Caramel Mocha	$ 3.50		
Beverages/Snacks			
Gatorade	$ 1.30		
Snapple	$ 1.30		
Red Bull	$ 1.30		
Starbucks Frappuccino	$ 1.30		
Bagels	$ 1.30		
Muffins	$ 1.30		
Ramen Noodles	$ 1.20		
Mrs. Field's Cookies	$ 1.20		
Starburst Candy	$ 1.20		
Granola Bar	$ 1.20		

The coffee cart appears to be dominant in the specialty coffee service on campus. This dominance can be attributed to the exclusivity and the social gathering environment. There are only two places for coffee within several blocks of the campus, the coffee cart and the cafeteria. The campus is gated on all sides, creating a fortress-like environment. The neighborhood surrounding the campus is not well defined, and the image is not reflective of the student body population. These factors further contribute to the exclusive campus coffee business. There is a center across the street from Loyola that would be inviting to students, and it would be a different place to gather socially.

The cafeteria is focused on food service more than beverages. The cafeteria is full-service with a grill and cook, salad bar, soda machine, ice machine, refrigerated drinks, grab-'n-go stand, and a condiment bar. The hours of operation are Monday through Thursday from 7:30 A.M. to 8:30 P.M. and Friday from 7:30 A.M. to 2:30 P.M. Prices range from $2.25 to $4.25 for sandwiches and grilled meals and $0.80 to $3.25 for beverages and snacks. It is a place for social gathering but eating is the primary activity.

Company Environs

The company is not established, and a main purpose of this report is exploratory. The client is in a position of understanding the wants and needs of the student body at Loyola Law School, as he is a student as well. What the client noted was the need for coffee service in the evenings for the students attending night class. He felt that a coffee shop would cater to both day and night students and offer an alternate location for social gathering and for studying. Many of the students will drive to locations that offer an environment more suitable to their likes for social gathering such as the Hotel Figueroa. This location is within a mile of the school but lacks the convenience of a location closer to campus (such as this location, which is across the street from campus).

TARGET MARKET

There are two target market groups, a primary and a secondary. The primary target market is the student body at Loyola Law School. The secondary target market is the residential population as detailed on the census map at the end of this appendix, in section A2-3, "Target Market," *Total Person Map*.

Cultural, Ethnic, and Racial Groups

The primary market is a diverse population with a 39 percent minority student population (http://www.princetonreview.com/). In an interview with the Assistant Director of Admissions, Betty Vu, she noted that the majority of the ethnic population is Asian with African-Americans and Latino next (Betty Vu). The secondary market is 87 percent Hispanic/Latino, 8 percent Asian, and the balance Caucasian and African American (http://www.census.gov/).

Social Classes

Although the primary market is made up of students, the majority of those students come from middle, upper-middle, and upper class social classes. Seventy percent of the student population pays for their tuition without the need for financial aid or scholarships (Betty Vu). Their families range from white-collar salaried to the wealthy. The secondary market consists of basic wage earners, skilled workers, and unskilled labor from the lower social class. Eighty-three and a half percent of the population rents housing while 16.5 percent own their dwellings. The renter occupied unit average size is 3.28 people, and the owner occupied unit average size is 2.81 people.

Demographics

The students at Loyola Law School are from 23 to 26 years of age on average. There are 1,351 students enrolled. Women make up 49 percent of the student body (http://www.princetonreview.com/). The majority of the student body is single with no children, and they are college graduates. The students are on a semester system with over 1,200 attending fall and spring and under 300 students attending summer (Betty Vu). The surrounding neighborhood population is 3,607. Women make up 49 percent of the population. Family households make up 63.4 percent of the population, and 31.7 percent of the nonfamily households are people under age 65 living alone. There are a number of businesses in the area on Olympic Boulevard. These businesses are considered part of the secondary market. The businesses include:

- Karate studio
- CPA offices
- UPS processing station
- Real estate agent
- Copy services
- Carpet sales
- Health/diet services
- Elderly day care

A detailed summary of the demographic population for the neighborhood can be found at the end of this appendix, in section A2-3, "Target Market," *Demographics*.

Decision Makers

In the primary target market, the decision makers and purchasers are the students. They are not hindered by spouses or child-related influences. They are free to spend their income at school, as they desire. The secondary market could be hindered by a spouse or child in the decision-making process. The neighborhood is lower-income skilled and unskilled labor. A wife might have something to say to her husband about buying a $3.00 cup of coffee.

Risk Perception

The price of coffee for the primary and secondary market has a lower risk associated with the purchase. The risk in buying coffee is in the quality of the coffee and the perceived customer service. The buyer could feel cheated if the quality and service were less than adequate.

Disposable Income

The primary target audience has a moderate disposable income. The price of coffee and a social gathering place is minor for this group. Men and women in this group are more likely to drink specialty coffee. The secondary market has less disposable income.

Wants and Needs

Specialty coffee is considered a want for both the primary and secondary market. Snacks, soft drinks, and meal items meet the basic needs of hunger and thirst. One of the primary needs that will be met is the psychological need of socializing. This will be most evident with the primary market. It is attainable with the secondary market as well.

Product Description

The Legal Beagle will offer beverage and food services. Quality service and quality product are paramount in the specialty coffee industry. Consumers expect a friendly and inviting environment in a specialty coffee shop. The industry leaders have set these standards, and consumers have come to expect them in a specialty coffee shop.

Size of Target Market

The primary market is 1,351 and the secondary market is 3,607, totaling roughly 5,000 people.

Growth Trends

Growth is not expected in the primary market. The population drops to less than 300 during the summer session at Loyola. Quantitative growth information on the secondary market is not available. In an interview with a business owner in the neighborhood, growth was discussed and none was expected. The neighborhood is about a half mile away from the Los Angeles Staples Sports Arena. The businesses in the area expected growth when the arena was being developed, but this expectation was never met.

OPPORTUNITIES AND PROBLEMS

Opportunities

The number one opportunity for the Legal Beagle specialty coffee shop is that there is no other coffee shop in the surrounding area other than the Loyola Law School coffee cart and cafeteria. Students will drive off campus or walk up to a mile for socializing or studying off campus. A location on Olympic Boulevard, across from Loyola Law School, will be convenient for the students. The cafeteria space is small, and it can be a little noisy at times. The resin chairs placed around the outdoor coffee cart are not comfortable, and one is open to the elements such as rain and cold weather.

A specialty coffee shop will benefit the businesses in the neighborhood. People arriving to work in the morning will be able to walk to the new location for a café latte, and people from the karate studio on the same block will be able to get a hot cup of java in the evening before their workout. The elderly daycare clients can get away for a moment and enjoy a morning or afternoon coffee and maybe read a book. Coffee service can be offered to the businesses as well. Carafes filled with coffee can be brought to the offices in the morning and picked up in the afternoon or early evening. The residents in the neighborhood will have a social gathering place and a place to purchase quality coffee. The shop will create an opportunity for social interchange between the students of Loyola and the residents in the neighborhood.

After the first six months, the Legal Beagle can further develop its business by expanding into meal items that cater to the students during the fall and spring semester and to the neighborhood residents during the summer months. In addition to meal items, other retail items such as schoolbooks and accessories can be sold. Roasted coffee beans can be sold for home use. There is great opportunity for vertical and horizontal integration of services and retail products.

Problems

One of the most challenging difficulties is the demographic population of the school and neighborhood. The students can support the business during the weekdays during the fall and spring session. The number of students patronizing the shop on the weekends will drop dramatically. The residents in the neighborhood are lower income, skilled, and unskilled workers with less than moderate disposable income. To cater to this population, specific menu items can be developed.

The dominant competitor is the coffee cart on campus. Students patronize the cart, and some will remain loyal clients because they enjoy the convenience, service, and quality of products. The tables and chairs near the coffee cart create a welcome social environment, especially on sunny days. We recommend directly targeting the customers of this business.

Finding a space in the neighborhood is a challenge. The flower shop across the street has a for-sale sign in front. Unfortunately, we did not receive any return phone calls on the property. The proprietor of the flower shop had a husband who was killed in a shooting last year. This could be one of the reasons why we did not receive a return phone call. Also, the property may not be available, and the sign may have been left there inadvertently.

The start-up costs are also a challenge. Due to the requirements by the city and county for design and layout of a restaurant, construction costs can be at a minimum $80,000. In an interview with a contractor, he discussed the challenges that come with a coffee shop. We recommend gathering estimates from two to three different contractors once the space and location are decided upon.

Parking on Olympic Boulevard is another problem. The students at Loyola will not have a problem, but customers from the neighborhood and customers driving by will not have convenient available parking due to street restrictions. The north side of Olympic Boulevard prohibits parking from 7 A.M. to 10 A.M. and 3:30 P.M. to 7 P.M. The south side of Olympic Boulevard prohibits parking from 7 A.M. to 9 A.M. and 3 P.M. to 7 P.M. There is side-street parking, but it is out of the way and inconvenient for people who want to quickly stop and go.

MARKETING OBJECTIVES AND GOALS

The Legal Beagle will provide a coffee experience to its customers that enhances their appreciation of coffee and espresso, in an environment where they can relax and enjoy what we have to offer.

Mission Statement

The Legal Beagle will operate as an ethical and safe business, free of prejudices and insisting upon the utmost respect for both customers and employees. In no circumstance shall we forgo safety and exceptional service to our clients and employees. Business operations will be conducted in a safe and legal manner as prescribed by all laws pertaining to this type of venture, while maximizing profits.

Objectives of the Legal Beagle

- Establish a sole proprietorship under the Laws of the state of California.
- Achieve and maintain maximum profits and minimum tax burden.
- Achieve sales of $150,000 by end of year two.
- Achieve sales of $250,000 by end of year three.
- Develop market share of at least 25 percent.

MARKETING STRATEGY

In general, coffee drinkers abound in Los Angeles. Though our market is small, this venture will prove successful in targeting the Loyola student body and the neighboring area. Our products, location, and strength in service will prove a winning combination for the Legal Beagle. Critical to our success is to form a strong relationship with our customers and endeavor to have each one return to give the Legal Beagle repeated business.

Sales in the coffee beverages market keep growing, and the current economic conditions do not seem to have any effect on coffee consumption. The Legal Beagle is poised for growth. As our financial statements show, we are ready to grow dramatically in three years, while providing a superior product and not compromising on flavor or quality of service.

The Legal Beagle will pursue a semiaggressive strategy. Students at Loyola have typically inelastic price sensitivities, which is beneficial to us since we will not be able to do much with pricing. Instead, we will position ourselves with quality and ambience. We will have a "law-themed" coffee shop providing great tasting, different flavored, and high-quality coffee beverages and snacks and sandwiches.

We will use cleanliness, high-quality equipment, and impeccable service, along with the ambience, as our main differential advantage. We will provide shelter if it rains, unlike the Loyola Coffee Cart. The Legal Beagle will be a relaxing yet invigorating hot spot to have a beverage, snack, lunch, or all three—in a fun, law-themed atmosphere. Our customers can expect only the best.

Advantages of the Legal Beagle include:

- Sufficient growth potential
- Sufficient market size and buying power
- No threat from competitors
- Convenient, strategic location
- Our "Legal Beagle Loyalty List" promotion, which would be permanent

MARKETING TACTICS

The market size, income, and purchasing power and the limited existing competition in the market provide sufficient income and growth potential in a venture such as this one, especially at the desired location.

Product

We will have an atmosphere where students, since they are our primary target, can enjoy coffee and relax after class, before class, and as a way to escape from the humdrum atmosphere of the campus.

We will provide excellent coffee, espresso, soft drinks, snacks, and sandwiches in a "law-themed" atmosphere. The Legal Beagle will have excellent equipment and facilities, a well-trained, courteous staff, and convenient hours of operation.

The coffee and espresso equipment will be capable of producing enough coffee to meet the demand. Our coolers and refrigerators will be in excellent working condition with plenty of capacity. The display cases will adequately display the wares while keeping pests and dust off. A list of prices and sources can be found at the end of this appendix, in section A2-4, "Marketing Tactics," *Product*.

The clean environment will be a selling point. We will have the necessary sinks, drainage, vents, and storage in order to maintain a spotless preparation area. The staff will be put on a strict cleaning schedule, as cleanliness will be a top priority of the Legal Beagle.

The staff will be hired selectively and trained on using the equipment. Also, they will be taught proper cleaning/garbage disposal methods.

The hours of operation will meet the schedule of the Loyola Law School. We will have staff ready to service the morning/breakfast customers as well as the lunch and the evening customers who take night classes. The schedules will be adjusted for when school is out of session and for weekends.

Price

Our prices will match those of the Loyola Cafeteria and the Loyola Coffee Cart. The population of the school does not seem to be very price conscious. We do not want to compete on the basis of price since that might hamper the image of the Legal Beagle. We will be providing the ambience as well as quality products; hence, we can match the prices of the competition in order to be a genuine contender in the coffee arena in the neighborhood. For the first six months of operations, we recommend the same menu as shown in Table A2.4. This menu conveys familiarity and creates parity with the coffee cart.

Place/Distribution

The Legal Beagle will be conveniently located across the street from Loyola Law School. As discussed in the opportunities section, this will be an exclusive location in the neighborhood outside of the coffee cart and cafeteria at Loyola.

As part of the décor, we can also have some small posters, in the form of books opened to a page, with phrases exalting coffee flavors and various coffee descriptions. For example, "The quality and flavor of our coffee is determined by the brewing process we use and by the type and quality of coffee we have selected. We have coffees and coffee blends from various countries and different varieties of coffee." Or, "Do you favor a dark roast coffee, a light blend, or something in between? Legal Beagle offers your choice. No matter what coffee you choose, we follow guidelines that guarantee you will drink the best cup of coffee possible. We optimize the taste and quality of every cup of coffee we prepare for you."

Promotion

The budget for advertising is limited since this is a small-scale operation. We will depend heavily on word-of-mouth promotion. It will be hard to incorporate television, radio, and newspaper advertising. The school's paper will be the main form of advertising, apart from flyers and the building's sign.

Flyers will be designed to bring customers into the store. Colored paper with coffee pictures can be included. It must be attractive and clearly state the business we are in. A sample of the flyer can be found at the end of this appendix, in section A2-4, "Marketing Tactics," *Promotional Flyer.*

In order to keep customers coming back, we can implement a loyalty program in which after so many purchases, the customer gets a free coffee or sandwich, or other drink. A sample of the customer loyalty card can be found at the end of this appendix, in section A2-4, "Marketing Tactics," *Customer Loyalty Card.*

We could also have daily drink specials, or "meal deals" whereby the customer gets a coffee and sandwich at a set price, especially for breakfast, when most people are short of time.

During the summer, since school will be out for several weeks and the number of students attending summer classes is small, the Legal Beagle will have to vary the menu and coffee offerings in order to attract not only those few remaining students, but also the neighborhood patrons who are in search of summer beverages. The menu during this period could include iced coffees and frozen snacks.

The cost to include frozen drinks will not increase dramatically. We must budget for the cost of the ice and for obtaining different cups to hold the beverages. We will already have the coffee, syrups, and the equipment to brew the coffee; hence, costs will be kept relatively stable.

It would be a novel idea to name a few of the drinks after Supreme Court justices (both living and dead), for example "Ruth B. Ginsberg Chocolate Decision" or "Marshall's Hazelnut Madness."

A promotional budget is located at the end of this appendix, in section A2-4, "Marketing Tactics," *Promotion Budget.*

IMPLEMENTATION AND CONTROL

Start-Up Costs

A new venture such as the Legal Beagle has high start-up costs. From obtaining the permits from the city to stocking for opening day, each step is volatile and crucial to success. The next few pages discuss in detail the costs involved and the potential rewards. There are separate discussions on start-up costs, break-even point, detailed projected first-year cash flow statement and income statement, a three-year outlook, and some ideas on helping to control costs.

We start off by outlining some of the start-up costs. Table A2.5 shows a list of expected costs. A more detailed list can be found at the end of this appendix, in section A2-5 "Implementation and Controls," *Start-Up Costs.* The information on permits and requirements can be obtained from the Web sites of the different departments of the city of Los Angeles, or by calling the respective departments. The bid on the remodeling and reconstruction of the space to fit the needs for this venture is a low bid from a contractor. Contractors will normally pull the permits and include them in their bid. In Table A2.5, the permit costs are itemized to show which ones will be needed. The cost of all the equipment is an estimated average, since the actual needs may be different once the plans for reconstruction are considered and since the sizes, styles, and models vary widely. The averages are considered using the estimated capacity to achieve the break-even number of cups of coffee.

Table A2.5 Start-Up Costs

Building Lease		1,800
Permits:		
Construction—Remodeling**		74,769
Health Dept. Upgrades	1,006	
Electrical (approx. 900 sq. ft.)	1,250	
Mechanical (HVAC)	1,700	
Plumbing	1,275	5,231
Espresso Equipment Lease		186
Refrigerator Purchase		1,250
Cooler Purchase		1,000
Display Cases		1,000
Espresso Machine Purchase		5,800
Coffee Makers Purchase		750
Other Equipment Purchase		1,446
Supplies Purchase		1,500
Security Deposits:		
Gas Company	50	
Electric Company	50	
Telephone Company	50	150
Water Softening Maintenance*		100
General Espresso Maintenance*		300
Filtration System Maintenance*		320
Fictitious Business Name Registration**		90
Sign Purchase**		500
Total		96,192

Monthly Cash Flow

In keeping with our goal of providing maximum income for the client, the costs for supplies have been kept low by seeking the lowest-priced providers, while keeping quality higher than expected. We have examples of detailed lists of options at the end of this appendix, in section A2-5, "Implementation and Controls," *Monthly Cash Flow.*

Because the need for maintenance on the equipment in a coffee shop is great, we have also worked equipment maintenance contracts into the costs. Labor is key to running a successful business. Following is a sample of an employee schedule we feel might work for the Legal Beagle. At this point, we are only including salaries and Worker's Compensation in the cost of labor. At a later date, the owner might consider health insurance or bonuses or other motivation factors in order to keep his most productive employees. Staff will be at minimum wage, or $6.00 per hour. We have developed the following schedule for consideration:

Mon–Fri

6am–12pm	**2 employees × 6 hours × 5 days**	**= 60 hours**
6am–3pm	**1 employee × 8 hours × 5 days**	**= 40 hours**
1pm–10pm	**1 employee × 8 hours × 5 days**	**= 40 hours**
4pm–10pm	**1 employee × 6 hours × 5 days**	**= 30 hours**

Sat–Sun

6am–12pm	**1 employee × 6 hours × 2 days**	**= 12 hours**
6am–3pm	**1 employee × 8 hours × 2 days**	**= 16 hours**
1pm–10pm	**1 employee × 8 hours × 2 days**	**= 16 hours**
4pm–10pm	**1 employee × 6 hours × 2 days**	**= 12 hours**

226 hours × $6.00 × $1,356.00

State Worker's Compensation averages 20 percent of wages paid.

Income Statement

The income statement is detailed at the end of this appendix, in section A2-5, "Implementation and Controls," *Income Statement*. It shows the first year having a net loss of over $102,000. The reason for this is the high cost of start-up. The Three-Year Projected Income Statement is also at the end of this appendix, in section A2-5, "Implementation and Controls," *Three-Year Projected Income Statement*. It shows increasing sales and a decreasing loss, but in years two and three the owner will start withdrawing money from the business, keeping with this goal of increasing his income and reducing his personal tax burden. Year three shows a small loss of just under $8,500 and the owner should be in the black by year four. In year four, the owner might consider increasing his withdrawals.

Interest on the SBA loan is being considered at 5 percent per year and will start repayment the month after procurement. On the Cash Budget, it is detailed as interest payment and principal payments.

Break-Even Analysis

For the break-even analysis, we have used the cost of equipment and lease as fixed costs. The average variable cost was calculated assuming an average variable cost per cup at end of first year, including labor and promotion costs—arriving at an average of $0.83 per cup. Table A2.6 details the analysis:

Table A2.6 Break-Even Analysis

Break-Even = Fixed cost/Price − Variable Cost	117,792	128,035
	$1.75–0.83	
OR	2462	Cups per Week

This volume appears high since it is for coffee only and does not indicate other items sold. This is because it is more complicated to calculate the break-even for the sandwiches and snacks that will be sold, and coffee is the main product we will be selling.

Balance Sheet

Upon looking at the Balance Sheet at the end of this appendix, in section A2-5, "Implementation and Controls," *Balance Sheet*, one can notice that owner's equity is small at this point and debt is large. Since the entrepreneur's available personal investment is small, it will be necessary for him to start his venture on large debt. The balance sheet is assumed at the beginning of the venture, incorporating only major purchases and the procurement of the loan.

BIBLIOGRAPHY

Al Akkad, Hamid, Real Estate. Personal Interview, February 10, 2003.
Anonymous, "11th Annual Flavor Survey." *Tea & Coffee Trade Journal,* February 20, 2002.
Anonymous. "Peet's Takes Out Elite Niche in High-End Coffees." *Reuters,* March 17, 2002.
Bachman, S.L. "Coffee Price Drop Hurts Farmers." *Mercury News,* May 28, 2002.
Baum, James, Contractor. Personal Interview, February 18, 2003.
Bendall, Dan. "Coffee and Espresso Equipment." *Food Management,* May 2001.
Brown, Suzanne J. "New Flavors and Uses." *Tea & Coffee Trade Journal,* January 20, 2002.
Coffee Science Source. "From Seed to Cup: Facts & Figures, Perceptions/Attitudes about Coffee by Age." Available: http://www.coffeescience.org/factage.html.

Coffee Science Source. "From Seed to Cup: Facts & Figures, Trends in Coffee Consumption." Available: http://www.coffeescience.org/factrendhtml.

"La Pavoni Espresso Machines." *Crossroads Espresso* Online. Internet January 28, 2003. Available: http://www.coffeefest.com/cgi-bin/vbbridge3/vg_.dll?VBEXE=F:/users/festival/www.crossroadsespresso.html.

Pasquini, Guy, Principal, Pasquini Espresso Equipment. Personal Interview, February 2, 2003.

Russo, Ed. "Eugene, Ore., Firm Finds Tasty Work in Coffee Consulting." *Knight Ridder Tribune Business News,* December 10, 2001.

"Starbucks Corporation." *Factiva* Online. Internet. February 2, 2003. Available: http://www.global.factiva.com/en/arch/print_results.asp.

U.S. Agency for International Development, "Coffee Price Crisis Response, Draft January 31, 2002." Available: http://www.usaid.gov/regions/lac/rural/reference_documts/Coffee.document.pdf.

Vu, Betty, Assistant Director Admissions, Loyola Law School. Personal Interview, February 2, 2003.

Walkup, Carolyn. "Second-Tier Specialty Coffee Contenders Brew Up Strategies in Order to Chase Starbucks." *Nations Restaurant News,* June 26, 2000.

"Wild Oats, Market, Inc. and Green Mountain Coffee Roasters Launch Nation's Leading Organic Fair Trade Coffee Program in Wild Oats Stores." *PR Newswire,* October 10, 2002.

FURTHER INFORMATION

A2-1 LOS ANGELES COUNTY DEPARTMENT OF HEALTH SERVICES PLAN CHECK CONSTRUCTION GUIDE

Source: http:lapublichealth.org

Plan Check Program Service Areas

E-Mail-plancheck@dhs.co.la.ca.us

SERVICE AREA I

ADMINISTRATIVE HEADQUARTERS
5050 Commerce Dr
Baldwin Park, California 91706
(626) 430-5560

METROPLEX
3530 Wilshire Blvd. 9th Floor
Los Angeles, California 90010-2313
(213) 351-7352

SERVICE AREA II

WEST HEALTH CENTER
6053 Bristol Pkwy. 2nd Floor
Culver City, California 90230
(310) 665-8482
Phone hours 8:00 a.m.–10:00 a.m.

SOUTH BAY
122 W. 8th Street, Room 20-A
San Pedro, California 90731
(310) 519-6081

SERVICE AREA III

WEST VALLEY HEALTH CENTER
6851 Lennox Ave., 3rd Floor
Van Nuys, California 91405
(818) 902-4409
Phone hours 8:00 a.m.–10:00 a.m.

SERVICE AREA V

LANCASTER HEALTH CENTER
335-A East Avenue, K-6, Room 23
Lancaster, California 93534
(661) 723-4551
Phone hours 8:00 a.m.–10:00 a.m.
E-Mail-plancheck@dhs.co.la.ca.us

The Importance of Planning

The proper layout and construction of a food establishment is an important element in a successful and profitable business. It assures that you will meet all structural and operational requirements of the applicable health laws and, at the same time, meet the objective of serving clean, wholesome food to the public. This was written to help you meet these goals.

BEFORE CONSTRUCTING, ENLARGING, ALTERING, OR CONVERTING ANY BUILDING FOR USE AS A FOOD ESTABLISHMENT, SUBMIT THREE (3) SETS OF COMPLETE CONSTRUCTION AND EQUIPMENT INSTALLATION PLANS FOR REVIEW AND APPROVAL BY THE COUNTY OF LOS ANGELES DEPARTMENT OF HEALTH SERVICES.

Plans shall be easily readable and drawn to scale,
For example, 1/4″ = 1′, and shall include:

1. Complete floor plan with plumbing, electric, and equipment details.

2. Complete exhaust ventilation plans including make-up air. Indicate the type of comfort cooling in building, e.g., "building is cooled by refrigerated air conditioning," "evaporative cooling," or "no coding system is installed."

3. Finish schedules for floors, walls, and ceilings that indicate the type of material, the surface finish, the color, and the type of coved base at the floor-wall juncture.

PLANS THAT ARE INCOMPLETE, AND PLANS THAT HAVE A MULTITUDE OF CHANGES WILL BE RETURNED FOR REVISION BEFORE APPROVAL AFTER THE PLANS HAVE BEEN APPROVED AND STAMPED, TWO (2) COPIES WILL BE RETURNED TO THE PERSON SUBMITTING THE PLANS, AND THE THIRD (3RD) COPY WILL BE KEPT ON FILE WITH THE HEALTH DEPARTMENT UNTIL CONSTRUCTION HAS BEEN COMPLETED. THE APPROVED PLANS RETURNED MUST BE KEPT AT THE JOB SITE UNTIL THE FINAL INSPECTION PRIOR TO OPENING HAS BEEN MADE. ANY REVISIONS SHALL BE RE-SUBMITTED FOR APPROVAL.

Fee Schedule

The following fees for Plan Check services are current for the fiscal year ending June 30, 2003.

Food Market Retail/Wholesale

10–50 sq.ft.	$253.00
51–1999 sq.ft.	$386.00
2000–5999 sq.ft.	$510.00
6000 or more sq.ft.	$639.00

Restaurant (Includes fast food, take out, & retail bakeries)

0–60 seats	$605.00
61–200 seats	$907.00
201 or more seats	$969.00

Retail Food Processing Establishment

1–1999 sq.ft.	$401.00
2000–5999 sq.ft.	$639.00
6000 or more sq.ft.	$936.00

Other Fees

Food Warehouse (Wholesale Distribution)	$281.00
Minor Remodeling (less than 300 sq.ft.)	$219.00

Mail payments to:
Department of Health Services
Plan Check Program
5050 Commerce Dr
Baldwin Park, CA 91706
(626) 430-5560

Floors

The floor surfaces, in all areas in which food is prepared, packaged, or stored, where any utensil is washed, where refuse or garbage is stored and where janitorial facilities are located, and in all toilet and handwashing areas, shall be smooth and of such durable construction and non-absorbent material as to be easily cleaned.

These floor surfaces shall be coved at the juncture of the floor and wall, with a three-eighths inch (3/8") minimum radius coving, and shall extend up the wall at least four inches (4"), except in areas where food is stored only in unopened bottles, cans, cartons, sacks, or other original shipping containers. Vinyl topset is not acceptable.

Floor Drains shall be installed in floors that are water-flushed for cleaning, and in areas where pressure spray methods for cleaning equipment are used. Floor surfaces in these areas shall be sloped one-eighth inch (1/8") per foot to the floor drains.

Please contact your plan checker for a list of approved clear, grease, and acid-resistant floor sealers.

NOTE: Sealers must be reapplied every six months to remain effective.

Walls and Ceilings

The walls and ceilings of all rooms, except for bars, rooms where food is stored in unopened containers, dining and sales areas, shall be of a durable, smooth, non-absorbent, washable surface. Walls and ceilings of food preparation and utensil washing areas, and interior surfaces of walk-in refrigeration units, shall also be light colored. Wall areas adjacent to bar sinks shall be smooth and easily cleanable. Conduits of all types shall be installed within walls as practicable. When otherwise installed, they shall be mounted or enclosed so as to facilitate cleaning.

Lighting

In every room and area in which food is prepared, processed, or packaged, or in which utensils are cleaned, lighting shall be provided to produce an intensity of not less than 20 footcandles as measured thirty inches (30") above the floor, except that the working surfaces on which alcoholic beverages are prepared, or where utensils used in the preparation or service of alcoholic beverages are cleaned, shall be provided with at least 10 footcandles of light. Light fixtures in areas where food is prepared, or where open food is stored, or where utensils are cleaned, shall be of shatterproof construction or shall be protected with shatterproof shields and shall be easily cleanable.

Ventilation

Ventilation shall be provided to remove toxic gases, heat, grease, vapors, and smoke from the food establishment. All areas shall have sufficient ventilation to facilitate proper food storage, and to provide a reasonable condition of comfort for any employee, consistent with the job performed by the employee.

Mechanical Exhaust Ventilation shall be provided at or above all newly-installed cooking equipment, such as ranges, griddles, ovens, deep fat fryers, barbecues, and rotisseries, and 180°F rinse water dishwashers. Toilet rooms and dressing rooms shall be vented to the outside air by means of an openable, screened window, on air shaft, or a light-switch activated exhaust fan, consistent with the requirements of local building codes.

Flies, Rodents, and Vermin

Continuous masonry foundation is required. A food facility shall at all times be so constructed, equipped, maintained, and operated as to prevent the entrance and harborage of animals, birds and vermin, including, but not limited to, rodents and insects.

Windows: Openable windows shall be screened with no more than 16 mesh screening. All food service pass-through openings to the outside shall be limited to a maximum size of 216 square inches. The minimum distance between the openings shall not be less than eighteen inches (18").

Delivery Doors: All delivery doors leading to the outside shall be self-closing. Large cargo-type doors shall not open directly into a food preparation area.

Entrance Doors: All entrance doors leading to the outside shall be self-closing. Air curtains or fly fans may be used as auxiliary fly control but are not substitute devices to permit a door to remain open.

Garbage and Trash Area: An area shall be provided for the storage and cleaning of garbage and trash containers. The walls, floor, and ceiling of this room or area shall be constructed so as to be smooth, impervious and easily cleanable.

Vector Control: Openings at the base and side of exterior doors shall not exceed on-fourth inch (1/4"). All exterior wall pipe or other openings shall be tightly sealed. All exterior wall vents shall be properly screened with one-fourth inch (1/4") hardware cloth screening.

Lavatories/Hand Washing Sinks

Hand washing facilities shall be provided within, or adjacent to, toilet rooms and shall be equipped with an adequate supply of hot and cold running water under pressure. Hand washing cleanser and single-use sanitary towels, or hot-air blowers, shall be provided in wall-mounted dispensers at all hand washing facilities. **Hand washing facilities shall be provided within each food preparation area.**

Toilet Facilities

In each food establishment, there shall be provided toilet facilities for use by employees. The number of toilet facilities required shall be in accordance with local building and plumbing codes. Toilet rooms shall be separated from other portions of the food establishment by well-fitting, self-closing doors.

Toilet facilities shall be provided for patron, guests, or invites in each food establishment with more than 20,000 square feet of floor space. There shall be at least one separate toilet facility for men and one separate toilet facility for women. Hand washing facilities shall be equipped with hot and cold running water. Hand washing detergent, or soap, and sanitary towels, or hot-air blowers, shall be provided at hand washing facilities in permanently installed dispensing devices.

Where **alcoholic beverages** are sold or given away for consumption on the premises, there shall be provided, for use by the public, separate toilet rooms for each sex with at least one urinal for men, and at least one lavatory in conjunction with, and convenient to, each toilet. The restrooms must be located within the food establishment and accessible without going through a food preparation or storage area.

Dressing Rooms

A room, enclosure, or designated area, separated from toilets, food storage, food preparation areas, and utensil washing areas, shall be provided where employees may change and store clothes. No employee shall store clothing or personal effects in any other area on the premises. A dressing room (minimum 18 square feet) shall be well lighted, provided with exterior ventilation, and have smooth, durable, washable walls.

Food Service Equipment

All equipment shall meet or be equivalent to applicable National Sanitation Foundation (NSF) Standards. That includes **all** shelving and countertop equipment such as sushi cases, espresso machines, microwave ovens, coffee makers, and cutting boards.

Utensil Washing Sink: All food establishments in which food is prepared (including coffee or beverages) or in which multi-service kitchen utensils are used shall have a minimum three-compartment metal sink with two integral metal drainboards. The sink must be N.S.F. approved, all metal and free standing (not installed in cabinets). When installed next to a wall, a metal "backsplash" (minimum eight inches [8"]), extending up the wall shall be formed as an integral part of the unit and sealed to the wall. The sink compartments and drain-boards shall be large enough to accommodate the largest utensil used.

Food Preparation Sinks: Depending on the type of operation, a minimum one-compartment food preparation sink may be required. Food preparation sinks **must drain indirectly to a floor sink**.

Dishwashing Machines: Machine washing of utensils in machine using a hot water, or chemical sanitizing rinse shall conform to applicable National Sanitation Foundation (NSF) Standards, and shall be installed and operated in accordance with those standards.

Janitorial Sink (Mop Sink):   A room, area, or cabinet, separated from any food preparation or storage area or utensil washing area, shall be provided for the storage of cleaning equipment and supplies, such as mops, buckets, brooms, cleaners, and waxes;

and shall be equipped with at least one of the following, to be used for general cleaning purposes and for the disposal of mop bucket wastes and other liquid wastes:

* A one-compartment, non-porous janitorial sink/mop sink (stainless steel, porcelain, or fiberglass).

* A slab, basin, or floor constructed of concrete or equivalent material, curbed and sloped to a drain. Such facilities shall be connected to approved sewerage, and provided with hot and cold running water, through a mixing valve, and protected with a backflow protection device.

Garbage Disposal: Garbage disposal may be installed in drainboards, if the drainboard is lengthened to accommodate the disposal cone, in addition to the minimum required drainboard size. A garbage disposal may not be installed under a sink compartment, unless an additional compartment is provided for it.

Refrigeration: Drainage from refrigeration units shall be conducted in a sanitary manner to a floor sink, or other approved device by an indirect connection, or be self-evaporative.

Food Storage

Adequate and suitable space shall be provided for the storage of food. Approximately 25 percent (25%) of the food preparation area and at least 96 lineal feet of approved shelving for each 100 square feet of storage area are considered adequate **(excluding refrigeration)**. Except for large or bulky food containers, all food shall be stored at least six inches (6") off the floor. Containers may be stored on dollies, racks, or pallets not meeting this height requirement, provided these items are easily movable. Shelving to be constructed so as to be easily cleanable. Recommend shelves installed on a wall have at least a one inch (1") open space between the back edge of the shelf or should be sealed to the wall with silicone sealant or equivalent. The lowest shelf to be at least six inches (6") above the floor, with a clear, unobstructed area below. All shelves located below a counter or work surface to be set back at least two inches (2") from the drip line of the surface above. Recommend shelves supported by legs on the floor be of a round metal equipment type leg.

Installation of Equipment

All equipment shall meet National Sanitation Foundation (NSF) Design and installation requirements or its equivalent.

At the Floor: All equipment shall be either easily movable (i.e., on casters), light enough so as to be easily moved by one person (i.e., a light table), installed on raised minimum six inch (6") rounded metal legs, or sealed to minimum two inch (2") solid masonry island with minimum three-eighths inch (3/8") coved radius. If on an island, it shall overhang the base at least two inches (2"), but not more than the height of the island. Sealing to the floor is acceptable **only** if no other means are available, such as beer coolers behind bars, refrigerators, and large bakery ovens.

Gaps and spaces between equipment base and top of islands shall be sealed with a non-hardening silicone sealant. All equipment on counters, tables, and shelves that are not easily lifted are to be installed on approved four-inch (4") legs, or sealed to table, shelves that are not easily lifted, are to be installed on approved four-inch (4") legs, or sealed to table, shelves, etc. Dipper wells with running water shall be provided for ice cream or other frozen dessert scooping operations. All equipment, flashings, and backsplashes are to be adequately sealed to the wall and abutting equipment, or moved away from the wall six inches (6") for every four (4) linear feet of equipment frontal length, or away from each other. Soldering, welding, approved sealants, or "T" cap molding may be used. A minimum of thirty inches (30") clearance is to be provided for all aisles and working areas.

Plumbing

All plumbing and plumbing fixtures shall be installed in compliance with local plumbing ordinances, shall be maintained so as to prevent any contamination, shall be kept clean, be fully operative, and in good repair. All liquid wastes shall be disposed of through the plumbing system, which shall discharge into the public sewerage or into an approved private sewage disposal system.

Steam tables, ice machines and bins, food preparation sinks, display cases, walk-in refrigerators and other similar equipment which discharge liquid waste, shall have this waste conveyed by a sewer line and disposed therein by an **INDIRECT CONNECTION INTO A FLOOR SINK**, funnel drain, or equivalent device. Indirect waste receptors shall be located as to be readily accessible for inspection and cleaning. Drain lines shall not cross any aisle, traffic area, or door opening.

As of July 1st, 1999, Los Angeles City, all unincorporated areas of Los Angeles County, and most incorporated cities have adopted the California Plumbing Code. These jurisdictions will require that all utensil/pot washing sinks shall be connected DIRECTLY to the drainage system.

Special Requirements: INSPECTIONS

All construction and equipment installation are subject to on-site inspections. During the course of construction, and particularly well before you plan to open, you are advised to call if you have any questions. The Building Department is generally responsible for inspections relating to enforcement of the **Building, Plumbing, Mechanical, Electrical Codes and Handicap Requirements**. The Department of Health Services is responsible for inspections relating to equipment. Before commencing installation of any equipment, be sure that the equipment plan and the data regarding the type of equipment and the method of installation have been approved by the Department of Health Services Plan Check Program.

FINAL INSPECTIONS

Final inspections and approval is required prior to beginning operation. The Department requires **AT LEAST THREE WORKING DAYS PRIOR NOTICE TO ARRANGE FOR FINAL INSPECTION**.

WARNING

IT IS A MISDEMEANOR VIOLATION TO BEGIN OPERATION WITHOUT A FINAL INSPECTION AND VALID HEALTH PERMIT. YOUR HEALTH PERMIT WILL BE ISSUED BY THE PLAN CHECKER <u>AT THE JOB SITE</u>. REMODELED AREAS OF EXISTING FOOD ESTABLISHMENTS MUST ALSO HAVE A FINAL INSPECTION.

OTHER DEPARTMENTS

BEFORE STARTING CONSTRUCTION, A BUILDING PERMIT MUST BE OBTAINED FROM YOUR BUILDING AND SAFETY DEPARTMENT. Any new construction, alteration, or remodeling shall be in accordance with applicable building codes.

GENERAL COMMENTS

1. Consult with the Department of Health Services;
2. get equipment plans approved;
3. install equipment according to plans and requirements; purchase only approved equipment (see **Equipment**).

When the installation is completed and the grand opening date is set, there will be no delays in obtaining an approval from the Department of Health Services.

A2-2 ENVIRONMENTAL HEALTH SELF-INSPECTION GUIDE

Source: http:lapublichealth.org/eh

_____

FOOD PREPARATION AREA

Temperature Monitoring of Potential Hazardous Foods (sanitize thermometer)

- food holding temperatures (60°F–125°F) (SC 1)
- food holding temperatures (42°F–59°F/126–139°F) (SC 17)
- holding pooling shelled eggs in danger zone (SC 2)
- internal cooking temperatures not reached or verified (SC 3)
- improper reheating method (SC 4)
- inadequate rapid cooling practices (SC 5)
- lack of a probe thermometer to measure food temperatures (SC 56)

Food Preparation

- food not under diligent preparation (SC 20)
- improper thawing of PHF (SC 21)
- refreezing thawed PHF (SC 41)
- cross contamination of food-contact surfaces (SC 6 or SC 32)
- food prepared in an unapproved area (SC 22)
- food prepared with bare hands, where utensils or gloves should be used (SC 22)
- food prepared at home or not from an approved source (SC 26)
- food adulterated/spoiled (SC 6 or SC 39)
- not storing wiping rag in sanitizing solution when used more than once (SC 54)

EMPLOYEE PRACTICES

Hand Washing

- employee did not wash hands as required (SC 8)
- hand washing sink lacks single-service soap, towels/hot air (SC 8 or SC 28)
- lack of hot/cold water (SC 13, SC 14, or SC 63)
- employee using soiled wiping rag for handwashing (SC 8)
- no handwashing sign posted (SC 80)

Personal Practice/Hygiene

- employee with a communicable disease is preparing food (SC 7)
- employee observed eating/drinking/smoking in the food preparation area (SC 30)
- employee observed wearing soiled clothes and/or lacking hair restraints (SC 44)
- employee with open wound observed contacting food and food-contact surfaces without wearing gloves. (SC 7 & SC 8)
- employee with artificial nails, nail polish or dirty finger nails observed contacting food and food-contact surfaces without wearing gloves (SC 44)

REFRIGERATION AND FREEZER UNITS

Food Storage

- raw meats/seafood/eggs stored above produce and ready-to-eat food products (SC 24 or SC 6)
- food items uncovered &/or not properly elevated (SC 23)
- food items stored in unapproved containers &/or on unapproved shelving (SC 53)

Food Temperatures

- food holding temperatures (60°F–125°F) (SC 1)
- food holding temperatures (42°F–59°F) (SC 17)
- thermometer missing, broken, or inaccurate (SC 56)
- inadequate rapid cooling practices (SC 5)

Equipment Condition

- refrigeration units, fan guards not maintained clean (SC 31)
- unapproved food shelving (SC 53)
- rusted, deteriorated shelving (SC 51)
- unapproved type, improper use or improper installation (SC 53)
- lack of light shields (SC 69)
- refrigeration unit not draining to an approved device (SC 64)

Walls/Floors/Ceilings

- walls, ceilings, and floors not maintained clean (SC 58)
- walls, ceilings, and floors not approved (SC 57)

PHYSICAL INSPECTION OF FOOD PREPARATION AREA

Equipment/Utensils/Shelving/Cabinets

- not maintained clean or free of grease build-up (SC 31)
- in disrepair (SC 51)
- unapproved, improperly installed, improperly used (SC 53)
- stored in unapproved area (SC 52)
- liquid waste from equipment (steam table, etc.) not draining into a floor sink or other approved device (SC 64)

Walls/Ceiling/Floors

- not maintained clean (SC 58)
- deteriorated/unapproved materials/facility not fully enclosed (SC 57)
- unapproved or pitted floors or floors in disrepair (SC 57)

Ventilation

- hood not clean, in disrepair, missing filters (SC 66)
- equipment not under hood, improper hood type (SC 67)
- lack of ventilation to facilitate reasonable comfort (SC 68)
- unapproved or inadequate exhaust system (SC 67)

Lighting/Light Shields

- missing light shields or shatterproof light bulbs, where required (SC 69)
- inadequate amount of lighting to clean or inspect (SC 69)

Vermin

- fresh rodent droppings or other evidence observed in the facility (SC 9 or SC 59)
- live cockroaches and evidence of cockroaches (SC 10 or SC 60)
- flies, food-infesting, insects or other insects observed in the facility (SC 11 or SC 61)
- dog, bird, or fowl in facility (SC 50)
- air curtain in disrepair and not fully operable (SC 62)
- exterior doors gaps exceed 1/4" (SC 59)
- doors maintained open (SC 62)

Food Preparation Sink

- directly connected to drain line (SC 64)

UTENSIL WASHING AND SANITIZING

Sanitizing multi-use consumer utensils

- observed not washing and sanitizing consumer utensils, as required (SC 12)
- lack of mechanical or manual equipment to properly wash and sanitize multi-use utensils (SC 12)
- water heater booster not working properly (SC 13 or SC 34)
- improper method of manual dishwashing (SC 55)

Sanitizing kitchen utensils

- not properly sanitizing food-contact surfaces (SC 32)

Sanitizer

- lack of approved sanitizer on the premises (SC 56)
- sanitizing solution at improper concentration (SC 56)
- sanitizing kit missing, incomplete, or misused (SC 56)

Water

- lack of hot/cold water at all sinks (SC 13 or SC 14)
- lack of cold or hot water at one sink (SC 34)
- water temperature less than 120°F but greater than 110°F (SC 65)
- water temperature less than 110°F at all sinks (SC 14)

Plumbing/Fixtures/Drainage

- leaking, no water at faucet (SC 34)
- lack of backflow or back siphonage device at faucet where a hose is connected (SC 33)
- leaking P-trap, overflowing/clogged grease trap (SC 64)
- clogged floor sink, floor drain (SC 15 or SC 64)
- sewage overflow (contamination of food prep area) (SC 15)

Vermin

- fresh rodent droppings or other evidence observed in the facility (SC 9 or SC 59)
- live cockroaches and evidence of cockroaches (SC 10 or SC 60)
- flies, food-infecting insects, or other insects observed in the facility (SC 11 or SC 61)

FOOD STORAGE AREA

Food Storage

- food stored in unapproved area (SC 22)
- food stored in unclean environment (SC 31)

- food stored in opened/unlabeled containers (SC 23)
- damaged or returned food not stored in a separate area (SC 48)
- food not elevated at least 6" (SC 23)
- spoiled and adulterated food found in facility (SC 6 or SC 39)
- food from unapproved source (SC 26)
- shellfish tags not maintained as required (SC 45)

Equipment Condition

- unapproved floor shelving (SC 53)
- not maintained clean (SC 31)

Ventilation

- lack of ventilation to facilitate proper storage (SC 68)

Vermin

- fresh rodent droppings or other evidence observed in the facility (SC 9 or SC 59)
- live cockroaches and evidence of cockroaches (SC 10 or SC 60)
- flies, food-infesting insects, or other insects observed in the facility (SC 10 or SC 61)

UTENSIL STORAGE AREA

Equipment/Utensil Condition

- not maintained clean (SC 31)
- unapproved, domestic-type utensils (SC 53)

Storage

- stored in unapproved area (SC 52)

Vermin

- fresh rodent droppings or other evidence observed in the facility (SC 9 or SC 59)
- live cockroaches and evidence of cockroaches (SC 10 or SC 60)
- flies, food-infesting insects, or other insects observed in the facility (SC 10 or SC 61)

FOOD SERVICE AREA

Hot/Cold Holding Unit (e.g., steam table, salad bar)

- food holding temperatures (60°F–125°F) (SC 1)
- food holding temperatures (42°F–59°F/126–139°F) (SC 17)
- liquid waste from equipment (steam table, etc.) not draining into a floor sink or other approved device (SC 64)

Food Display

- food displayed without proper sneeze guards or approved dispensing devices (SC 25)
- prepackaged food items not properly labeled (SC 35)

Condiment/Table Service

- re-serving food after having been served to a customer (SC 27)
- reusing food previously served to a customer in the preparation of another food (SC 27)
- utensils not stored with handles up in customer area (SC 40)

Vermin

- fresh rodent droppings or other evidence observed in the facility (SC 9 or SC 59)
- live cockroaches and evidence of cockroaches (SC 10 or SC 60)
- flies, food-infesting insects, or other insects observed in the facility (SC 10 or SC 61)

DELIVERY, TRANSPORTATION, AND RECEIVING

Temperature Monitoring of Potentially Hazardous Foods (sanitize thermometer)

- food holding temperatures (60°F–125°F) (SC 1)
- food holding temperatures (42°F–59°F/126–139°F) (SC 17)

Food Condition

- food not inspected upon receipt (SC 42)
- food being transported in unclean container (SC 31)
- food being transported in unapproved containers (SC 53)
- vermin evidence observed on packaging (SC 6 or SC 39)
- adulterated food (SC 6 or SC 39)

Purveyor/Source

- no invoice (SC 26)

FACILITIES

Lavatories

- lack of adequate, pressurized potable cold or hot water (SC 14 or SC 34)
- water temperature less than 120°F but greater than 110°F (SC 65)
- water temperature less than 110°F (SC 13)
- hand washing sink in disrepair (SC 34 or SC 63)
- hand washing sink lacks approved single-service soap or towels (SC 28 or SC 43)
- no single-service soap or towel dispenser (SC 43)

Toilet Rooms

- toilet facilities not maintained clean and in disrepair (SC 70)
- lack of toilet paper and/or dispenser (SC 70)
- missing/broken self-closing device at bathroom door (SC 70)
- toilet room not properly vented either by an openable window or a light-switch activated exhaust fan (SC 68)

Miscellaneous Storage

- storing non-facility items on the premises (SC 47)
- soiled linen not stored in a separate area (SC 47)

Janitorial Storage Area

- lack of adequate, pressurized potable cold or hot water (SC 14 or SC 63)
- water temperature less than 120°F but greater than 110°F (SC 65)
- water temperature less than 110°F (SC 13)
- lack of an area for the storage of cleaning supplies (SC 72)
- lack of a janitorial sink or an unapproved basin (SC 63)
- janitorial sink in disrepair (SC 63)

Hazardous Materials/Chemical Storage Area

- chemicals, pesticides, or cleaning compounds stored in unapproved area (SC 29 or SC 46)
- chemicals, pesticides, or cleaning compounds not properly labeled or used improperly (SC 29 or SC 46)

Employee Storage Area

- dressing room is cluttered, unclean, or non-existent (SC 71)
- employees observed storing personal items in unapproved area (SC 71)

Vermin

- fresh rodent droppings or other evidence observed in the facility (SC 9 or SC 59)
- live cockroaches and evidence of cockroaches (SC 10 or SC 60)
- flies, food-infesting insects, or other insects observed in the facility (SC 10 or SC 61)
- exterior doors not rodent proofed (SC 59)

Living Quarters

- using food facility to sleep (SC 49)

EXTERIOR PREMISES

Trash

- overflowing trash cans in the food preparation area (SC 73)

- trash area unclean and trash observed on the floor (SC 73)
- trash not disposed of in leak-proof and rodent-proof containers (SC 73)
- exterior trash cans or bins not covered (SC 73)
- recyclables stored inside the food preparation area (SC 73)

Premises

- cast-off items stored at the exterior of the facility (SC 74)
- parking lot not maintained clean (SC 74)

A2-3 TARGET MARKET

Total Person Map

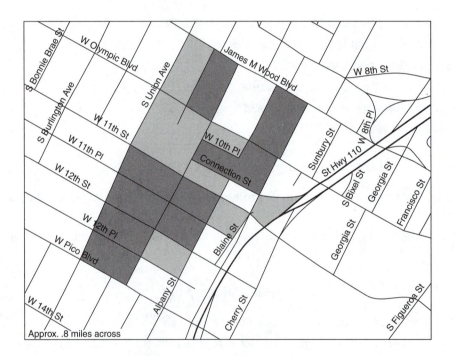

Data Classes

Total Persons
- 0–0
- 37–59
- 107–160
- 190–275
- 414–440

Features
- Major Road
- Street
- Stream/Waterbody
- Stream/Waterbody

Demographics

Source: http://www.census.gov/
DP-1: Profile of General Demographic Characteristics: 2000
Data Set: Census 2000 Summary File 1 (SF 1) 100-Percent Data
Geographic Area: Census Tract 2100.10, Los Angeles County, California
NOTE: For information on confidentiality protection, nonsampling error, and definitions, see
http://factfinder.census.gov/home/en/datanotes/expsf1u.htm.

Subject	Number	Percent
Total population	3,607	100.0
SEX AND AGE		
Male	1,839	51.0
Female	1,768	49.0
Under 5 years	330	9.1
5 to 9 years	367	10.2
10 to 14 years	292	8.1
15 to 19 years	303	8.4
20 to 24 years	346	9.6
25 to 34 years	618	17.1
35 to 44 years	462	12.8
45 to 54 years	335	9.3
55 to 59 years	97	2.7
60 to 64 years	93	2.6
65 to 74 years	152	4.2
75 to 84 years	152	4.2
85 years and over	60	1.7
Median age (years)	27.7	(X)
18 years and over	2,457	68.1
Male	1,249	34.6
Female	1,208	33.5
21 years and over	2,251	62.4
62 years and over	419	11.6
65 years and over	364	10.1
Male	109	3.0
Female	255	7.1
RACE		
One race	3,410	94.5
White	1,179	32.7
Black or African American	83	2.3
American Indian and Alaska Native	56	1.6
Asian	286	7.9
Asian Indian	9	0.2
Chinese	9	0.2
Filipino	41	1.1
Japanese	11	0.3
Korean	199	5.5
Vietnamese	4	0.1
Other Asian 1	13	0.4
Native Hawaiian and Other Pacific Islander	2	0.1
Native Hawaiian	1	0.0
Guamanian or Chamorro	1	0.0
Samoan	0	0.0
Other Pacific Islander 2	0	0.0
Some other race	1,804	50.0
Two or more races	197	5.5
Race alone or in combination with one or more other races 3		
White	1,341	37.2
Black or African American	96	2.7
American Indian and Alaska Native	93	2.6
Asian	305	8.5
Native Hawaiian and Other Pacific Islander	13	0.4
Some other race	1,983	55.0
HISPANIC OR LATINO AND RACE		
Total population	3,607	100.0
Hispanic or Latino (of any race)	3,150	87.3
Mexican	2,108	58.4
Puerto Rican	9	0.2

Subject	Number	Percent
Cuban	10	0.3
Other Hispanic or Latino	1,023	28.4
Not Hispanic or Latino	457	12.7
White alone	96	2.7
RELATIONSHIP		
Total population	3,607	100.0
In households	3,607	100.0
Householder	1,126	31.2
Spouse	432	12.0
Child	1,275	35.3
Own child under 18 years	1,005	27.9
Other relatives	488	13.5
Under 18 years	121	3.4
Nonrelatives	286	7.9
Unmarried partner	71	2.0
In group quarters	0	0.0
Institutional population	0	0.0
Noninstitutionalized population	0	0.0
HOUSEHOLDS BY TYPE		
Total households	1,126	100.0
Family households (families)	714	63.4
With own children under 18 years	458	40.7
Married-couple family	432	38.4
With own children under 18 years	298	26.5
Female householder, no husband present	179	15.9
With own children under 18 years	119	10.6
Nonfamily households	412	36.6
Householder living alone	357	31.7
Householder 65 years and over	218	19.4
Households with individuals under 18 years	508	45.1
Households with individuals 65 years and over	313	27.8
Average household size	3.20	(X)
Average family size	4.07	(X)
HOUSING OCCUPANCY		
Total housing units	1,176	100.0
Occupied housing units	1,126	95.7
Vacant housing units	50	4.3
For seasonal, recreational, or occasional use	1	0.1
Homeowner vacancy rate (percent)	1.6	(X)
Rental vacancy rate (percent)	4.3	(X)
HOUSING TENURE		
Occupied housing units	1,126	100.0
Owner-occupied housing units	186	16.5
Renter-occupied housing units	940	83.5
Average household size of owner-occupied unit	2.81	(X)
Average household size of renter-occupied unit	3.28	(X)

(X) Not applicable

1 Other Asian alone, or two or more Asian categories.

2 Other Pacific Islander alone, or two or more Native Hawaiian and Other Pacific Islander categories.

3 In combination with one or more other races listed. The six numbers may add to more than the total population, and the six percentages may add to more than 100 percent because individuals may report more than one race.

Source: U.S. Census Bureau, Census 2000 Summary File 1, Matrices P1, P3, P4, P8, P9, P12, P13, P17, P18, P19, P20, P23, P27, P28, P33, PCT5, PCT8, PCT11, PCT15, H1, H 3, H4, H5, H11, and H12.

A2-4 MARKETING TACTICS

PRODUCT

		Price	Lease 36mo	Lease 48mo.
Cimbali	Automatic w/direct brew M29 Selectron DT2 Tall/includes grinder, knockout system, and water softener. Makes 1000 cups per day. Requirements: 1. Drainage. Drain into a solid PVC terminating in floor 2. Waterline. One-quarter inch line. 3. Electrical. 30 amp service within 5 feet.	$ 5,800	$ 186	$ 130
Pasquini	Annual Water Softening Maintenance	$ 35		
Pasquini	Annual General Maintenance, including steam seals.	$ 150		
Pasquini	Filtrations System	$ 160		
Pasquini	Organic Coffee Beans price per pound Usage: 64 coffees per pound	$ 6		
Pasquini	Coffee Cups S-12oz, M-16oz, L-20oz per case of 1000 Usage: 4.5 cases per month (majority M & L) or 150 per day Average Price Per cup is $0.32, which includes cup and beans.	$ 58		

PROMOTION

Promotional Flyer

ENJOY YOUR COFFEE!

AT

The Legal Beagle

We optimize the taste and quality of every cup of coffee we prepare for you.

Bring this flyer in and get a FREE Legal Beagle Loyalty Card and 50% off your coffee purchase.

We offer Coffee, Espresso, Latte, Snacks, Sandwiches, Soft Drinks and More!

The best Coffee House West of the Supreme Court.

TASTING THE COFFEE
Will Prove us Guilty!

Please Insert Address Here.

Fresh roasted coffee is essential to a superb cup of coffee.

CUSTOMER LOYALTY CARD

The Legal Beagle Loyalty List

ENJOY YOUR COFFEE!

How to Join:
1. Buy a coffee Drink.
2. Get a Loyalty Card
3. Buy 4 more Drinks
4. Get one free!

The five drinks can be any of the coffee Drinks we make.

Name:_____
Joined the Legal Beagle Loyalty List on: _____
# of coffee Drinks: 1 ● 2 ● 3 ● 4 ● 5 ●

JAVA ~ JOE ~ COFFEE ~ CAFE

PROMOTION BUDGET

	AUG	SEP	OCT	NOV	DEC	JAN	FEB	MAR	APR	MAY	JUN	JUL	YEAR
Loyalty Card	$200	$200	$200	$200	$200	$200	$200	$200	$200	$200	$200	$200	$2,400
Flyers	$400	$400		$400		$400		$400		$400		$400	$2,800
Campus Newspaper	150	150	150	150	150	150	150	150	150	150	150	150	$1,800
Totals	$750	$750	$350	$750	$350	$750	$350	$750	$350	$750	$350	$750	$7,000

Promotion Type			Monthly Expense by week				
		Week 1	Week 2	Week 3	Week 4	Monthly Total
Flyers	Developing, Printing, and Distribution:	$100	$100	$100	$100	$400
Loyalty Card Promo	Developing, Printing, and Distribution:	50	50	50	50	$200
Campus Newspaper	Advertising, Developing Ad, cost per print:	0	75		75	$150
Total by Week		$150	$225	$150	$225	$750
Monthly Total		$750				

Notes:
*Loyalty Card Promotion will run indefinitely.
*Campus Newspaper Advertising will run when school is in session and there is an issue being printed.
*Flyers will run every other month, but steady for the first two months.
*In second year, a review of what Promotion is working should be done, and budget adjusted accordingly.

A2-5 IMPLEMENTATION AND CONTROLS

START-UP COSTS

The Legal Beagle
Estimated Start-Up Costs Summary

Cash Available:		
Loan		100,000
Personal Financing		10,000
Total Available for Expenditures		110,000
Less:		
Start-Up Costs:		
Building Lease		1,800
Permits:		
Construction-Remodeling**		74,769
Health Dept. Upgrades	1,006	
Electrical (appr/900 sq. ft.)	1,250	
Mechanical (HVAC)	1,700	
Plumbing	1,275	5,231
Espresso Equipment Lease		186
Refrigerator Purchase		1,250
Cooler Purchase		1,000
Display Cases		1,000
Espresso Machine Purch.		5,800
Coffee Makers Purch.		750
Other Equipment Purch.		1,446
Supplies Purchase		1,500
Security Deposits:		
Gas Co.	50	
Electric Co.	50	
Telephone Co.	50	150
Water Softening Maintenance*		100
General Espresso Maintenance*		300
Filtration System Maintenance*		320
Fictitious Business Name Registration**		90
Sign Purchase**		500
Total		96,192
Balance Available:		13,808

*Denotes Annual Cost
**Denotes One-Time Cost

MONTHLY CASH FLOW

Year 1 Cash Flow Estimates

	AUG	SEP	OCT	NOV	DEC	JAN	FEB	MAR	APR	MAY	JUN	JUL	YEAR
Cash, Beginning Balance	—	3,234	(9,089)	(16,688)	(20,044)	(24,929)	(27,180)	(22,424)	(18,631)	(11,506)	(6,787)	(7,994)	(162,036)
Add Receipts:													
Personal Financing	10,000	—	—	—	—	—	—	—	—	—	—	—	10,000
Sales	1,750	2,888	5,342	10,684	10,684	10,684	18,697	20,566	20,566	18,510	13,882	10,412	144,663
Total Available for Expenditures	11,750	6,122	(3,747)	(6,004)	(9,361)	(14,245)	(8,483)	(1,857)	1,935	7,004	7,095	2,418	(7,373)
Less Disbursements:													
Start-Up Costs	96,192	—	—	—	—	—	—	—	—	—	—	—	96,192
Lease	1,800	1,800	1,800	1,800	1,800	1,800	1,800	1,800	1,800	1,800	1,800	1,800	21,600
Additional Supplies Needed	100	50	50	50	50	50	50	50	50	50	50	50	650
Coffee/Espresso	750	1,000	1,250	1,750	2,000	2,000	2,000	1,500	1,500	1,250	1,000	1,000	17,000
Pastries	500	750	750	1,000	1,000	1,000	1,000	1,000	1,000	1,000	1,000	1,000	11,000
Sandwich Ingredients	1,000	1,250	1,250	1,250	1,250	1,250	1,250	1,250	1,250	1,250	1,250	1,250	14,750
Soft Drinks	500	250	250	250	250	250	250	250	250	500	500	500	4,000
Utilities	1,350	1,350	1,350	1,350	1,350	1,350	1,350	1,350	1,350	1,350	1,350	1,350	16,200
Labor	5,424	5,424	5,424	5,424	4,068	4,068	5,424	5,424	5,424	5,424	4,068	4,068	59,664
Worker's Compensation	—	2,170	—	—	2,983	—	—	2,983	—	—	3,254	—	11,390
Cleaning Supplies	150	—	50	—	50	—	50	—	50	—	50	50	400
Promotions	750	750	350	750	350	750	350	750	350	750	350	750	7,000
Owner's Withdrawals	—	—	—	—	—	—	—	—	—	—	—	—	—
Total Disbursements	#####	14,794	12,524	13,624	15,151	12,518	13,524	16,357	13,024	13,374	14,672	11,768	259,846
Cash Available	(96,766)	(8,672)	(16,271)	(19,628)	(24,512)	(26,763)	(22,007)	(18,215)	(11,089)	(6,370)	(7,577)	(9,350)	(267,219)
Financing:													
Borrowing (at Beginning)	#####												100,000
Repayments (at ending)		(21)	(21)	(21)	(21)	(21)	(21)	(21)	(21)	(21)	(21)	(21)	(229)
Interest		(396)	(396)	(396)	(396)	(396)	(396)	(396)	(396)	(396)	(396)	(396)	(4,354)
Total Financing	#####	(417)	(417)	(417)	(417)	(417)	(417)	(417)	(417)	(417)	(417)	(417)	95,417
Cash Balance, Ending	3,234	(9,089)	(16,688)	(20,044)	(24,929)	(27,180)	(22,424)	(18,631)	(11,506)	(6,787)	(7,994)	(9,767)	(171,803)

Disbursements

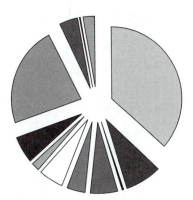

- ☐ Start-Up Costs
- ■ Lease
- ■ Additional Supplies Needed
- ■ Coffee/Espresso
- ■ Pastries
- ☐ Sandwich Ingredients
- ☐ Soft Drinks
- ■ Utilities
- ☐ Labor
- ■ Worker's Compensation
- ■ Cleaning Supplies
- ☐ Promotions

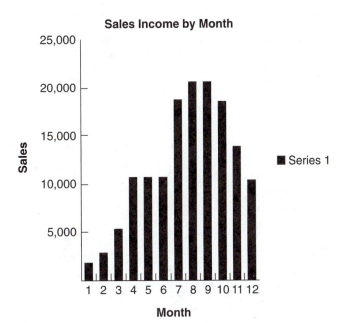

INCOME STATEMENT

Year 1-Budgeted Income Statement	
Net Sales	122,536
Less: Cost of Goods Sold	45,950
Selling & Admin Exp.	163,654
Operating Profit before Depr	(87,068)
Less: Depreciation	18,249
Earnings Before Interest & Taxes	(105,317)
Less: Interest	4,354
Earnings Before Taxes	(109,671)
Less: Taxes	—
Net Income After Taxes	(109,671)

THREE-YEAR INCOME STATEMENT

	YR-1	YR-2	YR-3
Net Sales	122,536	183,804	275,706
Less: Cost of Goods Sold	45,950	52,843	63,411
Selling & Admin Exp.	163,654	188,202	206,217
Operating Profit before Depr	(87,068)	(57,241)	6,078
Less: Depreciation	18,249	18,249	18,249
Earnings Before Interest & Taxes	(105,317)	(75,490)	(12,171)
Less: Interest	4,354	4,572	4,354
Earnings Before Taxes	(109,671)	(80,062)	(16,525)
Less: Taxes	—	—	—
Net Income After Taxes	(109,671)	(80,062)	(16,525)

Notes:

-In Years 2 and 3, the owner will start withdrawing some cash, making Selling and Administrative costs rise more dramatically. Also, as sales increase, Cost of Goods Sold increases and so do Selling and Administrative costs.

-Taxes will remain at $0 since we are not showing a profit by the end of year 3.

-Owner's Withdrawals are included in Selling and Administrative expenses and may have some Personal Income Tax implications for the owner.

-Depreciation is assumed using the Straight-Line Method, for 5 years.

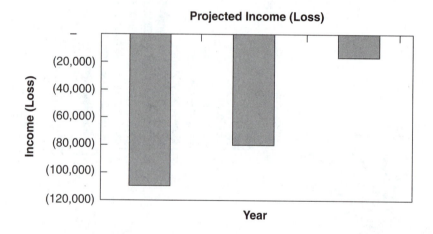

Projected Income (Loss)

A3

OPENAXIS

Developed by
CARLOS D. AGUAYO
AREG BOYAMYAN
LISA CHIN
DIEM-CHI PHUNG
DANIEL HUA YANG

Contents

EXECUTIVE SUMMARY

Computer software is a rapidly evolving technology. Statistics show that 80 percent of computer users in the business world utilize only 20 percent of what an application is capable of performing.[1] OpenAxis, Incorporated, based in Monterey Park, California, is a unique IT provider, derived from a small consulting firm owned by Shunji Muso with only six employees. OpenAxis provides management consulting services to clients based on packaged application programs. One such application is accounting software, ACCPAC Advantage Series (AAS).

OpenAxis is geared to provide you with the best-fit solution for your business, backed by a smooth, successful implementation. As a Microsoft Certified Partner, as well as an ACCPAC Business Partner, OpenAxis has the objective of increasing consulting services and increasing sales of the AAS software.

OpenAxis distinguishes itself from competitors by providing in-depth training classes at competitive prices. The ACCPAC Advantage Series distinguishes itself from competitors by providing superior "architecture." With four editions, each with increasing levels of functionality, the program makes it simple to upgrade your business management system as your business grows, while retaining the valuable history of transactions for your analysis.

The market is targeted toward small to medium-size businesses located in Los Angeles County who employ accounting/bookkeeping skills. To date, OpenAxis will be the only third-party provider of ACCPAC Advantage Series to offer training classes on the use of the application in the Los Angeles area.

The initial investment will be $20,000. The venture is projected to break even in about 3.54 months with a profit of $9,545 after-tax by the end of the first six months. The three-year projected income should be $143,194 after-tax. Through efficient training classes and referrals, OpenAxis will be able to build upon the existing clientele.

INTRODUCTION

Accounting is aptly called the "language of business" (Anthony, Hawkins, and Merchant, 1999). It is a system of gathering, summarizing, and communicating financial information (Keith, 2002). It enables decision makers to interpret financial information and to use the results to plan for the future. Informed decisions can then be made about such matters as production, marketing, and financing. Accounting also entails bookkeeping that involves recording financial transactions and maintaining financial records. As the number of jobs in many accounting fields grows, increasingly sophisticated management techniques demand information that can be provided most efficiently by accountants.

In today's competitive markets, companies of all sizes are dedicating substantial resources toward software solutions that streamline and reduce costs associated with key business functions. "International Data Corp. (IDC), an independent provider of information technology data, estimates that the worldwide market for financial accounting software will grow from approximately $5.3 billion in 1997 to approximately $10.4 billion in 2002."[2] While consumers seek out software that provides functionality, flexibility, and reliability to meet their needs, technology, industry standards, and product innovations must constantly change to meet those demands. The computer software business is extremely competitive.

OpenAxis, Inc., is a management consulting provider located in Monterey Park, California. Headed by Shunji Muso with only six employees under his wing, their more than a quarter century of experience in IT solutions is dedicated to providing businesses with customized solutions for the implementation and support of various program applications. OpenAxis's primary business partner, ACCPAC International, is a leading provider of financial accounting and business management software solutions to the small business and midsize/corporate markets. They have been in service since 1979. As of June 30, 1998, ACCPAC International had a client base consisting of over 350,000 in the United States and Canada. In addition, there are registered clients of ACCPAC International in more than 100 other countries.[3] With approximately 3,000 valued resellers and qualified installers, ACCPAC International relies on its business partners to sell their products. They offer their business partners extensive hands-on training in the installation, implementation, and maintenance of their products.

Among several ACCPAC products that OpenAxis vends, one product in particular is the focus of this new venture, ACCPAC Advantage Series (AAS). *CPA Magazine* rates ACCPAC as the number one accounting software, and ACCPAC Advantage Series has been awarded the highest rating by *CPA Software News.*[4] The modular design of AAS allows businesses to tailor the application to match their needs. The design includes system manager, general ledger, accounts receivable, accounts payable, inventory control, order entry, purchase order, payroll, general ledger consolidation, and intercompany transactions. With AAS, customers get a powerful accounting information system that provides such features as high-speed transaction processing, fault tolerance and data integrity, user-definable security, and system scalability. In addition, the general ledger module has a unique subaccount structure allowing for improved reporting by department, profit center, cost center, and activity. The application can integrate with Financial Reporter, Excel, and Crystal Reports. AAS has been designed with industry standard tools including Microsoft's Visual Basic and SQL database technology. From financial decision making to processing payrolls, from sales force automation to redefining processes via the Net, only AAS puts business critical information at your fingertips and turns it into a competitive advantage.

There are four resellers of AAS in Los Angeles area, but only two resellers that provide training classes for the program, including OpenAxis itself. Our competition, Micro Madness, is another management consulting firm located in Anaheim, California. Micro Madness provides separate distinct classes for each module of the application (general ledger, accounts receivable, accounts payable, order entry, inventory control, financial reporter, system manager, year-end, U.S. payroll) at $379 each full-day class. OpenAxis, Inc., provides only three classes:

- Basic Bookkeeping Class, which includes general ledger, accounts receivable/payable, and financial reporter
- Two different Advanced Accounting Classes, which include inventory control, purchase order, and order entry

Each class is offered at only $199, and each class is three hours per day for two days; this is especially advantageous for those who have time constraints.

The following business plan will include a more in-depth analysis of the marketing environment, target market, and an analysis on problems/opportunities. Also discussed will be OpenAxis's marketing objectives, strategies, and implementation and control.

Sales projections and cash flows on a monthly basis for three years are provided. The break-even analysis will give you a more precise projection as to how quickly this venture will produce profits.

ENVIRONMENTAL ANALYSIS

Situated in California, OpenAxis, Inc., provides management consulting services to clients based on packaged application programs. At OpenAxis, the focus is on implementation of IT solutions for small and medium-sized businesses. Our solutions include accounting systems and computer-based operation and management systems. One of the types of software promoted by OpenAxis is provided by ACCPAC International Corporation. Since this business plan primarily focuses on marketing OpenAxis's accounting software solutions, provided by ACCPAC International, the information covered in this marketing plan will relate only to the training seminars OpenAxis will conduct in order to increase awareness of ACCPAC accounting software and ultimately increase sales of AAS. Besides the commission OpenAxis receives from selling various ACCPAC software products, OpenAxis generates a sufficient amount of revenues from providing consulting services to the customer who purchases ACCPAC software.

The Marketing Environment

Competitive Forces Surrounding OpenAxis Although the competition in the specialty advertising industry is very strong nationwide and locally, we believe that advertisement of our product, mainly training seminars for ACCPAC software, should not be such a difficult task. Currently, there is only one competitor in the Orange County area who offers the services we do but at a higher price. There is also much competition nationwide, but since we are focusing our marketing efforts on local communities, we are not concerned with nationwide competition.

Although OpenAxis does not foresee any major competition in the marketing environment for the training seminars, we certainly acknowledge the competition ACCPAC software faces. The competitive forces surrounding ACCPAC software are inherited by Open Axis because our potential customers must first get attracted to ACCPAC products before they can try our services. Therefore, it is worthwhile to look at some of the competitive forces that influence ACCPAC product line.

Competitive Forces Surrounding ACCPAC ACCPAC has experienced competition to date from both established and emerging software companies that offer similar products targeted at businesses with ACCPAC's markets. ACCPAC's products compete with those from several vendors servicing a range of markets, from the corporate to small businesses. ACCPAC currently faces competition in the small-business market from Automatic Data Processing, Inc.'s MAS90 and Solomon IV, among others. Certain competitors may have greater financial, technical, and marketing resources and name recognition than ACCPAC. In addition, competitors may lower their prices, which may force ACCPAC to match price cuts and thereby decrease the profitability of ACCPAC software, plus the profitability of OpenAxis, which is trying to sell the software and provide consulting service for the software. We believe that the above-mentioned competitive forces surrounding the ACCPAC product line directly influences OpenAxis's ability to market the training seminars that this marketing plan advocates.

Economic Forces Due to the economic crisis our country is currently facing, many companies have reduced their overall promotion budgets. Although we have sustained some growth through these hard times and have remained profitable, OpenAxis does not have the resources to support a major advertising campaign. While the overall promotion budget at OpenAxis has shrunk significantly, we are ready to divert a large percentage of our promotion budget to sales promotions and specialty advertising by means of training seminars. We are anticipating this trend to continue since the slow-growing, weak economy has forced us to become more interested in the "value" from the promotion dollar. We believe that specialty advertising, through the training seminars that will increase ACCPAC software awareness and help us generate revenues through sales and consulting services, will provide us with the best "value" from the promotion dollar.

Political Forces   Currently, we do not anticipate any political forces that may influence our goal of increasing sales revenues through training seminars advocating various ACCPAC products.

Legal and Regulatory Forces   One of our methods of introducing the training seminars to the public is through the distribution of flyers. In recent years, the public has become somewhat speculative and annoyed by flyers advertising specialty products, partly due to the emergence of hundreds of phony companies and products and the worldwide increase and dependence on the Internet. While this label could be attached to the type of product we are trying to promote, we do not consider this a major threat because our plan is to attract potential customers to the training seminars, and it is through the training seminars that we plan to increase sales revenues and consulting business.

Technological Forces   Although OpenAxis does not face technological forces for the services it is providing to potential customers, we believe that the technological forces surrounding ACCPAC products could have a direct impact on OpenAxis's profitability.

In the "Competitive Forces Surrounding ACCPAC" section of this marketing plan, we already introduced numerous competitors that the ACCPAC product line faces. It is only logical that these competitors also pose great technological challenges to ACCPAC and, since we are advocating the ACCPAC product line, these challenges could have an impact on our success.

The computer software business in which ACCPAC competes is rapidly evolving and can be expected to evolve further in the future as a result of changing technology, industry standards, product innovations, and client requirements: There can be no assurance that ACCPAC's technology will meet, or be adaptable to meet, these standards. ACCPAC's ability to compete effectively will depend upon its ability to anticipate and react to changes in its markets in a timely manner. Our success is very much dependent on ACCPAC's ability to stay technologically advanced and innovative. ACCPAC gives us no assurance that substantial resources in product development and enhancement will not be required in the future and that ACCPAC will be able to successfully develop and bring to market new products and services in a timely manner. In addition, we believe that there may be reluctance in certain marketplaces to accept these new technologies, making it difficult for OpenAxis to effectively market ACCPAC software and our consulting services related to it.

Sociocultural Forces   Since this business plan focuses on providing training seminars to increase awareness of ACCPAC accounting software tailored to meet requirements of small businesses, we believe that understanding the sociocultural forces surrounding these sectors could have an impact on our success. Small businesses are leveraging increasing PC power, declining PC costs, and the availability and ease of use of software applications to manage financial functions that have traditionally required specialized training or were delegated to outside professionals. By using accounting software packages, small businesses can automate daily bookkeeping tasks, reduce costs, and improve business decision making by providing timely access to critical business information. In addition, accountants and auditors of small businesses often support the use of accounting software because it can reduce the time and costs required to perform audits and prepare tax returns.

Small businesses typically use PCs within simple peer-to-peer or small-networked systems as their primary technology platform. Small businesses employ accounting software applications to save time, reduce costs, and increase the ability to access and share information in a timely manner. Small businesses demand more robust functionality than is provided by off-the-shelf software. In addition, small businesses frequently demand the flexibility to generate customized reports. They look for software solutions that can be scaled to meet the needs of a growing company, have an affordable cost of ownership over the life of the product, and can be implemented with ease and relative speed.

TARGET MARKET

The great attraction to accounting software products lies in its widespread use. Companies of all sizes, whether personal or corporate, use accounting/bookkeeping skills to monitor their finances and for management purposes. The target market is small and mid-sized businesses that use accounting processes. There is a population of 9,802,800 in Los Angeles County and a population of 2,925,700 in the Orange County area as of January 1, 2001 (Flaxman, Kitchens, 2001). OpenAxis has a larger population base, being located just 10 minutes east of Downtown Los Angeles, than Micro Madness, our competitor. In a "Labor Market Information Study" produced by the City of Long Beach Workforce Development Bureau, the occupational forecast for bookkeepers, accountants, and auditing clerks shows that there will be a population of 52,200 in the year 2000, down from 52,309 in 1999 (Flaxman, Kitchens, 2001). Due to the recent economic crisis, there is only a −0.04 percent slow decline in the occupations. Employers in the sample indicated that new positions in the occupation expanded by 4 percent over the past twelve months. Most of the firms sampled (64 percent) expected employment to remain stable over the next two years. Employers are noted to have some difficulty finding qualified applicants at times. Advancement in the firms may depend upon specific qualifications such as accuracy, education, and computer and software skills.

With that in mind, the training classes offered by OpenAxis will provide not only exposure for OpenAxis's consulting business, but also training/education for those who already have the AAS or those who are looking for this type of integrative software to fulfill their business needs. There is also an incentive to take the class in groups due to special group discount rates.

PROBLEMS/OPPORTUNITIES

Problems

Competition As discussed in the "Marketing Environment" section, since most businesses already have accounting software, the market is not easy to penetrate. We intend to advertise through flyers, newspaper ads, and word-of-mouth the training class offered at the low price to introduce the AAS. ACCPAC International is continually expanding its list of business partners, which creates fear of increased competition. So far, there are only two companies in the Southern California region that provide the training classes for AAS, and OpenAxis is by far the more competitive price.

Consumer Risk Although the classes to be imparted will cover the required knowledge, consumers may still not want to pay for the classes at the set price of $199 each class. To help ease their financial worries, we will be offering the classes at group discount rates. For instance, if a firm already has the software but needs to train its employees in how to better use the application, it could send its employees to these classes for a discounted rate.

Intracompany Risk The instructors for the classes must be ACCPAC certified per OpenAxis's regulations. The instructors for the classes are already ACCPAC certified. There is a risk that these instructors will depart from the company, and to train any additional instructors will cost the company $5,000 for the first person and $3,000 each additional person. OpenAxis's instructors will be paid a competitive wage of $900 per week for the two certified instructors. One instructor is already employed with the company; the other instructor is hired just for this purpose. To eliminate turnover of these two instructors, for every AAS software sold for the company, OpenAxis will pay the consultant 50 percent of the profit from the sale, and the internal employee will receive a 10 percent wage increase per year.

Resource Risk The current classroom facility only holds a maximum of five students. Once the business grows, we will need to look for bigger classroom space with additional computers. With a break-even point at 3.54 months, we must limit our classes to five students until profits start to come in, allowing us the available financial resources to expand.

Opportunities

Expansion OpenAxis is a well-organized, experienced company. It has substantial experience in consulting, advising, and implementing software systems. It is an established company with five years of service to the community. The partnership of OpenAxis with other leading agencies provides a well-supported and leading organization (ACCPAC, MISys, Edisoft, Microsoft Certified). With the experience in the industry, we can expand the network of applications to train individuals, bringing in more profits. As noted in the introduction, the worldwide market for financial accounting software will have doubled in 2002 to approximately $10.4 billion.

Monopoly There are only four resellers in the Los Angeles area, OpenAxis being one of them. We are the only provider of training classes for AAS in Los Angeles County. This gives us a head start in the business and will allow us to eventually expand to Orange County and San Bernardino County with a larger list of clientele than any new competition.

Double Marketing We market not only the AAS software, but also the consulting skills and the name of OpenAxis. Through existing and new clientele referrals, OpenAxis can broaden its name recognition, which will increase consulting services for the company.

MARKETING OBJECTIVES AND GOALS

OpenAxis's short-term goal is to reach the break-even point in 3.54 months and then to expand classes and advertisements to Orange County and San Bernardino County. Open Axis's long-term goal is to make a profit of $9,545 by the end of the first six months, allowing the expansion of the training classes to include more software products. OpenAxis, as well as its business partner, ACCPAC International, intends to keep up with the technological advances in the computer software industry. Provided in Table A3-1 are the financial goals for the next three years.

Table A3-1.   Financial Goals for the Next Three Fiscal Years

	2002	2003	2004	2005
Net income after taxes	$9,545	$67,320	$104,095	$143,194

MARKETING STRATEGIES

Targeted toward small and medium-sized businesses, OpenAxis will focus on three levels of training classes. These classes are tailored to different client needs. The classes generate income from class fees, purchase of software itself, and possible consultant service fees. Quite often potential customers want to know the functionality of the product before committing to purchase the product or the service. The training class is merely the milestone to attract those who are interested in AAS software. But it has a very important part in helping to generate income in the long term. There are no other competitors that offer training classes within fifty miles. Even if they do, the price we offer is unbeatable and refundable with the purchase of AAS software.

Costs are fixed for start-up costs, which include the following:

- Mailing 1,100 training class flyers to businesses and individuals
- Paying ACCPAC for a direct-mail campaign of mailing 3,000 flyers to businesses
- Preparing for training class
- Handling advance advertising and staff salary (from April to May in first year)

Total start-up costs will be $14,303. OpenAxis needs to increase its net working capital to cover the start-up costs and annual operating costs of this marketing plan.

The training class is based on the mail campaign and advertising at newspapers. We estimate that in the first year OpenAxis can attract ten individuals to take part in the class every week. Then we will have two training classes, a total of eight classes a month. Each class has five students. Every student will pay $199 for a class. The costs of the training class mainly will come from instructors. OpenAxis needs two instructors to teach in each training class. One instructor is OpenAxis's employee. Because OpenAxis has paid wages to him and teaching in the training class is only a part of his job, his cost will be considered as $150 per class. Another instructor will be hired at $750 per class.

ACCPAC software sales and consulting services are based on the training class. We anticipate that every twenty-four classes will award OpenAxis one ACCPAC package sales and one consulting service.

The detailed sales and expense forecasts presented are listed in Table A3-2.

Break-Even Analysis

According to sales and expense forecasts, in the first year OpenAxis will get revenue from the training class weekly and get revenue from ACCPAC software sale and consulting services every three months. In order to do break-even analysis we transfer them as monthly data. Because advance advertising has been considered as a fixed cost, break-even analysis will begin from June of this year.

Figure A3-1 illustrates OpenAxis's breakeven point, the point at which the total sales equals total costs.

Table A3-2. Sales and Expense Forecasts

Revenue:	Unit Price	Selling Quantity	Per Week	Per Month
Accounting systems training class	$ 995.00	2/week	$1,990.00	$ 7,960.00
ACCPAC software sales	$12,695.00	1/24 classes	$1,057.92	$ 4,232.00
Consulting service	$ 7,617.00	1/24 classes	$ 634.75	$ 2,539.00
Total revenue for first year			**$3,683.00**	$14,731.00

Expense:
Fixed Costs

	Unit Price			
Design—training class flyer	$ 3,125.00			
ACCPAC direct mailing campaign (3,000 pc)	$ 3,000.00			
Flyer distribution cost	$ 253.00			
Design—class material and printing	$ 3,125.00			
Advance advertising and staff salary	$ 4,800.00			
Total fixed costs	**$14,303.00**			

Variable Costs	Unit Price	Selling Quantity	Per Week	Per Month
Advertising	$800/month		$ 200.00	$ 800.00
Labor cost of marketing	$1,600/month		$ 400.00	$ 1,600.00
Rent—computer and facilities	$650/month		$ 163.00	$ 650.00
Instructor (staff $150/class)	$150/class	1 class/week	$ 150.00	$ 600.00
Instructor (consultant $750/class)	$750/class	1 class/week	$ 750.00	$ 3,000.00
COG-ACCPAC software cost	$8,252.00	1/24 classes	$ 687.67	$ 2,751.00
Labor cost of consulting	$3,808.50	1/24 classes	$ 317.38	$ 1,270.00
Class material	$2.50/class		$ 5.00	$ 20.00
Total variable costs			**$2,673.00**	$10,690.00

FIGURE A3-1. Total Cost, Revenues, and Break-Even Point

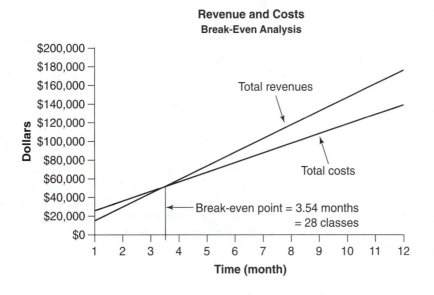

OpenAxis is expected to get its revenue from training classes, ACCPAC sales, and consulting services. The estimation of the breakeven point will be based on time.

As it is readily noticeable from Figure A3-1, the equation of the line that represents Total Revenues is

$$\textbf{Total Revenues} = 14{,}731 * T$$

where **T** is time measured in **months**

The equation of the line in Figure A3-1 that represents Total Costs is

$$\textbf{Total Cost} = \textbf{TFC} + (\textbf{TVC} * T)$$

where **TFC** is **Total Fixed Costs**
TVC is **Total Variable Costs**
T is time measured in **months**

$$\textbf{Total Cost} = 14{,}303 + (10{,}690 * T)$$

The break-even point is measured to be the time it takes for Total Revenues to equal Total Costs.

$$\textbf{Total Revenues} = \textbf{Total Costs}$$
$$14{,}731 * T = 14{,}303 + (10{,}690 * T)$$

Solving for **T** yields **Break-even Point**　　　**T = 3.54 Months**

This means that OpenAxis will arrive at its breakeven point at 3.54 months or after twenty-eight classes. Judging from the financial projections we have made concerning the costs of implementing this marketing plan and the revenues OpenAxis stands to gain from successful implementation, we believe that implementing this marketing plan could prove to be a very successful venture for OpenAxis. From the break-even analysis, we believe that the plan would pay for itself within the first four months of implementation.

Income Statement Projections and Cash Flow Projections

See the attached income statement projections for the years 2002, 2003, 2004, and 2005. Each chart also contains cash flow projections for corresponding years.

BIBLIOGRAPHY

Anthony, Robert N., Hawkins, David F., & Merchant, Kenneth A. *The Nature and Purpose of Accounting.* Accounting test and cases. (Boston: Irwin-McGraw Hill Companies, 1999), p. 10.

Cohen, William A. *Model Business Plan for Service Businesses.* (New York: John Wiley & Sons, 1995), pp. 9.1–9.17.

Cohen, William A. *Model Business Plans for Product Businesses.* (New York: John Wiley & Sons, 1995).

Flaxman, Gary, & Kitchens, Rachelle. "Occupational Outlook." *Los Angeles County: The California Cooperative Occupational Information System.* February 2001. (Long Beach, CA), pp. 18–19.

Keith, Robert M. "Accounting." *World Book Online American Edition.* http://www.aolsvc.world-book.al.com/wbol/wbPage/na/ar/co/002440. Accessed February 4, 2002.

Pride, William, & Ferrell, O. C. *Marketing* (Boston: Houghton Mifflin, 2000).

http://www.accountingsoftwarenews.com.

http://www.accpac.com.

http://www.ci.la.ca.us.

http://www.openaxis.com.

http://www.paloalto.com.

http://www.sec.gov.

NOTES

1. http://www.openaxis.com/solutions.html. Accessed January 25, 2002.
2. http://www.sec.gov/Archives/edgar/data/1063239/0001047469-98-032299.txt. Accessed January 26, 2002.
3. http://www.sec.gov/Archives/edgar/data/1063239/0001047469-98-032299.txt. Accessed January 26, 2002.
4. http://www.mispl.com.sg/Home.asp. Accessed February 11, 2002.

Income Statement Projections—2002

	January	February	March	April	May	June	July	August	September	October	November	December	Year-to-Date
Revenue													
Accounting system training fees						7,960	7,960	7,960	7,960	7,960	7,960	7,960	55,720
ACCPAC Advantage Series sales								12,695			12,695		25,390
Consultant fees								7,617			7,617		15,234
Total Sales	—	—	—	—	—	7,960	7,960	28,272	7,960	7,960	28,272	7,960	96,344
Cost of Goods Sold								8,252			8,252		16,504
Gross Margin from Sales	—	—	—	—	—	7,960	7,960	20,020	7,960	7,960	20,020	7,960	79,840
Operating Expenses													
Setup cost				9,503									9,503
Advertising				800	800	800	800	800	800	800	800	800	7,200
Staff salary				1,600	1,600	2,200	2,200	2,200	2,200	2,200	2,200	2,200	18,600
Rent—computer and facilities						650	650	650	650	650	650	650	4,550
Prof. fee—instructor						3,000	3,000	3,000	3,000	3,000	3,000	3,000	21,000
Prof. fee—consulting								3,809			3,809		7,618
Class material						20	20	20	20	20	20	20	140
Total Operating Expense	—	—	—	11,903	2,400	6,670	6,670	10,479	6,670	6,670	10,479	6,670	68,611
Income Before Tax	—	—	—	(11,903)	(2,400)	1,290	1,290	9,542	1,290	1,290	9,541	1,290	11,230
Income Tax	—	—	—									1,684	1,684
Net Income	—	—	—	(11,903)	(2,400)	1,290	1,290	9,542	1,290	1,290	9,541	(394)	9,545
Cash Flow Projections													
Beginning cash				20,000	8,097	5,697	6,987	8,277	17,819	19,109	20,399	29,940	
Cash receipts				—	—	7,960	7,960	20,020	7,960	7,960	20,020	7,960	
Cash paid out													
Operating expenses				11,903	2,400	6,670	6,670	10,479	6,670	6,670	10,479	6,670	
Accounts payable													
Dividend													
Income taxes												1,684	
Total Cash Out	—	—	—	11,903	2,400	6,670	6,670	10,479	6,670	6,670	10,479	8,354	
Net Cash Flow	—	—	—	(11,903)	(2,400)	1,290	1,290	9,542	1,290	1,290	9,541	(394)	
Ending Cash	—	—	—	8,097	5,697	6,987	8,277	17,819	19,109	20,399	29,940	29,545	

Income Statement Projections—2003

	January	February	March	April	May	June	July	August	September	October	November	December	Year-to-Date
Revenue													
Accounting system training fees	7,960	7,960	7,960	7,960	7,960	11,940	11,940	11,940	11,940	11,940	11,940	11,940	123,380
ACCPAC Advantage Series sales		12,695			12,695		12,695			12,695			50,780
Consultant fees	1,000	8,617	1,000	1,000	9,617	2,000	9,617	2,000	2,000	9,617	2,000	2,000	50,468
Total Sales	**8,960**	**29,272**	**8,960**	**8,960**	**30,272**	**13,940**	**34,252**	**13,940**	**13,940**	**34,252**	**13,940**	**13,940**	**224,628**
Cost of Goods Sold		8,252			8,252		8,252			8,252			33,008
Gross Margin from Sales	8,960	21,020	8,960	8,960	22,020	13,940	26,000	13,940	13,940	26,000	13,940	13,940	191,620
Operating Expenses													
Setup cost													
Advertising	800	800	800	800	800	800	800	800	800	800	800	800	9,600
Staff salary	2,200	2,200	2,200	2,200	2,200	3,080	3,080	3,080	3,080	3,080	3,080	3,080	32,560
Rent—computer and facilities	650	650	650	650	650	650	650	650	650	650	650	650	7,800
Prof. fee—instructor	3,000	3,000	3,000	3,000	3,000	3,000	3,000	3,000	3,000	3,000	3,000	3,000	36,000
Prof. fee—consulting		3,809			3,809		3,809			3,809			15,236
Class material	20	20	20	20	20	30	30	30	30	30	30	30	310
Total Operating Expense	**6,670**	**10,479**	**6,670**	**6,670**	**10,479**	**7,560**	**11,369**	**7,560**	**7,560**	**11,369**	**7,560**	**7,560**	**101,506**
Income Before Tax	**2,290**	**10,541**	**2,290**	**2,290**	**11,541**	**6,380**	**14,631**	**6,380**	**6,380**	**14,631**	**6,380**	**6,380**	**90,114**
Income Tax			2,722			3,638			8,217			8,217	22,794
Net Income	**2,290**	**10,541**	**(432)**	**2,290**	**11,541**	**2,742**	**14,631**	**6,380**	**(1,837)**	**14,631**	**6,380**	**(1,837)**	**67,320**
Cash Flow Projections													
Beginning cash	29,545	26,835	32,376	26,944	24,234	30,775	28,517	38,148	39,528	32,691	42,322	43,702	
Cash receipts	8,960	21,020	8,960	8,960	22,020	13,940	26,000	13,940	13,940	26,000	13,940	13,940	
Cash paid out													
Operating expenses	6,670	10,479	6,670	6,670	10,479	7,560	11,369	7,560	7,560	11,369	7,560	7,560	
Accounts payable	5,000	5,000	5,000	5,000	5,000	5,000	5,000	5,000	5,000	5,000	5,000	5,000	
Dividend													
Income taxes			2,722			3,638			8,217			8,217	
Total Cash Out	11,670	15,479	14,392	11,670	15,479	16,198	16,369	12,560	20,777	16,369	12,560	20,777	
Net Cash Flow	(2,710)	5,541	(5,432)	(2,710)	6,541	(2,258)	9,631	1,380	(6,837)	9,631	1,380	(6,837)	
Ending Cash	26,835	32,376	26,944	24,234	30,775	28,517	38,148	39,528	32,691	42,322	43,702	36,865	

Income Statement Projections—2004

	January	February	March	April	May	June	July	August	September	October	November	December	Year-to-Date
Revenue													
Accounting system training fees	11,940	11,940	11,940	11,940	11,940	15,920	15,920	15,920	15,920	15,920	15,920	15,920	171,140
ACCPAC Advantage Series sales	12,695		12,695			12,695		12,695		12,695			63,475
Consultant fees	10,617	3,000	10,617	3,000	3,000	10,617	4,000	11,617	4,000	11,617	4,000	4,000	80,085
Total Sales	**35,252**	**14,940**	**35,252**	**14,940**	**14,940**	**39,232**	**19,920**	**40,232**	**19,920**	**40,232**	**19,920**	**19,920**	**314,700**
Cost of Goods Sold	8,252		8,252			8,252		8,252		8,252			41,260
Gross Margin from Sales	27,000	14,940	27,000	14,940	14,940	30,980	19,920	31,980	19,920	31,980	19,920	19,920	273,440
Operating Expenses													
Setup cost													
Advertising	800	800	800	800	800	800	800	800	800	800	800	800	9,600
Staff salary	3,080	3,080	3,080	3,080	3,080	5,874	5,874	5,874	5,874	5,874	5,874	5,874	56,518
Rent—computer and facilities	650	650	650	650	650	650	650	650	650	650	650	650	7,800
Prof. fee—instructor	3,000	3,000	3,000	3,000	3,000	3,000	3,000	3,000	3,000	3,000	3,000	3,000	36,000
Prof. fee—consulting	3,809		3,809			3,809		3,809	3,809	3,809			19,045
Class material	30	30	30	30	30	40	40	40	40	40	40	40	430
Total Operating Expense	**11,369**	**7,560**	**11,369**	**7,560**	**7,560**	**14,173**	**10,364**	**14,173**	**10,364**	**14,173**	**10,364**	**10,364**	**129,393**
Income Before Tax	**15,631**	**7,380**	**15,631**	**7,380**	**7,380**	**16,807**	**9,556**	**17,807**	**9,556**	**17,807**	**9,556**	**9,556**	**144,047**
Income Tax			6,956			7,892			11,076			14,029	39,952
Net Income	**15,631**	**7,380**	**8,675**	**7,380**	**7,380**	**8,915**	**9,556**	**17,807**	**(1,520)**	**17,807**	**9,556**	**(4,473)**	**104,095**
Cash Flow Projections													
Beginning cash	36,865	44,496	43,876	44,551	43,931	43,311	44,226	45,782	55,589	46,070	55,877	57,433	
Cash receipts	27,000	14,940	27,000	14,940	14,940	30,980	19,920	31,980	19,920	31,980	19,920	19,920	
Cash paid out													
Operating expenses	11,369	7,560	11,369	7,560	7,560	14,173	10,364	14,173	10,364	14,173	10,364	10,364	
Accounts payable													
Dividend	8,000	8,000	8,000	8,000	8,000	8,000	8,000	8,000	8,000	8,000	8,000	8,000	
Income taxes			6,956			7,892			11,076			14,029	
Total Cash Out	19,369	15,560	26,325	15,560	15,560	30,065	18,364	22,173	29,440	22,173	18,364	32,393	
Net Cash Flow	7,631	(620)	675	(620)	(620)	915	1,556	9,807	(9,520)	9,807	1,556	(12,473)	
Ending Cash	44,496	43,876	44,551	43,931	43,311	44,226	45,782	55,589	46,070	55,877	57,433	44,959	

Income Statement Projections—2005

	January	February	March	April	May	June	July	August	September	October	November	December	Year-to-Date
Revenue													
Accounting system training fees	15,920	15,920	15,920	15,920	15,920	19,900	19,900	19,900	19,900	19,900	19,900	19,900	218,900
ACCPAC Advantage Series sales	12,695	—	—	12,695	—	12,695	—	12,695	—	12,695	—	12,695	76,170
Consultant fees	12,617	5,000	5,000	12,617	5,000	12,617	6,000	13,617	6,000	13,617	6,000	6,000	104,085
Total Sales	**41,232**	**20,920**	**20,920**	**41,232**	**20,920**	**45,212**	**25,900**	**46,212**	**25,900**	**46,212**	**25,900**	**38,595**	**399,155**
Cost of Goods Sold	8,252			8,252		8,252		8,252		8,252		—	41,260
Gross Margin from Sales	32,980	20,920	20,920	32,980	20,920	36,960	25,900	37,960	25,900	37,960	25,900	38,595	357,895
Operating Expenses													
Setup cost													
Advertising	800	800	800	800	800	800	800	800	800	800	800	800	9,600
Staff salary	5,874	5,874	5,874	5,874	5,874	7,260	7,260	7,260	7,260	7,260	7,260	7,260	80,190
Rent—computer and facilities	650	650	650	650	650	650	650	650	650	650	650	650	7,800
Prof. fee—instructor	3,000	3,000	3,000	3,000	3,000	3,000	3,000	3,000	3,000	3,000	3,000	3,000	36,000
Prof. fee—consulting	3,809			3,809		3,809		3,809		3,809		3,809	22,854
Class material	40	40	40	40	40	50	50	50	50	50	50	50	550
Total Operating Expense	**14,173**	**10,364**	**10,364**	**14,173**	**10,364**	**15,569**	**11,760**	**15,569**	**11,760**	**15,569**	**11,760**	**15,569**	**156,994**
Income Before Tax	18,807	10,556	10,556	18,807	10,556	21,391	14,140	22,391	14,140	22,391	14,140	23,026	200,901
Income Tax			7,185			12,689			15,201			22,632	57,707
Net Income	**18,807**	**10,556**	**3,371**	**18,807**	**10,556**	**8,703**	**14,140**	**22,391**	**(1,061)**	**22,391**	**14,140**	**394**	**143,194**
Cash Flow Projections													
Beginning cash	44,959	53,766	54,322	47,693	56,500	57,056	55,759	59,899	72,290	61,228	73,619	77,759	
Cash receipts	32,980	20,920	20,920	32,980	20,920	36,960	25,900	37,960	25,900	37,960	25,900	38,595	
Cash paid out													
Operating expenses	14,173	10,364	10,364	14,173	10,364	15,569	11,760	15,569	11,760	15,569	11,760	15,569	
Accounts payable													
Dividend	10,000	10,000	10,000	10,000	10,000	10,000	10,000	10,000	10,000	10,000	10,000	10,000	
Income taxes	—	—	7,185	—	—	12,689	—	—	15,201	—	—	22,632	
Total Cash Out	24,173	20,364	27,549	24,173	20,364	38,258	21,760	25,569	36,961	25,569	21,760	48,201	
Net Cash Flow	8,807	556	(6,629)	8,807	556	(1,298)	4,140	12,391	(11,061)	12,391	4,140	(9,606)	
Ending Cash	53,766	54,322	47,693	56,500	57,056	55,759	59,899	72,290	61,228	73,619	77,759	68,154	

A4

MCM POWERSPORTS

Developed by
MISTY IWATSU
AHMET MURAT MENDI
CAROLINE YEUNG

Contents

EXECUTIVE SUMMARY

MCM Powersports will be a Los Angeles–based, privately held new service corporation promoting offshore endurance racing for the Personal Watercraft and Mini Jet boat industries. It will plan and coordinate a National Tour for the powersports racing industry in nine states and ten racing locations per year. The company's competitive advantage is that it will be the first and only sanctioned promoter in the market of PWC and Mini Jet boat endurance racing at a national level.

Each of the owners will invest $5,000 as capital for start-up costs and predicted cash shortages due to the cyclical nature of the business. MCM Powersports' main source of fund income will be from sponsorships through local and national corporations, ticket sales, and parking space fees and loans.

MCM Powersports has analyzed the PWC industry, and through secondary research, the findings are as follows: predicted sales are estimated to grow 12 percent annually through the year 2000. PWC will be the entry-level product purchase for most consumers rather than larger, more traditional watercrafts. An estimated amount of more than two million PWCs are currently being used in U.S. waters. This incredible rate of market growth also boosts the demand for PWC racing. Current promoters are far away from fulfilling the existing needs of the market, especially in endurance racing.

Start-up costs are estimated to be $124,440. The break-even dollar value for the corporation is $3,081,826. The firm expects to break even by twelve months. The return on investment is expected to be 61 percent and 72 percent in years 2 and 3 respectively, and a cash flow of $186,431 is projected by the first year of operation.

INTRODUCTION

Within the last decade, the number of Personal Watercraft (PWC) enthusiasts who demand an environment to test their skills and to compete with other PWC enthusiasts has increased dramatically. This created a great opportunity for an industry where promoters of the sport could conduct races all over the United States. MCM Powersports will be established as a Los Angeles-based offshore endurance promoter that conducts a

National Tour for the PWC and Mini Jet Boat endurance racing industries. The races will be longer than closed-course races since they measure the racer's endurance level rather than their speed. MCM Powersports will run both the Amateur and pro divisions in PWC and Mini Jet Boats, as well as free-style competition. MCM Powersports will tour nine states, ten racing spots per year, which are planned as follows: Northern California, Southern California, Colorado, Florida, Illinois, New Jersey, Ohio, Texas, Virginia, and Washington. MCM Powersports' objective is to foster and encourage competition, as it will give riders and enthusiasts of all skill levels the opportunity to test themselves in regulated, safe environments.

MCM Powersports plans to contact local and national associations, manufacturers, dealerships as well as other companies that are leaders in their industry and are interested in sponsoring sport activities to sponsor part of the events' funding. In return, the sponsors will have the opportunity to display new products/services to approximately forty thousand people per event or four hundred thousand total at the booths that MCM Powersports will provide. The tour will be nationally televised, and the sponsors will have numerous opportunities to advertise their name during all ten events (see Appendix A).

SITUATIONAL ANALYSIS

Situation Environs

Business Conditions   The first PWC was introduced as a stand-up model in 1968 by Clayton Jacobson II. Kawasaki, in 1975, launched the first mass produced stand-up model for the consumer market. Over the past three decades, several manufacturers have entered the market. The five biggest are Yamaha, Bombardier, Kawasaki, Polaris, and Tigershark.

PWC use has dramatically increased over the past few years. Today, there are more than two million watercraft registered in the United States. PWC sales, in dollar terms, were estimated to grow at a 12 percent annual rate through the year 2000 and will turn out to be the entry-level product for larger, more traditional craft like boats.

The value of PWC shipments, excluding Mini Jet Boats, was forecast to almost double from $364 million in 1995 to $660 million in 2000. The total U.S. recreational boating market, including propulsion systems and accessories, will increase at approximately an 8 percent annual rate through the year 2005, from almost $9.5 billion in sales in 1995, to $13.6 billion in 2000 and $19.6 billion in 2005.

As the number of PWC enthusiasts proliferate, the number of people who want to test their PWCs as well as their skills will also increase. Under the current situation, the existing promoters are far from fulfilling the existing needs of the market, especially in endurance racing due to limitations such as finances, lack of knowledge, and lack of manpower.

State of Technology   Last year, forty-seven new models of PWC were offered on the market. Models have evolved from two-seaters to three-seaters. In addition, the newer models are faster and safer, where the watercraft can move to speeds in excess of 70 mph and is equipped with a lanyard-type engine cutoff switch. This results in an increasing number of categories in which PWC enthusiasts can race.

Currently, none of the promoters in the industry use technology efficiently to improve their services, such as electronic scoring, which is crucial in getting accurate race results to satisfy customer needs.

Demand Trends   Demand for owning one or more PWC as well as using them as both racing and recreational purposes is much stronger than the demand trend for all other types of boats. Affordability (average price is approximately $5,700), high performance, and maneuverability have brought scores of new customers into the PWC market. Consumers want to enjoy using their PWC and demand new and improved products with better and more efficient features (top speed, predictable handling, and comfort).

Laws and Regulations   As the number of PWC on the water increases, public concerns about pollution and noise, accidents related to careless usage, speeding, and increasing number of fatal injuries have come to the forefront in media and legislation. These factors forced a majority of the states to take restrictive actions against the use of PWC in the local waterways. The current trend of increasing regulations and bans on the usage of PWC may have a direct and indirect adverse effect on MCM Powersports.

PWC are subject to the same rules and requirements as any other powerboats plus additional requirements specific to PWC due to its maneuverability, speed, and limited protection, which can be a dangerous combination for the racers as well as for other people using the same waterways. In addition to the general regulations in effect for motorboats, PWC racing promoters must also be aware that there are local laws and ordinances around the country that regulate racing conditions. There are many primary regulations that MCM Powersports as a race promoter will have to enforce and abide by. A few provisions include: all racers must wear U.S. Coast Guard–approved personal flotation devices; a PWC cannot be operated from one half hour after sunset to one half hour before sunrise; and a lanyard-type engine cutoff switch must be attached to the racer.[1] For a detailed list of other regulations that MCM Powersports will have to enforce, please refer to Appendix B.

Neutral Environs

There are many organizations that have concerns about the use of PWC. They include such groups as the Environmental Protection Agency, Personal Watercraft Industry Association (PWIA), environmental interest groups, and other organizations. Each has its own concerns and could help or hinder MCM Powersports.

Environmental Issues   The PWC racing industry has been attacked over many environmental issues, such as toxic pollutants released into the environment by their use. As a result, MCM Powersports will have to force racers to refuel on land to reduce chances of gas spillage into the water, and to check and clean their engines well away from shorelines.

Another concern is turbidity. In shallow waters where PWCs can easily operate, the bottom becomes stirred up, suspending sediment that cuts down on light penetration and depletes oxygen. This can affect bird and fish feeding.

Vegetation is another concern for environmental issues. In coastal areas, MCM Powersports will be aware of low tide. Low water levels expose sea grass beds and other delicate vegetation. Disturbances can cause erosion and long-lasting damage.

A PWC near shore can also interrupt feeding and nesting wildlife, and cause animals to deviate from their normal behavior, which is illegal. Mammals such as otters, manatees, and whales can be injured by direct contact with a boat, and it is believed that the noise from watercraft can adversely influence breeding cycles and cause birth defects.

Personal Watercraft Industry Association (PWIA)   The Personal Watercraft Industry Association (PWIA) was formed in 1987 as an affiliate of the National Marine Manufacturers Association. It was created to bring together companies that manufacture or distribute PWC in order to promote safe and responsible operation. The PWIA is actively involved in numerous consumer education and informational campaigns designed to raise awareness about proper operation of and regard for safety, and appropriate behavior. In addition, it monitors local issues; race promoters and its members strive to work proactively to minimize waterway-use conflicts. Therefore, it will closely monitor MCM Powersports' operations to ensure it is promoting proper operation in regard to safety and appropriate behavior during the course of its race tours and competitive events.

U.S. Park Service The U.S. National Park Service is under pressure from the National Parks and Conservation Association (NPCA) to regulate PWC. (NPCA is a private special interest group of park patrons.) As a result, the U.S. National Park Service is developing new rules to make it easier for PWC to be banned in National Parks. The agency has proposed a rule that would direct local park officials to determine the appropriateness of PWC use in each park and restrict or ban the boats if necessary. There has been a growing concern among many park superintendents about the impact of PWC on the tranquility of parks. This will hinder MCM Powersports, since it will be prohibited from promoting racing events in parks.

TARGET MARKET

Demographics

The target audience for MCM Powersports are single men between the ages of twenty-one and thirty-nine years old, with an average annual household income of $60,000 and over.[2]

Psychographics

The majority of PWC owners use their PWC for recreational riding; 9 percent of the PWC owners race and 16 percent of all PWC owners belong to some type of PWC club or association. In addition, MCM Powersports will provide a Web site as a part of its customer service, since two-thirds of the target market have computers and 78 percent use modems.[3]

Geographics

MCM Powersports will tour nine states, ten racing spots per year, which are planned as follows: San Francisco, California; Orange County, California; Boulder, Colorado; Orlando, Florida; Chicago, Illinois; Seaside Heights, New Jersey; Cincinnati, Ohio; Dallas, Texas; Virginia Beach, Virginia; and Richland, Washington. MCM Powersports will use the IJSBA Regional Breakdown list and provide at least one event in each region.

Product Usage

There are more than 2.4 million watercraft registered in the United States. There are potentially two million owners. The target market may initially buy PWC for themselves; however, statistics show that 32 percent[4] of watercraft owners share their PWC with family and friends. MCM Powersports will have a potential market of 2.6 million people.

Competitor and Company Environs

Company	Current Strategy	Strengths	Weaknesses	Competitive Advantage	Pricing
International Jet Sports Boating Association (IJSBA)	1. Looks for new ways to promote the sport 2. Increases exposure for sponsors and the participants 3. Provides an expansive media package for their sponsors and racers 4. Expands the scope and reach of their TV package for 1998 5. Continues cooperative relationships with regional event promoters	1. Well known in the industry for conducting national closed-course racing tours 2. As the international sanctioning organization, it promotes PWC racing	1. Lacks knowledge and experience of setting up endurance races as it solely sets up closed course races 2. There is a conflict of interest. IJSBA is the sanctioning organization as well as a race promoter. Its own interests can interfere with their neutrality toward governing PWC issues	1. As the international sanctioning organization, it promotes PWC racing	$20/day for spectator, $10/day for parking
Baja Promotions Racing (BP Racing)	1. Relies heavily on publicity and race coverage in featured magazines 2. Relies on radio and TV programs 3. Utilizes extensive and accurate computerized scoring programs	1. Well known in the industry 2. Has diverse business activities to help eliminate cash-flow shortages from the cyclical nature of the business 3. Had experience in holding endurance races	1. Has, other businesses aside, not concentrated solely on PWC race promoting 2. Does not have the ability or the expertise in setting up large events 3. Does not advertise; relies solely on publicity	1. First regional offshore endurance race promoter	No areas for spectator viewing
CT Sports	1. Relies on word of mouth 2. Publishes own newsletter once a month	1. Well known in the industry 2. Has a strong financial support 3. Experience in holding closed-course races	1. New at setting up endurance races. It is very expensive, and time consuming to organize 2. Does not have the ability or the expertise in setting up large events	1. In business over 10 years	No areas for spectator viewing

Competitor and Company Environs (continued)

Company	Current Strategy	Strengths	Weaknesses	Competitive Advantage	Pricing
MCM Power-sports	1. New entrant into the industry 2. Corporate structure enables the transfer of ownership to a third party easily in case of financial difficulty. Hence, the exit strategy would be to transfer the ownership to another promoter in case of financial distress.	1. Advantages of being a corporation: limited liability, specialized management, easy to raise capital, unlimited life, ease of ownership transferability to avoid double taxation 2. Misty Iwatsu and Taylor LeClaire: years of racing and promoting experience 3. Implements the latest technology 4. Has strong image positioning	1. Organizing a corporation is complicated, costly, and time-consuming 2. Corporations are bombarded with more government rules and regulations than are the sole proprietorship or partnership	1. First into the national PWC endurance racing market 2. Will audit accounts once a year 3. Environmentally conscious company 4. High-quality event 5. Affordable prices 6. New products are shown at each event for purchase 7. Extensive TV coverage 8. Leader in technology 9. Misty Iwatsu and Taylor LeClaire: years of racing and promoting experience 10. Has strong image positioning	<u>1998</u> 1 Day: Ticket—$7 Parking—$5 Two Day: Ticket—$10 Parking—$8 <u>1999</u> One Day: Ticket—$8 Parking—$5 Two-Day: Ticket—$12 Parking—$8 <u>2000</u> Two-Day: Ticket—$9 Parking—$5 Two-day: Ticket—$15 Parking—$8

PROBLEMS, THREATS, AND OPPORTUNITIES

Problems

Problems that may be encountered in the Mini Jet Boat and the PWC industries are:

- Upcoming regulations of PWC and Mini Jet Boats.

  Since there are 2.4 million PWC operated annually, and the Mini Jet Boat has just surfaced in the market, laws and regulations will be more stringent. This is due to organizations wanting to ban PWC in lakes, oceans, and waterways. To help stop the bans, MCM Powersports will provide an opportunity for watercraft enthusiasts to be heard by placing a booth where people can write to their legislator. They will also be able to sign petitions to stop bans on their favorite lake or waterway.

- High injury rate for the PWC and Mini Jet Boats.

  The injury rate has gone down during the last year. However, the negligent use of PWC by uneducated users has provided a serious concern for the sport of watercraft riding. MCM Powersports will help the PWC industry by offering water safety certificate courses free of charge. Each person attending the program will receive a certificate stating that they completed the water safety course provided by the U.S. Coast Guard.

There are many environmental issues that may become problems for MCM Powersports. They are the following:

- A concern is turbidity.

  To avoid it, MCM Powersports will encourage its racers to operate their PWC in deeper water. If racers do have to traverse shallow water, they should run at idle speed.

- PWC can interrupt feeding and nesting wildlife, as well as disturb water fowl and other marine animals, which causes animals to deviate from their normal behavior, and is illegal.

  MCM Powersports will abide by state-enacted noise ordinances/legislation and help to reduce the noise pollution that could cause harmful results to various marine life.

Threats

- Inclement weather may become a threat for MCM Powersports.

  People may not be willing to attend an open-air event if it is raining. To handle this threat, it may be necessary to keep extra tarps and canopies available for distribution to vendors and to put on the stands for spectators.

- New promoters may try to capitalize on the events.

  To handle this threat, MCM Powersports will invite local promoters to participate in the event. MCM Powersports will gain valuable experience from other promoters and promote a positive presence to the industry.

- MCM Powersports will be vulnerable to inflation or depression.

  If the discretionary income becomes tighter, MCM Powersports will streamline costs to be even more cost-effective. During depressionary or inflationary conditions, the first thing people cut from their spending is the expensive leisure activities. MCM Powersports will try to overcome this problem by implementing an affordable ticket policy. (See Appendix C.)

- There may also be other major trade shows, such as car shows, in the area operating at the same time as an MCM Powersports event.

  MCM Powersports will provide space for its sponsors as well as other PWC manufacturers and local dealers to display their new product offerings from PWC to Mini Jet Boats and their accessories. This allows sponsors to reach their consumers without extra cost.

Opportunities

- The need in the market for a national endurance race tour is not currently being met.

  Several regional promoters are holding local offshore endurance races, but they do not have the technical knowledge or support to put on an event of this magnitude. MCM Powersports is a premier promoter, so it will be able to support and advance the sport of offshore endurance racing to the national level.

- The media is a powerful force that can influence society as a whole.

  In order to use the power of the media, contributing reporters will write stories for all the PWC magazines and newspapers across the country. Press releases will be implemented to provide maximum coverage for the event. This will enable free publicity for the company as well as PWC endurance racing.

- The staff has firsthand knowledge of the PWC industry, racing, and promotion.

  Several members of MCM Powersports have been in the PWC industry for several years and are well known in the industry. Through networking and other race events, several members of MCM Powersports have been mentioned in magazines and newspapers. This can enable MCM Powersports to find sponsors and raise capital to support its activities easier than expected.

- MCM Powersports will provide the latest technology through the integrated technology systems that will be developed.

  MCM Powersports will be able to capture all of the PWC enthusiasts who come to the events for further development of mailing lists and to segment the target population by advertising to them directly. With the use of laptops, the site event crew can maintain contact with the home office via e-mail. MCM Powersports will use the latest technology in scoring the races. A Web page will also be set up where PWC enthusiasts can not only find the latest news about events and activities, but also find the latest developments in laws and regulations, technology, and product offerings of major manufacturers. MCM Powersports will also provide an e-mail address for people to make comments, suggestions, or ask questions that MCM Powersports will answer.

- MCM Powersports can easily adapt to change.

  Being a relatively small company, MCM Powersports does not have a large bureaucracy, nor will it allow itself to be set in its ways. MCM Powersports wants to provide premier watercraft racing at a low cost for the whole family. In order to be able to do this, it must be able to adapt to the needs of the target market.

- MCM Powersports will just specialize in promoting endurance race nationally, which will enhance specialization.

MARKETING OBJECTIVE AND GOALS

Mission Statement

To market and grow as the only existing national offshore racing promotions company in the United States while continuously improving consumer attractiveness and profitability.

Objectives

- Establish a premier national offshore endurance race series.
- Be the number-one promoter in the United States and bring promoting to a new level of competition.
- Achieve maximum return of investment by keeping costs low and promoting heavily.
- Achieve high audience participation.
- Provide cost-effective entertainment for the whole family.
- Promote and function as an environmentally conscious company.
- Provide a commodity for sponsors and investors by hiring an independent auditing firm to report to them.
- Break even by the end of the first year.
- Create a healthy organizational structure with an effective, loyal sponsorship, and establish necessary networking connections for the future success of the firm.
- Expand the tour to twelve events from ten by the end of the third year.

Goals

- Achieve break-even at $3,081,826 by the end of the first year.
- MCM Powersports' staff expects to gain experience, discover and remedy any unforeseen problems with operations, marketing, and sales.
- MCM Powersports will have a goal of forty thousand spectators with five thousand cars per event.
- MCM Powersports expects to have eighty racers per event.
- Achieve the following returns on investment per year, which is calculated by the ratio of net income to average total assets:

Year 1:	Year 2:	Year 3:
ROA: 3%	ROA: 61%	ROA: 72%
Profits: $1,958	Profits: $156,306	Profits: $435,380

- Its long-term goals are to create a strong financial structure and a strong image/position among the industry and among PWC enthusiasts by increasing its total assets to $866,432.
- Improve the negative images of PWC through incorporating safety classes and community involvement. This will bring awareness to safe PWC operations.
- Help watercraft enthusiasts ages sixteen and over at all skill levels compete in a safe racing environment.
- Promote the sport of PWC racing as a fun event for everyone to enjoy.

MARKETING STRATEGY

- MCM Powersports will be first in the market. Spectators and businesses will see and test out these events for further participation and support.
- The niche market for MCM Powersports will also be the target market. There are currently over 2.6 million people in this market to advertise to.
- MCM Powersports can capitalize on the unique expertise of the management team. Misty Iwatsu and Taylor LeClaire have been able to make many contacts in the PWC industry and have numerous years of racing experience.

- MCM Powersports will have the financial resources of a corporation. By being a corporation, it will provide numerous benefits and compete at a level no other promoter can match.
- MCM Powersports will position itself as affordable family entertainment with spectator participation for the general public and a premier race promoter to the race participants and sponsors by offering low prices and high-quality entertainment.

MARKET TACTICS

Product

The following classes have been set for amateurs: Open, 785, Sport, Ski, Women, Veterans, Free-style, Mini Jet Boat 1 engine, and Mini Jet Boat 2 engines. The following program for Pros is as follows: Open, 785, Sport, Ski, Women's, Veterans, Freestyle, Mini Jet Boats 1 engine, and Mini Jet Boats 2 engine.

For spectator entertainment, the course will be set up as an extended closed course. It will be approximately a two-mile track. There will be two options set up for the amateurs, which consist of option 1, fewer buoy turns but longer distance, and option 2, more buoy turns but shorter distance. In the Pro course setup there will be four options: options 1 and 2 are the same as above, and option 3 is going a longer distance around buoys, or option 4, which is jumping a ramp. (See Appendix D.)

For audience participation, MCM Powersports will select five volunteers to judge the free-style competition each day. MCM Powersports will provide a twenty-minute training program on the difficulty ratings of each maneuver performed. In return for their participation, MCM Powersports will offer them free gifts. The compound will be set up for ease of traffic flow and high visibility of the racecourse.

MCM Powersports will be the leader in technological advances since it will use magnetic stripe cards for its race and audience participants. Each person will be able to swipe his/her card to enter raffles, to vote for his/her favorite racer, and to visit booths. As each person swipes his/her card, pertinent and crucial information such as name, telephone number, address, and identification number (if applicable), as well as psychographic and behavioral data will be recorded on a database system for organizing better events in the future. This database will also create an opportunity to rent the names to mailing-list companies, major PWC manufacturers, and local dealers for additional income.

Place

Because a service is intangible, unlike physical products, it needs personal contact with its customers. Therefore, MCM Powersports will implement a direct channel of distribution to reach its target market.

MCM Powersports will be conducting its racing across the United States in ten different locations. Each location will consist of a two-day event. The first day will be amateur racing, and the second day will be pro racing.

In order to meet the demands of the different segments of its target market and to challenge the participants, MCM Powersports will conduct its races in several kinds of waterways. In choosing the waterways, MCM Powersports will give the maximum importance to protecting nature and the environment.

Promotion

Being an environmentally sound company, MCM Powersports will organize two beach clean-ups to promote the clean environment—one before the event starts, to have a fresh startup, and one after the event is over, to clean up the mess we caused. To help implement this, MCM Powersports plans to contact local colleges and universities for volunteers to help make these events a success.

MCM Powersports will emphasize keeping the waterways safe; hence, it will host water-safety courses offered by the U.S. Coast Guard. The course teaches people safe boating habits and will be offered several times during the weekend. Each person completing the course will receive a certificate of completion. This will enable the watercraft community to create a positive image to the public in addition to providing a public service for the industry. The goal for the first year will be to award 100 certificates, and 150 and 200 certificates for the second and third years, respectively.

MCM Powersports plans to contact local dealerships, the Chamber of Commerce, local businesses, and local promoters to help assist in the events, to give them a new outlet for advertising, and to offer them forty thousand potential new contacts for their business.

As part of the added promotion benefits, MCM Powersports plans on having a meet and greet event for the racers and manufacturers. At each event there will be a different pro racer and manufacturer for a question-and-answer period to answer questions about themselves and the products they sell. The registration for pros will be kept to a minimum during the first year with a 100 percent pro payback purse for the first-place winners. This is to entice professional riders to attend the events and attract more spectators.

Taking the seasonality of the product into consideration, ten months a year the company is planning to advertise heavily in PWC magazines such as *Splash, Personal Watercraft Illustrated, Watercraft World,* and *Jet Sports,* on local radio stations, and on local cable TV stations carrying ESPN, ESPN2, FoxSports, and Sports Network prior to and during the events, as well as conducting live interviews.

MCM Powersports will also use direct mail campaigns from lists provided by the IJSBA and DMV boater registration to inform potential consumers of the events and Web site where they can receive the latest up-to-date information on each event.

MCM Powersports will hire an independent firm to audit the financial accounts once a year. In addition, an annual report will be issued for its sponsors to explain the activities done and where the money was spent.

Price

MCM Powersports learned from competitors' mistakes of pricing too high. MCM Powersports will be able to reduce risk by entering at a low price. In addition, being first in the market will discourage competition. See Appendix C for ticket and booth prices.

ORGANIZATION, EVALUATION, CONTROL, AND IMPLEMENTATION

Organization

The company will have four managing partners:

Misty L. Iwatsu, President	A. Murat Mendi, VP of Finance
Taylor LeClaire, VP of Operations	Caroline Yeung, VP of Marketing

Detailed organizational chart and product development schedule can be found in the Appendix (see Appendices E and F).

Break-Even Analysis

The following assumptions are used to calculate the break-even point: In calculating the unit price, the money from sponsors, accessory sales, and video cassette sales was deducted from total revenues. The revenue used to calculate unit price is found as $3,779,600. Since the assumptions are that the total number of participants will be 400,000 and cars coming will be 50,000, and other items will have 1,109, it is assumed that total units involved will be 451,109. Therefore, the unit income will be:

$$\frac{\$3,779,600}{451,109} = \$8.38$$

MCM Powersports has found that variable cost will be $631,342. This figure was divided into total units involved. Therefore, the unit variable cost will be:

$$\frac{\$631,342}{451,109} = \$1.40$$

After calculating the unit revenue, unit cost, and fixed cost, the break-even point was found by using the following formula:

$$BE = \frac{FC}{P - VC}$$

Then, percentages of each item such as ticket sales revenues and parking fee revenues in total revenues are used to break down this figure. The following table summarizes the results.

Break-Even Analysis		Break Down of Break-Even Figure	
Average price per unit	$8.38	# of tickets sold	39,156 (88.67%)
Average variable cost per unit	$1.40	# of parking spaces sold	4,894 (11.08%)
Fixed Cost	$3,081,826	# of racers registered	59 (0.13%)
Break-Even Point	44,159	# of booths rented	49 (0.11%)
		# of mailing lists rented	1 (0.00%)

Cash Flow

Pro forma cash flows have been calculated for 36 months. The following figures are found as year-end cash flows for three years (see Appendix G).

Year 1:	**Year 2:**	**Year 3:**
$186,431	$618,122	$1,459,702

Profit-and-Loss Statement

Pro forma income (profit-and-loss) statements have been prepared to figure out the net income for each year. Findings are summarized below (see Appendix H).

$1,958 **(year 1)** $156,306 **(year 2)** $435,380 **(year 3)**

Balance Sheets

Pro forma balance sheets are prepared for three years. The depreciation of the fixed assets is calculated using the straight-line method over a period of three years. Total assets of the company will be (see Appendix H):

$147,640 **(year 1)** $378,002 **(year 2)** $866,432 **(year 3)**

SUMMARY

MCM Powersports will be a premier promoter in the United States and expects to be successful in the business by promoting and implementing the strategies that will take advantage of the expertise found in all of the partners.

Through the mission statement, MCM Powersports hopes to have a competitive advantage over other promoters in the United States.

By making the initial investment, MCM Powersports hopes to attract sponsors and venture capitalists to invest in the organization. Each partner will invest $5,000 in order to cover part of the start-up costs. Net income for each year would be:

- $1,958 (year 1)
- $156,306 (year 2)
- $435,380 (year 3)

MCM Powersports' competitive advantage is that it will tap into the PWC endurance racing market, which other competitors have not done. In addition, MCM Powersports will be the only IJSBA-sanctioned national offshore endurance race promoter. The company will be able to gain in this market and cater to PWC enthusiasts who seek the thrill and competitive edge of endurance races.

BIBLIOGRAPHY

Alger, A. "Here They Come Again (Controversy over the Use of the Jet Skis)," *Forbes* (June 3, 1996), p. 182.

Alger, A., and Flanigan, W. G. "Snowmobiles of the Sea," *Forbes* (August 28, 1995), p. 304.

Argetsinger, A. "Deaths Rise as More People Ride the Waves," *Washington Post* (August 27, 1995).

Berkowitz, E. N., Kerin, R., Hartley, S., and Rudelius, W. *Marketing*. Irwin, 1994.

Cohen, William A. *The Marketing Plan*. Wiley, 1995.

Cohen, William A. *Model Business Plans for Service Businesses*. Wiley, 1995.

Department of Boating & Waterways. *PWC News* (Sacramento, CA, 1997), p. 7.

Fiataff, J. "Clearing the Pipeline," *Watercraft Business* (January 1997), p. 2.

Harris, J. C. *Personal Watercraft*. Crestwood House, 1988.

Henschen, D. "New Jersey Passes Mandatory Education: PWC Bill," *Boating Industry* (March 1996), p. 11.

International Jet Sports Boating Association. *1997 Official Competition Rule Book* (Santa Ana, CA, 1997), p. 10.

Media Kit. *Splash Magazine* (1997).

Napier, J. "Napier Predicts Slight Sales Growth in 1997," *Boating Industry* (November 1996).

Paulsen, B. "Squeezing PWC: More States Are Finding Ways to Restrict Their Use," *Yachting* (May 1996), p. 32.

"PWC: Many Challenges in Taking a Line," *Boating Industry* (June 1996), p. 50.

Steven, S. "Water Bikes Are Losing Some Speed." *Wall Street Journal,* September 17, 1996.

Stewart, R. L. "The Wonderful World of 'Wet and Wild' Water-Sports," *Rough Notes* (May 1993), pp. 30–32.

Weeth, C. "Water Events Facing New Environmental Regulations," *Amusement Business* (February 20, 1995), p. 28.

APPENDIX A

$1,000,000 for Title Sponsorship

This is for the title of the tour. This will be one sponsor with no other competing companies. This sponsor will receive the title of the event in their name as well other perks. For example, they will have free booth space and free advertising on all of the materials distributed, and the Web site will feature their name and logo. They will have unlimited access to the VIP booth at all events, as well as all-event access, and free ad space on the TV monitors that will be stationed around the event compound. MCM Powersports will showcase them at all events, and be available for promotional need if necessary. Banners with the sponsor name will be prominently displayed throughout the event, and in addition the buoys at the start/ finish line will feature their name. There will be a hospitality suite available for their use at each of the events. All mass media advertising will prominently display the name of the title sponsor. There will also be numerous benefits other than just the ones stated here.

$500,000 for Exclusive Sponsorship

These will be noncompetitive companies. The benefits for this sponsor are as follows: they will receive free booth space and free advertising on all promotional materials distributed, the Web site will list them as sponsors, and they will have access to the VIP booth at all events as well other perks. For example, they will have free booth space and free advertising on all of the materials distributed, and the Web site will feature their name and logo. They will have unlimited access to the VIP booth at all events as well as all-event access, and they will have free ad space on the TV monitors that will be stationed around the event compound. MCM Powersports will showcase them at all events and be available for promotional needs if necessary. Banners with the sponsor name will be prominently displayed throughout the event, and in addition the buoys at the start/finish line will feature their name. There will be a hospitality suite available for their use at each of the events. All mass media advertising will prominently display the name of the title sponsor. There will also be numerous benefits other than just the ones stated here.

$500,000 for Exclusive Sponsorship

These will be noncompetitive companies. The benefits for this sponsor are as follows: they will receive free booth space, free advertising on all promotional materials distributed, the Web site will list them as sponsors, and they will have access to the VIP booth at all events as well as all event access and free ad space on the TV monitors that will be stationed around the event compound. MCM Powersports will showcase them at all events, and be available for promotional need if necessary. Banners with the sponsor name will be prominently displayed throughout the event and, in addition, some of the buoys will feature their name. There will be a hospitality suite for their use at each of the events. All mass media advertising will display the names of the sponsors. There will also be numerous benefits other than just the ones stated here.

$250,000 for Official Sponsorship

These will be noncompetitive companies. The benefits for this sponsor are as follows: they will receive free booth space and free advertising on all promotional materials distributed, the Web site will list them as sponsors, they will have access to the VIP booth at all events as well as all event access, and they will have several free ad spots on the TV monitors that will be stationed around the event compound. MCM Powersports will announce them at all events. Banners with the sponsor name will be prominently displayed throughout the event, and some buoys will feature their name. There will be a hospitality suite available for their use at each event. All mass media advertising will display the names of the sponsors. There will also be numerous benefits other than just the ones stated here.

$100,000 for Associate Sponsorship

The benefits for this sponsor are as follows: they will receive free booth space and free advertising on all promotional materials distributed, the Web site will list them as sponsors, and they will have limited access to the VIP booth at all events, as well as limited all-event access, and ad space on the TV monitors that will be stationed around the event compound. MCM Powersports will announce them at all events. Banners with the sponsor name will be displayed throughout the event as well as on some of the buoys that will feature their name. There will be a hospitality suite available for their use at each event.

APPENDIX B

Laws and Regulations

Regulations for Race Promoters   The following are the primary regulations that MCM Powersports as a race promoter will have to enforce and abide by:[5]

- PWC racers must wear U.S. Coast Guard–approved personal flotation devices.
- PWC racers are prohibited from operating a PWC from one half-hour after sunset to one half-hour before sunrise.
- A lanyard-type engine cutoff switch must be attached to the racer in case the racer is displaced from the craft or if the craft is not upright.
- No PWC shall exceed a noise level of 90 decibels when subjected to a stationary, on-site sound level test, or 75 decibels when subjected to a shoreline test.
- All PWC racers have to abide by "no negligent operation" statutes.

The following IJSBA criteria/regulations are required for PWC and Mini Jet boat race promoters:

Body of Water

- Predictable water level or favorable tidal fluctuation
- Must secure event area from boat traffic
- Race course water depth minimum of 4 feet—maximum 50 feet

Land Area

- 1,400 feet long × 150 feet wide (pits 1,000 feet, spectator area 400 feet)
- Authority to charge admission and install security fencing
- No signage restrictions

Parking

- Safe and secure participant parking area located adjacent to race site. Able to accommodate at least one thousand vehicles, including fifth-wheel trailers, with separate parking for VIPs
- Parking for ambulance and staff equipment trucks near race site

Regulations for Pre-event Planning   Pre-event planning is essential to conducting a successful event. Therefore, the following regulations set up by the IJSBA are required for PWC race promoters.[6]

Red Cross Courses

The Race Director, Course Marshals, and safety boat personnel must take the American Red Cross Standard First Aid course and Basic Water Safety course.

Event Site

The following event site criteria must be followed:

- The location must be large enough to safely accommodate all types of events (e.g., endurance race and freestyle).
- Beach and adjacent land areas for pit locations, launching facilities, spectator viewing; rider and spectator parking; and overall access to the water for both spectators and riders should be considered.

Coast Guard/Coast Guard Auxiliary

- The promoter must contact the Coast Guard or Coast Guard Auxiliary several months prior to the event to investigate their regulations and complete a marine event application.

Fire Department

Contact the Fire Marshal for criteria requirements prior to and during the event because they have the authority to cancel an event at any time. Criteria include such things as posting no-smoking signs, keeping fire lanes open, and acquiring certificates of fire retardation for tents that exceed a certain limit.

Office of the City Clerk

Contact the Office of the City Clerk in the city where the event will be held several months in advance. The promoter may be required to purchase a city business license and complete an application for special event or temporary use permit.

State Department of Revenue

Contact the Department of Revenue in the state where the event will be held. The promoter may have to complete a tax application and pay an application fee. After the event, the promoter may have to pay a tax based on ticket sales, exhibitor booth sales, and any other revenue specified by the Department of Revenue.

Parks and Recreation Department

Contact the Parks and Recreation Department, which may require a land use fee.

Fish and Game

Contact the Fish and Game Department, which may have a list of regulations regarding the use of the facility.

Emergency Response Vehicle

The race promoter must supply an emergency response, rescue, and transport vehicle(s) (e.g., ambulance) that meets the requirements of the authorizing local jurisdiction, as stated in the IJSBA sanction agreement.

One vehicle must be present at all times during the entire event. The event must stop if the vehicle leaves the event site. Racing may resume once the vehicle or a replacement returns.

Emergency response vehicle personnel must consist of one driver and one medical attendant capable of providing care at the basic life support level.

Exhibit Sales

The race promoter must check with the Facility Manager for approval to sell exhibit space. Some facilities may not allow the promoter to sell exhibit space due to existing concession contracts.

Insurance Coverage

Promoters will purchase insurance coverage for personal injuries. The insurance costs $630 for the first day and $380 for the second day, and it covers two-day setup before the event (Thursday, Friday), the weekend, and one-day teardown after the event (Monday). The coverage includes:

- $200,000 participant (racer or pit crew)
- $7,500 in excess medical benefits
- $7,500 in accidental death or dismemberment
- $1,000,000 single limit liability per occurrence

Regulations for Racing   The following regulations are required for those who are interested in PWC racing:

- Using a PWC approved by the International Jet Sports Boating Association (IJSBA)
- A competition-level membership in the IJSBA
- A properly fitting wetsuit meeting U.S. specifications and full-coverage helmet with chin, eye, feet, and mouth protection
- Knowledge of the IJSBA competition rules and regulations

APPENDIX C

The following table summarizes the pricing for tickets and parking fees.

MCM Powersports	1998		1999		2000	
Event	1 day	2 days	1 day	2 days	1 day	2 days
Ticket Sales	$7	$10	$8	$12	$9	$15
Parking	$5	$8	$5	$8	$5	$8

The following table summarizes the booth rental prices for each event.

MCM Powersports	10 x 10	10 x 20
Regular	$200	$300
IJSBA Affiliated	$175	$275
All 10 Events	$100	$150

APPENDIX D—A SAMPLE EVENT SCHEDULE DAY AT THE RACES FOR AMATEURS

6:00–8:00 A.M. Sign-Up/Registration/Tech Inspection

This is when the amateur racers go to the sign-up area to register for the day's events. The amateur racers will fill out the entry form, present their IJSBA membership card, and pay their entry fees. The IJSBA provides many benefits to its members, especially the right to race (all racers must be members of the IJSBA). This can be done at the registration booth during sign-up. Registration closes at 8:00 A.M. All racers must then proceed to the tech inspection area to have their PWC checked out for any infractions of the rules and regulations of the IJSBA boat specifications.

Note: All events will allow preregistration either the Saturday before the race or weeks in advance. Check out MCM Powersports' Preregistration Information Page, which can be accessed from our Web page. Since the space is limited, preregistration is highly recommended.

8:00 A.M. Riders Meeting

All amateur racers will be called to a designated area by the race director to go over information such as the course layout, starting procedures, course officials, caution flags, and what to do if they have a question or complaint. The practice and race order will also be posted at this time.

8:30 A.M. Practice

All amateur racers will be given a chance to learn the course and become comfortable with it. A course official will lead a group of amateur racers around the course for one lap; it is up to the amateur racers to know the course.

9:00 A.M. Morning Session Racing Begins

Three out of seven classes will race in the morning. These are: 785 and Sport/Ski (combined). The first of three classes will be called to the starting line by 9:00 A.M. While the first sets of racers are on the line, the next group of racers will already be making their way toward the starting line. This early preparation is to ensure races flow smoothly without having to wait for racers to make their way to the starting line. Each race will be ninety minutes long; two races are scheduled for the morning session. Before the afternoon session starts, the free-style competition will take place.

12:30 P.M. Afternoon Session Racing Begins

The rest of the classes will race at this session. These are Open, Women/Vets, Mini Jet Boats 1 engine/2 engines. Open, and Women/Vets will go first in the first part of the afternoon session. There will be a half-hour break at 3:30 P.M. for resetting the course for Mini Jet Boat races. The races are scheduled to end at 5:30 P.M.

8:00 P.M. Award Ceremony

Top five finishers in each class will be awarded. Raffle prizes for racers from sponsors will also be given at that time.

APPENDIX E

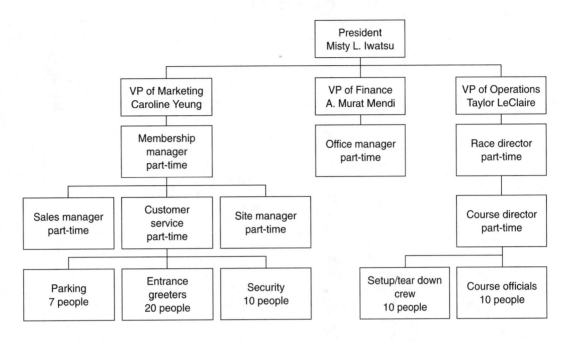

APPENDIX F

Product Development Schedule Year 1

Month	January					February				March				April					May				June				July					August				September				October					November				December			
Week	1	8	15	22	29	5	12	19	26	5	12	19	26	2	9	16	23	30	7	14	21	28	4	11	18	25	2	9	16	23	30	6	13	20	27	3	10	17	24	1	8	15	22	29	5	12	19	26	3	10	17	24

Task

- Setting up the firm
- Development of Policy and Procedures Manual
- Sponsor connections
- Sponsor follow-up
- Place reservations
- Site logistics
- Race course logistics
- Purchase Equipment
- Inviting Pros
- Plan Advertising Cmp.
- Advertising
- Safety Program Guidelines
- Web site setup
- Prepare event 1
- Setup event 1
- Event 1
- Prepare event 2
- Setup event 2
- Event 2
- Prepare event 3
- Setup event 3
- Event 3
- Prepare event 4
- Setup event 4
- Event 4
- Prepare event 5
- Setup event 5
- Event 5
- Prepare event 6
- Setup event 6
- Event 6
- Prepare event 7
- Setup event 7
- Event 7
- Prepare event 8
- Setup event 8
- Event 8
- Prepare event 9
- Setup event 9
- Event 9
- Prepare event 10
- Setup event 10
- Event 10

Product Development Schedule Year 2

Month →	January					February				March				April					May				June				July					August				September				October				November				December			
Task \ Week	1	8	15	22	29	5	12	19	26	5	12	19	26	2	9	16	23	30	7	14	21	28	4	11	18	25	2	9	16	23	30	6	13	20	27	3	10	17	24	1	8	15	22	29	5	12	19	26	3	10	17	24
Sponsor follow-up											▓	▓	▓	▓	▓	▓	▓	▓	▓	▓	▓	▓	▓	▓	▓	▓	▓	▓	▓	▓	▓	▓	▓	▓	▓	▓	▓	▓	▓	▓	▓	▓	▓	▓	▓	▓	▓	▓	▓	▓	▓	▓
Place reservations											▓	▓	▓	▓																																						
Site logistics						▓	▓	▓	▓	▓																																										
Race course logistics						▓	▓	▓	▓	▓																																										
Purchase Equipment												▓	▓																																							
Inviting Pros										▓	▓	▓	▓																																							
Plan Advertising Cmp.						▓	▓	▓	▓																																											
Advertising											▓	▓	▓	▓	▓	▓	▓	▓	▓	▓	▓	▓	▓	▓	▓	▓	▓	▓	▓	▓	▓	▓	▓	▓	▓	▓	▓	▓	▓	▓	▓	▓	▓	▓	▓	▓	▓	▓	▓	▓	▓	▓
Safety Program Guideines						▓	▓	▓	▓																																											
Web site setup						▓	▓	▓	▓																																											
Prepare event 1						▓	▓	▓																																												
Setup event 1																		▓																																		
Event 1																			▓																																	
Prepare event 2						▓	▓	▓																																												
Setup event 2																				▓																																
Event 2																					▓																															
Prepare event 3						▓	▓	▓																																												
Setup event 3																						▓																														
Event 3																							▓																													
Prepare event 4						▓	▓	▓																																												
Setup event 4																								▓																												
Event 4																									▓																											
Prepare event 5						▓	▓	▓																																												
Setup event 5																										▓																										
Event 5																											▓																									
Prepare event 6						▓	▓	▓																																												
Setup event 6																												▓																								
Event 6																													▓																							
Prepare event 7						▓	▓	▓																																												
Setup event 7																														▓																						
Event 7																															▓																					
Prepare event 8						▓	▓	▓																																												
Setup event 8																																▓																				
Event 8																																	▓																			
Prepare event 9						▓	▓	▓																																												
Setup event 9																																		▓																		
Event 9																																			▓																	
Prepare event 10						▓	▓	▓																																												
Setup event 10																																				▓																
Event 10																																					▓															

Product Development Schedule Year 3

Month	January					February				March				April				May				June				July					August				September				October					November				December			
Week	1	8	15	22	29	5	12	19	26	5	12	19	26	2	9	16	23	7	14	21	28	4	11	18	25	2	9	16	23	30	6	13	20	27	3	10	17	24	1	8	15	22	29	5	12	19	26	3	10	17	24

Task

- Sponsor follow-up
- Place reservations
- Site logistics
- Race course logistics
- Purchase Equipment
- Inviting Pros
- Plan Advertising Cmp.
- Advertising
- Safety Program Guideines
- Web site setup
- Prepare event 1
- Setup event 1
- Event 1
- Prepare event 2
- Setup event 2
- Event 2
- Prepare event 3
- Setup event 3
- Event 3
- Prepare event 4
- Setup event 4
- Event 4
- Prepare event 5
- Setup event 5
- Event 5
- Prepare event 6
- Setup event 6
- Event 6
- Prepare event 7
- Setup event 7
- Event 7
- Prepare event 8
- Setup event 8
- Event 8
- Prepare event 9
- Setup event 9
- Event 9
- Prepare event 10
- Setup event 10
- Event 10

Management Team

Misty Iwatsu is the president of MCM Powersports. She has more than thirteen years of retail management experience. She has been a Personal Watercraft endurance racer for more than seven years. She has also assisted promoters in organizing watercraft events. She has been a team manager for several race teams and was responsible for gaining sponsorship and media recognition. She has earned several national titles in the Personal Watercraft endurance racing field. She is achieving her B.S. degree at California State University, Los Angeles, in marketing, management, with a minor in economics. She attended the Fashion Institute of Design and Merchandising and received her A.A. degree in marketing management.

Ahmet Murat Mendi is the vice president of finance. He has more than four years of experience in the finance field. He received his B.A. degree in management at Bogazici University and will achieve his master's degree at California State University, Los Angeles. He has also done extensive research in the economic and risk management fields.

Caroline Yeung is the vice president of marketing. She has more than three years of experience in the marketing field. She earned her B.S. degree in marketing management at California State University, Los Angeles. She has done numerous marketing plans and advertising campaigns for highly visible companies.

Taylor LeClaire is the vice president of marketing. She has more than ten years in the retail management field. She has been in the Personal Watercraft industry for more than three years. She has assisted promoters in staffing events and has earned a national title in Personal Watercraft endurance racing.

APPENDIX G

Cash Flow Analysis	Month 1	Month 2	Month 3	Month 4	Month 5	Month 6	Month 7	Month 8	Month 9	Month 10	Month 11	Month 12
Beginning Balance	$ 20,000	$ 112,700	$ 1,245,560	$ 975,933	$ 773,057	$ 639,976	$ 506,894	$ 373,813	$ 218,232	$ 262,440	$ 237,104	$ 211,768
Loan	$ 100,000											
Sources of Funds												
Sponsorship		$ 1,150,000		$ 690,000	$ 690,000	$ 690,000	$ 690,000	$ 690,000				
Ticket sales				$ 620,000	$ 620,000	$ 620,000	$ 620,000	$ 620,000				
Parking				$ 57,500	$ 57,500	$ 57,500	$ 57,500	$ 57,500				
Racer registration			$ 1,000	$ 7,000	$ 7,000	$ 7,000	$ 7,000	$ 6,000				
Booth rental			$ 21,500	$ 21,500	$ 21,500	$ 21,500	$ 21,500					
Mailing list					$ 49,920	$ 49,920	$ 49,920	$ 49,920	$ 49,920			
Accessory sales				$ 18,750	$ 37,500	$ 37,500	$ 37,500	$ 37,500	$ 18,750			
Videocassette					$ 1,125	$ 1,125	$ 1,125	$ 1,125	$ 1,125			
Total Sources	$ —	$ 1,150,000	$ 22,500	$ 1,414,750	$ 1,484,545	$ 1,484,545	$ 1,484,545	$ 1,462,045	$ 69,795	$ —	$ —	$ —
Uses of Funds												
Startup costs												
New promoter fee	$ 300											
Establishing firm	$ 5,000											
Salary												
Full time		$ 8,000	$ 8,000	$ 8,000	$ 8,000	$ 8,000	$ 8,000	$ 8,000	$ 8,000	$ 8,000	$ 8,000	$ 8,000
Part time			$ 2,240	$ 2,240	$ 2,240	$ 2,240	$ 2,240	$ 2,240	$ 2,240	$ 2,240	$ 2,240	$ 2,240
Temporary hires				$ 11,400	$ 11,400	$ 11,400	$ 11,400	$ 11,400				
Insurance												
Equipment		$ 2,500	$ 2,500	$ 2,500	$ 2,500	$ 2,500	$ 2,500	$ 2,500	$ 2,500	$ 2,500	$ 2,500	$ 2,500
Event		$ 2,000		$ 2,060	$ 2,060	$ 2,060	$ 2,060	$ 2,060				
Permit fees												
Interest paid		$ 873	$ 873	$ 873	$ 873	$ 873	$ 873	$ 873	$ 873	$ 873	$ 873	$ 873
Computer equipment												
Computers		$ 1,852	$ 1,852	$ 1,852	$ 1,852	$ 1,852	$ 1,852	$ 1,852	$ 1,852	$ 1,852	$ 1,852	$ 1,852
Software for magnetic cards			$ 5,000									
Magnetic card readers			$ 61,000									
Magnetic cards		$ 1,944										
Other office equipment				$ 18,000	$ 18,000	$ 18,000	$ 18,000	$ 18,000				
Office supplies		$ 500	$ 500	$ 500	$ 500	$ 500	$ 500	$ 500	$ 500	$ 500	$ 500	$ 500

Cash Flow Analysis	Month 1	Month 2	Month 3	Month 4	Month 5	Month 6	Month 7	Month 8	Month 9	Month 10	Month 11	Month 12
TV cameras				$1,500,000	$1,500,000	$1,500,000	$1,500,000	$1,500,000				
AT & T Business 1 Rate for 1–888 numbers		$222	$222	$222	$222	$222	$222	$222	$222	$222	$222	$222
Advertising												
Prepare TV commercial			$75,000									
Air the TV commercial				$5,000	$5,000	$5,000	$5,000	$5,000				
Design magazine ad			$1,500									
Print ad space				$7,900	$7,900	$7,900	$7,900	$7,900	$7,900	$7,900	$7,900	$7,900
Record radio commercial			$500									
Air the radio commercial				$4,500	$4,500	$4,500	$4,500	$4,500				
Equipment												
Personal watercraft			$120,000									
Course equipment			$9,440									
PWC maintenance				$3,000	$3,000	$3,000	$3,000	$3,000				
Transportation												
Setup and tear-down				$20,000	$20,000	$20,000	$20,000	$20,000				
Travel				$11,780	$11,780	$11,780	$11,780	$11,780				
Hotel				$2,100	$2,100	$2,100	$2,100	$2,100				
Plaques, gifts, prizes				$3,700	$3,700	$3,700	$3,700	$3,700				
Rent tents				$10,000	$10,000	$10,000	$10,000	$10,000				
Utilities	$1,000	$250	$500	$1,000	$1,000	$1,000	$1,000	$1,000	$500	$250	$250	$250
Miscellaneous	$1,000	$1,000	$1,000	$1,000	$1,000	$1,000	$1,000	$1,000	$1,000	$1,000	$1,000	$1,000
Lawyer fees												
Total Uses	**$7,300**	**$17,140**	**$292,126**	**$1,617,626**	**$1,617,626**	**$1,617,626**	**$1,617,626**	**$1,617,626**	**$25,586**	**$25,336**	**$25,336**	**$25,336**
Earnings Before Taxes	$(7,300)	$1,132,860	$(269,626)	$(202,876)	$(133,081)	$(133,081)	$(133,081)	$(155,581)	$44,209	$(25,336)	$(25,336)	$(25,336)
Less: Tax			$—		$—		$—		$—			
Earnings After Taxes	$(7,300)	$1,132,860	$(269,626)	$(202,876)	$(133,081)	$(133,081)	$(133,081)	$(155,581)	$44,209	$(25,336)	$(25,336)	$(25,336)
Net Cash Flow	**$112,700**	**$1,245,560**	**$975,933**	**$773,057**	**$639,976**	**$506,894**	**$373,813**	**$218,232**	**$262,440**	**$237,104**	**$211,768**	**$186,431**

Cash Flow Analysis	Month 1	Month 2	Month 3	Month 4	Month 5	Month 6	Month 7	Month 8	Month 9	Month 10	Month 11	Month 12
Beginning Balance	$186,431	$160,750	$1,283,486	$1,195,509	$1,014,520	$925,407	$836,293	$747,180	$635,566	$699,914	$672,650	$645,386
Sources of Funds												
Sponsorship		$1,150,000		$690,000	$690,000	$690,000	$690,000	$690,000				
Ticket sales				$720,000	$720,000	$720,000	$720,000	$720,000				
Parking				$57,500	$57,500	$57,500	$57,500	$57,500				
Racer registration			$1,000	$11,000	$11,000	$11,000	$11,000	$10,000				
Booth rental			$21,500	$21,500	$21,500	$21,500	$21,500					
Mailing list					$72,000	$72,000	$72,000	$72,000	$72,000			
Accessory sales				$18,750	$37,500	$37,500	$37,500	$37,500	$18,750			
Videocassette					$1,125	$1,125	$1,125	$1,125	$1,125			
Total Sources	$ –	$1,150,000	$22,500	$1,518,750	$1,610,625	$1,610,625	$1,610,625	$1,588,125	$91,875	$ –	$ –	$ –
Uses of Funds												
Salary												
Full time	$8,000	$8,800	$8,800	$8,800	$8,800	$8,800	$8,800	$8,800	$8,800	$8,800	$8,800	$8,800
Part time	$2,240	$2,464	$2,464	$2,464	$2,464	$2,464	$2,464	$2,464	$2,464	$2,464	$2,464	$2,464
Temporary hires				$12,540	$12,540	$12,540	$12,540	$12,540				
Insurance												
Equipment	$2,500	$2,625	$2,625	$2,625	$2,625	$2,625	$2,625	$2,625	$2,625	$2,625	$2,625	$2,625
Event				$2,163	$2,163	$2,163	$2,163	$2,163				
Permit fees			$2,100									
Interest paid	$873	$873	$873	$873	$873	$873	$873	$873	$873	$873	$873	$873
Computer equipment												
Computers	$1,852	$2,037	$2,037	$2,037	$2,037	$2,037	$2,037	$2,037	$2,037	$2,037	$2,037	$2,037
Magnetic cards				$18,900	$18,900	$18,900	$18,900	$18,900				
Office supplies	$500	$625	$625	$625	$625	$625	$625	$625	$625	$625	$625	$625
TV cameras				$1,575,000	$1,575,000	$1,575,000	$1,575,000	$1,575,000				
AT & T Business 1 Rate for 1–888 numbers	$222	$233	$233	$233	$233	$233	$233	$233	$233	$233	$233	$233
Advertising												
Prepare TV commercial			$78,750									
Air the TV commercial				$5,250	$5,250	$5,250	$5,250	$5,250				
Design magazine ad			$1,575									
Print ad space $ 8,295	$7,900	$8,295	$8,295	$8,295	$8,295	$8,295	$8,295	$8,295	$8,295	$8,295	$8,295	$8,295
Record radio commercial			$525									
Air the radio commercial				$4,725	$4,725	$4,725	$4,725	$4,725				
Equipment												
PWC maintenance				$3,150	$3,150	$3,150	$3,150	$3,150				
Transportation												
Setup and tear-down				$21,000	$21,000	$21,000	$21,000	$21,000				
Travel				$12,369	$12,369	$12,369	$12,369	$12,369				
Hotel				$2,205	$2,205	$2,205	$2,205	$2,205				
Plaques, gifts, prizes				$3,885	$3,885	$3,885	$3,885	$3,885				
Rent tents				$10,500	$10,500	$10,500	$10,500	$10,500				
Utilities	$250		$525	$1,050	$1,050	$1,050	$1,050	$1,050				
Miscellaneous	$1,000	$263		$1,050	$1,050	$1,050	$1,050	$1,050	$525	$263	$263	$263
Auditing fees	$50,000								$1,050	$1,050	$1,050	$1,050
Lawyer fees	$25,000	$1,050	$1,050									
Total Uses	$25,336	$27,264	$110,477	$1,699,739	$1,699,739	$1,699,739	$1,699,739	$1,699,739	$27,527	$27,264	$27,264	$27,264
Earnings Before Taxes	$(25,336)	$1,122,736	$(87,977)	$(180,989)	$(89,114)	$(89,114)	$(89,114)	$(111,614)	$64,348	$(27,264)	$(27,264)	$(27,264)
Less: Tax	$346		$ –			$ –			$ –			$ –
Earnings after taxes	$(25,682)	$1,122,736	$(87,977)	$(180,989)	$(89,114)	$(89,114)	$(89,114)	$(111,614)	$64,348	$(27,264)	$(27,264)	$(27,264)
Net Cash Flow	$160,750	$1,283,486	$1,195,509	$1,014,520	$925,407	$836,293	$747,180	$635,566	$699,914	$672,650	$645,386	$618,122

Cash Flow Analysis	Month 1	Month 2	Month 3	Month 4	Month 5	Month 6	Month 7	Month 8	Month 9	Month 10	Month 11	Month 12
Beginning Balance	$ 618,122	$ 506,259	$ 1,627,758	$ 1,534,384	$ 1,447,908	$ 1,477,307	$ 1,506,705	$ 1,536,104	$ 1,558,107	$ 1,645,205	$ 1,616,704	$ 1,588,203
Sources of Funds												
Sponsorship		$ 1,150,000		$ 690,000	$ 690,000	$ 690,000	$ 690,000	$ 690,000				
Ticket sales				$ 900,000	$ 900,000	$ 900,000	$ 900,000	$ 900,000				
Parking				$ 57,500	$ 57,500	$ 57,500	$ 57,500	$ 57,500				
Racer registration			$ 1,000	$ 11,000	$ 11,000	$ 11,000	$ 11,000	$ 10,000				
Booth rental			$ 21,500	$ 21,500	$ 21,500	$ 21,500	$ 21,500					
Mailing list					$ 96,000	$ 96,000	$ 96,000	$ 96,000	$ 96,000			
Accessory sales				$ 18,750	$ 37,500	$ 37,500	$ 37,500	$ 37,500	$ 18,750			
Videocassette					$ 1,125	$ 1,125	$ 1,125	$ 1,125	$ 1,125			
Total Sources	$ –	$ 1,150,000	$ 22,500	$ 1,698,750	$ 1,814,625	$ 1,814,625	$ 1,814,625	$ 1,792,125	$ 115,875	$ –	$ –	$ –
Uses of Funds												
Salary												
Full time	$ 8,800	$ 9,680	$ 9,680	$ 9,680	$ 9,680	$ 9,680	$ 9,680	$ 9,680	$ 9,680	$ 9,680	$ 9,680	$ 9,680
Part time	$ 2,464	$ 2,710	$ 2,710	$ 2,710	$ 2,710	$ 2,710	$ 2,710	$ 2,710	$ 2,710	$ 2,710	$ 2,710	$ 2,710
Temporary hires				$ 13,794	$ 13,794	$ 13,794	$ 13,794	$ 13,794				
Insurance												
Equipment	$ 2,625	$ 2,756	$ 2,756	$ 2,756	$ 2,756	$ 2,756	$ 2,756	$ 2,756	$ 2,756	$ 2,756	$ 2,756	$ 2,756
Event				$ 2,271	$ 2,271	$ 2,271	$ 2,271	$ 2,271				
Permit fees			$ 2,205									
Computer Equipment												
Computers	$ 2,037	$ 2,241	$ 2,241	$ 2,241	$ 2,241	$ 2,241	$ 2,241	$ 2,241	$ 2,241	$ 2,241	$ 2,241	$ 2,241
Magnetic cards				$ 19,845	$ 19,845	$ 19,845	$ 19,845	$ 19,845				
Office supplies	$ 625	$ 781	$ 781	$ 781	$ 781	$ 781	$ 781	$ 781	$ 781	$ 781	$ 781	$ 781
TV cameras	$ 233	$ 245	$ 245	$ 245	$ 245	$ 245	$ 245	$ 245	$ 245	$ 245	$ 245	$ 245
AT & T Business 1 Rate for 1-888 numbers				$ 1,653,750	$ 1,653,750	$ 1,653,750	$ 1,653,750	$ 1,653,750				
Advertising												
Prepare TV Commercial			$ 82,688									
Air the TV commercial				$ 5,513	$ 5,513	$ 5,513	$ 5,513	$ 5,513				
Design magazine ad			$ 1,654									
Print ad space	$ 8,295	$ 8,710	$ 8,710	$ 8,710	$ 8,710	$ 8,710	$ 8,710	$ 8,710	$ 8,710	$ 8,710	$ 8,710	$ 8,710
Record radio commercial			$ 551									
Air the radio commercial				$ 4,961	$ 4,961	$ 4,961	$ 4,961	$ 4,961				
Equipment												
PWC maintenance				$ 3,308	$ 3,308	$ 3,308	$ 3,308	$ 3,308				
Transportation												
Setup and tear-down				$ 22,050	$ 22,050	$ 22,050	$ 22,050	$ 22,050				
Travel				$ 12,987	$ 12,987	$ 12,987	$ 12,987	$ 12,987				
Hotel				$ 2,315	$ 2,315	$ 2,315	$ 2,315	$ 2,315				
Plaques, gifts, prizes				$ 4,079	$ 4,079	$ 4,079	$ 4,079					
Rent tents				$ 11,025	$ 11,025	$ 11,025	$ 11,025					
Utilities	$ 263	$ 276	$ 551	$ 1,103	$ 1,103	$ 1,103	$ 1,103	$ 1,103	$ 551	$ 276	$ 276	$ 276
Miscellaneous	$ 1,050	$ 1,103	$ 1,103	$ 1,103	$ 1,103	$ 1,103	$ 1,103	$ 1,103	$ 1,103	$ 1,103	$ 1,103	$ 1,103
Auditing fees	$ 50,000											
Lawyer fees	$ 25,000											
Repay loan												$ 100,000
Total Uses	$ 101,391	$ 28,501	$ 115,874	$ 1,785,226	$ 1,785,226	$ 1,785,226	$ 1,785,226	$ 1,770,122	$ 28,777	$ 28,501	$ 28,501	$ 28,501
Earnings Before Taxes	$ (101,391)	$ 1,121,499	$ (93,374)	$ (86,476)	$ 29,399	$ 29,399	$ 29,399	$ 22,003	$ 87,098	$ (28,501)	$ (28,501)	$ (128,501)
Less: Tax	$ 10,471		$ –			$ –			$ –			$ –
Cash Flow After taxes	$ (111,863)	$ 1,121,499	$ (93,374)	$ (86,476)	$ 29,399	$ 29,399	$ 29,399	$ 22,003	$ 87,098	$ (28,501)	$ (28,501)	$ (128,501)
Net Cash Flow	$ 506,259	$ 1,627,758	$ 1,534,384	$ 1,447,908	$ 1,477,307	$ 1,506,705	$ 1,536,104	$ 1,558,107	$ 1,645,205	$ 1,616,704	$ 1,588,203	$ 1,459,702

APPENDIX H

Income Statement	Year 1	Year 2	Year 3
Net Income	$ 8,572,725	$ 9,203,125	$ 10,223,125
Less: Cost of Goods Sold	$ 8,298,495	$ 8,536,248	$ 8,938,698
Sell., Gen. and Adm. Exp.	$ 198,200	$ 299,369	$ 421,905
Operating Profit Before Depr.	***$ 76,030***	***$ 367,508***	***$ 862,522***
Less: Depreciation	$ 64,128	$ 128,256	$ 192,384
Earnings Before Interest and Taxes	***$ 11,902***	***$ 239,252***	***$ 670,138***
Less: Interest	$ 9,599	$ 10,471	$ 10,471
Earnings Before Taxes	***$ 2,303***	***$ 228,780***	***$ 659,667***
Less: Tax Paid	$ 346	$ 72,474	$ 224,287
Net Income after taxes	***$ 1,958***	***$ 156,306***	***$ 435,380***

Balance Sheet	Year 1	Year 2	Year 3
Current Assets			
Cash and Equivalent	18,889	313,321	865,810
Account Receivable	—	—	—
Inventories	495	553	622
Total Current Assets	*19,384*	*313,874*	*866,432*
Fixed Assets	192,384	192,384	192,384
Depreciation	64,128	128,256	192,384
Total Assets	**147,640**	**378,002**	**866,432**
Current Liabilities			
Accounts Payable	15,096	16,000	16,111
Salaries Payable	10,240	11,264	12,390
Taxes Payable	346	72,474	224,287
Total Current Liabilities	*25,682*	*99,738*	*252,788*
Long-Term Debt	100,000	100,000	—

NOTES

1. International Jet Sports Boating Association, *1997 Official Competition Rule Book* (Santa Ana, CA, 1997), p. 10.
2. "PWC: Many Challenges in Taking a Line." *Boating Industry* (June 1996), p. 50.
3. Media Kit. *Splash Magazine* (1997).
4. Department of Boating & Waterways. *PWC News* (Sacramento, CA, 1997), p. 7.
5. International Jet Sports Boating Association. *1997 Official Competition Rule Book* (Santa Ana, CA, 1997), 10.
6. *Ibid.,* p. 13.

A5

BIRRALEE PRIMARY SCHOOL (AUSTRALIA)

Developed by
QUAH SUAT HONG
WELLY TEHUNAN
VANESSA YAU

Contents

EXECUTIVE SUMMARY

This plan analyzes the industry environment of the Victoria Primary School sector, in particular, Birralee Primary School. Other factors that aid in the analysis of the industry, include the changing trends in the environment, industry life cycle, industry attractiveness and structure, and competition. These helped to formulate and develop the corporate and marketing objectives, strategies, and tactics for Birralee Primary School.

The corporate objectives of Birralee Primary School are to increase the school's market share, in terms of student number, from 5.46 percent in 1998 to 6 percent by January 2002 and to improve the school reputation among all the primary schools in the same region from a current rating of 2.73 to a rating of 3.5 by the end of 2002. To achieve this, Birralee has to pursue a corporate strategy by horizontal growth. Tactics such as targeting the promotional activities to a new area of coverage, fostering good relationships with external organizations (local businesses and kindergartens), and increasing the range of teaching programs are used to enforce the corporate strategy.

In the marketing plan, more specific objectives, strategies, and tactics are developed, with an aim of aiding the school in achieving its corporate objectives. The marketing objectives of Birralee Primary School are to increase student enrollment from 185 in 1999 to 205 by the end of 2001, and to improve the school reputation among all the primary schools in the same region from a current rating of 2.73 to a rating of 3.5 by the end of 2001. Several marketing strategies are used to obtain these objectives. They include promotional strategy of fund raising, sponsorship from local business and developing good relationship with local kindergartens, product strategy of introducing the Asian language program, and place strategy of exploring new mediums for information distribution. The tactics in achieving the strategies are carrying out two major fund-raising events per year (during March 2000 and 2001, and October 2000 and 2001), instead of several ones; drafting a proposal to seek sponsorship from local businesses; forming a visiting team to organize shared activities between Birralee and the kindergartens; applying for local subsidies from Community Development Grant Program through the Manningham City Council; and developing a Web site with general information of the school.

Once the marketing tactics and strategies are implemented in the year 2000 and 2001, they are expected to generate about $15,000 in projected income (mainly from the fund-raising events) and $11,800 in expenses, thus creating a surplus of $38,700 from the available fund of $35,500. Also, once the student enrollment increases, there is a possibility of an increase in the government funding of an unspecified amount.

STRATEGIC PLAN

Mission Statement

Birralee Primary School is committed to providing a quality education with a supportive, friendly, caring environment to enhance the students with a range of learning experiences and to develop their self-esteem, confidence, and independence.

Corporate Objectives

- To increase the school's market share (in terms of student number) from 5.46 percent (see Appendix 1) in 1998 to 6 percent by January 2002 (6 percent market share is a revised objective—refer to the gap analysis).
- To improve the school reputation among all the primary schools in the same region from a current rating of 2.73 to a rating of 3.5 by the end of 2002 (see Appendix 2—survey of the people in the area).

Situation Analysis

Market Size   There were 1,694 primary schools in Victoria in February 1998, 24 fewer than in 1997. Most of the change in school numbers occurred in the government sector.[1]

Table A5-1   Number of Schools by School Type and Sector, February 1997–1998.

	Government		Catholic		Independent		All schools	
School Type	1997	1998	1997	1998	1997	1998	1997	1998
Primary Schools	1270	1253	386	384	62	57	1718	1694

Industry Segmentation   Primary education offers students general information and prepares them for further education, and a valued role in society. The providers of primary school services include state and territory governments, Catholic dioceses, and other nongovernment schools (refer to Appendix 3).

Industry Life Cycle   Primary education industry in Victoria is in mature phase (shown in Figure A5-1), for the following reasons:

- Number of primary school students is stable at a lower rate from 1992 to 1999 when compared to the trend from 1989 to 1991 (Figure A5-1).

FIGURE A5-1. The Life Cycle of Primary School Industry in Victoria[2]

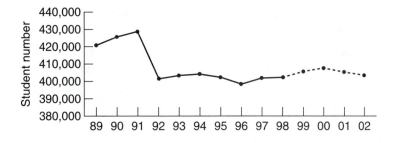

- The average rate of the real growth in industry gross product for the whole Australia (2.1 percent in 1997–1998; see Appendix 4) is below that of real growth in the general economy (the rate of growth in GDP is 4.7 percent in 1997–98).[3] It is assumed that this trend will be reflected in Victoria for a number of periods.
- The number of primary schools being established has been in a phase of decline. Over the five years to 1998, the number of primary schools in Victoria decreased by 1.17 percent on average (see Appendix 5).
- The population's demographics (a decline in the primary school-age students), combined with the compulsory nature of the primary level education, impose a natural market limit.

Industry Attractiveness

FIGURE A5-2. Porter's Five Forces Model

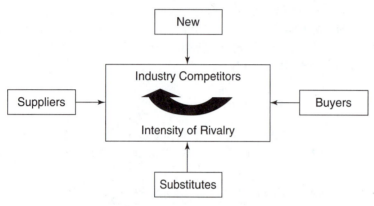

Summary of industry attractiveness (refer to Appendix 6).

- The industry is not attractive due to the high intensity of competition.
- The government plays a central role in the industry.
- Despite the medium level of bargaining power by suppliers and buyers, the mature state of the industry, future availability of teaching staff, and low growth of the primary school students will affect the industry's well-being in the long run.

Driving Forces and Trends

- There is an increasing usage of technology-based teaching in the schools as more schools are using computers in the classrooms, as well as facilitating work in the office.
- The movements in the level of mean gross weekly income (increase from $596 in 1994–95 to $625 in 1996–97)[4] affect parents' selection of nongovernment schools.
- Community perception of the quality and desirability of government, private, or church-associated education affect the parents' schools of choice.
- The number of primary schools enters into a decline phase due to government budgeting pressures and consequent relationship of the education system. Over the five years to 1993, the number of government primary schools decreases by 1.6 percent overall.[5]
- The government's commitment to improve literacy and numeracy standards is set for a boost with the development of a new Curriculum and Standards Framework for Victorian schools, thus forcing primary schools to improve their teaching quality.
- Students are moving to private schools because of the increased concern about the perceived falling standards of government schools. The attendance rate in government primary schools is 70 percent in 1998.[6]

Critical Success Factors

- Location of the schools. Primary-aged children normally attend schools in close proximity to their homes. Therefore, schools need to be located in a geographical location within close proximity to a large number of primary school-age children.

- Status and reputation of the schools. Schools with a good reputation improve parents' perception, and thus they are more likely to consider the schools as one of their choices. Status and reputation are directly related to the school's tradition, quality, and level of teaching staff, facilities of the schools, educational programs, and other equipment.

- Adequate public relations and marketing skills. This is important to increase public awareness, attract students, and maintain a positive image of the schools.

- Number of students. There are economies of scale available to schools with larger student numbers. In Victoria, government schools with low student numbers need to be closed due to the limited government educational budget.

Main Customers of the Industry

- Main customers are households with young children studying in kindergarten and reaching the age of primary education.

- The student population for primary schools is classified according to the age, level of schooling, religion, and genders.

Gap Analysis

FIGURE A5-3. Gap Analysis for Birralee Primary School

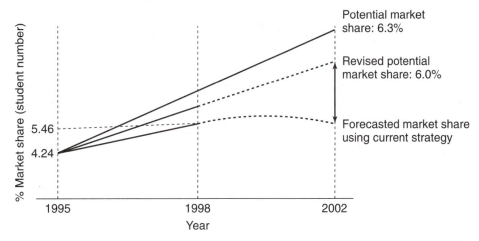

The gap analysis identified the gap between the revised potential market share and Birralee's projected market share (in terms of student number). The revised market share is obtained after conducting situation analysis of the school. The gap indicates huge opportunities for Birralee to grow and gain market share. Birralee has a desire to grow and increase its market share. However, due to the limited resources and captivity, which the organization has, Birralee needs to develop new strategies to attract more students.

Ansoff Matrix As for the old format, the school is adopting an existing product within the existing market strategy, which is dependent on the children reaching primary school age living within 500 m of the Birralee School. The school currently wants to extend into the new market (area within 1 km of the school and with the increased Asian families in the region) and continuously attract children in the existing area to enroll in the school. Therefore, Birralee needs to develop the growth strategy in order to achieve this aim.

FIGURE A5-4. Ansoff Matrix Model for Birralee Primary School

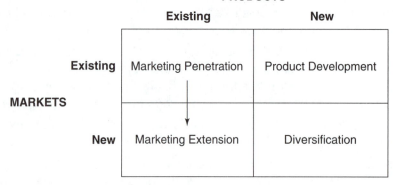

Corporate Strategy and Tactics

Strategy

Birralee corporate strategy is to achieve horizontal growth by expanding the school's market into a wider coverage area, as well as improved promotional activities to increase awareness and improve the school's reputation.

Tactics

- Target the promotional activities to a new area of coverage (refer to Appendix 2).
- Foster good relationship with external organizations (local businesses and kindergartens) to increase awareness and reputation.
- Increase the range of teaching programs to attract more students.

Assumptions

- Children reaching the primary school age will go to primary schools in Victoria and not in other states. Therefore, it is assumed that the primary school industry in this marketing plan is Victorian industry.
- The plan considers only nine primary schools, which are considered to be direct competitors of Birralee.
- The latest ABS census data (1996) is assumed to be relevant in aiding our analysis and strategy formulation.

MARKETING PLAN

School Profile

The following table provides the general information for the Birralee Primary School:

Table 2 Birralee Primary School Profile

Birralee Primary School Profile	Details
Year of Establishment	• Established in 1971
Current Enrollment No.	• Currently has 185 students and will have a confirmed enrollment number of 190 students in the 1st semester of 2000
District	• Manningham District
Location	• Doncaster
Market Coverage Area	• Doncaster, Box Hill North, and Balwyn North

(Continues)

Table A5-2   *(Continued)*

Birralee Primary School Profile	Details
Staff No.	• Currently has 15 teachers and administration staff
Facilities	• Playground, canteen, library, Art/Craft room, two computers with Internet access per classroom, sick bay, multi-purpose hall
Teaching Programs	• Eight major curriculum—English, Maths, Science, Technology, Health and Physical Education, Arts, Study of societies and environment, LOTE (Italian)
Other Programs' Activities	• Prep A program operates as a specialized program for young school-age children (from kindergarten to prep) who may not be mature enough to join the prep class
	• Art & craft lessons held for one hour per week for every grade. The areas of painting, drawing, printing, modeling, constructions, textiles, collage and art appreciation are covered in a developmental progression.
	• Out-of-hours childcare is held at school from 7:15 A.M. to 8:45 A.M. and from 3:30 P.M. until 6:00 P.M. every weekday. Snacks and drinks are provided for children under the child-care services.
	• At least one exclusion is held per term. Other camping and exclusion programs may take place depending on circumstances.
	• Perceptual Motor program (PMP) is held for all children from Prep A to grade 2, with an aim to give children an opportunity to learn and develop confidence in the fundamental skills.
	• Swimming lessons are conducted at the Aquarena in either term 3 or 4 of each school year.
	• Tennis skills program is held for each grade once per fortnight within the school grounds.
	• Pastoral care services
	• Religious education
	• Annual school concert

Birralee Life Cycle

FIGURE A5-5. Birralee Primary School Life Cycle

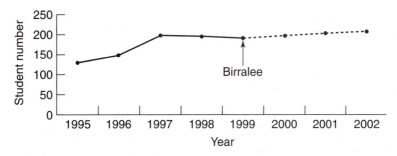

An organization is said to be in a competitive turbulence stage if the sale is slowing down and profit per unit is declining. In the case of Birralee Primary School, our analysis shows that it is in this stage because (refer to Table A5-3):

*   The growth rate from 1997 to 1998 is −1.56 percent as compared to the previous years (16.54 percent and 29.73 percent in 1995–96 and '96–97, respectively).

*   The 1999 and 2000 enrollment number is 185 and 190 students, respectively (growth rate of −2.12 percent in '98–99 and 2.7 percent in 1999–2000), resulting in low growth rate compared to the previous years and the average growth rate.

Competitor Analysis

The schools listed below have been identified as the main competitors of Birralee Primary School.

Table A5-3 Analysis of School Enrollment

Name/Year	1995	1996	1997	1998	% change 95–96	% change 96–97	% change 97–98	Average growth rate (%)
Birralee Primary School	127	148	192	189	16.54	29.73	−1.56	14.9
Doncaster Garden Primary School	300	307	316	305	2.33	2.93	−3.48	0.59
Doncaster Primary School	303	342	410	480	12.87	19.88	17.07	16.61
Greythorn Primary School	498	502	486	519	0.80	−3.19	6.79	1.47
Templestowe Valley Primary School	189	181	165	191	−4.23	−8.84	15.76	0.89
Manningham Park Primary School	165	145	191	173	−12.12	31.72	−9.42	3.39
Anderson's Greek Primary School	352	354	377	409	0.57	6.50	8.49	5.18
Mont Albert Primary School	572	580	582	580	1.40	0.34	−0.34	0.47
Boroondara Park Primary School	290	306	373	400	5.52	21.90	7.24	11.55
Box Hill North Primary School	197	212	216	213	7.61	1.89	−1.39	2.70

Summary of data analysis from the table above:

- Birralee Primary School held a market share of 4.24 percent, 4.81 percent, 5.80 percent, and 5.46 percent in 1995, 1996, 1997, and 1998, respectively.
- Most of the schools experienced an increase in their enrollment numbers. A few schools experienced a slight decrease, including Birralee Primary School.
- In terms of average growth rate from 1995 to 1998, most schools experienced little growth in their level of enrollment. However, a few schools like Birralee have an average growth rate of 14.9 percent, which is second highest among the group.

  For general information on the competitors, please refer to Appendix 7.

Birralee Customer Profile

- Households with low to medium income level, with young children aged 5+.[7]
- Living within the school suburb of approximately ten minutes' drive.[8]

SWOT Analysis

Strength

- The children were taught in small classes, which allow individual students to receive more attention. Moreover, the smaller classes encourage better class interaction and reduce incidents of bullying and lack of attention from teachers.
- The school is located in a quiet neighborhood, which is conducive to learning.

Weaknesses

- The location of Birralee Primary School is isolated and not really accessible by public transport.
- The school lacks sufficient facilities (such as computer laboratory and separate music room) to be perceived by potential parents as a high-quality school for their children.

Opportunities

- There is an increase in the number of Asian families who live in the area of Doncaster (about 7.1 percent of the residents in the Manningham district are of Asian origin; see Appendix 8). They can be regarded as an untapped market for Birralee Primary School.

Threats

- There is a decreasing number of Italian families[9] (who are Birralee's "traditional customers") living in the area of Doncaster, thus affecting enrollment.

- The increase of elderly people living in the area of Doncaster (about 30 percent of the residents in the Manningham district are fifty years old and above, whereas the percentage of people under the age of eighteen is only 23 percent; see Appendix 8) means fewer students of primary school age in the area.

- The trend toward smaller families means fewer children for primary schools.

- Smaller family size and the increase in general level of disposable income means that more parents can afford to send their children to private schools instead of government schools like Birralee.

Financial Position

Table A5-4 Summary of Financial Position in Accordance with 1999 School Global Budget (see Appendix 9 for Full Details)

Annual Budget Expenses	Amount ($$$)	%
Leadership and Teaching	464,000	59.9
Teaching Support	69,000	8.9
Premises	39,000	5.0
On Costs	78,000	10.1
Disability and Impairment	63,000	8.1
English as Second Language	11,000	1.4
Priority Programs	51,000	6.6
Total School Global Budget	**775,000**	**100**

The budget shown is partially funded by the government. The school itself has to raise the remaining amount, via voluntary donations in the form of school fees ($135 per student), local sponsorship, and various fund-raising activities (such as Sausage Sizzle and Chocolate Drive). The school generally spends about $500 per year on promotional activities, including brochures and advertisements in local newspapers.

GE Screening Grid

FIGURE A5-6. GE Screening Grid for Birralee Primary School

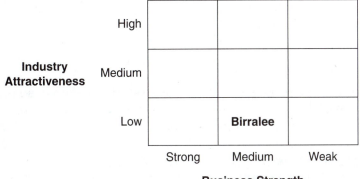

According to the analysis, industry attractiveness is low because of:

- Unfavorable growth rate (see Appendix 5)
- High competitive intensity
- Extensive control by the government in terms of school budgets and teaching curriculum

Business strength is medium because of:

- Small relative market share of 0.33 (see Appendix 1)
- High average growth rate (refer to Table A5-4)
- Strong customer loyalty from parents[10]

Marketing Objectives

- To increase student enrollment from 185 in 1999 to 205 by the end of 2001.
- To improve the school reputation among all the primary schools in the same region from a current rating of 2.73 to a rating of 3.5 by the end of 2001 (see Appendix 2).

The marketing objectives are similar to the corporate objectives due to the small size of the organization.

Marketing Strategy

- *Promotional strategy:* to increase the school's public exposure (eventually its enrollment) via fund raising, sponsorships from local business, and developing good relationships with local kindergartens.
- *Product strategy:* to introduce an Asian language program to attract students from an increasing number of Asian families living in the area as specified in the strategic plan.
- *Place strategy:* to improve the distribution of information using new mediums in order to disseminate information about the school quickly and effectively to existing and potential parents.

Marketing Program and Tactics

Fund Raising A fund-raising committee will be formed to organise two major fund-raising events per year (during March 2000 and 2001, and October 2000 and 2001). The nature of these events will be such that they involve greater participation from the public other than the school's population. Each event will incorporate different activities, which may include the existing ones, such as the Chocolate Drive, food stalls, and second-hand book sale. Kathy Sweeny will be in charge of the team, which is composed of the new principal, Mr. Graham Gordon, members of the Parents Committee, and all teachers. For each event, the estimated costs will be $5,000 and the projected income will be $7,500.

Sponsorship from Local Business A proposal should be drafted to seek sponsorship from local businesses. The project will involve all parents, who will seek new contacts in exchange for "intangible rewards" from the school, such as publishing their names in the school's newsletter. Parents will be informed of the details in a "special" parents meeting, which will take place on November 1, 1999, at 7:30 P.M. (subject to change). Mr. Graham Gordon and Rhonda Zerbi, vice president of the School Council, will be in charge of who will supervise the progress of the program. The details of the proposal should be finalised by October 25, 1999. Should the project succeed, the school will continue this with similar details in the year 2001.

Create a Good Relationship with the Local Kindergartens   A number of local kindergartens are contacted to explore the opportunities of working together. A "visiting team" is formed to organise activities such as the Buddy system between kindergarten students and students from Birralee Primary Schools, teachers promoting the school in the local kindergartens, and other shared activities. The team consists of teachers and will be closely supervised by the school principal and Rhonda Zerbi, especially in terms of objectives and details of this program. This program will take place several times during the year, starting from the beginning of the study term in 2000. The program will initially incur the cost of $300 including transport and promotional activities such as brochures. Any additional expenses will be revised in the near future.

Offer Asian Language Program   The school applies for local subsidies from the Community Development Grant Program 2000–01 by the Manningham City Council (see Appendix 10 for the copy of the application form). The application is to be submitted by September 17, 2000 (subject to change by the Manningham City Council).

Prior to the approval of the applications, the members of the school board and the principal will meet and discuss plans to be conducted after the approval from the Manningham City Council has been given. If this is the case, the language program will be introduced as early as the beginning of 2001.

Explore Other Mediums of Promotions   The school develops a Web site with general information about the school and is updated regularly for any current events and policy changes. Any staff in the schools or parents who have knowledge of creating a Web site and are willing to do the job voluntarily will be in charge of it. The Web site will be completed by the end of 1999. Brochures emphasizing the benefits of the small-school environment will be distributed to the households living in the school-targeted area. Mr. Graham Gordon will prepare all the printing and distribution of the brochure before the start of the study period in 2000. All distribution and printing costs will amount to $200.

For a summary of the marketing tactics and program, please refer to Appendix 11.

Budgeting

The financial budget for 2000–01 is shown as follows:

	Year		
	2000	*2001*	*Total*
Available Fund			
Funds from: School Council Reserve	$5,000	$5,000	$10,000
Fund Raising	$4,000	$4,000	$8,000
Printing	$1,000	$1,500	$2,500
Advertising	$500	$500	$1,000
Telephone	$4,500	$4,500	$9,000
Copy Paper	$2,500	$2,500	$5,000
Total fund			**$35,500**
Projected Income			
Fund Raising	$7,500	$7,500	$15,000
Projected Expenditure			
Fund Raising	$5,000	$5,000	$10,000

(Continues)

Projected Expenditure *(Continued)*

Meeting Expenses (refer to section 2.10 – Sponsorship)	$100	$100	$200
Transportation and Promotional Kits (refer to Section 2.10 – Kindergarten)	$300	$300	$600
Promotion and Advertising	$500	$500	$1,000
Total Costs			**$11,800**
Surplus			**$38,700**

These budgets are subject to change according to the financial adjustments from the school.

Contingency Plan

If the current planning environment changes substantially during the life of this marketing plan, the following contingency plans will be considered.

- To pursue the stabilize strategy. Birralee can choose to maintain its operation, with the small student enrollment, and continue to serve the people within the school's distance.
- To pursue the harvest strategy. Birralee primary school should cease its operations due to the lack of competitive advantage and the poor fit with the future direction of the school.

Implementation

This marketing plan is to be presented by the planners (Welly Tehunan, Quah Suat Hong, and Vanessa Yau) to Ken Grant (acting as marketing advisor to Birralee Primary School) and the representatives of Birralee Primary School on October 18, 1999. The presentation will take place at Monash University, between 7 P.M. and 9 P.M.

Having heard the presentation, the school's representatives are to present the plan to the school board at the designated time and venue. The school board will further assess the plan on criteria such as availability of resources required to carry out the plan.

Assuming that the plan is approved, the school board will arrange a special meeting (a week after the school board meeting) with representatives from local kindergartens and small businesses, parents, and members of the Parents Committee. The aim is to communicate the plan to the participants and to obtain their feedback to be used for further improvement on the plan.

The planners can be contacted to assist the schools in any stage of the plan, especially in terms of answering questions and presenting the plan to the school board during the special meeting. We can be contacted at 03-95760182 and 04-12182806.

Evaluation, Monitoring, and Control

Evaluation of the marketing plan will provide a feedback loop to the next marketing plan. This evaluation is the start and the end of the marketing plan. The evaluation can be used to find new opportunities and threats, keep performance in line with expectations, and also to solve specific problems that may occur.

A marketing audit will be conducted yearly to evaluate whether the plan still offers the best tactics. This will be conducted by the Program manager (the person in charge of each proposed strategy) in conjunction with the other staff members.

To ensure the marketing plan was implemented properly, it is to be monitored every six months. The monitoring process should take place in June 2000 and December 2000. The plan will be monitored by analysing the number of students enrolled in the school. The enrollment number will be monitored every half year to ensure that it is increasing.

A survey of parents and the people living within close proximity to the school is to be conducted to measure the effectiveness of the strategy (such as fund raising) and any change in the reputation of the school.

In addition, the school should conduct external analysis on an annual basis to detect any changes in the external environment (such as competitors and population demography).

BIBLIOGRAPHY

Summary Statistics, Victoria School, February 1998, Department of Education Victoria, 1998.
Australian Economic Indicators, Australian Bureau of Statistics, July 1999.
IBIS Industry Report 1997–98, Small Business Victoria, 1998.
Internet Access
  Household Income, http://www.abs.gov.au, 1998.
Personal Interview
  Interview with Sue Rathbone (Principal of Birralee Primary School), on September 17, 1999.
  Interview with Kathy Sweeny (President of the Community Relations Committee), September 24, 1999.
  Interview with Rhonda Zerbi (Vice President of the School Council), on September 27, 1999.

NOTES

1. *Summary Statistics—Victoria School Feb. 1998*, Department of Education Victoria, 1998, p. 5.
2. *Summary Statistics—Victoria School Feb. 1998,* loc. cit. p. 12.
3. *Australian Economic Indicators,* Australian Bureau of Statistics, July 1999, p. 22.
4. *Household Income,* http://www.abs.gov.au, 1998.
5. *IBIS Industry Report 1997–98, Small Business Victoria,* 1998, p. 5.
6. *Ibid.*
7. Interview with Sue Rathbone (Principal of Birralee Primary School), on September 17, 1999.
8. *Ibid.*
9. Interview with Sue Rathbone, Kathy Sweeny, and Rhonda Zerbi, on September 17, 1999, September 24, 1999, and September 27, 1999, respectively.
10. Interview with Kathy Sweeny and Rhonda Zerbi, on September 24, 1999 and September 27, 1999, respectively.

APPENDICES

APPENDIX 1

Analysis of Schools' Enrollment and Their Market Share

Name/Year	1998	% of Market Share	Relative Market Share
Birralee Primary School	189	5.46	0.33
Doncaster Garden Primary School	305	8.81	0.53
Doncaster Primary School	480	13.88	0.83
Greythorn Primary School	519	15	0.89
Templestowe Valley Primary School	191	5.52	0.33
Manningham Park Primary School	173	5	0.30
Anderson's Creek Primary School	409	11.82	0.71
Mont Albert Primary School	580	16.77	3.07
Boroondara Park Primary School	400	11.56	0.69
Box Hill North Primary School	213	6.16	0.37
Total	3,459	100	———

Calculation of market share in percent:

(Number of students in a particular school/Total number of students) × 100

Calculation of relative market share:

(Number of students in a particular school/The number of students in the largest competitor's school)

APPENDIX 2

Summary of Survey

Likert scale:	1	2	3	4	5
	very poor	poor	average	good	very good

- Twenty-five adults in the nearby area (see Appendix 11—the area within the orange line) were interviewed on September 20–21, 1999.

- Sixty-five percent (17 people) of the interviewees are aware of the existence of large primary schools listed in Appendix 6 (those schools with more than 300 students). These schools tend to be more heavily advertised than smaller primary schools.

- When measured against the Likert scale, Birralee Primary School scored an average of 2.73 in terms of its general reputation.

- When asked about the things that determine good primary schools, the interviewees frequently mentioned three things: facilities of the schools, location of the schools, and teaching standards. Birralee Primary School was ranked quite low in the first two because of its small size and the fact that the school is quite isolated.

- While the survey is not conclusive, it serves as an indication as to where the school currently stands in the public's perception.

APPENDIX 3

Segmentation of Primary School
(*Source: IBIS Industry Report 1997–1998.* Small Business Victoria, 1998)

1.   Government Schools

These primary schools are established on the basis of population criteria, whose students' composition is determined by the local community profile. Ideally, this profile is the establishment of appropriate curriculum emphasis, and the budget allocation to different programs within the schools such as literacy and English as a second language.

2.   Catholic Schools

The Catholic education system is managed and run by the National Catholic Education Commission, its state subsidiaries, and local Catholic dioceses. Most teachers in Catholic schools are now laypeople, and many have no affiliation to the Catholic faith.

3.   Other Nongovernment Schools

These schools may have religious affiliations, particularly Anglican, or be independent nondenominational schools. The larger nongovernment schools tend to be old, well-established schools with excellent reputations and strong traditions.

APPENDIX 4

Real Growth for the Primary Education Industry in Australia (in $ term)

	'95–'96 (%)	'96–'97 (%)	'97–'98 (%)
Industry Turnover	3.4	2.5	2.1
Industry Gross Product	3.4	2.5	2.1
Employment	1.0	0.8	0.4
No. of Establishments	−0.3	−0.3	−0.4
Domestic Demand	3.4	2.5	2.1
Total Wages	3.4	2.5	2.1

Source: IBIS Industry Report 1997–98, Small Business Victoria, 1998.

APPENDIX 5

Estimation of Average Percent Change of Victoria Primary Schools over the Past Five Years

School Type	Year				
	1994	1995	1996	1997	1998
Primary (All Primary Schools)	1,776	1,750	1,741	1,718	1,694
Percent Change	N/A	−1.46	−0.51%	−1.32	−1.40

Source: Summary Statistics Victoria Schools 1994–1998, Department of Education.

• According to the table above, the average percent change of the number of primary schools in Victoria is calculated as follows:

$$-(1.46\% + 0.51\% + 1.32\% + 1.40\%) \div 4 = -1.1725\%$$

APPENDIX 6

Porter's Five Forces

Threat of New Entrants: Low

- The cost of facilities and equipment is high.

- Each school must attract a sufficient number of students to achieve economic viability.

- Each school must have high-quality teaching and other staff to attract students' enrollment.

- The tradition and reputation of existing schools are already established and long lasting.

- The government restricts the establishment of new primary schools, and thus it is more difficult to obtain government funding.

Bargaining Power of Suppliers: Medium to High

- The government plays an important role in the industry, since it provides the guidelines for teaching and administration. This is even the case with the government schools, since the government allocates funds for each school.

- For each type of supplier (see Appendix 13), primary schools are able to choose the services from a number of services. Thus, the switching cost is low.

Bargaining Power of Buyers: Medium

- Parents are able to choose from a number of primary schools within a particular area. For example: there are sixteen primary schools within the Manningham District in Victoria to choose from (see Appendix 12).

- The switching cost is high due to the time, money, and effort involved in getting a new school for students.

Availability of Substitutes: Low

- There is almost no substitute for primary educating due to its compulsory nature.

Intensity of Rivalry: High

- A large number of schools are competing within the same region. As mentioned earlier, sixteen primary schools are competing with one another within the Manningham District.

- The exit barrier is high since it involves a large investment in the schools, as well as its reputation and tradition.

Other Factors to Consider

- The primary education industry is in a mature stage, with the number of schools established decreasing (growth rate of −0.3 percent in 1995–1996, to −0.4 percent in 1997–1998), as well as the domestic demand for primary school (growth rate of 3.4 percent in 1995–1996, to 2.1 percent in 1997–1998). (See Appendix 4.)

- There is a possibility that the growth prospects of the industry may be hampered by the availability of teaching staff. A study conducted for university deans of education predicts that there will be a shortage of 4,700 primary and secondary teachers nationally by the year 2000.

- The rate of growth in the population of primary school students in Australia is low (an average rate of 0.55 percent per year) compared to the growth in the overall percent population (1.3 percent per year), due mainly to a declining female fertility rate, an aging population, and high elder immigration to Australia.[*]

[*] IBIS Industry Report, Small Business Victoria, 1997–1998.

APPENDIX 7

Major Competitors Profile

- Nine schools are identified as the major competitors to the Birralee Primary School. All these schools are located in three different districts, namely, Boroondara District, Manningham District, and Whitehorse District.

School in Boroondara District

Name (Primary School)	Boroondara Park Primary School	Greythorn Primary School
Year of Establishment	1989	1953
Current Enrollment No.	400	519
Location	North Balwyn	North Balwyn
Facilities	• Extensive playing fields	• School hall
	• Two large ovals	• Computerised library
	• Performance/Arts department	• Well-equipped gym
	• Air-conditioned and portable classroom	• Uniform and swap shop
	• Computer room	
	• Computerised library	• French room
	• Recreation hall/gymnasium	• Extensive outdoor play areas
	• Art room	• Art room
	• Open, airy classroom	• Canteen
	• Canteen	
Teaching Programs	• Eight major curriculum	• Eight major curriculum
		• LOTE (French)
Other Activities	• Educational enhancement	• Christian religious education
	• Cultural and artistic programs	• After-school care program
	• Sporting and leisure programs	• Camp and exclusion
	• Leadership and decision-making programs	• House system
	• Pastoral care and concealing programs	
	• Religious activities and services	
	• Camps and exclusion	

Schools in Whitehorse District

Name (Primary School)	Box Hill North Primary School	Mont Albert Primary School
Year of Establishment	N/A	1917
Current Enrollment No.	213	580
Location	Box Hill North	Mont Albert
Facilities	• Library	• Library
	• Canteen	• Art room
	• Playground	• Performing art centre
	• Computer lab	• Canteen
		• Computer centre
		• Hall
Teaching Programs	• Eight major curriculum	• Eight major curriculum
		• LOTE (Italian)
Other Activities	• After-school care program	• After-school care program
	• Religious education program	• Reading recovery program
		• Art/craft studies
		• Music/drama studies
		• Swimming program
		• Camping and touring program
		• Gifted and talented student program
		• Teacher-student relationship meeting

Schools in Manningham District

Name (Primary School)	Anderson's Creek Primary School	Doncaster Gardens Primary School	Doncaster Primary School	Manningham Park Primary School	Templestowe Valley Primary School
Year of Establishment	N/A	N/A	1860	N/A	N/A
Current Enrollment No.	409	305	480	173	191
Location	Warrandyte	Doncaster East	Doncaster	Lower Templestow	Lower Templestow
Facilities	• Full-size breakfast stadium • Computer labs • Computerised library • Playground • Canteen	• Computer labs • Computerised library • Playground • Canteen • Library	• 100-seat theatre • Full-size gymnasium • Basketball courts • Music room • Art/craft centre • Extensive playground • Full-size oval • Computer lab • Canteen	• Video conferencing facilities • Art room • Fully computerised library • 300-seat hall • General purpose room • Canteen	• Computer lab • Library • Canteen • Language room • Playground
Teaching Programs	• Eight major curriculum • LOTE (Italian)	• Eight major curriculum	• Eight major curriculum • LOTE (Chinese)	• Eight major curriculum • LOTE (Japanese/Italian)	• Eight major curriculum
Other Activities	• After-school child care program • Early years literacy intervention program • Reading recovery program • Buddy system	• After-school care program • Dancing class • Singing class • Drama and musical performance • Buddy system	• After-school care program • Visual Arts studies • Student welfare and discipline program • Reading recovery program • Media studies • Drama class • Instrumental music program • Instrumental music program • Cultural awareness program • Study enrichment programs • Swimming program • Religious education program	• After-school care program • Individualised special needs program • Parents and friends club • Perceptual motor program	• Big Friends/Little Friends program • After-school care program • Camping program • House system

APPENDIX 8

Statistics of Population and Housing in Manningham District

According to the Australian Bureau of Statistics Census of Population and Housing 1996, the estimated percentage of Asian residents in Manningham District is calculated as follows:

2.0% (China) + 2.8% (Hong Kong) + 2.0% (Malaysia)
+ 0.3% (Vietnam) = 7.1%

The percentage of elderly people is calculated as follows:

14.7% (Age 50–59) + 8.5% (Age 60–69)
+ 5.6% (Age 70–84) + 1.2% (Age 85+) = 30%

The percentage of people under 17 years old is calculated as follows:

5.2% (Age 0–4) + 17.8% (Age 5–17) = 23.0%

- The chart below shows the trend of the nine primary schools' enrollment numbers from 1995 to 1998.

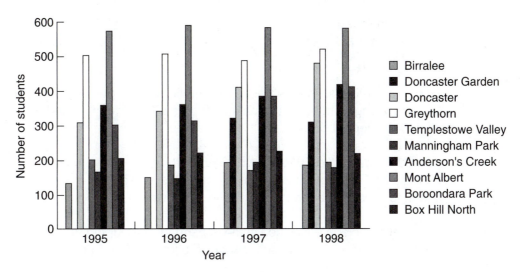

Source: Summary Statistics Victoria Schools 1995–1998.

APPENDIX 9

1999 School Global Budget

MEMORANDUM

TO: Principals and Head Teachers
General Managers (Schools)

FROM: B J Beaumont, General Manager
School Personnel and Resources

SUBJECT: **CONFIRMED 1999 SCHOOL GLOBAL BUDGETS**

DATE: April 8, 1999

Please find enclosed the confirmed 1999 School Global Budget (SGB) for your school. The Principal Classification Budget and principal class entitlements for 1999 are also included.

As usual, the confirmed SGB is based on enrollments as per the February census. Revisions resulting from new information, such as Enrollment audits, will be issued periodically to affected schools.

An updated *Guide to the 1999 School Global Budget* is being issued separately to all schools. The Guide outlines the major changes reflected in the confirmed SGB. The changes have also been highlighted in the covering memo to the Guide.

In addition, allocations are included in the confirmed SGB for the Victorian Early Years Literacy Program for all Primary schools which completed an Early Literacy plan.

CASES reports will reflect the confirmed SGB from pay 9822.

Contact telephone numbers for enquiries are included in the *Guide to the School Global Budget.*

for B J BEAUMONT
General Manager
School Personnel and Resources

DEPARTMENT OF EDUCATION
SCHOOL GLOBAL BUDGET
1999 CONFIRMED-SUMMARY

Budget Version: 2   **Version Date: 09/04/1999**

Version Time: 16:28:42

Host School: 4991   **Birralee Primary School**   **Total Enrollment:** 186.0

Region: 33   School Type: Primary

Enrollment P-2:   95.0   Enrollment 3–6:   91.0   Primary Ungraded: 0.0   **Total Primary:**   186.0

Enrollment 7–10   0.0   Enrollment 11–12   0.0   Secondary Ungraded: 0.0   **Total Secondary:**   0.0

Summary

Total Core	$650,633.35
Total Disability and Impairment	$63,478.00
Total English as a Second Language	$10,882.00
Total Priority Programs	$51,079.80
TOTAL SCHOOL GLOBAL BUDGET	**$776,073.15**
Notional Cash Allocation	$87,847.10
Notional Credit Allocation	$688,226.05

PRINCIPAL CLASSIFICATION BUDGET

TOTAL SCHOOL GLOBAL BUDGET	776,073.15
WorkCover:	−462.25
Superannuation Charge:	−44,955.00
Principal Class Salary Variation	13,168.08
Principal Classification Budget	743,823.98

PRINCIPAL CLASSIFICATION ENTITLEMENT

Range   645,750.00–819,000.00   Principal Class IIB   Assistant Principal Class IA   Asst Prin Entitlement   100

The 1999 Principal Classification Budget is calculated by adjusting the School Global Budget to exclude workcover and superannuation.

A further adjustment, the Principal Class Salary Variation, represents two factors:

The increase or decrease in principal class salary entitlements that would result in the event of these positions being vacated where the encumbent position differs from the new entitlement

A correction factor, which enables principal class positions in schools which have a total PCB near the top of a PCB range to be automatically classified according to the next highest range

DEPARTMENT OF EDUCATION
SCHOOL GLOBAL BUDGET
1999 CONFIRMED-SUMMARY

Budget Version: 2

Version Date: 09/04/1999

Version Time: 16:28:42

Host School: 4991   **Birralee Primary School**   **Total Enrollment:** 186.0

Region: 33   School Type: Primary

Enrollment P-2:	95.0	Enrollment 3–6:	91.0	Primary Ungraded:	0.0	**Total Primary:**	186.0
Enrollment 7–10	0.0	Enrollment 11–12	0.0	Secondary Ungraded:	0.0	**Total Secondary:**	0.0

School: 4991   Birralee Primary School   TYPE: Primary

Particulars	Type	EFT/SQ.M STUDENT	RATE	AMOUNT $
SLN-Index: 0.569	Location_Index: 0:00	Expenses Code		

Core

Leadership and Teaching

Particulars	Type	EFT/SQ.M STUDENT	RATE	AMOUNT $
Principal Class I	Credit	1.00	$57,925.00	$57,925.00
Assistant Principal Class IA	Credit	1.00	$57,925.00	$57,925.00
Leading Teachers – Level 2	Credit	1.00	$51,731.00	$51,731.00
Level 1 Teachers	Credit	6.00	$45,400.00	$272,400.00
Performance Incentives & Special Payments	Credit	0.00	$0.00	$11,544.00
Core – Primary Relief Teacher	Cash	9.00	$1,430.90	$12,878.10
				$464,403.10

Teaching Support

Particulars	Type	EFT/SQ.M STUDENT	RATE	AMOUNT $
Teaching Support – Credit	Credit	0.00	$0.00	$35,992.86
Teaching Support – Cash	Cash	0.00	$0.00	$29,572.51
Literacy Allocation	Cash	186.00	$20.00	$3,720.00
				$6,928.37

Premises

Particulars	Type	EFT/SQ.M STUDENT	RATE	AMOUNT $
Contract Cleaning – Normal Use (sq.m)	Cash	897.00	$16.70	$14,979.90
Contract Cleaning – Low Use (sq.m)	Cash	504.00	$3.45	$1,738.80
Grounds Allowance (sq.m)	Cash	19,576.00	$0.16	$3,132.16
Utilities	Cash	0.00	$0.00	$10,340.96
Maintenance and Minor Works Funding	Cash	0.00	$0.00	$8,915.87
				$39,107.69

On Costs

Particulars	Type	EFT/SQ.M STUDENT	RATE	AMOUNT $
WorkCover Premium	Credit	0.00	$0.00	$462.25
Revised/New Scheme Superannuation Charge	Credit	9.00	$4,995.00	$44,955 00
Core – Payroll Tax (%)	Credit	487,517.86	$6.65	$32.419 94
				$77,837.19

Total Core				$650,633.35

(Continues)

DEPARTMENT OF EDUCATION
SCHOOL GLOBAL BUDGET *(Continued)*
1999 CONFIRMED-SUMMARY

Budget Version: 2

Version Date: 09/04/1999

Version Time: 16:28:42

Host School: 4991   **Birralee Primary School**   **Total Enrollment:** 186.0

Region: 33   School Type: Primary

Enrollment P-2:	95.0	Enrollment 3–6:	91.0	Primary Ungraded:	0.0	**Total Primary:** 186.0
Enrollment 7–10	0.0	Enrollment 11–12	0.0	Secondary Ungraded:	0.0	**Total Secondary:** 0.0

School: 4991   Birralee Primary School   TYPE: Primary

Particulars	Type	EFT/SQ.M STUDENT	RATE	AMOUNT $
SLN-Index: 0.569	Location_Index: 0:00	Expenses Code		
Disability and Impairment				
New Integration Students – Level 2	Credit	0.00	$0.00	$8,530.00
New Integration Students – Level 4	Credit	0.00	$0.00	$54,948.00
Total Disability and Impairment				63.478.00
English as a Second Language				
ESL – Level 1	Credit	28.00	$264.00	$7,392.00
ESL – Level 2	Credit	5.00	$340.00	$1,700.00
ESL – Level 3	Credit	3.00	$422.00	$1,266.00
ESL – Level 4	Credit	1.00	$524.00	$524.00
Total English as a Second Language				$10,882.00
Priority Programs				
LOTE Allocation	Credit	0.00	$0.00	$13,950.00
Literacy Coordination	Credit	0.00	$0.00	$16,758.00
Reading Recovery	Credit	0.00	$0.00	$17,803.00
Teacher Professional Development	Cash	0.00	$0.00	$2,568.80
Total Priority Programs				$51,079.80
School Total				$776,073.15

APPENDIX 10

Copy of Community Development Grant Program

MANNINGHAM
BALANCE OF CITY AND COUNTRY

COMMUNITY DEVELOPMENT GRANT PROGRAM 1999/00
Application Form

Please read the *Community Development Grant Program Guidelines* prior to applying for funding. Applicants are required to complete each section. Please attach additional information if required. Typed applications are preferred. Faxed and late applications *will not* be accepted.

**An information session will be held 6.30pm – 7.30pm on
Thursday 26 August, 1999
"THE FUNCTION ROOM"
MANNINGHAM CITY COUNCIL
699 Doncaster Road
Doncaster Vic 3108**

Closing date for applications is 5.00pm Friday 17 September, 1999

SECTION 1 – ORGANIZATION DETAILS

1.1 Organization Name . . . .

1.2 Contact Person . . . .

1.3 Address . . . .

  Postcode . . . .

1.4 Telephone Number. . . . . Facsimile Number . . . .

1.5 Names and Positions of Principal Office Bearers . . . .

  . . . .

  . . . .

  . . . .

1.6 Is the organization incorporated? Yes/No Registration Number . . . .

1.7 If the organization is **not** Incorporated, which organization will auspice your organization? . . . . .

  . . . .

  Registration Number . . . .

1.8   Purpose of your organization

SECTION 2 – APPLICATION SUMMARY

2.1   Name of Project/Program . . . .

2.2   Total Amount of Funding Requested $ . . . .

SECTION 3 – PROJECT/PROGRAM INFORMATION

3.1   Description of Project/Program.
      In this section please provide the following information about the project/program:
      - Description.
      - Commencement and completion dates.
      - Location.
      - Target Group/s.
      - Expected number of participants.
      - Other organization/groups who will be involved in your activity *(explain how they will be involved)*.

3.2   Objectives of the Project/Program.

3.3   List three expected outcomes of the project/program *(the outcomes need to be specific, achievable and measurable).*

<u>**SECTION 4 – FINANCIAL INFORMATION**</u>

		Supplied
4.1	Please supply a copy of your organization's last audited financial statement.	**Yes/No**
4.2	Has other financial assistance been sought for this project/program? If yes, please give details. This may include sponsorship or government funding.	**Yes/No**

| 4.3 | Have you received funding from Council in the last three years? If yes, please give details. | **Yes/No** |

4.4   Program/Project Budget:

(A)   Income – list all sources and amounts of income (including anticipated income) for example: donations, fees, charges, grants, organization contributions. [Income (A) and Expenditure (B) must balance.]

Source	Amount
....	$ ....
....	$ ....
....	$ ....
....	$ ....
....	$ ....
....	$ ....
....	$ ....
....	$ ....
....	$ ....
.... Total Income	$ ....

(B)   Expenditure – list all costs of the program/project. [Income (A) and Expenditure (B) must balance.]

Item of Expenditure	Amount
....	$ ....
....	$ ....
....	$ ....
....	$ ....
....	$ ....
....	$ ....
....	$ ....
....	$ ....
....	$ ....
.... Total Income	$ ....

Total Amount of funding requested from Council $ ....

4.5   **Organizations Contribution**

Applicants must demonstrate their contribution to the project. Please list all non-financial contributions, for example: volunteer hours, facilities or equipment. [Financial contributions should be included in 4.4 (A).]

....

....

....

....

....

4.5 I hereby apply for funding through the ***Community Development Grant Program*** on behalf of:

Organization:...

Signed:...

Position: ....

Date: ....

CLOSING DATE FOR APPLICATIONS IS 5.00PM FRIDAY 17 SEPTEMBER 1999

Send applications to:

Customer Service Officer
Cultural and Leisure Services Unit
MANNINGHAM CITY COUNCIL
PO Box 1
DONCASTER VIC 3108

MANNINGHAM
BALANCE OF CITY AND COUNTRY

If you have any queries please contact:
Customer Service Officer
Telephone: 9840 9393

Manningham City Council
COMMUNITY DEVELOPMENT GRANT PROGRAM
FUNDING GUIDELINES 1999/00

Introduction

The *Community Development Grant Program* is conducted annually by Council in recognition of the importance and value of community development in the City of Manningham. This is reflected in the *Corporate Plan 1998–2001,* which states:

- *Culture and Leisure.* Promote, facilitate and provide a diverse range of quality cultural and leisure facilities, programs and services, based on community development principles, to residents of and visitors to the City of Manningham which enhance cultural heritage, quality of life, community development and healthy lifestyles.

- *Social and Community Services.* Facilitate the equitable distribution of a range of diverse, quality social and community services to all sections of the community by maximising the use of available resources and encouraging community activity based on community principles.

- *Health and Well-Being.* Promote and support the optimum physical, psychological and emotional health and well-being of the community.

Council has allocated **$68,525** for the 1999/00 *Community Development Grant Program.* Grants are offered **once** a year.

Information about other Council grant programs is available on request.

Purpose

The purpose of the *Community Development Grant Program* is to facilitate and support non-profit community organisations in the City of Manningham to develop projects and programs which benefit and meet the needs of the community.

Objectives

The objectives of the Community Development Grant Program are to:

- Strengthen community identity, promote Manningham and Manningham City Council through a diverse range of projects and programs.

- Facilitate opportunities to participate in a broad range of activities which promote community development, for example in the areas of:
  - community service
  - leisure and recreation
  - arts, culture and heritage
  - welfare
  - information
  - health
  - education
  - environmental education and interpretation
  - natural heritage

- Support community projects and programs that address demonstrated needs in specific areas, for example: people with disabilities, people of non English speaking backgrounds (NESB) and from specific ethnic populations, and Aboriginal and Torres Strait Islanders.

- Promote and integrate environmentally sustainable practices.

- Encourage the innovative and effective use of community resources.

- Reflect and promote the cultural richness and diversity of the City of Manningham, including the heritage and environmental qualities.

- Support and encourage community organisations to develop partnerships and networks with fellow agencies, businesses, schools and local government, thereby enhancing the sense of community and effective use of resources.

- Provide opportunities for the development of a range of skills through the management and participation in projects and programs.

Eligibility

- Applicants must make and demonstrate their financial and non financial contribution to the project or program, for example: staff resources, volunteer hours, funds, facilities, equipment, sponsorship or donations.

- The project or program must be located within the City of Manningham.

- Preference will be given to applications from organisations located within the City of Manningham.

- Priority will be given to cooperative ventures between two or more community organisations.
- Organisations must be non profit and incorporated. If the organisation is not incorporated it must be auspiced by another organisation that is incorporated (this arrangement must be confirmed by written agreement).
- Preference will be given to applications that demonstrate effective planning (including financial planning and sustainable practices), clear objectives and evaluation processes.
- Funds will only be allocated for direct program or project costs, for example:
  - materials
  - workers costs (not ongoing salaries)
  - advertising & promotion
  - venue rental
  - equipment/equipment hire
  - transport

Eligibility Exclusions

The following will **not** be considered eligible:

- Capital works.
- Ongoing costs, e.g. staff salaries, administration, maintenance.
- Applicants who have not met the requirements of previous grants from Council, for example: have not completed the evaluation forms or acknowledged Council support in publicity and promotion.
- Organisations who request funding for a program or project that is the responsibility of other levels of government.
- Community organisations who already receive Council funds to undertake a specific activity for which funding is being sought.
- Programs or projects that are seen as a duplication of existing programs or projects in the municipality.

Assessment

- An independent Assessment Panel consisting of: a Councilor, representatives from relevant Council Advisory Committees and appropriately skilled community representatives, will assess applications and allocate funds. The Assessment Panel will consist of a maximum of six people.
- Council officer(s) will provide advice to the Assessment Panel.
- Assessment Panel members must declare any pecuniary interest.
- The Assessment Panel reserves the right to recommend the transfer of an application to a more appropriate grant program.

Conditions of Grant

Grants are allocated to community organizations from the *Community Development Grant Program* according to the following conditions:

- Programs and projects will not be funded retrospectively.
- Funds will be allocated **once** a year.
- Only one application per community organisation/project will be considered in any year. Therefore any organisations jointly applying for funds should submit only one application.
- Acknowledge Manningham City Council in all promotional material including: media, programs, flyers, advertisement, billboards and banners etc. The Council logo must be reproduced according to the corporate style guide, which is available from the Marketing Unit.
- Utilise funding only for the stated purpose.
- Allocation of funds to a community organisation for any purpose, in any funding round, must not be taken as a commitment of subsequent funding.
- The recipients of the *Community Development Grant Program* shall take out, and keep current a liability insurance policy in a form approved by Council, in the joint names of the Manningham City Council and the recipient for a minimum sum of $5 million (or more), insuring Council and the recipient against all actions, costs, claims, charges, expenses, and damages whatsoever which may be brought or made or claimed against them arising out of, or in relation to, the said activity. The policy shall also contain a cross liability clause.
- Programs and projects must be completed within twelve months of funding, unless an alternative written agreement has been reached with the Cultural Development Officer.
- Within two months of completing the program or project an evaluation report must be submitted on the supplied form, incorporating a financial statement of income and expenditure of the total project or program.
- Grant recipients are required to sign a proforma agreeing to the above *Conditions of Grant* prior to receiving the grant.
- Grants will be paid by cheque.
- If funding is not utilized for the stated purpose, the organisation receiving the funding must guarantee repayment in full, plus interest earned.
- Funding must be deposited and maintained in a Bank approved by Council and not invested outside that Bank without written approval. (List supplied with *Conditions of Grant*.)
- Grant recipients must be willing (on request) to supply a complete copy of the program/project, accounts/books for examination by the Council auditor.

Applications

- An information session for intending applicants will be held:

THURSDAY
26 August 1999
6:30–7:30 P.M.
in the Function Room
Municipal Offices
699 Doncaster Road,
Doncaster 3108

It is recommended that all potential applicants, particularly first time applicants, attend this session.

- *Community Development Grant Program* Application Forms are available from the Cultural and Leisure Services Unit or the Social and Community Services Unit, Manningham City Council.

- If you require an application package, further information or assistance in completing your application please contact:

Cultural and Leisure Services Unit
or
Social and Community Services Unit
MANNINGHAM CITY COUNCIL
699 Doncaster Road
DONCASTER VIC 3108
9840-9393
9840-9269
9840-9426
9840-9257

- Application packages are available by Email on request.
- Upon request Funding Guidelines will be available in community languages.

Applications close
at 5:00 P.M.

FRIDAY 17 SEPTEMBER 1999

Applications will not be accepted after this date.

All applications must be on the designated application form.

Faxed applications will not be accepted.

Schedule

- Advertise the availability of the grants week beginning 16 August 1999.
- Information session conducted 6:30–7:30 P.M., Thursday 26 August 1999.
- Applications close 5:00 P.M. Friday 17 September 1999.
- Applications will be assessed and funds allocated by mid November 1999.
- Applicants advised of the outcome of their applications at the end of November 1999.
- Signing of agreements to grant conditions and distributions of grants during December 1999.
- *The schedule may be affected by the number of applications and vary accordingly.*

APPENDIX 11

Summary of the Strategy and Tactics

Strategy	Aim	Action Plan	Person-In-Charge	Time	Cost
Conduct fund-raising activities	• To raise public awareness of the school • To increase fund to finance additional school activities and improve existing facilities	• Fund-raising committee will be formed to organise 2 major fund-raising events per year, instead of several ones. The nature of these events will be such that they involve greater participation from the public other than the school's population. • Each event will incorporate different activities which may include the existing ones, such as the Chocolate Drive, food stalls, and second books selling, etc.	• Kathy Sweeny will be in charge of the team. • The fund-raising committee will consist of the principal, Mr. Graham Gordon, members of Parents Committee and all teachers.	• The fund-raising events will occur twice a year: during March 2000 and 2001, and October 2000 and 2001.	• For each event, the estimated costs will be $5,000, and the projected income will be $7,500.
Sponsorship from local businesses	• To increase fund to finance additional school activities and improve existing facilities • To raise public awareness of the school	• A proposal should be drafted to seek sponsorship from local businesses. • All parents will be involved to seek new contacts in exchange of "intangible rewards," such as publishing their names in the school's newsletter. • Parents will be informed of the details in "special" parents' meeting.	• Mr. Graham Gordon and Rhonda will be in charge. • Mr. Gordon and Rhonda, with the help of parents' committee member, will be following up on the developments of each participating parent.	• The details of the proposal should be finalised by October 25, 1999. • The parents meeting will take place on November 1, 1999 at 7:30 P.M. (subject to change). • Should the project succeed, the school will continue this with similar details in 2001.	• Beverages (tea and coffee) and stationaries for the meeting: $60.

Strategy	Objectives	Actions	Responsibility/Timing	Costs
Create good relationship with the local kindergartens	• Create a good working relationship with the local kindergartens. • To increase awareness of the school among the "potential students."	• A number of local kindergartens are contacted to explore the opportunities of working together. • A "visiting team" is formed to organise activities such as Buddy system between kindergarten students and students from Birralee Primary Schools, teachers promoting the school in the local kindergartens, and other shared activities.	• The school principal and Rhonda will be supervising this activity in terms of objectives and details of this program. • The "visiting team" will consist of teachers.	• This program will occur several times during the year, starting from the start of study term, and right throughout the year 2001.	• $300 including transport, promotional.
Offer Asian language program	• To attract potential students from the Asian families living in the area. • To improve the prestige of the school.	• The school applies for local subsidies from Community Development Grant Program 2000/2001 by the Manningham City Council (see Appendix 10). • The discussed plan will be adjusted accordingly once the subsidy is granted.	• The details of the program will be discussed among the members of the school board and the principal.	• The application should be submitted by 17 September, 2000 (subject to change by the Manningham City Council). • If successful, the language program will be introduced as early as the beginning of 2001.	• No projected costs at this point of time.
Explore other mediums of promotions	• To increase the awareness of the school • To improve the perception (technology advanced) of the schools from the community.	• Develop a Web site with general information about the school, and update regularly for any current events and policy changes. • Brochures emphasising the benefits of small school environment are distributed to local household's letterbox. • Publication in the local newspaper should be maintained and continued.	• Any staff in the school who has the knowledge to develop the Web site will be in charge of it. If not, ask for the help from parents who have the knowledge and volunteer to do it. • Mr. Graham Gordon will be in charge of all the printing and distribution of the brochure, and of the publication in the local newspaper.	• The Web site should be completed by the end of 1999. • Distribution of brochures and publication in local newspaper will be carried out before the start of the study period in 2000 and will continue throughout the whole year.	• No obvious fee for setting up a Web site. There is considerable free Web hosting in the Internet. • $200 including printing, distribution costs, etc.

APPENDIX 12

Schools in Manningham District of Victoria

(*Source:* Victorian Government Schools, http://www.softweb.vic.edu.au schools melbdist.htm, 1998)

- Anderson's Creek Primary School
- Beverley Hills Primary School
- Birralee Primary School
- Bulleen Heights Schools
- Donburn Primary School
- Doncaster Garden Primary School
- Doncaster Primary School
- Doncaster Secondary College
- Manningham Park Primary School
- Milgate Primary School
- Park Orchards Primary School
- Serpell Primary School
- Templestowe College
- Templestowe Heights Primary School
- Templestowe Park Primary School
- Warrandyte High School
- Warrandyte Primary School
- Wonga Park Primary School

APPENDIX 13

Suppliers for the Primary Schools

(*Source: IBIS Industry Report 1997–98. Small Business Victoria,* 1998)

Preschool education
- Suppliers of potential students for primary schools

Government administration
- Provides guidelines, budgets, and teaching curriculum

Electronic equipment manufacturing
- Provides schools with the necessary laptops, computers, and photocopier to aid the teaching of the students

Newspaper, books, and stationery retailers
- Provide publicity, the necessary textbooks, teaching materials, and office equipment

Nonresidential building constructions
- Provide building construction for the schools

Child-Care services
- Provide child care for busy parents whose children are left in the schools

APPENDIX 14

Criteria for Choosing Primary Schools

(Source: IBIS Industry Report 1997–98, Small Business Victoria, 1998)

Each parent has a different set of criteria for making a decision in their choice of their children's primary schools. Below are the common factors that affect their decisions.

- Convenience of the location of primary schools.
- The quality of teaching staffs and programs.
- The quality of facilities and equipment in the schools.
- The proximity of the primary schools to the desired secondary schools. Some primary schools may compete with combined primary and secondary schools which can provide continuity of education.
- The reputation, tradition, and status of the schools.
- The cost of education, which is influenced by the level of government funding to nongovernment schools, and the extent of extra facilities and opportunities provided by the schools. Catholic-affiliated schools tend to receive higher government grants and charge significantly lower fees than other nongovernment primary schools.
- The schools' religious affiliation.
- The degree of promotional activities being conducted to increase parents' awareness of the schools' existence.

A6

OAKSTREAM HOMES

Developed by
JONATHAN J. BURSON

Contents

EXECUTIVE SUMMARY

OakStream Homes is a real estate brokerage and management company that offers a unique perspective to real estate sales and management. CEO and President Willard Burson is a licensed real estate broker who sponsors real estate agents in Columbus, Ohio. He and his wife are the primary agents who are supported by a small staff of office workers and construction crews.

OakStream Homes began as Home Rite Realty in 1980 as a real estate brokerage and investment company. The owner, Will Burson, had been a practicing realtor since 1969. In 2001, the company changed its name to OakStream Homes to reflect a change in the company's direction and to give the company a new image.

The primary goal of OakStream is to purchase investment real estate in the Columbus, Ohio area for clients, make capital improvements to those properties, and then manage the newly acquired assets so that its clients will have investment income. Oakstream's agents have a combined experience of over 50 years in real estate sales, investment, and management that allows them to provide excellent deals and service to their clients.

SITUATIONAL ANALYSIS

2.1 Situational Analysis Summary

Columbus is a growing city that delivers capital gains from real estate investments as well as an easy market to receive positive cash flow from rents received. Due to its position as the state capital, county seat, and central Ohio location, Columbus offers more to real estate investors and other businesses than many other similar cities. While there are several real estate investment firms in Franklin County, few tender the unique aspects that OakStream brings to the table.

2.2 The Marketing Environment

2.2.1 Demographics Franklin County has a population of over 1 million people, putting the Columbus metropolitan area in the top 15 most populated urban areas in the

United States. Over 75 percent of the population is white and almost 20 percent are African-American with a small percentage being of Asian descent or other nationalities (*Ohio QuickFacts,* 2004, pg. 1). The county's population has been growing steadily, as indicated in Figure A6-1.

2.2.2 Household Incomes   The per capita income was $23,059 in Franklin County in 1999, but median household income was $42,734 (*Ohio QuickFacts,* 2004, pg. 2). "The Bureau of Labor Statistics reports that an average American 'consumer unit'—defined as a family, a single person who's financially independent or two people living together who share major expenses—spends $38,050 a year" (Lobb, 2002, pg. 1). Since the average American consumer unit spends this much, it means that the median household in Franklin County has approximately an additional $4,500 to spend. However, the cost of living in Columbus is slightly lower (3 percent) than the rest of the country, meaning that that extra $4,500 goes even further (*Cost of Living Index,* 2002, pg. 3).

Figure A6-2 shows the per capita personal income statistics (not household income statistics, which would be higher) for Franklin County.

What is important to note in Figures A6-1 and A6-2 is the steady increase in not only the nominal incomes, but also the adjusted incomes. While Oakstream Homes is primarily concerned with the income of the household as a whole, these figures show that the spending ability of the average individual in Franklin County has been steadily increasing.

2.2.3 Housing   In the 2000 census, Franklin County had a 56.9 percent homeownership rate. That means that 43.1 percent of people rented their dwelling places in 2000. The total number of housing units available in 2002 was 489,851. Of those, 37.5 percent were in multiunit structures. The median value of owner-occupied house was $116,200 (*Ohio QuickFacts,* 2004, pg. 2).

From 1970 to 2000, the price of the average home in Columbus rose 6 percent every year, on average. Thus a home costing $25,000 in 1970 would have cost $143,587 in 2000. While the appreciation of the average home was not exactly 6 percent every year, the growth was fairly consistent and has resulted in significant capital gains for many homeowners.

FIGURE A6-1.   Population Over Time

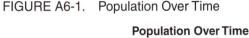

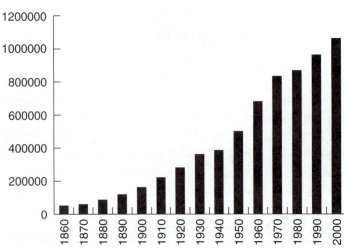

Source: Ohio Department of Development, Office of Strategic Research; Extension Data Center, Dept of HCRD, The Ohio State University

FIGURE A6-2. Per Capita Personal Income

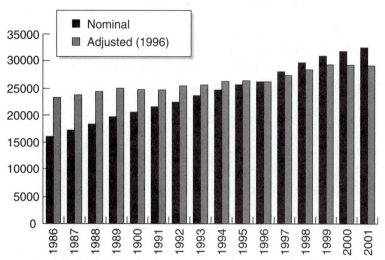

Per Capita Personal Income

Source: Bureau of Economics Analysis; Extension Data Center, Dept of HCRD, The Ohio State University

These statistics are important for a number of reasons. First, they show that the rental business in Columbus is strong, so purchasing real estate there should allow the buyer to have income. Second, the consistent rise in home prices indicates an increase in not only the value of houses, but other types of property as well. While OakStream Homes deals primarily with dwelling units, it also works with investors who prefer commercial real estate.

2.2.4 Government The role that the government plays in investment real estate is significant. Some states and counties generally side with landlords, while others tend to stand for tenants. Then there are a few states that are relatively neutral. Franklin County tends to be a neutral county. Tenants have won cases and landlords have won cases. Thus, having to remove a troublesome tenant from the premises, while it may take time due to the legal process, is not extremely difficult for a management company. In other states, such as California, the tenant is almost always right, making it much more cumbersome for the landlord to remove an undesirable tenant.

Not only do the courts have a noteworthy role in the investment of real estate, the legislative branch does as well. It is the legislative branch of the state and county that decides how properties of foreclosed mortgages will be sold. In Wyoming, a buyer of a foreclosed property cannot get title to or possession of the property for at least 60 days, and in many cases, 90 days. However, in Ohio, thanks to different laws, purchasers of foreclosed properties can get title in just a few days. This makes buying foreclosed homes in Ohio much more appealing than that of states with laws similar to Ohio.

What makes Ohio even more attractive for the real estate investor is that not all the money is due up front for a foreclosed property. In Wyoming for example, the purchaser must pay the entire price of the property the day it is sold and then wait 60 to 90 days before getting title to the property. In Ohio, the buyer places a down payment for the house, gets title to it, and then is able to obtain a mortgage for the remainder of the purchase price.

These laws and judicial tendencies are helpful to OakStream Homes, since the company purchases numerous properties every month from foreclosure sales and has had to manage several units that have required tenants to be removed from the premises.

2.2.5 Businesses When it comes to business economics, Franklin County is doing well. Centrally located in Ohio and the Midwest, Columbus is an excellent place for distribution centers:

> Greater Columbus offers unparalleled access to U.S. and Canadian markets. That's why Greater Columbus has been a focal point of distribution for well over a century. Today, the area is home to more than 120 million square feet (11 million square meters) of warehouse and distribution space.
>
> Within a one-day truck drive of Greater Columbus are:
> 58 percent of the U.S. population
> 50 percent of the Canadian population
> 61 percent of U.S. manufacturing capacity
> 80 percent of U.S. corporate headquarters (*Access to Markets,* pg. 1).

Perhaps it is because of location that the headquarters to many well-known companies, including Wendy's, Big Lots, Nationwide Insurance, American Electric Power, Value City Department Stores, Abercrombie & Fitch, and the Limited, which owns Victoria's Secret and Bath & Body, are located in Franklin County.

The location of Columbus may have originally lent itself for distribution purposes, but the business atmosphere has grown far beyond location, and people are noticing. *Entrepreneur* magazine ranked Columbus in the number 15 spot for best business climate in the United States and the number 1 spot for the Midwest.

The climate and growth of business in Columbus is significant to OakStream Homes because it affects the appreciation of property values and price of rents.

2.2.6 Competitors As in any large metropolitan area, there are hundreds of real estate companies in Columbus. However, few would be seen as competitors to OakStream Homes' unique niche in real estate investing. While many real estate brokerages sell residential houses as personal residences, only a few sell any type of real estate as investments. In fact, OakStream is the only physical agency I know of that purchases foreclosed homes for investors and manages them. Thus, the competition is limited.

2.3 TARGET MARKETS

2.3.1 High-Income Families

Being the home to so many company headquarters, Columbus has numerous wealthy individuals. As such, many of those individuals have large amounts of disposable income that could be used to invest. OakStream Homes can give these families advice and select properties in which that money could be invested.

2.3.2 Middle-Income Families

The majority of households in Franklin County fit into this target market. Many of these families are looking for ways to make a few extra hundred dollars a month. OakStream Homes provides that way through the vehicle of investment real estate.

2.3.3 Low-Income Families

OakStream Homes does not like to see people suffer to stay on top of bill payments, nor do they want the people who rent their properties to lose out on the benefits of home ownership. Many of the low-income families could use a property bought at a foreclosure sale for their personal residence due to the much lower cost of acquiring foreclosed property. Once these families see the benefits of real estate, they could use real estate to move into the high-income category and leave behind their worries of not being able to pay the bills.

2.3.4 Individuals

While the primary users of Oakstream's services are couples with children, there are several individuals who also purchase investment properties. These individuals fall into all three levels of income, but do not have a significant other with whom decisions must be made. As such, they have much more liberty to purchase higher risk investments and potentially increase the amount of income received from such investments.

SWOT ANALYSIS

3.1 Strengths

OakStream Homes' major strengths lie in the knowledge and experience of its owner. Will Burson has been a licensed realtor since 1969. With 35 years of experience in the Columbus area, he understands the market. Furthermore, Will has an accounting degree from The Ohio State University. This degree gives him the knowledge he needs to accurately and quickly process numbers and give quality investment advice to clients. His degree and his real estate experience helped him in establishing his own business in 1980, which has further deepened his investment knowledge and experience.

3.2 Weaknesses

The weaknesses of a company may be numerous to an insider, but only some of the most obvious ones may be noticed from the outside. One of the major weaknesses of OakStream is a lack of accountability. No independent auditing firm checks the financials of the company. There are no autonomous financial planners or paid advisers who do an annual review of the company's progress. Without these types of objective reviews of the company, it is difficult for OakStream to see where it has been and where it is going.

Because there is no accountability, it creates other weaknesses for OakStream Homes, such as its lack of the "big picture view." While Will often has plans for the 1-, 5-, and 10-year points, it is difficult for him to track where he has been and where he is going since he is the primary worker in every aspect of the company. In fact, in many cases he can get side-tracked for months while working on a single project. Rather than doing such jobs, he should hire others to do the work and keep his focus on the big picture. But it is hard for him to see this weakness because the company is not periodically reviewed by an outside agency.

Another weakness of OakStream Homes is the lack of technology and tech support. In one of its more prosperous years, the company had a Web site, but it was little more than an informational site about the company. The company uses computers that are networked, but there is no dedicated technology employee and the company has not hired an outside agency to be its support.

3.3 Opportunities

OakStream Homes has a number of opportunities that have become available with the advent of the Internet. One such opportunity is Web-based management of properties. The company's Web site could be set up similar to an online bank. An owner of a property that OakStream manages could log on to get details about his property—when rent was paid, when money was last deposited into his bank account, when taxes and insurance were paid, all the information about the tenants, if there is a problem with the property, and more. Likewise, a tenant in any property that OakStream manages could log onto the Web site to see when his rent is due, what the exact wording of the rental agreement says, how soon he will receive a gift for paying his rent early every month, and so forth. Such a Web-based program would allow tenants to pay their bills online, give suggestions online, and receive automated responses online. It would simplify and clarify communication between tenants, owners, and OakStream.

Another opportunity that is available would also be through the Web site. Current owners could send money to OakStream via the Internet to purchase additional investment properties. Other clients could use a fee-based portion of the Web site to access the company's research on foreclosures. Using the Web site as a portal to sell foreclosure real estate could have enormous potential for profits.

Along with the selling and managing of real estate online comes the instruction of how to buy investment real estate. OakStream could sell its real estate investment seminar online and use its seminar to promote its management and sales of foreclosed properties.

On the physical side, OakStream Homes has the opportunity to increase the number of real estate agents that work under the licensed broker. Since Columbus is continuing to grow, the number of real estate agents required will also grow. Taking advantage of this opportunity would allow the broker to have more time overseeing the company while earning a profit from his agents' sales.

3.4 Threats

With the increase in the popularity of real estate investing due to such men as Robert Kiyosaki, author of the Rich Dad series, Robert Allen, author of *Multiple Streams of Income* and *Nothing Down: How to Buy Real Estate with Little or No Money Down*, and Carleton Sheets, creator of the *No Down Payment* system, more and more individuals are becoming interested in purchasing foreclosed real estate. As more individuals show up to foreclosure sales, it is increasingly difficult to purchase good deals for clients without having a fair amount of competition.

Another threat is that of another real estate agency providing the same services for less and doing a better job. Unless OakStream is able to refine its management process, it would make sense for an investor to let another agency manage his properties because other agencies often do a better job.

OBJECTIVES AND GOALS

1. Acquire and retain five new investment clients this year.
2. Sell 36 traditional (non-foreclosure) properties this year.
3. Purchase, for the company or clients, 36 foreclosure properties this year.
4. Reestablish a company Web site to have a presence on the Internet.

MARKETING STRATEGIES

5.1 Product Differentiation

The services offered by OakStream Homes appeal to real estate investors, renters, home sellers, and home buyers. Each of these categories holds members of each of the markets that OakStream targets (high income, middle income, low income, and individuals). Figure A6-3 shows the approximate percentage of users of OakStream's services.

5.2 Market Segmentation

OakStream Homes uses various means to communicate its unique real estate niche to its targeted market. OakStream uses rental ads in the local newspaper, flyers, signs, and investment seminars to convey to the Columbus area how its real estate services put it above other real estate agencies.

5.3 Positioning

Personalized attention, meeting the needs of every income, and covering every facet of real estate from buying and selling to renting and investing to remodeling and rehabilitating—OakStream has it all. Unlike most other real estate agencies, OakStream is committed to delivering great investment deals and quality property management.

MARKETING TACTICS

6.1 Products and Services

OakStream offers a unique service to clients through its foreclosure investment and management services. These services offered by OakStream could be streamlined and marketed more effectively using the Internet.

6.2 Price

OakStream prices its services competitively with other real estate agencies and management companies in the Columbus areas. It is common for agencies to take a percentage of the sales price of a home, from 3 to 5 percent depending on the value of the home. On these deals, OakStream's commission is generally lower than the average. Management services

FIGURE A6-3.   Percentage of Users of OakStream's Services

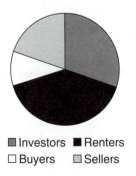

■ Investors ■ Renters
□ Buyers   ■ Sellers

are priced as a percentage of the monthly rental income. Ten percent is on the high end of this percentage, and OakStream generally charges 7 to 8 percent. These services offered by OakStream could be streamlined and marketed more effectively using the Internet.

6.3 Promotion

Newspaper ads, flyers, and signs are the top three ways in which OakStream promotes its services. The company's investment seminar, while it is a service, also acts as a promotion for the company's other services.

IMPLEMENTATION

7.1 Organization

The organization of OakStream Homes is rather simple. Will Burson is the CEO, President, and Broker-agent. Underneath him, the company is divided into the office and the field. In order to offer the company's services over the Internet, a technology staff should be hired either as an internal division or an outsourced division.

7.2 Activities and Responsibilities

The responsibilities of the Broker-agent are to buy and sell foreclosed properties, acting as a buying or selling real estate agent, and meeting with current and prospective investors. While final CEO type decisions are part of the job description, the Broker-agent should not be making the day-to-day minor decisions that are the responsibilities of the office staff.

The office workers have the responsibilities of scheduling, including the showing of housing and managing dispatches for customer problems, managerial paperwork, accounting, traditional promotion, and general day-to-day operations of the company.

The field workers are responsible for dispatching to solve customer problems such as plumbing leaks or electrical problems as well as remodeling and repairing properties in preparation for a tenant move in.

The technology staff would be responsible for company communication, including mobile phones and land lines, Internet promotion and Web site, and technology hardware, including computers and PDAs.

EVALUATION AND CONTROL

8.1 Performance Standards and Monitoring Procedures

The goals of the company are the standards of performance for the company. An analysis every six months will help the company determine whether or not it is on the path to meeting those goals. The analysis will be accomplished by an annual audit of the company and then six months later by an annual financial plan review.

8.2 Financial Data

Right now, OakStream's primary sources of income are from rent received from real estate owned and fees from selling properties. If, however, OakStream were to increase

FIGURE A6-4.   Income from Property Management

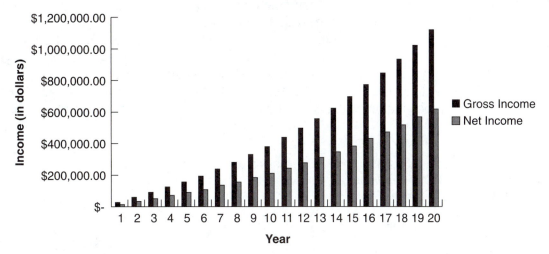

the number of properties it manages for investors every year, the company could act solely as a management firm. Figure A6-4 shows how OakStream could change its primary source of income to management fees.

The following are the assumptions of Figure A6-4:

- The company starts managing 30 properties in this year and adds 30 properties every year thereafter.
- The average value of the properties that are managed is $150,000.
- The company expects the average value of the properties to increase 4 percent every year.
- The monthly rental income from all the properties is a percentage of the value of the property (0.70 percent).
- The company takes a percentage of the monthly rental income (7 percent) as its fee.
- The company calculates its expenses and taxes as a percentage of the monthly rental income (15 percent and 35 percent, respectively).

FIGURE A6-5.   Contribution Margin Income Statement
For the year ended December 31, 2002

	# of Properties	Average Fee	Totals
REVENUE			
Sales	50	$2,625.00	$131,250.00
TOTAL REVENUE			**$131,250.00**
VARIABLE EXPENSES	# of Properties	Cost/Property	Totals
Labor	50	$50.00	$2,500.00
Paperwork	50	$300.00	$15,000.00
Phone	50	$100.00	$5,000.00
TOTAL VARIABLE EXPENSES		$450.00	$22,500.00
CONTRIBUTION MARGIN		$2,175.00	$108,750.00
FIXED EXPENSES	# of Weeks	Cost/Week	Totals
Labor	50	50	$2,500.00
Paperwork	50	50	$2,500.00
Phone	52	50	$2,600.00
Mortgage	52	1500	$78,000.00
TOTAL FIXED EXPENSES			**$85,600.00**
NET INCOME			**$23,150.00**

In just six years, the company could net over $100,000 just from management fees. While this is just speculation, it represents a significant opportunity for OakStream if the company could streamline its management process.

As shown in Figure A6-5, the margin income statement shows that OakStream is currently receiving from traditional real estate brokerage activities (i.e., acting as a buyer's or seller's agent). Compare this to Figure A6-4 to see what they could be earning.

Consider how much work OakStream would need to do if traditional real estate brokerage activities remained the company's only source of income, as shown in Table A6-1.

Table A6-1. Break-Even Analysis

Total Fixed Costs per Year	$ 85,600.00
Contribution Margin per Property	$ 2,175.00
Break-Even Quantity	**39**
Total Fixed Costs per Year	$ 85,600.00
Desired Income	$100,000.00
Contribution Margin per Property	$ 2,175.00
Total Quantity Needed for Desired Income	**85**

REFERENCES

"Access to Markets." Greater Columbus. www.greatercolumbus.org, accessed June 1, 2004.

"Cost of Living Index." (2002). Nd.placementmanual.com, accessed June 1, 2004.

Lobb, A. (2002). "How does your spending stack up? From housing to child care, we all spend our money differently. Find out what your neighbors spend." *CNNMoney.* Money.CNN.com, accessed June 1, 2004.

Ohio QuickFacts. (2004). U.S. Census Bureau. Quickfacts.census.gov, accessed June 1, 2004.

"Top 25 Cities—business climate—Directory." (2002). *Entrepreneur.* Articles.findarticle.com, accessed June 1, 2004.

B

SOURCES OF SECONDARY RESEARCH

Following are hundreds of research sources and links which, due to secondary links found on the Web sites, are further connected to probably tens of thousands of others. The first group is based on bibliographies originally put together by Lloyd M. DeBoer, then Dean of the School of Business Administration at George Mason University, Fairfax, Virginia, and the Office of Management and Training of the SBA and published by the Small Business Administration as a part of two booklets, *Marketing Research Procedure, SBB 9,* and *National Directories for Use in Marketing SSB 13.* More recently others, including Internet links, were compiled by the author and my then research assistant, Misty Iwatsu.

U.S. GOVERNMENT PUBLICATIONS

The publications in this section are books and pamphlets issued by federal agencies and listed under the issuing agency. Where availability of an individual listing is indicated by the Government Printing Office (GPO), the publication may be ordered from the Superintendent of Documents, U. S. Government Printing Office, Washington, DC 20402 or ordered over the Internet at http://www.gpoaccess.gov/index.html. When ordering a GPO publication, give the title and series number of the publication, and the name of the issuing agency. You can also order by phone by calling (202) 783-3238. Contact the GPO for current prices.

Publications should be requested by the title and any number given from the issuing agency. Most libraries have some listings to identify currently available federal publications. Some keep a number of selected government publications for ready reference through the Federal Depository Library System.

American Statistics Index: A Comprehensive Guide and Index to the Statistical Publications of the United States Government. Washington, DC

Congressional Information Service, 1973–. Monthly, with annual cumulations. This is the most comprehensive index to statistical information generated by the federal agencies, committees of

Congress, and special programs of the government. Approximately 7,400 titles of 500 government sources are indexed each year. The two main volumes are arranged by issuing breakdown, technical notes, and time period covered by publication. Separate index volume is arranged by subject and title and also includes the SIC code, the Standard Occupation Classification, and a list of SMSAs (standard metropolitan statistical areas).

Bureau of the Census, Department of Commerce, Washington, DC 20230; http://www.census.gov

Contact the Public Information Office for a complete listing of publications. The following is a sample.

Catalog of U.S. Census Publications   Published monthly with quarterly and annual cumulations. A guide to census data and reports. This catalog contains descriptive lists of publications, data files, and special tabulations.

Census of Agriculture   Performed in years ending in 4 and 9. Volumes include information on statistics of country; size of farm; characteristics of farm operations; farm income; farm sales; farm expenses; and agricultural services.

Census of Business   Compiled every five years (in years ending in 2 and 7).

Census of Construction Industries   Information from industries based on SIC codes. Included is information about the number of construction firms; employees; receipts; payrolls; payments for materials, components, and work supplies; payments for machinery and equipment; and depreciable assets.

Census of Governments   Done in years ending in 2 and 7. This is the most detailed source for statistics on government finance.

Census of Housing   Provides information on plumbing facilities, whether a unit is owned or rented, value of home, when built, number of bedrooms, telephones, and more.

Census of Manufacturers   Compiled every five years (in years ending in 2 and 7). Reports on 450 classes of manufacturing industries. Data for each industry includes information on capital expenditures, value added, number of establishments, employment data, material costs, assets, rent, and inventories. Updated yearly by the *Annual Survey of Manufacturers*.

Census of Mineral Industries   Covers areas of extraction of minerals. Information on employees, payroll, work hours, cost of materials, capital expenditures, and quantity and value of materials consumed and products shipped.

Census of Population   Compiled every ten years (in years ending in 0). Presents detailed data on population characteristics of states, counties, SMSAs, and census tracts. Demographics data reported include age, sex, race, marital status, family composition, employment income, level of education, and occupation. Updated annually by the *Current Population Report*.

Census of Retail Trade   This report presents statistics for more than 100 types of retail establishments by state, SMSAs, counties, and cities with populations over 2,500. It includes data on the number of outlets, total sales, employment, and payroll. Updated each month by *Monthly Retail Trade*.

Census of Selected Services   Provides statistics similar to those reported by the *census of Retail Trade* for retail service organizations such as auto repair centers and hotels. Does not include information on real estate, insurance, or the professions. Updated monthly by *Monthly Selected Service Receipts.*

Census of Transportation Information on four major phases of U.S. travel. (1) National Travel Survey, (2) Truck Inventory and Use of Survey, (3) Commodity Transportation Survey, and (4) Survey of Motor Carriers and Public Warehousing.

Census of Wholesale Trade Statistics for more than 150 types of wholesaler categories. The data detail the number of establishments, payroll, warehouse space, expenses, end-of-year inventories, legal form of organization, and payroll. Updated each month by *Monthly Wholesale Trade.*

Statistical Abstract of the United States Published annually. This is a useful source for finding current and historical statistics about various aspects of American life. Contents include statistics on income, prices, education, population, law enforcement, environmental conditions, local government, labor force, manufacturing, and many other topics.

State and Metropolitan Area Data Book A *Statistical Abstract* supplement. Presents a variety of information on states and metropolitan areas in the United States on subjects such as area, population, housing, income, manufacturers, retail trade, and wholesale trade.

County and City Data Book Published every five years. Supplements the *Statistical Abstract.* Contains 144 statistical items for each county and 148 items for cities with a population of 25,000 or more. Data is organized by region, division, states, and SMSAs. Contains standard demographics in addition to harder-to-find data.

County Business Patterns Annual. Contains a summary of data on number and type (by SIC number) of business establishments as well as their employment and taxable payroll. Data are presented by industry and county.

Bureau of Economic Analysis, Department of Commerce, Washington, DC 20230; http://www.bea.doc.gov

Business Statistics This is the biennial supplement to the *Survey of Current Business* and contains data on 2,500 series arranged annually for early years, quarterly for the last decade, and monthly for the most recent five years.

Bureau of Economic Analysis, Department of Commerce, Washington, DC 20230; http://www.bea.gov

United States Industrial Outlook Projections of sales trends for major sectors of the United States economy including business services, consumer services, transportation, consumer goods, and distribution; http://www.ita.doc.gov/td/industry/otea/outlook.

Economic and Statistics Administration, Department of Commerce, Washington, DC 20230; http://www.stat-usa.gov and http://www.stat-usa.gov/hometest.nsf/ref/Products

County and City Data Book Published every other year; supplements the *Statistical Abstract.* Using data taken from censuses and other government publications, it provides breakdowns by city and county for income, population, education, employment, housing, banking, manufacturing, capital expenditures, retail and wholesale sales, and other factors.

Measuring Markets: A Guide to the Use of Federal and State Statistical Data   Government Planning Office. Provides federal and state government data on population, income, employment, sales, and selected taxes. Explains how to interpret the data to measure markets and evaluate opportunities.

Selected Publications to Aid Business and Industry   Listing of federal statistical sources useful to business and industry.

Statistics of Income   Annual. Published by the Internal Revenue Service of the Treasury Department. This publication consists of data collected from tax returns filed by corporations, sole proprietorships and partnerships, and individuals.

State Statistical Abstract   Every state publishes a statistical abstract, almanac, or economic data book covering statistics for the state and its counties and cities. A complete list of these abstracts is in the back of each volume of the *Statistical Abstract* and *Measuring Markets*.

International Trade Administration, Department of Commerce, Washington, DC 20230; http://www.ita.doc.gov

Country Market Survey   These reports describe market sectors and the markets for producer goods, consumer goods, and industrial material.

Global Market Surveys   Provides market research to verify the existence and vitality of foreign markets for specific goods as well as Department of Commerce assistance to U.S. businesses to help in market penetration.

Foreign Economic Trends   Prepared by U.S. embassies abroad. Each volume has a table of key economic indicators and other data on the current economic situation and trends for the country under discussion.

Overseas Business Reports   Analysis of trade opportunities, marketing conditions, distribution channels, industry trends, trade regulations, and market prospects are provided.

Trade Opportunity Program (TOP)   Weekly indexes of trade opportunities by product as well as by type of opportunity.

U.S. Small Business Administration, Washington, DC 20416; http://www.sba.gov

The SBA issues a wide range of management and technical publications designed to help owner–managers and prospective owners of small business. For general information about the SBA office, its policies and assistance programs, contact your nearest SBA office.

A listing of currently available publications can be obtained free from the Small Business Administration, Office of Public Communications, 409 Third Street, SW, Washington, DC 20416 or from 1-800-U-ASK-SBA. The SBA offers fifty-one publications currently. One particular publication, *Basis Library Reference Sources*, contains a section on marketing information and guides to research. Get the latest *Directory of Publications* by writing or calling the 800 number. You can also obtain a free booklet, *Your Business and the SBA*, which gives you an overview of all SBA services and programs. A listing is also available at the U.S. Small Business Administration Web site: http://www.sbaonline.sba.gov/library/pubs.html.

Management Aids (3- to 24-page pamphlet) This series of pamphlets is organized by a broad range of management principles. Each pamphlet discusses a specific management practice to help the owner–manager of a small firm with management problems and business operations. A section on marketing covers a wide variety of topics from advertising guidelines to marketing research to pricing.

PERIODICALS

Economic Indicators United States. Council of Economic Advisors. Washington, DC: Government Printing Office. Monthly. Statistical tables for major economics indicators are included. Section on credit is useful for marketers. Statistics quoted annually for about six years and monthly for the past year.

Export America: The Magazine of International Trade United States. International Trade Administration. Monthly. Activities relating to private sector or the Department of Commerce are covered including exports and other international business activities. http://www.export.gov/exportamerica.

Federal Reserve Bulletin United States. Board of Governors of the Federal Reserve System. Washington, DC: Government Printing Office. Monthly. Contains official statistics on national banking, international banking, and business. http://www.federalreserve.gov/pubs/bulletin/default.htm.

Monthly Labor Review United States. Bureau of Labor Statistics. Washington, DC: Government Printing Office. Monthly. This publication covers all aspects of labor including wages, productivity, collective bargaining, new legislation, and consumer prices. http://www.bls.gov/opub/mlr/mlrhome.htm.

Survey of Current Business United States. Department of Commerce. Bureau of Economic Analysis. Washington, DC: Government Printing Office. Monthly with weekly supplements. The most useful source for current business statistics. Each issue is divided into two sections. The first section covers general business topics; the second, "Current Business Statistics," gives current data for 2,500 statistical series or topics. Also, indexed in *Business Periodicals Index*. http://www.bea.doc.gov/bea/pubs.htm.

Treasury Bulletin United States. Department of the Treasury. Washington, DC: Government Printing Office. Monthly. Statistical tables are provided on all aspects of fiscal operations of government as well as money-related activities of the private sector. Useful for consumer background or from a monetary view. http://www.fms.treas.gov/bulletin.

DIRECTORIES

The selected national directories are listed under categories of specific business or general marketing areas in an alphabetical subject index.

When the type of directory is not easily found under the alphabetical listing of a general marketing category, such as "jewelry," look for a specific type of industry or outlet, such as "department stores."

Apparel

Hat Life Directory   Annual. Includes renovators, importers, classified list of manufacturers, and wholesalers of men's headwear. Hat Life Directory, 66 York Street, Jersey City, NJ 07302-000; Phone: 201-434-8322; Fax: 201-434-8277.

American Sportswear & Knitting Times—Buyers Guide Issue   Annual. Lists manufacturers and suppliers of knitted products, knit goods, materials, supplies services, etc. National Knitting & Sportswear Association, 386 Park Avenue South, New York, NY, 10016; Phone: 212-683-7520; Fax: 212-532-0766; E-mail: nksa@pop.interport.net; http://www.asktmag.com.

Nationwide Directory of Men's & Boy's Wear Buyers (exclusive of New York metropolitan area)   Annually in August. More than 20,000 buyers and merchandise managers for 6,100 top department, family clothing, and men's and boys' wear specialty stores. Telephone number, buying office, and postal zip code are given for each firm. Also available in individual state editions. Salesman's Guide, 121 Chanlon Road, New Providence, NJ 07974-0000; Phone: 908-464-6800; Toll-free: 800-521-8100; Fax: 908-665-2894. Also publishes *Metropolitan New York Directory of Men's and Boys' Wear Buyers*. Semiannually in May and November. (Lists same information for the metropolitan New York area as the nationwide directory.)

Nationwide Directory of Women's & Children's Wear Buyers (exclusive of New York metropolitan area)   Annually in October. Lists more than 25,000 buyers and divisional merchandise managers for about 6,100 leading department, family clothing, and specialty stores. Telephone number and mail zip code given for each store. Also available in individual state editions. Salesman's Guide, 121 Chanlon Road, New Providence, NJ 07974-0000; Phone: 908-464-6800; Toll-free: 800-521-8100; Fax: 908-665-2894.

Appliances, Household

Appliance Dealers—Major Household Directory   Annual. Lists manufacturers and distributors in home electronics, appliances, kitchens. Gives complete addresses and phone. Compiled from Yellow Pages. American Business Directories Inc., American Business Information Inc., 5711 South 86th Circle, PO Box 27347, Omaha, NE 68127; Phone: 402-593-4600; Toll-free: 800-555-6424; Fax: 402-331-5481; E-mail: directory@abii.com; Web site: http://www.abii.com.

Automatic Merchandising (Vending)

NAMA Directory of Members   Annually in June. Organized by state and by city, lists vending service companies who are NAMA members. Gives mailing address, telephone number, and products vended. Also includes machine manufacturers and suppliers. National Automatic Merchandising Association, 20 North Wacker Drive, Chicago, IL 60606; Phone: 312-346-0370; Toll-free: 888-337-8363; Fax: 312-704-4140; Web site: http://www.vending.org/store/search.html.

Automotive

Automotive Service Industry Assoc.—Guide to Manufacturer's Representatives Irregular. A geographical listing of about 300 representatives including name, address, telephone number, territories covered, and lines carried. Automotive Service Industry Association, 25 Northwest Point, No. 425, Elk Grove Village, IL 60007-1035; Phone: 847-228-1310; Fax: 847-228-1510; E-mail: http://www.asiaassistankmktusa.org.

Automotive Warehouse Distributors Association Membership Directory Annually in April. Includes listing of manufacturers, warehouse distributors, their products, personnel, and territories. Automotive Warehouse Distributors Association, 9140 Ward Parkway, Kansas City, MO 64114; Phone: 816-44-3500; Fax: 816-444-0330; Web site: http://www.awda.org.

Aviation

World Aviation Directory Published twice a year in March and September. Gives administrative and operating personnel of airlines, aircraft, and engine manufacturers and component manufacturers and distributors, organizations, and schools. Indexed by companies, activities, products, and individuals. Aviation Week-McGraw Hill, Inc., 1200 G Street NW, Suite 900, Washington, DC 20005; Phone: 202-383-2484; Toll-free: 800-551-2015; Fax: 202-383-2478; E-mail: wad@mcgraw-hill.com; Web site: http://www.wadaviation.com.

Bookstores

Book Trade Directory, American Annually in June. Lists more than 25,000 retail and wholesale booksellers in the United States and Canada. Entries alphabetized by state (or province), and then by city and business name. Each listing gives address, telephone numbers, key personnel, types of books sold, subject specialties carried, sidelines and services offered, and general characteristics. For wholesale entries gives types of accounts, import–export information and territory limitations Cahners Business Information, 121 Chanlon Road, New Providence, NJ 07974-0000; Phone: 908-464-6800; Toll-free: 800-521-8100; Fax: 908-665-2894; E-mail: info@bowker.com.

Business Firms

D&B Million Dollar Directory—Top 50,000 Companies Annually in March. Lists about 50,000 top corporations. Arranged alphabetically. Gives business name, state of incorporation, address, telephone number, SIC numbers, function, sales volume, number of employees, and name of officers and directors, principal bank, accounting firm, and legal counsel. Dun & Bradstreet, 3 Sylvan Way, Parsippany, NJ 07054-3896; Phone: 973-605-6442; Toll-free: 800-526-0651; Fax: 973-605-6911; E-mail: dnbmdd@dnb.com; Web site: http://www.dnbmdd.com.

China and Glassware

American Glass Review—Glass Factory Directory Issue Annually in March. Issued as part of subscription (thirteenth issue) to *American Glass Reviews*. Lists companies manufacturing flat glass, tableware glass, and fiberglass, giving corporate and plant addresses, executives, and type of equipment used. Doctorow Communications, Inc., 1011 Clifton Avenue, Clifton, NJ 07013-0000; Phone: 973-779-1600; Fax: 973-779-3242.

City Directories Catalog

Municipal Yearbook (U.S.) Annual. Contains a review of municipal events of the year, analyses of city operations, and a directory of city officials in all the states. International City/Council Management Association, 777 North Capitol Street NE, Suite 500, Washington, DC 20002-4201; Phone: 202-962-6700; Toll-free: 800-745-8780; Fax: 202-962-3500; Web site: http://www.icma.org.

College Stores

Directory of College Stores Annual. Published every two years. Lists about 3,000 college stores geographically with manager's name; kinds of goods sold; college name; number of students, whether it's a school for men, women, or both; whether the store is college owned or privately owned. B. Klein Publications, PO Box 6578, Delray Beach, FL 33482; Phone: 407-496-3316; Fax: 407-496-5546.

Confectionery

Candy Buyer's Directory Annually in January. Lists candy manufacturers, importers, and U.S. representatives, and confectionery brokers. Manufacturing Confectioner Publishing Co., 175 Rock Road, Glen Rock, NJ 07452-0000; Phone: 201-652-2655; Fax: 201-652-3419; Web site: http://www.themc@gomc.com.

Construction Equipment

Construction Equipment Buyer's Guide Annually in November. Lists 1,500 construction equipment distributors and manufacturers; includes company names, names of key personnel, addresses, telephone numbers, branch locations, and lines handled or type of equipment produced. Cahners Business Information, 1350 East Touhy Avenue, Des Plaines, IL 60018; Phone: 847-635-8800; Toll-free: 800-446-6551; Fax: 847-299-8622; Web site: http://www.coneq.com.

Conventions and Trade Shows

Directory of Conventions—Regional Edition Annually in January. Contains more than 18,000 cross-indexed listings of annual events, gives dates, locations, names and addresses of executives in charge, scope, and expected attendance. Bill Communications, 355 Park Avenue South, New York, NY 10010-1789; Phone: 212-592-6505; Toll-free: 800-266-4712; Fax: 212-592-6650.

Dental Supply

Hayes Directory of Dental Supply Houses Annually in August. Lists wholesalers of dental supplies and equipment with addresses, telephone numbers, financial standing and credit rating. Edward N. Hayes, Publisher, PO Box 3436, Mission Viejo, CA 92690-1436.

Department Stores

Sheldon's Retail Annual. Lists 1,500 large independent department stores, 600 major department store chains, 150 large independent and chain home furnishing stores, 700 large independent women's specialty stores, and 450 large women's specialty store chains alphabetically by states. Gives all department buyers with lines bought by each buyer, and addresses and telephone numbers of merchandise executives. Also gives all New York, Chicago, Dallas, Atlanta, and Los Angeles buying offices, the number and locations of branch stores, and an index of all store/chain headquarters. Todd Publications, PO Box 635, Nyack, NJ 10960; Phone: 914-358-6213; Toll-free: 800-747-1056; Fax: 914-358-1059; E-mail: toddpub@aol.com.

Discount Stores

Directory of Discount & General Merchandise Stores   Annual. Lists headquarters address, telephone number, location, square footage of each store, lines carried, leased operators, names of executives and buyers (includes Canada). Also special section on leased department operators. Chain Store Guide Information Services, 3922 Coconut Palm Drive, Tampa, FL 33619; Phone: 813-627-6800; Toll-free: 800-927-9292; Fax: 813-627-6882; E-mail: info@csgis.com; Web site: http://www.csgis.com.

Drug Outlets—Retail and Wholesale

Chain Drug Stores Guide, Hayes   Annually in September. Lists headquarters address, telephone numbers, number and location of units, names of executives and buyers, and wholesale drug distributors. Edward N. Hayes, Publisher, PO Box 3436, Mission Viejo, CA 92690-1436.

Drug Store Market Guide   Annually in March. Lists about 53,000 retail and 700 wholesale druggists in the United States, giving addresses, financial standing, and credit rating. Also publishes regional editions for one or more states. Computerized mailing labels available. Melnor Publishing Inc., 1739 Horton Avenue, Mohegan Lake, NY 10547; Phone: 914-528-7147; Fax: 914-528-1369; E-mail: melnor@prodigy.net.

Redbook (Drugs & Pharmaceuticals)   Annually in March. Gives information on wholesale drug companies, chain drug stores headquarters, department stores maintaining toilet goods or drug departments, manufacturers' sales agents, and discount houses operating toilet goods, cosmetic, proprietary medicine, or prescription departments. Medical Economics Co., 5 Paragon Drive, Montvale, NJ 07645-1725; Phone: 201-358-7500; Toll-free: 800-223-0581; Fax: 201-573-8999; E-mail: http://www.customer-service@medec.com.

National Wholesale Druggists' Association Membership and Executive Directory   Annually in January. Lists 800 American and foreign wholesalers and manufacturers of drugs and allied products. National Wholesale Druggists' Association, 1821 Michael Faraday Drive, Suite 400, Reston, VA 20190; Phone: 703-787-0000; Fax: 703-787-6930.

Electrical and Electronics

ECN's Electronic Industry Telephone Directory   Annually in August. Contains 23,000 listings of manufacturers, representatives, distributors, government agencies, contracting agencies, and others. Cahners Business Information, 201 King of Prussia Road, Radnor, PA 19087-5114; Phone: 610-964-4000; Fax: 610-964-4273; E-mail: ecn-info@chilton.net; Web site: http://www.ecnmag.com/eitd.

Electrical Wholesale Distributors, Directory of   Detailed information on 3,400 companies with more than 7,630 locations in the United States and Canada, including name, address, telephone number, branch and affiliated houses, and products handled. Intertec

Publishing Corp., 9800 Metcalf Avenue, Overland Park, KS 66212; Phone: 913-341-1300; Toll-free: 800-262-1954; Fax: 800-633-6219; Web site: http://www.ecmbook.com.

Electrical Utilities

Electrical Power Producers, Electrical World, Directory of Annually in November. Complete listings of electric utilities (investor-owned, municipal, and government agencies in the United States and Canada), giving their addresses and personnel and selected data on operations. UDI/McGraw Hill Co., 1200 G Street NW, Suite 250, Washington, DC 20005; Phone: 202-942-8788; Toll-free: 800-486-3660; Fax: 202-942-8789; Web site: http://www.electricalworld.com/enestore.

Embroidery

Annual Laces & Embroideries Directory Annually in November. Alphabetical listing with addresses and telephone numbers of manufacturers, merchandisers, designers, cutters, bleacheries, yarn dealers, machine suppliers, and other suppliers to the Schiffli lace and embroidery industry. Schiffli Lace & Embroidery Manufacturers Association, 596 Anderson Avenue, Suite 203, Cliffside Park, NJ 07010-1828; Phone: 201-943-7757; Fax: 201-943-7793.

Export and Import

American Export Register Annually in September. Includes more than 30,000 importers and exporters and products handled. Thomas Publishing Co., International Division, 5 Penn Plaza, New York, NY 10001; Phone: 212-629-1177; Fax: 212-629-1140.

Canadian Trade Directory, Fraser's Annually in May. Contains more than 42,000 Canadian companies. Also lists more than 14,000 foreign companies that have Canadian representatives. Fraser's Trade Directories Co. Ltd., 777 Bay Street, Toronto, Ontario, Canada, MSW 1A7; Phone: 416-596-5086, Fax: 416-593-3201.

Flooring

Flooring Buying & Resource Guide Issue Annually in October. References to sources of supply, giving their products and brand names, leading distributors, manufacturers' representatives, and associations. Douglas Publications, Inc., 2807 North Parham Road, Suite 200, Richmond, VA 23294; Phone: 804-762-9600; Fax: 804-217-8999.

Food Dealers—Retail and Wholesale

Food Brokers Directory Annually in July. Arranged by states and cities, lists member food brokers in the United States and Europe, giving names and addresses, products they handle, and services they perform. American Business Information, Inc., 5711 South 86th Circle, PO Box 27347, Omaha, NE 68127; Phone: 402-593-4600; Toll-free: 800-555-6124; Fax: 402-331-5481; E-mail: directory@abii.com; Web site: http://www.abii.com.

National Frozen Food Association Directory Annually in January. Lists packers, distributors, supplies, refrigerated warehouses, wholesalers, and brokers; includes names and addresses of each firm and their key officials. Contains statistical marketing data. National Frozen Food Association, Inc., 4755 Linglestown Road, Suite 300, Harrisburg, PA 17112; Phone: 717-657-8601; Fax: 717-657-9862; E-mail: info@nffa.org; Web site: http://www.nffa.org.

Thomas' Food Industry Registry, Thomas' Annually in May. *Volume 1* lists super-market chains, wholesalers, brokers, frozen food brokers, exporters, warehouses. *Volume 2* contains information on products and services; manufacturers, sources of supplies, importers. *Volume 3* has an A–Z index of 48,000 companies. Also, a brand name/trademark index. Thomas Publishing Co., 5 Penn Plaza, New York, NY 10001; Phone: 212-696-0500; Fax: 212-290-7206; E-mail: ortertr@thomasregister.com; Web site: http://www.tfir.com.

Uker's International Tea & Coffee Directory & Buyers Guide Annual. Includes revised and updated lists of participants in the tea and coffee and allied trades. Lockwood Trade Journal, Inc., 130 West 42nd Street, 10th Floor, New York, NY 10036; Phone: 212-391-2060; Fax: 212-827-0945; E-mail: http://www.teacof@aol.com.

Gas Companies

Brown's Directory of North American & International Gas Co. Annually in November. Includes information on every known gas utility company and holding company worldwide. Energy Publications Division, Advanstar Communications, 7500 Old Oak Boulevard, Cleveland, OH 44130-3369; Web site: http://www.advanstar.com.

LP/Gas—Industry Buying Guide Issue Annually in March. Lists suppliers, supplies, and distributors. Advanstar Communications, 131 West First Street, Duluth, MN 55802; Toll-free: 800-346-0085; E-mail: fulfill@superfil.com.

Gift and Art

Nationwide Directory of Gift, Housewares & Home Textile Buyers Annually with semiannual supplement. For 7,000 types of retail firms lists store name, address, type of store, number of stores, names of president, merchandise managers, and buyers for gift-wares and housewares. State editions also available. Douglas Publications, Inc., 2807 North Parham Road, Suite 200, Richmond, VA 23294; Phone: 804-762-9600; Fax: 804-217-8999; E-mail: info@douglaspublications.com.

Home Furnishings

National Antique & Art Dealers Assoc. of America-Membership Directory Annual. Lists 35,636 dealers with name, address, and phone number as well as size of advertisement and first year advertised in Yellow Pages. National Antique & Art Dealers Association, 12 East 56th Street, New York, NY 10022; Phone: 212-826-9707; Fax: 212-319-0471.

Home Fashions—Buyer's Guide Issue Annually in December. Lists names and addresses of manufacturers, importers, and regional sales representatives. Fairchild Publications, Capital Cities Media, 7 West 34th Street, New York, NY 10003; Phone: 212-630-4784; Toll-free: 800-247-2160; Fax: 212-630-4796.

Hospitals

Hospitals, Directory of Annually in January. Lists 12,173 hospitals, with selected data. SMG Marketing Group, 875 North Michigan Avenue, Chicago, IL 60611; Phone: 312-642-3026; Toll-free: 800-678-3026; Fax: 312-642-9729; Web site: http://www.smgusa.com.

Hotels and Motels

Hotels and Motels Directory   Annually. Lists more than 62,400 hotels and motels. American Hospital Publishing, 737 North Michigan Avenue, Suite 700, Chicago, IL 60611-2615; Phone: 312-440-6800; Toll-free: 800-621-6902; Fax: 312-951-8491.

OAG Business Travel Planner (North America)   Quarterly. Lists more than 26,000 hotels in the United States. Also lists 14,500 destination cities. Reed Travel Group, OAG Travel Services Division, 2000 Clearwater Drive, Oak Brook, IL 60521; Phone: 630-574-6000; Toll-free: 800-DIAL-OAG (342-5624); Fax: 630-574-6090; E-mail: info@oag.com; Web site: http://www.oag.com.

Housewares

MHMA Membership Directory   Annually in June. Compilation of resources of the housewares trade, includes listing of their products, trade names, and a registry of manufacturers' representatives. National Housewares Manufacturing Association, 6400 Shafer Street, Suite 650, Rosemont, IL 60018; Phone: 847-292-4200; Fax: 847-292-4211.

Jewelry

Jewelers' Circular/Keystone—Jewelers' Directory Issue   Annually in June. Lists manufacturers, importers, distributors, and retailers of jewelry; diamonds; precious, semi-precious, and imitation stones; watches, silverware; and kindred articles. Includes credit ratings. Reed Business Information (formerly Cahners Business Information), 360 Park Avenue South, New York, NY 10010, Phone: 646-746-6400; Web site: http://www.reed-business.com/index.asp?layout=cahnerscom; E-mail: corporatecommunications@reed-business.com.

Liquor

Wine and Spirits Wholesalers of America—Member Roster and Industry Directory   Annually in January. Lists names of 700 member companies; includes parent house and branches, addresses, and names of managers. Also has register of 2,200 suppliers and gives state liquor control administrators, national associations, and trade press directory. Wine & Spirits Wholesaler of America, 805 15th Street NW, Suite 430, Washington, DC 20005; Phone: 202-371-9792; Fax: 202-789-2405; Web site: http://www.wswa.org.

Mailing List Houses

Directory of Mailing Lists   Lists 1,800 firms, brokers, compilers, and firms offering their own lists for rent; includes the specialties of each firm. Arranged geographically. American Business Information, 5711 South 86th Circle, PO Box 27347, Omaha, NE 68127; Phone: 402-593-4600; Toll-free: 800-555-6124; Fax: 402-331-5481; E-mail: directory@abii.com; Web site: http://www.abii.com.

Mail Order Businesses

Mail Order Business Directory   Lists 10,000 names of mail order firms with buyers' names, and lines carried. Arranged geographically. B. Klein Publications, PO Box 6578, Delray Beach, FL 33482; Phone: 407-496-3316; Fax: 407-496-5546.

Manufacturers

MacRae's Blue Book (Manufacturers) Annually in March. In three volumes. Volume 1: Corporate Index lists company names and addresses alphabetically, with 40,000 branch and/or sales office telephone numbers. Volumes 2 and 3: Lists companies by product classifications. MacRAE'S BLUE BOOK Inc., 410 Park Avenue, 15th Floor, New York, NY 10022; Phone: 212-421-2595; Toll-free fax: 866-605-7333; E-mail: info@ macraesbluebook.com; Web site: http://macraesbluebook.com.

Manufacturers, Thomas' Register of American Annual. Volumes 1–14 list products and services; suppliers of each product category are grouped by state and city. Volumes 15–16 contain company profiles. Volumes 17–23 list manufacturers' catalogs. More than 150,000 firms are listed under 50,000 product headings. Thomas Publishing, 5 Penn Plaza, New York, NY 10001; Phone: 212-696-0500; Fax: 212-290-7206; E-mail: ortertr@thomasregister.com; Web site: http://www.tfir.com.

Manufacturer's Sales Representatives

Manufacturers Agents National Association Directory of Manufacturers Sales Agencies Annually in May/June. Contains individual listings of manufacturers' agents throughout the United States, Canada, and several other countries. Listings are cross-referenced by alphabetical, geographical, and product classification. Manufacturing Agent National Association (MANA), 23016 Mill Creek Road, PO Box 3467, Laguna Hills, CA 92654; Phone: 949-859-4040; Fax: 949-855-2973; E-mail: askmana@aol.com; Web site: http://www.manaonline.org.

Metalworking

Metalworking Directory, Dun & Bradstreet—Industrial Guide Annually in June. Lists about 78,000 metalworking and metal producing plants with twenty or more production employees. Arranged geographically. Dun & Bradstreet, 3 Sylvan Way, Parsippany, NJ 07054-2896; Phone: 973-605-6442; Toll-free: 800-526-0651; Fax: 973-605-6911; E-mail: dnbmdd@dnb.com.

Military Market

Military Market Magazine—Supply Bulletin Directory Annually in January. Lists manufacturers and suppliers of products sold in military commissaries. Also lists manufacturers' representatives and distributors. Army Time Publishing Co., 6883 Commercial Drive, Springfield, VA 22159-0001; Phone: 703-750-8197; Toll-free: 800-368-5718; Fax: 703-658-8314.

Paper Products

Sources of Supply Buyers' Guide Lists 1,700 mills and converters of paper, film, foil, and allied products, and paper merchants in the United States alphabetically with addresses, principal personnel, and products manufactured. Also lists trade associations, brand names, and manufacturers' representatives. Wm. O. Dannhausen Corp., PO Box 795, Parkridge, IL 60068; Phone: 847-823-3145; Fax: 847-696-3445; E-mail: wmdann@compuserve.com; Web site: http://www.dannhausen.com.

Physicians Supply Houses

Hayes Directory of Medical Supply Houses   Annually in August. Listings of 1,850 U.S. wholesalers doing business in physician, hospital, and surgical supplies and equipment; includes addresses, telephone numbers, financial standing, and credit ratings. Edward N. Hayes, Publisher, PO Box 3436, Mission Viejo, CA 92690-1436.

Premium Sources

Incentive Directory Issue   Annually in February. Contains classified directory of suppliers and list of manufacturers' representatives serving the premium field. Also lists associations, clubs, and trade shows. Bill Communications, 355 Park Avenue South, New York, NY 10010-1787; Phone: 212-592-6505; Toll-free: 800-266-4712; Fax: 212-592-6650.

Purchasing, Government

U.S. Government Purchasing & Sales Directory   Irregularly issued. Booklet designed to help small businesses receive an equitable share of government contracts, Lists types of purchases for both military and civilian needs; catalogs procurement offices by state. Lists SBA regional and branch offices. Office of Government Contracting, Small Business Administration, 409 3rd Street SW, Washington, DC 20416; Phone: 202-205-6460.

Refrigeration and Air Conditioning

Air Conditioning, Heating & Refrigeration News—Directory Issue   Annually in January. Lists 1,900 manufacturers and 3,000 wholesalers and factory outlets in refrigeration, heating, and air-conditioning. Business News Publishing Co., 755 West Big Beaver Road, Suite 1000, Troy, MI 48084; Phone: 248-362-3700; fax: 248-362-5103; E-mail: peruccae@bnp.com; Web site: http://www.bnp.com/the-news.

Selling Direct

Direct Selling, World Directory   Annually in April. About forty direct selling associations and 750 associated member companies. Includes names of contact persons, company product line, and method of distribution. World Federation of Direct Selling Association, 1666 K Street NW, Suite 1010, Washington, DC 20006; Phone: 202-293-5760; Fax: 202-463-4569; E-mail: info@wfdsa.org; Web site: http://www.wfdsa.org.

Shopping Centers

Shopping Center Directory   Annual. Alphabetical listing of 34,000 shopping centers, with location, owner/developer, manager, physical plant (number of stores, square feet), and leasing agent. National Research Bureau, 330 West Wacker Drive, Suite 900, Chicago, IL 60606; Phone: 312-541-0100; Toll-free: 800-456-4555; Fax: 312-541-1492.

Specialty Stores

Phelon's Women's Apparel Stores   Lists more than 7,000 women's apparel and accessory shops with store headquarters' name and address, number of shops operated,

New York City buying headquarters or representatives, lines of merchandise bought and sold, name of principal and buyers, store size, and price range. Phelon, Sheldon, & Marsar, Inc., 330 Main Street, Ridgefield Park, NJ 07660-0000; Phone: 201-440-9096; Toll-free: 800-234-8804; fax: 201-440-8568.

Sporting Goods

Nationwide Directory of Sporting Goods Buyers   Including semiannual supplements. Lists more than 7,500 top retail stores with names of buyers and executives, for all types of sporting goods, athletic apparel and athletic footwear, hunting, and fishing, and outdoor equipment. Salesman's Guide, 121 Chanlon Road, New Providence, NJ 07974; Phone: 908-464-6800; Toll-free: 800-521-8110; Fax: 908-665-2894.

Textiles

Davison's Textile Blue Book   Annually in March. Contains more than 8,400 separate company listings (name, address, etc.) for the United States and Canada. Firms included are cotton, wool, synthetic mills, knitting mills, cordage, twine, and duck manufacturers, dry goods commission merchants, converters, yarn dealers, cordage manufacturers' agents, wool dealers and merchants, cotton merchants, exporters, brokers, and others. Davison Publishing Co. Inc., PO Box 1289, Concord, NC 28026; Phone: 704-785-8700; Toll-free: 800-328-4766; Fax: 704-785-8701; E-mail: textiles@davisonbluebook.com; Web site: http://www.davisonbluebook.com.

Toys and Novelties

Playthings—Buyers Guide   Annually in June. Lists manufacturers, products, trade names, suppliers to manufacturers, supplier products, licensors, manufacturers' representatives, toy trade associations, and trade show management. Geyer-McAllister Publications, Inc., 51 Madison Avenue, New York, NY 10010-1603; Phone: 212-689-4411; Fax: 212-683-7929.

Small World—Directory Issue   Annually in December. Lists 200 wholesalers, manufacturers, manufacturers' representatives of toys, games, and hobbies for children and infants. Earn Shaw Publications, Inc., 225 West 34th Street, Room 1212, New York, NY 10122; Phone: 212-563-2742; Fax: 212-629-3249.

Trailer Parks

Woodall's Campground Directory   Annual. Lists and star-rates public and private campgrounds in North American continent alphabetically by town with location and description of facilities. Also lists more than 800 RV service locations. Regional editions available. American Business Information Inc., 5711 South 86th Circle, PO Box 27347, Omaha, NE 68127; Phone: 402-593-4600; Toll-free: 800-555-6124; Fax: 402-331-5481; E-mail: directory@abii.com; Web site: http://www.abii.com.

Trucking

Trucksource: Sources of Trucking Industry Information   Annually in November. Includes more than 700 sources of information on the trucking industry, classified by subject. American Trucking Association Inc. (ATA), 2200 Mill Road, Alexandria, VA 22314-4677; Phone: 703-838-1700; Toll-free: 800-282-5463.

Variety Stores

Directory of General Merchandise, Variety & Specialty Stores Annually in March. Lists headquarters address, telephone number, number of units and locations, executives, and buyers. American Business Information Inc., 5711 South 86th Circle, PO Box 27347, Omaha, NE 68127; Phone: 402-593-4600; Toll-free: 800-555-6124; Fax: 402-331-5481; E-mail: directory@abii.com; Web site: http://www.abii.com.

Warehouses

Affiliated Warehouse Companies—Directory Annually in July. Lists leading public warehouses in the United States and Canada, as well as major truck lines, airlines, steamship lines, liquid and dry bulk terminals, material handling equipment suppliers, ports of the world and railroad piggyback services and routes. Affiliated Warehouse Co. Inc., 54 Village Court, PO Box 295, Hazlet, NJ 07730; Phone: 732-739-2323; Fax: 732-739-4154; E-mail: http://www.sales@awco.com.

OTHER IMPORTANT DIRECTORIES

The following business directories are helpful to those persons doing marketing research. Most of these directories are available for reference at the larger libraries. For additional listings consult the *Guide to American Directories* at local libraries.

Bradford's Directory of Mkt. Research Agencies & Mgmt. Consultants in the US & the World Gives names and addresses of more than 2,400 marketing research agencies in the United States, Canada, and other countries. Lists service offered by agency, along with other pertinent data, such as date established, names of principal officers, and size of staff. Bradford's Directory, PO Box 2300, Centreville, VA 20122; Phone: 703-631-1500; Fax: 703-830-5303.

Consultants & Consulting Organizations Directory Contains 16,000 entries. Guides reader to appropriate organization for a given consulting assignment. Entries include names, addresses, phone numbers, and data on services performed. Gale Research, 27500 Drake Road, Farmington Hills, MI 48331-3535; Phone: 248-699-GALE (4253); Toll-free: 800-877-GALE (4253); Fax: 248-699-8069; E-mail: galeord@gale.com.

Research Centers Directory Lists more than 11,000 nonprofit research organizations. Descriptive information provided for each center, including address, telephone number, name of director, data on staff, funds, publications, and a statement concerning its principal fields of research. Has special indexes. Gale Research, 27500 Drake Road, Farmington Hills, MI 48331-3535; Phone: 248-699-GALE (4253); Toll-free: 800-877-GALE (4253); Fax: 248-699-8069; E-mail: galeord@gale.com.

Thomas' Food Industry Register Annually in May. Lists in two volumes wholesale grocers, chain store organizations, voluntary buying groups, food brokers, exporters and importers of food products, frozen food brokers, distributors and related products distributed through grocery chains. Thomas Publishing Co., 5 Penn Prize, New York, NY 10001; Phone: 212-696-0500; Fax: 212-290-7206; E-mail: ortertr@thomasregister.com; Web site: http://www.tfir.com.

Thomas' Register of American Manufacturers Annually in February. In 23 volumes. Volumes 1–14 contain manufacturers arranged geographically under each product, and capitalization or size rating for each manufacturer, under 50,000 product headings. Volumes 15 and 16 contain company profiles and a brand or trade name section with more than 112,000 listings. Volumes 17–23 are catalogs from more than 1,500 firms. Thomas Publishing, 5 Penn Plaza, New York, NY 10001; Phone: 212-696-0500; Fax: 212-290-7206; E-mail: ortertr@thomasregister.com; Web site: http://www.tfir.com.

INTERNET SOURCES

American Express Small Business Exchange

http://www.americanexpress.com/smallbusiness
Information on creating a business plan and managing a business, and expert advice on small business problems.

American Business Information

http://www.abii.com
Order an in-depth profile on any business. Get the address and phone number of any business.

American Demographics

http://www.demographics.com
Demographics of special interest to marketers.

Business Essentials Library

http://pasware.com
Sections on business planning, including sample plans, information on financing, and marketing, and plan outline.

Commercial Services of the U.S. Department of Commerce

http://www.ita.doc.gov/uscs
Numerous programs having to with export, including trade statistics abroad.

Dun and Bradstreet

http://www.zapdata.com/marketingintelligence/businessdirectory.jsp
Tips for using business directories and more.

Free Marketing Magazine for Consultants

http://www.hansonmarketing.com
Online help for consultants, marketing tips, and more.

Fortune 500

http://www.fortune.com/fortune/fortune500
Statistics and data on Fortune 500 companies. However, currently available only to *Fortune Magazine* subscribers.

Hoover's Online

http://www.hoovers.com
Company information and profiles on more than 40,000 companies, both public and private.

The Internet Invention Store

http://www.catalog.com/impulse/invent.htm
Information on new products.

Internet Links to Free Advertising

http://www.kosoma.com/FreeAdLinks.html

Kennedy Information Research Group

http://www.kennedyinfo.com

General information on consulting, trends, fees, and so forth.

Linkexchange

http://www.linkexchange.com

Banner exchange and help starting, promoting, and managing a Web site. Selling online and more.

Promotion Business Builders

http://promobusinessbuilder.com

Ideas, products, and promotion campaigns.

The Market Research Center

http://www.asiresearch.com

Links to any product or service category. Good source for information on competitive sites.

MCNI

http://www.mcni.com

Forums, free consultant listing, search service, bookstore, and more.

Small Business Advisor

http://www.isquare.com

Advice and short reports for small businesses.

Statistical Abstract of the United States

Numerous sites. Use a search engine and look up "*Statistical Abstract of the United States.*" Demographics of all types.

Trade Show Central

http://www.prnewswire.com/tech/tscsourc_tech.html

Search directory for 30,000 trade shows worldwide.

U.S. Small Business Administration

http://www.sbaonline.sba.gov

Information on starting a business, expanding one, local small business administration resources, shareware, and more.

Wholesale Directories

http://www.qualitybooks.com/director.htm

Sources of trade directories for purchase.

Valuable Internet Links

http://www.stuffofheroes.com

Leaders Free Online Library—provides links to more than one million articles and books and other research material.

http://www.mapnp.org/library

Free Management Library—provides links to tens of thousands of articles in different business areas.

Links to Libraries of More Than 100,000 Free Downloadable Books

Name	URL	Estimated number of Books
Bartleby.com	http://www.bartleby.com	500
Bibliomania	http://www.bibliomania.com	2,000
Book Rags	http://www.bookrags.com/ebooks	1,500
Ebook Directory	http://www.ebookdirectory.com	20,000
Franklin Free Library	http://www.franklin.com/freelibrary	5,000
Free Books	http://www.free-books.org	1,000
Free e-books.net	http://www.free-ebooks.net	100
Internet Classics Archive	http://classics.mit.edu	400
Internet Public Library	http://www.ipl.org/div/books	20,000
MemoWare	http:/www.memoware.com	10,000
Microsoft Reader	http://www.mslit.com/default.asp?mjr=FRE	1,500
National Academies Press	http://www.nap.edu	2,500
Online Books Page	http://digital.library.upenn.edu/books	18,000
Oxford Text Archive	http://ota.ahds.ac.uk	2,500
Page by Page Books	http://www.pagebypagebooks.com	1,000
Project Gutenberg	http://promo.net/pg	6,000
Qvadis Lilbrary	http://www.qvadis.com/exlibris/ebooks.html#library	6,000
University of California	http://www.ucpress.edu/scan/books.html	500
University of Virginia	http://etext.lib.virgina.edu/ebooks	1,800
World E-book Library	http://netlibrary.net/WorldHome.html	10,000

APPENDIX

C

EXAMPLES OF SIMPLE RESEARCH AND A MARKETING RESEARCH CHECKLIST

The kind of marketing research you do is limited only by your imagination. Some research, even of the primary type, can be done at very little cost except for your time. Here are some examples of simple research done by small businesses that greatly increased sales. These ideas were suggested by J. Ford Laumer Jr., James R. Hams, and Hugh J. Guffey Jr., all professors of marketing at Auburn University of Auburn, Alabama, in their booklet *Learning about Your Market,* published by the Small Business Administration.

1. *License plate analysis.* In many states, license plates give you information about where car owners live. Therefore, simply by taking down the numbers of cars parked in your location and contacting the appropriate state agency, you can estimate the area from which you draw business. Knowing where your customers live can help you in your advertising or in targeting your approach to promotion. By the same method you can find who your competitors' customers are.

2. *Telephone number analysis.* Telephone numbers can also tell you the areas in which people live. You can obtain customers' telephone numbers from sales slips, credit card slips, or checks. Again, knowing where they live will give you excellent information about their lifestyles.

3. *Coded coupons.* The effectiveness of your advertising vehicle can easily be checked by coding coupons that can be used for discounts or inquiries about products. You can find out the areas that your customers come from, as well as which vehicle brought them your message.

4. *People watching.* Simply looking at your customers can tell you a great deal about them. How are they dressed? How old are they? Are they married or single? Do they have children or not? Many owners use this method intuitively to get a feel about their customers. However, a little sophistication with a tally sheet for a week can provide much more accurate information simply, easily, and without cost. It may confirm what you've known all along, or it may completely change your picture of your typical customer.

CHECKLIST FOR APPRAISAL OF YOUR RESEARCH STUDY

1. Review of research objectives:
   a. In relation to the problem.
   b. In relation to previous research.
   c. In relation to developments subsequent to initiation of research.

2. Overall study design:
   a. Are the hypotheses relevant? Consistent?
   b. Is the terminology relevant and unambiguous?
   c. Is the design a logical bridge from problem to solution?
   d. Are there any biases in the design that may have influenced the results?
   e. Was care taken to preserve anonymity, if needed?
   f. Were proper ethical considerations taken into account?
   g. Was the study well administered?

3. Methods used:
   a. Were the right sources used (populations sampled)?
   b. Do any of the data collection methods appear to be biased?
   c. What precautions were taken to avoid errors or mistakes in data collection?
   d. If sampling was used, how representative is the sample? With what margin of error?
   e. Were the data processed with due care? What precautions were taken to assure good coding?
   f. Are the categories used in tabulation meaningful?
   g. Were any pertinent tabulations or cross-classifications overlooked? On the other hand, are the tabulations so detailed as to obscure some of the main points?
   h. Do the analytical (statistical) methods appear to be appropriate?
   i. Is the report well executed in terms of organization, style, appearance, etc.?

4. Review of interpretations and recommendations:
   a. Do they follow from the data? Are they well supported?
   b. Are they comprehensive? Do they relate to the whole problem or only part of it?
   c. Are they consistent with the data? With existing information, other studies, executives' experiences, etc.?
   d. Were any relevant interpretations overlooked?

5. Responsibility for action and follow-up:
   a. Will information receive due consideration from all those concerned?
   b. What are the implications of the results for action? Will all action possibilities be considered? (How do the results affect aspects of total operation outside the scope of the report?)
   c. Is an action program necessary? Will it be formulated?
   d. Is further information needed? If so, along what lines?
   e. Is responsibility for follow-up clearly assigned?
   f. Should a time be set for reevaluation of the action program (e.g., to reevaluate an innovation or test a new package after introduction)?

APPENDIX   D

HOW TO LEAD A TEAM

One of the most important and difficult challenges you face in developing a marketing plan is working on a team. Teamwork is never easy. You must work with different personalities, having different work schedules, different priorities, different motivation, and different ways of approaching the project. Further, someone may or may not be assigned as team leader. You may think that teamwork is something that you need to be concerned with only as a student. You may be under the impression that once you graduate, you need never be concerned with teamwork again. You would be very much mistaken. Most companies of all sizes use teams to accomplish work to some extent or another. Over the past ten years, there has been a dramatic increase in the use of team structures in companies due to the quality movement and the use of process action teams. Process action teams focus on improving the process of getting some type of work accomplished. But long before the quality movement, teams had already made important contributions in industry. In fact, back in 1987, management guru Tom Peters stated, "The power of the team is so great that it is often wise to violate apparent common sense and force a team structure on almost anything."[1]

To understand just how powerful teams are, please try to identify what kind of work has all of the following characteristics:

- The workers work very hard physically, including weekends, with little complaint.
- The workers receive no money and little material compensation for their services.
- The work is dangerous, and workers are frequently injured on the job.
- The work is strictly voluntary.
- The workers usually have very high morale.
- There are always more volunteers than can be used for the work.
- The workers are highly motivated to achieve the organization's goals.
- Not only is the work legal, but many community organizations encourage it.

Turn the page to identify this work. The work that has all of these characteristics is . . .

A HIGH SCHOOL FOOTBALL TEAM

What's So Great about a Team?

Yes, all of the characteristics of the football team are true. The operative word here is TEAM. Can you begin to see just how powerful and unique a team can be? Yet the basic concept of a team is very simple. A team is simply two or more individuals working together to reach a common goal.

Teams in industry have had some amazing achievements. One of General Electric's plants in Salisbury, North Carolina, increased its productivity by 250 percent compared to other General Electric plants making the same product, but without teams. General Mills plants with teams are 40 percent more productive than plants without teams. Westinghouse Furniture Systems increased productivity 74 percent in three years with teams. Using teams, Volvo's Kalimar facility reduced defects by 90 percent. In one hospital study of critical care, when patients receiving mechanical ventilation are managed by a multidisciplinary team that proactively oversees the weaning process of removing a tube used for breathing, it takes patients nearly two fewer days to become acclimated compared to the traditional process.[2]

A number of scientists have observed that when geese flock in a V formation to reach a destination, they are operating as a team. Their common goal is their destination. And by teaming, they extend their range by as much as 71 percent! Flocking also illustrates some other important aspects of effective teaming. One goose doesn't lead all the time. The lead position at the point of the V varies. Note that this is also true in football. On different plays, the leadership role varies. Also, at different times in football, different individuals may assume important leadership roles. At any given time, the head coach, line coach, team captain, quarterback, or someone else may have the most important leadership role on the team.

Getting back to our flock of geese, should a single goose leave formation, he or she soon returns because of the difficulty in flying against the wind resistance alone. Should a goose fall out of formation because it is injured, other "team members" will drop out and attempt to assist their teammate. You may have thought that the honking noise that geese make in formation serves no useful purpose. But scientific investigation found that honking was all part of their teamwork. The honking was the cheering that encouraged the leader to maintain the pace. Flocks of geese, football teams, and teams of students developing a marketing plan share the following characteristics if they are to be effective:

- They demonstrate coordinated interaction.
- They are more efficient working together than alone.
- They enjoy the process of working together.
- Responsibility rotates either formally or informally.
- There are mutual care, nurturing, and encouragement among team members and especially between leaders and followers.
- There are a high level of trust.
- Everyone is keenly interested in everyone else's success.

As you might expect, when you have a group acting together toward a common goal showing these characteristics, you see some very positive results. It becomes not just a team, but a winning team. The team members have a degree of understanding and acceptance not found outside the group. They produce a greater number of ideas, and these ideas are of higher quality than if they thought up some ideas individually and met to make a list of the total. Such a team has higher motivation and performance levels that offset individual biases and cover each others' blind spots.

If you saw the picture *Rocky*, you may remember the scene in which Rocky's girlfriend's brother demands to know what Rocky sees in his sister. "She fills spaces," answers Sylvester Stallone, playing the role of Rocky. "Spaces in me, spaces in her." Having fewer blind spots and performing together in such a way as to emphasize each member's strengths and make his or her weaknesses irrelevant, an effective team is more likely to take risks and innovative action that leads to success.

When a flock of geese becomes a winning team, they get to their destination quicker than other flocks. They get the most protective nesting areas, which are located closer to food and water. Their goslings are bigger, stronger, and healthier. They have a much better chance of survival and procreation. We see the winning football teams in the Super Bowl. And a winning marketing planning team? In class, this is the team that gets the "A" and has a lot of fun doing it. In real life, the winning team developing a marketing plan gets the resources needed and goes on to build a multibillion-dollar success in the marketplace.

Who Gets to Be the Team Leader?

Sometimes you will be assigned the position of team leader. Sometimes not. Sometimes no team leader assignment will be made. However, in some courses it is possible that you may be the only graduate student on a team with undergraduate students. Or, in your "other life," you are a company president. You are confident that your fellow team members will follow your lead. You go to several meetings and attempt to take charge. Guess what? Your teammates reject you in favor of someone else who isn't one-tenth as qualified. What do you do?

My advice is this: If you are assigned or selected as team leader by your teammates, do the job to the best of your ability. If you are not assigned or selected as team leader by your teammates, support whoever is team leader to the best of your ability. Never let your ego get in the way of doing the best you can for your team. Not only will this help your team become a winning team, but also you will earn the respect of your teammates and maintain your self-respect as well. A good leader can both lead and follow. He or she doesn't need to be the leader in order to make a major contribution to the team.

How Do I Lead If I Am the Leader?

There is no way of telling you how to be a leader in twenty-five words or fewer. There are volumes written about leadership. I should know. I wrote a couple. These were recommended by leaders from Mary Kay Ash, CEO emeritus of Mary Kay Cosmetics, and CEOs of major corporations to Senator Barry Goldwater and General H. Norman Schwarzkopf. I highly recommend these books to you.[3]

I will point out one critical fact. There is no question that as team leader, you have a major responsibility for the ultimate marketing plan that is produced. There is an old saying that it is better to have an army of lambs led by a lion than an army of lions led by a lamb. This emphasizes the extreme importance of the leader in getting the job done. There is no such thing as an excuse that "all my team members were lambs." A leader who says this is really saying that "I am a lamb." We really don't know what the team members were. They could have all been lions and still failed with a lamb as a leader.

Although I can't make you an expert leader in a few pages of suggestions, there are specific things I can tell you that you need to know about being a *team* leader. Psychologists and researchers in leadership have found that teams progress through four stages of development. Each stage has different characters, and in each stage members of teams tend to ask different questions. Partly because the concerns of the team tend to be different in each stage, the leader's focus, actions, and behavior must be different in each stage as well. This is extremely important because what might be the correct actions in one stage would be counterproductive and incorrect in another. For example, in the second stage of development members actually tend to be committed and even obedient. The leaders' focus during this stage must be on building relationships and facilitating tasks. But look out! In the next stage, members tend to challenge one another and even their leader. You've got to focus on conflict management and examining key work processes to make them better. If you are stuck in Stage 2 while your team is in Stage 3, you may lose your moral authority as leader.

So, as a team leader, you must first identify what stage the team is in. Then, pay attention to your focus and take actions to answer the concerns of your team while you help move them toward completing the project. With this in mind, here are the four stages of team development:

- Stage 1: Getting Organized
- Stage 2: Getting Together and Making Nice-Nice
- Stage 3: Fighting It Out
- Stage 4: Getting the Job Done

Now let's look at each in turn.

Stage 1: Getting Organized

When you first get together as a team, you're going to find that many of your team members may tend to be silent and self-conscious unless they have known one another previously. This is because they are uncertain. They don't know what is going to happen, and they may be worried about what is expected of them. The questions that may occur to your fellow team members include: Who are these other guys? Are they going to be friendly or to challenge me? What are they going to expect me to do? What's going to happen during this process? Where exactly will we be headed and why? What are our precise goals? Where do I fit in? How much work will this involve? Is this project going to require me to give up time that I need to put in elsewhere?

As the team leader, your primary focus during Stage 1 is just as the stage is named: to organize the team. Your actions should include making introductions, stating the mission of the team, clarifying goals, procedures, rules, and expectations, and answering questions. The idea is to establish a foundation of trust right from the start. You want an atmosphere of openness with no secrets. While members may disagree with one another or with you, everyone gets his or her say and everyone's opinion is listened to and considered.

To do this, you must model these expected behaviors yourself. If you aren't open, no one else will be. If you don't treat the opinions of others with respect, neither will anyone else. If you listen carefully, so will everyone else. If you argue and try to shout down others, so will those you are attempting to lead.

You may be interested in the characteristics of high-performance teams as distinguished from those that performed less well.[4] Keep these in mind as you organize your team.

- Clear goals
- Goals known by all
- Goals achieved in small steps
- Standards of excellence
- Feedback of results
- Skills and knowledge of everyone used
- Continuous improvement expected
- Adequate resources provided
- Autonomy

- Performance-based rewards
- Competition
- Praise and recognition
- Team commitment
- Plans and tactics
- Rules and penalties
- Performance measures

Remember, in Stage 1 your principal focus is on getting organized. At the same time, you are laying the foundations of trust and openness for the stages that follow.

Stage 2: Getting Together and Making Nice-Nice

Congratulations! You did a great job of getting your marketing planning team together at the first meeting. Now you have a different challenge. Members tend to ignore disagreements and conform obediently to the group standards and expectations, as well as your directions as leader. There is heightened interpersonal attraction, and at the end, everyone will be committed to a team vision. All of this is what you want.

Of course, team members still wonder and ask themselves questions. What are the team's norms and expectations? How much should I really give up and conform to the group's ideas? What role can I perform on this team? Where can I make a contribution? Will I be supported in what I suggest, or will others "put me down"? Where are we headed? How much time and energy should I commit to this project?

During this stage, you have several major challenges:

- Facilitating role differentiation
- Showing support
- Providing feedback
- Articulating and motivating commitment to a vision

To facilitate role differentiation, you need to continue to build relationships among your team members. You want your team members to contribute according to their strengths where they are most needed. You also want to assist them in whatever tasks they are working on. You can do this by asking about their strengths and about their preferences for tasks that need to be done. As they proceed, it is your responsibility to ensure they have the resources to do the job. When there are disagreements between team members, it is your responsibility to resolve the situation. As a task facilitator, you yourself may function in a variety of roles. At times you may give direction, or at least suggestions. You are sometimes an information seeker, and sometimes an information giver. You must monitor, coordinate, and oversee everything that is going on. Avoid blocking others from contributing, and don't let anyone else block either. People try to block others in a variety of ways. This includes by finding fault, overanalyzing, rejecting out of hand, dominating, stalling, and other tactics we might never anticipate. Don't let them do it!

You show support for others by building people up every chance you get. Build on their ideas, but give the credit to them for being the first to think them up. And as indicated above, let everyone be heard. Don't let someone who is more articulate, powerful, or popular block the ideas of some other team member who is less so.

Providing effective feedback is not easy. You must indicate what is going to work and what won't. To do this without offending, so this person maintains his or her self-respect and continues to contribute, is the real challenge. To best accomplish this, talk about behavior, not about personalities. Make observations, not judgments. Be as specific as possible. Share ideas and information. Don't set yourself up as a know-it-all who gives advice.

Learn the art of the possible. It is possible to give too much feedback at one time, especially if the feedback is more critical than congratulatory. In fact, critical feedback is always difficult. Look for ways of doing this that remove the sting of criticism. President Reagan once gave a small statue of a foot with a hole in it to his secretary of the interior when the secretary made a major public error. The statue was the "Shot Yourself in the Foot" award. There was a lot of laughter and good humor as President Reagan presented it. Still, it was criticism. You might establish a pot into which people have to put in a dollar if they show up late to a team meeting. The money could go toward a team party or for some other team purpose. Finally, remember that you give feedback for value to the team . . . not for personal emotional release. Not to show who's boss and not to show how clever you are.

Finally, you must focus on articulating and motivating commitment to a vision. A vision is sort of a mental picture of the outcome of the mission. Maybe the vision is to submit the best marketing plan in the class. Maybe it is to win a prize with the plan. Maybe it is to develop a plan for someone who is actually going to implement it. In any case, you should sell the outcome, the good things that will happen as a result of the team's work in precise terms. Motivating your team means making your vision their vision also. To do this, you must get them involved with it. Ask their opinions. Modify your vision as necessary. Ground the vision in core values. Also, people don't sacrifice to do small tasks. They sacrifice only for big tasks. So if you are preparing a marketing plan for a medical product that can do a lot of good, emphasize building a better world more than you do profitability. If you can get them involved with suggestions and ideas about the vision and how to achieve it, you will have attained two essential ingredients: public commitment and ownership. Get those, and you've gone a long way toward building a winning team.

Stage 3: Fighting It Out

When you enter Stage 3, the good news is that you have a team fully committed to a vision and fighting to get a first-class marketing plan developed, printed, and bound. Unfortunately, since individuals have invested so much of themselves, members in this stage can become polarized, form cliques, become overly competitive, and even challenge your authority as leader.

Clearly, you have your work cut out for you. Your focus must be on conflict management, continuing to ensure that everyone gets to express his or her ideas, examining key work processes to make them better, getting team members working together rather than against each other, and avoiding groupthink. All of these are pretty straightforward except for groupthink. What is groupthink?

Groupthink has to do with adopting some idea or course of action simply because the group seems to want it and not because it is a particularly good idea that has been thoroughly discussed and thought through. The most conspicuous example of groupthink has been popularized as a "Trip to Abilene." In a "Trip to Abilene," a family makes a miserable two-hour trip to Abilene and returns to a ranch in west Texas. The trip is made in a car without air conditioning on a hot, humid summer day on the suggestion of one of the family members. All members agreed on the trip, although later it turns out that they did so simply "to be agreeable." Whereupon, the member who suggested the idea states that he didn't want to go either. He had simply suggested the idea to make conversation.

To avoid groupthink, all ideas should be critically evaluated. You should encourage open discussion of all ideas on a routine basis. Some more sophisticated ideas can be evaluated better by calling in outside experts to listen or even by the rotating assignment of one member as a devil's advocate to bring up all the ideas against any proposed action. One idea that helps many teams avoid groupthink is a policy of second-chance discussions. With this technique, all decisions have their implementations deferred until one additional confirmation discussion at a later date.

During this stage, the questions on the minds of your fellow team members will include: How will we handle disagreements? How do we communicate negative information? Can the composition of this team be changed? How can we make decisions even though there is a lot of disagreement? Do we really need this leader? You may wish that your fellow team members were not asking themselves these questions, especially the last. However, it is better to be forewarned, so you can deal with these issues, than to be surprised.

You can take a number of actions to help your team during this stage. You can think up ways to reinforce and remotivate commitment to the vision. You can turn your fellow team members into teachers, helping others with problems they may be having. In fact, you should know that using others as teachers, or leaders, for subareas in the project helps generate their public commitment. You might think up ways to provide individual recognition, such as a small prize for having accomplished the most during the previous week. As arguments arise, you can work on being a more effective mediator. You can look for win/win opportunities and foster win/win thinking, where both sides of an argument or an issue benefit. One way to increase feelings of cohesion in the group is to identify a common "enemy." Other class teams competing for "best marketing plan" might constitute one such enemy.

There are plenty of challenges for you as a leader in this stage. You will learn a tremendous amount about leading groups. Do it right, and your team goes in to the final stage looking, acting, and performing like a real winner.

Stage 4: Getting the Job Done

Of course, your team is getting the job done during all four stages. But if you've done things right, when you get to Stage 4 you are really on a roll. How soon your team gets to this stage varies greatly. Clearly, it is to your advantage to get to this stage as soon as you can and to spend the bulk of your time working on your marketing plan in this stage. During this stage, team members show high mutual trust and unconditional commitment to the team. Moreover, team members tend to be self-sufficient and display a good deal of initiative. The team looks like an entrepreneurial company. As team leader, your focus should be on innovation, continuous improvement, and emphasizing and making most of what your team does best—its core competencies.

Team members' questions reflect this striving for high performance. How can we continuously improve? How can we promote innovativeness and creativity? How can we build further on our core competencies? What further improvements can be made to our processes? How can we maintain a high level of contribution to the team?

As team leader, your actions are in direct line with these questions. Do everything you can to encourage continuous improvement. Celebrate your team's successes. Keep providing feedback on performance. Sponsor and encourage new ideas and expanded roles for team members. And most importantly, help the team avoid reverting to earlier stages.

When Good Team Members Do Bad Things

As you progress through the four stages, you will occasionally be surprised by team members you considered first rate doing things to hurt the team. When that happens, you're going to have to take some kind of action. You might also consider the root cause. Why did this productive team member go wrong? Here are some of the more common reasons that good team members err:

- Inequity of effort.

  When one or more members of the team fail to work up to a certain standard of effort, you will soon find that others will do likewise. The erring team member thinks, "If this other person isn't working up to this effort, why should I?" This is one reason why you cannot allow one of the members to goof off and do less than his or her fair share. You must stop inequity of effort before it starts.

- No accountability.

  This occurs when members are allowed to "freewheel" and no feedback occurs. Since no one else seems to care, the member feels insignificant and unimportant. This can lead to general inequity of effort.

- Some reward to everyone

  This, too, is related to inequity of effort. The team member wonders why he or she should work harder than other team members when all get the same reward. What you want is for everyone striving to contribute to the maximum extent possible. Offering the same reward can lead to everyone trying to do the minimum. The solution is to set up a reward system, even if the "reward" is a simple public recognition of an action above the call of duty or a successful accomplishment.

- Coordination problems.

  There is no getting around it. The more people involved, the more coordination required. That can mean waiting for the work of others, having to get others' approval, and other delays. For someone who has always worked successfully alone, the inefficiencies are frustrating and painfully obvious. However, as already noted, the loss in efficiency of the individual can be more than made up by the synergistic effect. Team members can not only help one another, but also cheer one another on and rejoice in another individual's success. As team leader, you must make certain this happens. You must make it efficient and fun to be part of the team. Do this, and every member will see that they can accomplish more as a member of a group than they ever could individually.

SUMMARY

The focus of this book is how to put together a marketing plan. You will learn a lot from doing this. It is a skill that is worth a great deal to any corporation. You may get to work on a team. If so, you are going to learn a great deal from this also. It is an invaluable experience. If you are really lucky, you will have the responsibility of team leader. You have achieved a triple whammy. You are going to learn more than anyone else. It's not going to be easy. You will face the stiffest challenges and the most difficult work. You will bear the heaviest responsibility. It can also be one of the most rewarding experiences you have ever had. What is in this appendix can help you. However, only you can determine how to apply the information. Your success is up to you. Good luck!

NOTES

1. Tom Peters, *Thriving on Chaos* (New York: Knopf, 1987), p. 306.
2. Jeffrey R. Dichter, "Teamwork and Hospital Medicine: A Vision for the Future," *Critical Care Nurse* (June 2003).
3. William A. Cohen, *The New Art of the Leader* (Paramus, NJ: Prentice Hall, 2000); and *The Stuff of Heroes: The Eight Universal Laws of Leadership* (Marietta, GA, 1998).
4. F. Petrock, "Team Dynamics: A Workshop for Effective Team Building." Presentation at the University of Michigan Management of Managers Program, 1991.

APPENDIX

E

THE CONCEPT AND APPLICATION OF MARKETING STRATEGY[1]

One of the most important issues in marketing planning is developing marketing strategy, not simply documenting the use of various parts of product, price, promotion, and distribution. Numbers are important in the development of marketing strategy, for they act as important inputs to that greatest of computers and computer programming, the human brain. Yet, it is your judgment that enables the development of a strategy that works, not any assignment of numbers and percentages. These can never replace the ability of the human brain to integrate vast amounts of data, both qualitative and quantitative, and to reason to a solution that works and is optimal. This is better than any computer or computer program, no matter how sophisticated. In fact, we can introduce major error into the development of strategy when we attempt to assign numbers to elements that cannot and should not be quantified. This is because assigning numbers to qualitative aspects gives the appearance of truth and accuracy, when in reality we are simply cloaking judgment in a way to make it appear absolute. If you have heard of "the tyranny of numbers," this is what the term means.

WHY THIS APPENDIX IS NEEDED

Because we already looked at developing marketing strategy in Chapter 4, you may wonder why an additional chapter on strategy is necessary. The use of matrices for developing strategy really is an assist in developing strategy regarding a portfolio of products or businesses, thus its name, "portfolio management." Strategy using the product life cycle also helps you make certain strategic decisions regarding what you should do with products or services you have introduced. But strategy is an art. As an art, there is a concept of strategy that helps us make strategy (and tactical) decisions, no matter whether we are managing portfolios of products or businesses or considering what to do with a product or service in a certain stage of its life cycle. So, this appendix is for the real student of strategy, the student who wants to understand the underpinning and then apply it to any situation to achieve objectives and goals.

Although we're going to use principles as the core of our discussion, this does not mean that the application of these principles to strategy development cannot be scientific. The scientific method is a process that is a reliable, consistent, and nonarbitrary representation of the real world. It minimizes the influence of bias and prejudice. Because numbers are most easily controlled, we frequently assume that to be scientific requires quantifiable entering arguments. This is not necessarily true. What is true is that we must approach the solution in such a way that the output yields consistent results. In this way, we can avoid a repetition of past errors, capitalize on the greatest chances for success, and reach the predictable and repeatable conclusions we desire.

A scientific method is crucially important when employing judgment and in using strategy principles and to coordinate the many factors that must be considered in developing operational marketing strategy. It is painfully true when various principles conflict (which they often do) or when, under different conditions, one principle is more important than another, which is also true.

Principles, Resources, and Situational Variables

We face three aspects of any situation when we seek to apply principles of strategy. These are:

- The principles themselves
- The resources we have available
- The relevant variables found in the situation faced

Innumerable concepts have been put forth as the true basic principles of strategy. My own studies have resulted in ten principles I consider universal. These are:

1. Commitment to a Definite Objective—This refers to what you, as a marketing strategist, intend to accomplish.

2. Seizing and Maintaining the Initiative—This means that you, not your competitor, should be in control.

3. Economization and Mass—No company has unlimited resources. So you need to economize where the situation allows it and concentrate your resources where it is important to be strong.

4. Surprise—If your competitor does not know your plans, he cannot prepare to counter your marketing initiatives.

5. Simplicity—The simpler your strategy is, the easier it is to implement everything as you intend.

6. Multiple Simultaneous Approaches and Objectives—If you have alternate approaches and objectives, it becomes difficult, if not impossible, for a competitor to counter your strategic moves. If he blocks one way, you can go another.

7. The Indirect Approach—If you approach your objective indirectly, you have a greater chance of achieving it. Instead of competing on price, for example, you compete on delivery, like Domino's Pizza.

8. Environment—Select a strategy that matches your environment.

9. Timing and Sequencing—Doing the right thing at the wrong time is sometimes worse than not doing it or doing the wrong thing.

10. Exploitation of Success—Keep going until your goals are fully achieved.

The resources you have to work with may include manpower, capital, equipment, know-how, and quality of leadership. They are assets that you control. You can manipulate these resources to implement your strategy.

The relevant variables in the situation faced include situational or environmental (uncontrollable) variables—economic conditions, business conditions, the state of technology, politics, legal and regulatory requirements, social and cultural norms, and the competition—as well as the familiar marketing tactical variables we can control—product, price, promotion, and distribution.

An astute strategist first looks at all aspects of the situation and selects the relevant variables in it. Each variable must be avoided, overcome, ignored, used, or turned to an advantage. The strategist's purpose is to integrate the variables with the principles and to use the available resources to develop a plan to accomplish marketing objectives and goals.[2]

In the following table, I have prepared side-by-side lists of the aspects of strategy. Then we'll look at an example of how these aspects might be used.

Situational and Tactical Variables	Principles of Strategy	Available Resources
Economic and business conditions	Commitment to a definite objective	Manpower
State of technology	Seizing and maintaining the initiative	Capital
Politics	Economization to mass	Equipment
Legal and regulatory issues	Positioning	Special knowledge
Social and cultural norms	Surprise	Quality of leaders
Competition	Simplicity	Other relevant assets
Product	Multiple simultaneous alternatives	
Price	The indirect approach	
Promotion	Timing and sequencing	
Distribution	Exploitation of success	

Example: Attacking the Market Leader's Top Product

To illustrate the method, let's look at one of the most successful new product introductions ever undertaken against a market leader. In 1936, Lever Bros., number two in the soap business behind Procter & Gamble, introduced Spry vegetable shortening to compete against P&G's well-entrenched Crisco brand.[3] The smart money said "no way." Not only was Crisco firmly established, but it also had been on the market for twenty years. Despite the Great Depression, it appeared to be depression-proof, and sales were up. It had no serious challengers, despite that fact that lard and butter were far less expensive. The Crisco name had become synonymous with vegetable shortening and almost generic. When women asked for "Crisco," they meant vegetable shortening. Yet within one year of introduction, Spry had captured 50 percent of Crisco's market share. Moreover, there were no new ingredients used, and Spry was made from exactly the same raw materials as Crisco.

HOW LEVER BROS. DID IT

Lever Bros. was a subsidiary of Unilever of London, a giant worldwide corporation. Having been successful with a number of products in the United States in the late 1920s, it sought another new product to launch. The company first looked at all aspects of the situation. A vegetable shortening product seemed a good potential candidate. P&G had already proven there was a market. Although its potential competitor's product was well established, its dominance also meant there were no other major competitors or competitive products to contend with. At the time of the initial decision, both business and economic conditions were good.

Lever initiated a deeper look into its competitor's product and found some weaknesses. Although women liked the product, there were some things that they didn't like. If refrigerated, the product turned hard and was difficult to use. If left unrefrigerated, it turned rancid. The color was not consistent, and while housewives would have preferred the product in a pure white colorization, it tended to be a dirty white color. Moreover, the packaging was not uniform in the cans in which it was supplied, and the housewives didn't like that either.

Integrating the Principles

Looking at the principles of strategy, we can see how some were integrated with the situational variables. Lever Bros. seized the initiative and committed to a definite objective. It planned to concentrate resources at the strategic position of shortening. P&G thought its product, Crisco, was invulnerable, so it paid little attention and did no research with the consumer. In fact, it had even allowed quality control in manufacturing and packaging to get sloppy. As a consequence, the thought that a competitor, even a major one like Lever Bros., would introduce a product to compete with Crisco was totally unexpected, even unthinkable. Lever Bros. capitalized on this belief. Coupled with good security, the Spry product achieved complete surprise.

Looking at Resources

Lever Bros. decided which of the situational variables could be avoided, overcome, or taken advantage of. Moreover, it had the resources to support the general principles of strategy it was planning. Unilever had made major technological advances in Europe in the manufacture of soap, and the technology was directly transferable to the production of vegetable shortening due to hydrogenation, the major process common to both types of products. Thus, a vegetable shortening product was compatible with the Lever Bros.' experience, know-how, and technical advantage. Consumers' problems with Crisco were easy to overcome. Some had simply to do with a stricter quality control. Financial resources and know-how were on Lever Bros.' side, but it also had one additional major advantage.

Lever Bros.' Secret Weapon

Francis Conway had become president of Lever Bros. in 1913 when sales were but $1 million. By the late 1920s, sales were over $40 million due largely to his personal leadership. Conway had met every challenge thrown at him, and he had the confidence of the parent company's leadership back in England. Unilever invested the money to build the manufacturing plants to make the product. By the early 1930s, Lever Bros. was ready to go.

Enter the Great Depression

The depression began in October 1929 and preempted product launch. By mid-1930 it was clear this was not an economic condition that would change soon. Lever Bros. had planned on introducing the product by then. There was tremendous pressure from within the company and the parent corporation to do so. The company had sunk a lot of money in Spry and wanted to get on with it. However, Conway knew his strategy and the importance of timing. He made the decision to wait. Meanwhile, he noted that the sales of Crisco did not slow, and while Spry was shelved, fine-tuning went on and research began into the best promotional approach.

The Launch

In late 1935, lard and butter prices rose. This meant the higher-price shortening would be more price competitive. Lever Bros. did not intend to compete with P&G on price, a direct approach strategy. Instead, although it was competing with essentially an identical product, the approach was indirect in the sense that problems with Crisco, recognized by consumers but not by the manufacturer, were all corrected in Spry.

Again, Conway economized elsewhere to concentrate and initiate a massive promotional campaign. Until this time, conventional wisdom was to introduce advertising for a new product and let it be assimilated gradually by the consumer. Conway eschewed this approach and gave his campaign everything he had. This included tactics ranging from door-to-door salesmen distributing one-pound sample cans and free Spry cookbooks to discount coupons and advertising even in small-town newspapers. Conway even launched a mobile cooking school that went around the country doing two-hour demonstrations. P&G was stunned, and though it improved its product and manufacturing, it never recaptured the share it had lost. Conway and Lever Bros. integrated the relevant variables with the principles, and using the resources available, developed and initiated a plan that made Spry a success despite the advantages enjoyed by P&G with Crisco.

SUMMARY: APPLY THE PRINCIPLES SCIENTIFICALLY

Strategy is an art, but the principles are not applied haphazardly, but scientifically. The strategist analyzes his situation and identifies the relevant variables. He uses numbers, but he does not allow them to overrule his good judgment. Rather, he integrates the relevant variables with the principles. Using the resources he has available, he develops and then implements the marketing plan that will help him attain his goals and objectives.

NOTES

1. A more detailed explanation of the principles of strategy and their application can be found in William A. Cohen, *The Art of the Strategist: 10 Essential Principles for Leading Your Company to Victory* (New York: AMACOM, 2004).
2. This concept originated with J. F. C. Fuller as developed in Anthony John Trythall, *'Boney' Fuller* (New Brunswick, NJ: Rutgers University Press, 1977), p. 108.
3. Robert F. Harley, *Marketing Successes,* 2nd ed. (New York: John Wiley & Sons, 1990), pp. 68–78.

APPENDIX

F

USEFUL WORKSHEETS FOR MARKETING PLANNING

WORKSHEET 1
Potential Expenditure Summary

Purpose	Total Period 1	Total Period 2	Total Period 3
Advertising			
Car and truck expense			
Commissions			
Contributions			
Delivery expense			
Dues and publications			
Employee benefits			
Freight			
Insurance			
Interest			
Laundry and cleaning			
Legal and professional services			
Licenses			
Maintenance			
Miscellaneous expenses			
Office supplies			
Pension and profit-sharing plan			
Postage			
Rent			
Repairs			
Selling expenses			
Supplies			
Taxes			
Telephone			
Traveling and entertainment			
Utilities			
Wages			
Totals			

WORKSHEET 2

Inventory to Be Purchased

Date Needed	Inventory to Be Ordered	Estimated Date of Receipt	Amount Payable	Cash Available Confirmation
		Totals		

WORKSHEET 3

Employee Compensation Forecast

Date	Period Worked	Wage Rate per Period	Total Wages	Soc. Sec. Ded.	Fed. Inc. Tax Ded.	State Inc. Tax Ded.	Net to Be Paid
TOTALS							

WORKSHEET 4

Tax Obligations Forecast

Type of Tax	Due Date	Amount Due	Pay To	Cash Available Confirmation
Federal Taxes				
Social Security Tax				
Employee Income tax				
Owner's/Corporations Income Tax				
Unemployment Taxes				
State Taxes				
Income Taxes				
Sales Taxes				
Unemployment Taxes				
Franchise Tax				
Other				
Local Taxes				
Sales Tax				
Real Estate Tax				
Personal Property Tax				
Licenses				
Other				

WORKSHEET 5

Determining Source of Funding to Use

Step 1 Weight the following factors on a scale of 1 to 5, 1 being not very important to you and 5 being very important to you.

Cost of capital—How important is the cost of capital and its effect on earnings? _____
Risk—How important is the risk imposed by the source of funding? _____
Flexibility—How important is it that you have flexibility in use of the money
borrowed or your ability to borrow more money in the future? _____
Control—How important is it to retain control over your business? _____
Availability—How important is it to attain the capital easily? _____
Amount—How important is the amount you can borrow? _____

Step 2 Note the potential sources you are considering for your loan. For each source and factor, assign a value of 1 to 5, 1 signifying that a source is not very attractive on a particular factor; 5 signifying that a source is very attractive on that factor.

Potential Source 1. _____
Cost of capital—How attractive is the cost of capital and its effect on earnings? _____
Risk—How attractive is the risk imposed by the source of funding? _____
Flexibility—How attractive is it on the flexibility in use of the money
borrowed or your ability to borrow more in the future? _____
Control—How attractive is it in retaining control over your business? _____
Availability—How available is the capital from this source? _____
Amount—How attractive is the amount you can borrow from this source? _____

Potential Source 2. _____
Cost of capital—How attractive is the cost of capital and its effect on earnings? _____
Risk—How attractive is the risk imposed by the source of funding? _____
Flexibility—How attractive is it on the flexibility in use of the money
borrowed or your ability to borrow more money in the future? _____
Control—How attractive is it in retaining control over your business? _____
Availability—How available is the capital from this source? _____
Amount—How attractive is the amount you can borrow from this source? _____

Potential Source 3. _____
Cost of capital—How attractive is the cost of capital and its effect on earnings? _____
Risk—How attractive is the risk imposed by the source of funding? _____
Flexibility—How attractive is it on the flexibility in use of the money
borrowed or your ability to borrow more money in the future? _____
Control—How attractive is it in retaining control over your business? _____
Availability—How available is the capital from this source? _____
Amount—How attractive is the amount you can borrow from this source? _____

Potential Source 4. _____
Cost of capital—How attractive is the cost of capital and its effect on earnings? _____
Risk—How attractive is the risk imposed by the source of funding? _____
Flexibility—How attractive is it on the flexibility in use of the money
borrowed or your ability to borrow more money in the future? _____
Control—How attractive is it in retaining control over your business? _____
Availability—How available is the capital from this source? _____
Amount—How attractive is the amount you can borrow from this source? _____

Potential Source 5. _____
Cost of capital—How attractive is the cost of capital and its effect on earnings? _____
Risk—How attractive is the risk imposed by the source of funding? _____
Flexibility—How attractive is it on the flexibility in use of the money
borrowed or your ability to borrow more money in the future? _____
Control—How attractive is it in retaining control over your business? _____
Availability—How available is the capital from this source? _____
Amount—How attractive is the amount you can borrow from this source? _____

Potential Source 6. _____

Cost of capital—How attractive is the cost of capital and its effect on earnings?   _____

Risk—How attractive is the risk imposed by the source of funding?   _____

Flexibility—How attractive is it on the flexibility in use of the money   _____
borrowed or your ability to borrow more money in the future?   _____

Control—How attractive is it in retaining control over your business?   _____

Availability—How available is the capital from this source?   _____

Amount—How attractive is the amount you can borrow from this source?   _____

Potential Source 7. _____

Cost of capital—How attractive is the cost of capital and its effect on earnings?   _____

Risk—How attractive is the risk imposed by the source of funding?   _____

Flexibility—How attractive is it on the flexibility in use of the money   _____
borrowed or your ability to borrow more money in the future?   _____

Control—How attractive is it in retaining control over your business?   _____

Availability—How available is the capital from this source?   _____

Amount—How attractive is the amount you can borrow from this source?   _____

Potential Source 8. _____

Cost of capital—How attractive is the cost of capital and its effect on earnings?   _____

Risk—How attractive is the risk imposed by the source of funding?   _____

Flexibility—How attractive is it on the flexibility in use of the money   _____
borrowed or your ability to borrow more money in the future?   _____

Control—How attractive is it in retaining control over your business?   _____

Availability—How available is the capital from this source?   _____

Amount—How attractive is the amount you can borrow from this source?   _____

Step 3   Multiply the totals from the results from Step 1 and Step 2 for each source.

Potential Source 1. _____

	Step 1 Results ×	Step 2 Results =	
Cost of capital	_____ ×	_____ =	_____
Risk	_____ ×	_____ =	_____
Flexibility	_____ ×	_____ =	_____
Control	_____ ×	_____ =	_____
Availability	_____ ×	_____ =	_____
Amount	_____ ×	_____ =	_____

Potential Source 1 Total _____

Potential Source 2. _____

	Step 1 Results ×	Step 2 Results =	
Cost of capital	_____ ×	_____ =	_____
Risk	_____ ×	_____ =	_____
Flexibility	_____ ×	_____ =	_____
Control	_____ ×	_____ =	_____
Availability	_____ ×	_____ =	_____
Amount	_____ ×	_____ =	_____

Potential Source 2 Total _____

Potential Source 3. _____

	Step 1 Results ×	Step 2 Results =	
Cost of capital	_____ ×	_____ =	_____
Risk	_____ ×	_____ =	_____
Flexibility	_____ ×	_____ =	_____
Control	_____ ×	_____ =	_____
Availability	_____ ×	_____ =	_____
Amount	_____ ×	_____ =	_____

Potential Source 3 Total _____

Potential Source 4. _____

	Step 1 Results ×	*Step 2 Results* =	
Cost of capital	_____ ×	_____ =	_____
Risk	_____ ×	_____ =	_____
Flexibility	_____ ×	_____ =	_____
Control	_____ ×	_____ =	_____
Availability	_____ ×	_____ =	_____
Amount	_____ ×	_____ =	_____

Potential Source 4 Total _____

Potential Source 5. _____

	Step 1 Results ×	*Step 2 Results* =	
Cost of capital	_____ ×	_____ =	_____
Risk	_____ ×	_____ =	_____
Flexibility	_____ ×	_____ =	_____
Control	_____ ×	_____ =	_____
Availability	_____ ×	_____ =	_____
Amount	_____ ×	_____ =	_____

Potential Source 5 Total _____

Potential Source 6. _____

	Step 1 Results ×	*Step 2 Results* =	
Cost of capital	_____ ×	_____ =	_____
Risk	_____ ×	_____ =	_____
Flexibility	_____ ×	_____ =	_____
Control	_____ ×	_____ =	_____
Availability	_____ ×	_____ =	_____
Amount	_____ ×	_____ =	_____

Potential Source 6 Total _____

Potential Source 7. _____

	Step 1 Results ×	*Step 2 Results* =	
Cost of capital	_____ ×	_____ =	_____
Risk	_____ ×	_____ =	_____
Flexibility	_____ ×	_____ =	_____
Control	_____ ×	_____ =	_____
Availability	_____ ×	_____ =	_____
Amount	_____ ×	_____ =	_____

Potential Source 7 Total _____

Potential Source 8. _____

	Step 1 Results ×	*Step 2 Results* =	
Cost of capital	_____ ×	_____ =	_____
Risk	_____ ×	_____ =	_____
Flexibility	_____ ×	_____ =	_____
Control	_____ ×	_____ =	_____
Availability	_____ ×	_____ =	_____
Amount	_____ ×	_____ =	_____

Potential Source 8 Total _____

Step 4   Write in the eight totals below and compare. The highest totals are the best for your situation.

Potential Source 1 Total _____
Potential Source 2 Total _____
Potential Source 3 Total _____
Potential Source 4 Total _____
Potential Source 5 Total _____
Potential Source 6 Total _____
Potential Source 7 Total _____
Potential Source 8 Total _____

WORKSHEET 6

Checklist for Business Insurance

This checklist is based on a checklist originally developed by Mark R. Greene, Distinguished Professor of Insurance at the University of Georgia and published by the U.S. Small Business Administration.

Fire Insurance	Action
1. Add other coverages, such as windstorm, hail, smoke, explosion, vandalism, and malicious mischief to basic fire insurance	
2. If you need comphrehensive coverage, your best buy may be one of the all-risk contracts that offer the broadest available protection for the money.	
3. The insurance company may compensate you for your losses in different ways: (1) It may pay actual cash value of the property at the time of loss. (2) It may repair or replace the property with material of like kind and quality. (3) It may take all the property at the agreed or appraised value and reimburse you for your loss.	
4. You can insure property you don't own if you have a financial interest in the property when a loss occurs but not necessarily at the time the insurance contract is made.	
5. When you sell property, you cannot assign the insurance policy along with the property unless you have permission from the insurance company.	
6. Even if you have several policies on your property, you can still collect only the amount of your actual cash loss. All the insurers share the payment proportionately.	
7. Special protection other than the standard fire policy is needed to cover the loss by fire of accounts, bills, currency, deeds, evidences of debt, and money and securities.	
8. If an insured building is vacant or unoccupied for more than 60 consecutive days, coverage may be suspended unless you have a special endorsement to your policy canceling this provision.	
9. If, either before or after a loss, you conceal or misrepresent to the insurer any material fact or circumstance concerning your insurance or the interest of the insured, the policy may be voided.	
10. If you take any action that increases the hazard of fire, the insurance company may suspend your coverage even for losses not originating from the increased hazard.	
11. After a loss, you must use all reasonable means to protect the property from further loss or run the risk of having your coverage canceled.	
12. To recover your loss, you must furnish (unless an extension is granted by the insurance company) a complete inventory of the damaged, destroyed, and undamaged property within 60 days with complete details.	
13. If you and the insurer disagree on the amount of loss, the question may be resolved through special appraisal procedures provided for in the fire insurance policy.	
14. You may cancel your policy without notice at any time and get part of the premium returned. The insurance company also may cancel at any time with a five-day written notice to you.	
15. By accepting a coinsurance clause in your policy, you get a substantial reduction in premiums. A coinsurance clause states that you must carry insurance equal to 80 or 90 percent of the value of the insured property. If you carry less than this, you cannot collect the full amount of your loss, even if the loss is small. What percent of your loss you can collect will depend on what percent of the full value of the property you have insured it for.	

16. If your loss is caused by someone else's negligence, the insurer has the right to sue this negligent third party for the amount it has paid you under the policy. This is known as the insurer's right of subrogation. However, the insurer will usually waive this right upon request.	
17. A building under construction can be insured for fire, lightning, extended coverage, vandalism, and malicious mischief.	

Liability Insurance	Action
1. Beware of legal liability limits. $1 million or more is not considered high or unreasonable even for a small business.	
2. Most liability policies require you to notify the insurer immediately after an incident on your property that might cause a future claim. This is true no matter how unimportant the incident may seem at the time it happens.	
3. Most liability policies, in addition to bodily injuries, may cover personal injuries (libel, slander, and so on) if these are specifically insured.	
4. Under certain conditions, your business may be subject to damage claims even from trespassers.	
5. You may be legally liable for damages even in cases where you used "reasonable care."	
6. Even if the suit against you is false or fraudulent, the liability insurer pays court costs, legal fees, and interest on judgments in addition to the liability judgments themselves.	
7. You can be liable for the acts of others under contracts you have signed with them. This liability is insurable.	
8. In some cases you may be held liable for fire loss to property of others in your care. Yet, this property would normally not be covered by your fire or general liability insurance. This risk can be covered by fire legal liability insurance or through requesting subrogation waivers from insurers of owners of the property.	

Automobile Insurance	Action
1. When an employee or a subcontractor uses his own car on your behalf, you can be legally liable even if you don't own a car or truck yourself.	
2. Five or more automobiles or motorcycles under one ownership and operated as a fleet for business purposes can generally be insured under a low-cost fleet policy against both material damage to your vehicle and liability to others for property damage or personal injury.	
3. You can often get deductibles of almost any amount and thereby reduce your premiums.	
4. Automobile medical payments insurance pays for medical claims, including your own, arising from automobile accidents regardless of the question of negligence.	
5. In most states, you must carry liability insurance or be prepared to provide other proof (surety bond) of financial responsibility when you are involved in an accident.	
6. You can purchase uninsured motorist protection to cover your own bodily injury claims from someone who has no insurance.	
7. Personal property stored in an automobile and not attached to it (for example, merchandise being delivered) is not covered under an automobile policy.	

Workers' Compensation	Action
1. Common law requires that an employer (1) provide his employees a safe place to work, (2) hire competent fellow employees, (3) provide safe tools, and (4) warn his employees of an existing danger.	
2. If an employer fails to provide the above, under both common law and workers' compensation laws he is liable for damage suits brought by an employee.	

3. State law determines the level or type of benefits payable under workers' compensation policies.	
4. Not all employees are covered by workers' compensation laws. The exceptions are determined by state law and therefore vary from state to state.	
5. In nearly all states, you are now legally required to cover your workers under workers' compensation.	
6. You can save money on workers' compensation insurance by seeing that your employees are properly classified.	
7. Rates for workers' compensation insurance vary from 0.1 percent of the payroll for "safe" occupations to about 25 percent or more of the payroll for very hazardous occupations.	
8. Most employers in most states can reduce their workers' compensation premium cost by reducing their accident rates below the average. They do this by using safety and loss-prevention measures.	
Desirable Coverages	
Some types of insurance coverage, while not absolutely essential, will add greatly to the security of your business. These coverages include business interruption insurance, crime insurance, glass insurance, and rent insurance.	
Business Interruption Insurance	*Action*
1. You can purchase insurance to cover fixed expenses that would continue if a fire shut down your business—such as salaries to key employees, taxes, interest, depreciation, and utilities—as well as the profits you would lose.	
2. Under properly written contingent business interruption insurance, you can also collect if fire or other peril closes down the business of a supplier or customer and this interrupts your business.	
3. The business interruption policy provides payments for amounts you spend to hasten the reopening of your business after a fire or other insured peril.	
4. You can get coverage for the extra expenses you suffer if an insured peril, while not actually closing your business down, seriously disrupts it.	
5. When the policy is properly endorsed, you can get business interruption insurance to indemnify you if your operations are suspended because of failure or interruption of the supply of power, light, heat, gas, or water furnished by a public utility company.	
Crime Insurance	*Action*
1. Burglary insurance excludes such property as accounts, fur articles in a showcase window, and manuscripts.	
2. Coverage is granted under burglary insurance only if there are visible marks of the burglar's forced entry.	
3. Burglary insurance can be written to cover, in addition to money in a safe, inventoried merchandise and damage incurred in the course of a burglary.	
4. Robbery insurance protects you from loss of property, money, and securities by force, trickery, or threat of violence on or *off* your premises.	
5. A comprehensive crime policy written just for small-business people is available. In addition to burglary and robbery, it covers other types of loss by theft, destruction, and disappearance of money and securities. It also covers thefts by your employees.	
6. If you are in a high-risk area and cannot get insurance through normal channels without paying excessive rates, you may be able to get help through the federal crime insurance plan. Your agent or state insurance commissioner can tell you where to get information about these plans.	

Glass Insurance	Action
1. You can purchase a special glass insurance policy that covers all risk to glass panels.	
2. The glass insurance policy covers not only the glass itself, but also its lettering and ornamentation, if these are specifically insured, and the costs of temporary plates or boarding up when necessary.	
3. After the glass has been replaced, full coverage is continued without any additional premium for the period covered.	

Rent Insurance	Action
1. You can buy rent insurance that will pay your rent if the property you lease becomes unusable because of fire or other insured perils and your lease calls for continued payments in such a situation.	
2. If you own property and lease it to others, you can insure against loss if the lease is canceled because of fire and you have to rent the property again at a reduced rental.	

Employee Benefit Coverages	
Insurance coverages that can be used to provide employee benefits include group life insurance, group health insurance, disability insurance, and retirement income. Key-man insurance protects the company against financial loss caused by the death of a valuable employee or partner.	

Group Life Insurance	Action
1. If you pay group insurance premiums and cover all employees up to a set amount, the cost to you is deductible for federal income tax purposes, and yet the value of the benefit is not taxable income to your employees.	
2. Most insurers will provide group coverages at low rates even if there are 10 or fewer employees in your group.	
3. If the employees pay part of the cost of the group insurance, state laws require that 75 percent of them must elect coverage for the plan to qualify as group insurance.	
4. Group plans permit an employee leaving the company to convert his group insurance coverage to a private plan, at the rate for his age, without a medical exam if he does so within 30 days after leaving his job.	

Group Life Insurance	Action
1. Group health insurance costs much less and provides more generous benefits for the worker than individual contracts would.	
2. If you pay the entire cost, individual employees cannot be dropped from a group plan unless the entire group policy is canceled.	
3. Generous programs of employee benefits, such as group health insurance, tend to reduce labor turnover.	

Disability Insurance	Action
1. Workers' compensation insurance pays an employee only for time lost because of work injuries and work-related sickness—not for time lost because of disabilities incurred off the job. But you can purchase, at a low premium, insurance to replace the lost income of workers who suffer short-term or long-term disability not related to their work.	
2. You can get coverage that provides employees with an income for life in case of permanent disability resulting from work-related sickness or accident.	

Retirement Insurance	Action
1. If you are self-employed, you can get an income tax deduction for funds used for retirement for you and your employees through plans of insurance or annuities approved for use under the Employees Retirement Income Security Act of 1974 (ERISA).	
2. Annuity contracts may provide for variable payments in the hope of giving the annuitants some protection against the effects of inflation. Whether fixed or variable, an annuity can provide retirement income that is guaranteed for life.	
Key-Man Insurance	Action
1. One of the most serious setbacks that can come to a small company is the loss of a key man. But your key man can be insured with life insurance and disability insurance owned by and payable to your company.	
2. Proceeds of a key-man policy are not subject to income tax, but premiums are not a deductible business expense.	
3. The cash value of key-man insurance, which accumulates as an asset of the business, can be borrowed against and the interest and dividends are not subject to income tax as long as the policy remains in force.	

WORKSHEET 7

Designing a Marketing Research Questionnaire

Very basic classification data can usually be completed by the interviewer before the interview. Complicated or very personal data should go at the end of the questionnaire.	Name of Interviewer _____ Date _____ Name of Respondent _____ Phone _____ Address _____ Other (nonpersonal) relevant data_____

The introductory statement establishes rapport with the interviewee. It should not be read, but rather put in the interviewer's own words. This introduction will make the difference between success and failure for the interview.	Good morning, my name is _____, and I am conducting a marketing study for a new product (or service) called _____. The answers you give me to the following questions will help determine whether or not to introduce this new product (or service) idea, and what features to incorporate into the product. May I have a few minutes of your time?

Product description tells the interviewee about the product or service. It should be a complete description of the product. Do not try to oversell the product; that may bias the results.	The benefits of this product are: 1. _____ 2. _____ 3. _____

Initial impression questions should appear first. They should be noncomplicated, nonpersonal, closed-end questions. Attitude scales are used to determine the intensity of the respondents' feelings. Open-ended questions are useful for determining why the person feels the way he or she does.	1. What is your immediate reaction to this idea *Positive*　　　　　　　　*Negative* Great _____　　　　　　So-So _____ Like it very much _____　I do not particularly like it _____ Like it somewhat _____　I do not like it at all _____ Why do you say that? Please explain.

Buying intentions are important to determine. A person may like the idea, but not want to buy it. If one can determine why they would not, perhaps the product can be revised to better meet their demands.

2. Which of the following best expresses your feeling about buying this product if it were available to you?

Positive
I'm absolutely sure I would buy it ___
I'm almost sure I would buy it ___

I probably would buy it ___

Negative
I probably would not buy it ___
I am almost sure I would not buy it ___
I am absolutely sure I would not buy it ___

Why do you say that? Please explain.

Product appeals must be determined, so as to be able to effectively promote the product. Such information will indicate what to emphasize and what to de-emphasize.

3. Tell me, all things considered, what is there about this product idea that appeals to you most. What do you consider its most important advantages?

Appeals to Most
1.
2.
3.

Advantages
1.
2.
3.

Pricing is an important aspect. Here one can determine a relative demand curve for the product. It is difficult for the consumer to answer this question precisely, but it should at least give the entrepreneur an idea of the price range.

4. How much do you think such a product would cost?

The retail outlet where the product would be most likely to be found is important.

5. Where would you expect to buy such a product?

The advertising medium to use must also be determined. Sometimes consumers do not like a product for minor reasons, and when these reasons are eliminated, they will buy. The more difficult, tiring questions should be placed at the end of the interview.

6. Where would you expect such a product to be advertised?

Not infrequently the person you are interviewing will come up with good ideas and concepts you may have missed in your questionnaire.

7. Are there any suggestions you would care to make that you think might improve this product?

Classification data of a personal nature should be asked at the end of the interview. Never ask for a person's specific age or income directly, because they could resent it, feeling this information is too personal. Always use a range.

Classification data:

1. In what category does your age fall?
19 or below ___
20-29 ___
30-39 ___
40-49 ___
50-59 ___
60-69 ___
70 or older

2. In what category does your family income fall?
19,000 or below ___
20,000 – 39,999 ___
40,000 – 59,999 ___
60,000 – 79,999 ___
80,000 – 99,000 ___
100,000 or more

3. Check one: female   married ___ single ___
                 male   married ___ single ___

Always close with a friendly thank you. It's the right thing to do, and also you may want to interview them in the future.

Thank you for your cooperation!

WORKSHEET 8

Appraising a Primary Research Study

Follow this checklist to insure your marketing research study will be complete. If you use it, research should provide you with excellent results.

1. Review of research objectives	Yes	Needs Work
a. Research objectives are consistent with overall problem or question.		
b. Objectives consider prior research done and secondary research available.		

2. Overall study design	Yes	Needs Work
a. The concept of the research is relevant to what you want to find out.		
b. The terminology you use is easily understandable.		
c. The design of your study is a clear bridge from question to solution.		
d. You have eliminated biases in your questions that may influence results.		
e. If necessary, you have preserved the anonymity of respondents.		
f. Ethical considerations have been taken into account.		
g. Your organization for administrating the study is clear.		

3. Methods used	Yes	Needs Work
a. The right populations (market segments) will be sampled.		
b. The data collection methods planned are unbiased.		
c. You have anticipated potential errors or mistakes in data collection and eliminated them.		
d. If sampling was used, the sample is representative of your target market.		
e. The plan for processing the data is clear.		
f. The categories used in tabulation are meaningful for the results.		
g. The statistical methods you selected for the analysis are appropriate.		

4. Actions and Follow-Up	Yes	Needs Work
a. You have thought through potential results and how this will affect your actions or recommendations for actions to others.		
b. All action possibilities will be considered.		
c. There is no information needed for action that is lacking in your planned study.		
d. Potential actions that will be taken as a result of your study are within your organization's capability of being performed.		

WORKSHEET 9

Important Questions to Ask *Before* Developing a New Product*

Your Company Strengths	Yes	No
Is manufacturing your company's strength?		
Are your production personnel highly skilled?		
Do you prefer a product with a high ratio of labor to production costs?		
Do you have skilled industrial design expertise available?		
Do you have production equipment currently available?		
Is your production equipment currently underutilized?		
Do you currently have a strong sales force?		
Is your current product line too limited?		
Do you have a competitive advantage in a particular technology?		
Do you have significant cash or credit resources available?		
Do you have a reputation for high quality?		
Do you have a reputation for low cost or high value?		
Market Preference		
Do you prefer a particular industry?		
Do you prefer a product sold to retail consumers?		
Do you prefer a product sold to industrial users?		
Do you prefer a product sold to the government?		
Do you prefer a product with long usage?		
Do you prefer fad products?		
Do you prefer a consumable item?		
Do you prefer a particular method of distribution?		
Would you consider a product limited to a particular locality?		
Do you prefer a product for a specialty market?		
Do you prefer a product sold through mass merchandising?		
Do you intend to sell your product abroad?		
Have you determined the break-even point for this new product?		
Have you determined the Return on Investment (ROI) for this new product?		
Have you determined the payback period (how long it will take to recoup your investment for this new product?		
Is price range important to be consistent with your present or planned business?		
Have you set sales volume objectives over the next three years?		
At what sales volume does a product exceed your company's capability?		
Product Status		
Is the source of the new product idea important to you?		
Will you accept a product that cannot be protected through patent or copyright?		
Are you willing to license a patent, process, etc. from someone else?		
Are you willing to develop an idea or concept to a patentable stage?		
Are you willing to accept a product that has previously failed in the marketplace?		
Are you willing to enter a joint venture with another company?		
Would you merge with or buy a company that has good products but needs your company's strengths?		

Your Company Strengths	Yes	No
The Product Configuration		
Are there any maximum size limitations to a product you can manufacture?		
Are there any weight or size limitations?		
Is production time a factor?		
Do you prefer a product made of a certain material?		
Are there any manufacturing processes important to the type of product you select?		
Is quality control a significant factor?		
Finance		
Have you established an overall budget for this product?		
Have individual budgets been established for finding, acquisition, development, market research, manufacturing, and marketing the new product?		
Has a time period been established by which a new product must become self-supporting, profitable, or capable of generating cash?		
Does the new product require a certain profit margin to be compatible with your financial resources or company objectives?		
Has external long-range financing been explored for your new product?		
Have you determined average inventory to sales ratio for the new product?		
Have you determined average aging of accounts receivable for your new product?		
Does the product have seasonal aspects?		

*This checklist is based on a checklist originally developed by John B. Lang and published in *Finding a New Product for Your Company*, by the U.S. Small Business Administration.

WORKSHEET 10

Screening Questions*

Screening questions act as a shield to eliminate products that you shouldn't even consider before you waste a lot of time, money, or other resources. Your answers to these questions can lead to a well thought-out guide as to the acceptability of any potential new product. A short condensed profile helps communicate your needs. Such a profile also indicates a high degree of professional management that sources of new products will welcome.

Company Operations

- How compatible is the product concept with the current product lines? _____
- Does it represent an environmental hazard or threat to your production facility and to the facilities of your neighbors? _____
- Would it unreasonably interrupt manufacturing, engineering or marketing activities? _____
- Could you meet the after-sale service requirements that would be demanded by customers? _____

Potential Market

- What is the size of the potential market? _____
- Where is the market located? _____
- What would be your potential market share? _____
- How diversified is the need for the product? Is it a one-industry or multi-industry product? _____
- How fast do you anticipate the market for the concept to grow? _____
- How stable would such a market be in a recession? _____

Concept Marketability

- Who would be your competitors? _____
- How good is their product? _____
- How well capitalized are potential competitors? _____
- How important is their product to the survival of their business? _____
- How is your product differentiated from the competition's? Will the differentiation provide a market advantage? _____
- Could you meet or beat the competition's price? _____
- Is the product normally sold through your current distribution channels, or would you have to make special arrangements? _____
- Do you have qualified sales personnel? _____
- Do you have suitable means by which to promote the product? _____
- What would you anticipate to be the life expectancy of the product? Is it going to move through the various life cycle stages in six months, six years, or sixty years? _____
- Will the product be offensive to the environment in which it will be used? _____

Engineering and Production

- What is the technical feasibility of the product? _____
- Do you have the technical capability to design it? _____
- Can it be manufactured at a marketable cost? _____
- Will the necessary production materials be readily available? _____
- Do you have the production capabilities to build it? _____
- Do you have adequate storage facilities for the raw materials and completed product? _____
- Do you have adequate testing devices for proper quality control of the product? _____

Financial

- What is your required return on investment (ROI)? _____
- What is your anticipated ROI for this product? _____
- Do you have the available capital? _____
- What would be the pay-back period? _____
- What is your break-even point? _____

Legal

- Is the product patentable or is some other means of protecting your exclusivity available? _____
- Can you meet legal restrictions regarding labeling, advertising, shipment, etc.? _____
- How significant are product warranty problems likely to be? _____
- Is the product vulnerable to existing or pending legislation? _____

---

*Adapted from Tom W. White, "Use Variety of Internal, External Sources to Gather and Screen New Product Ideas," *Marketing News*, September 10, 1983; p.12.

WORKSHEET 11

Quick Go/No-Go Checklist

1. Does this product or service fit your needs, interests, background, and abilities? _____
   _____

2. What is your realistic assessment of the chances of success? _____

3. Do you know where to obtain the services of everyone needed to complete this project? _____
   _____

4. What advantage(s) will this product or service have over its competing products or services? _____
   _____

5. Is there a real market for the new or improved product or service? _____

6. Is this market profitable, and will you be able to defend it easily against competitors? _____
   _____

7. Do you really know how you will sell and distribute this product or service? _____
   _____

8. Does the product or service fit with your present line, or if you are not currently in business, can you easily expand this product or service into a full line? _____
   _____

9. Will the product fill a permanent or long-term need, or will it be a fad product or service? (*Note:* You can make money either way, but it is important that you know up front.) _____
   _____

10. Can the product be made with your present equipment? If not, what will the tooling cost and how soon and how easily will you be able to recoup your investment? _____
    _____

WORKSHEET 12

Selecting Products or Services from Many Opportunities

Step 1: Decide the relative importance of the factors listed. Assign a percentage value of importance to each. The total percentages for all factors must equal 100 percent. You may assign a value of 0 percent for factors that are completely unimportant. You may also add to the list of factors.

Step 2: Look at each factor individually. For each factor assign 0 to 10 points. Those products that seem very good in relation to a particular factor receive 10 points. Those that are very poor receive 0 points. Complete a separate sheet below for each product.

Step 3: Multiply the importance percentage times the points assigned for each factor. Put the results in the final value column.

Step 4: Add the final values for each factor and arrive at a total product/service value for that product or service.

Step 5: Repeat this process for each product or service being compared.

Step 6: Compare total product/service values for all products and services. That product or service with the highest total product/service value is the one that you should introduce.

Product or Service _____

Factors	Relative Importance Percentage	Point Value	Final Value
Demand for product			
Strength			
Period			
Need			
Market			
Size			
Location			
Competition			
Product			
Compatibility with current line			
Uniqueness of features			
Price			
Protection			
Company Strengths			
Marketing			
Location			
Special facilities			
Production			
Financial Considerations			
Capital budgeting			
ROI			
Pay-back			
Cash flow			
Product Development			
Technical risk			
Producibility			
Scheduling			

TOTALS   100%   ⬅   **TOTAL PRODUCT/SERVICE VALUE**

WORKSHEET 13

Things to Consider If New Product/Service Introduction Is Failing

If things are going wrong, action should be taken as soon as possible to correct the problem. If any of the following occur as you begin new product introduction or development, stop, heed, and take action as soon as possible.

SOURCE OF WARNING SIGNAL FEEDBACK	FEEDBACK	ACTION TO TAKE	ACTION NOTES
Consumer	Price	Find out if price is too low or too high and adjust price	
Consumer	Hard to use product	Modify product or educate	
Consumer	Not convinced of value	Modify advertising/promotion	
Retailer or Wholesaler	Low rate of turnover	Increase consumer advertising/promotion	
Retailer or Wholesaler	Fear of loss of current sales	Increase trade advertising and address issue	
Retailer or Wholesaler	Potential servicing problems	Modify product or address through promotion/salesmen	
Retailer or Wholesaler	Field already crowded	Increase trade advertising and promotion to address issue	
Retailer or Wholesaler	Hard to ship or display in store	Redesigning packaging or store display	
Retailer or Wholesaler	Product needs demonstration	Consider demonstration alternatives	
You	Difficult to get right materials	Focus on this issue	
You	Raw materials subject to price	Buy in larger quantities fluctuations or scarcity	
You	Production could slow down other products	Analyze alternatives and make decision	
You	Patent protection may not be possible	Consider alternative means of protection including getting to market first and establishing position	
You	Product difficult for salesman to demonstrate	Modify/change demonstration	
You	Competitor dominates market	Consider a niching strategy where you will dominate a small segment	

WORKSHEET 14*

Establishing Costs, Sales Volume, and Profits

For questions for which your answer is "no," decide whether you must carry out the action in order to establish your price. Disregard those not applicable to your business.

QUESTION	YES	NO
COSTS AND PRICES If you set the price by applying a small markup, you may be overlooking other cost factors that are connected with that item. The questions in this section will help you to collect the information to determine pricing on specific types of items.		
Do you know which of your operating costs remain the same regardless of sales volume?		
Do you know which of your operating costs decrease percentage-wise as your sales volume increases?		
Have you ever figured out the break-even point for your items selling at varying price levels?		
Do you look behind high gross margin percentages? (For example, a product with a high gross margin may also be a slow turnover item with high handling costs. Thus it may be less profitable than lower margin items that turn over faster.)		
When you select items for price reductions, do you project the effects on profits? (For example, if a food marketer considers whether to run canned ham or rump steak on sale, an important cost factor is labor. Practically none is involved in featuring canned ham; however, a rump steak sale requires the skill of a meat-cutter, and this labor cost might mean little or no profits.)		
PRICING AND SALES VOLUME An effective pricing program should also consider sales volume. For example, high prices might limit your sales volume while low prices might result in a large but unprofitable volume. The following questions should be helpful in determining what is right for your situation.		
Have you considered setting a sales volume goal and then studying to see if your prices will help you reach it?		
Have you set a target of a certain number of new customers for next year? (If so, how can pricing help you to get them?)		
Should you limit the quantities of low-margin items that any one customer can buy when they are on sale? (If so, will you advertise this policy?)		
What is your policy when a sale item is sold out before the end of the advertised period? Do you allow disappointed customers to buy the item later at the sale price?		
PRICING AND PROFITS Prices should help bring in sales that are profitable over the long haul. The following questions will help you think about pricing policies and their effect on your annual profits.		
Do you have all the facts on costs, sales, and competitive behavior?		

Do you set prices to accomplish definite objectives? (Example: a 1-percent profit increase over last year).		
Do you have a goal of a certain level of profits in dollars and in percent of sales?		
Do you keep records which will give you the needed facts on profits, losses, and prices?		
Do you review your pricing practices periodically to make sure that they are helping to achieve your profit goals?		
JUDGING THE BUYER, TIMING, AND COMPETITORS The questions in this part are designed to help you check your practices for judging the buyer (your customers), your timing, and your competitors.		
THE BUYER AND PRICING STRATEGY After you have your facts on costs, the next point must be the CUSTOMER—whether you are changing a price, putting in a new item, or checking out your present price practices. Knowledge of your customers helps you to determine how to vary prices in order to get the average gross margin you need for making a profit. (For example, to get an average gross margin of 35 percent, some retailers put a low markup—10 percent, for instance—on items that they promote as traffic builders and use high markup—sometimes as much as 60 percent—on slow-moving items.) The following questions should be helpful in checking your knowledge about your customers.		
Do you know whether your customers shop around or buy impulsively and for which items this is true?		
Do you know how your customers make their comparisons? (Example: newspaper ads, television, the Internet, hearsay?)		
Are you trying to appeal to customers who buy on price alone? To those who buy on quality alone? To those who seek the best value for their money?		
Do your customers tell you that your prices are comparable with those of your competitors, or higher or lower?		
Do you know which item (or types of items) your customers ask for even if you raise the price?		
Do you know which items (or types of items) your customers no longer buy when you raise the price?		
Do certain items seem to appeal to customers more than others when you run sales?		
Have you used your individual sales records to classify your present customers according to the volume of their purchases?		
Will your customers buy more if you use multiple pricing? (For example, 3 for 39 cents for products with rapid turnover.)		
Do your customers respond to odd prices more readily than even prices, for example, 99 cents rather than $1?		
Have you decided on a pricing strategy to create a favorable price image with your customers? (For example, a retailer with 8,000 different items might decide to make a full margin on all medium or slow movers while featuring—at low price levels—the remaining fast movers.)		

If you are trying to build a quality price image, do your individual customer records, such as charge account statements, show that you are selling a larger number of higher priced items than you were 12 months ago?		
Do your records of individual customer accounts and your observations of customer behavior in the store show price as the important factor in their buying under general or special conditions?		
TIME AND PRICING Effective merchandising means that you have the right product at the right place, at the right price, and at the right time. All are important, but timing is the critical element for the small retailer. The following questions should be helpful in determining what is the right time for you to adjust prices.		
Are you a "leader" or a "follower" in announcing your price reductions? (The follower, even though he matches his competitors, may create a negative impression on his customers.)		
Have you studied your competitors to see whether they follow any sort of pattern when making price changes? (For example, do some of them run clearance sales earlier than others.)		
Is there a pattern to the kinds of items that competitors promote at lower prices at certain times of the month or year?		
Have you decided whether it is better to take early markdowns on seasonal or style goods or to run a clearance sale at the end of the season?		
Have you made regular annual sales, such as Anniversary Sales, Fall Clearance, or Holiday Cleanup, so popular that many customers wait for them rather than buying in season?		
When you change a price, do you make sure that all customers know about it through price tags and so on?		
Do you try to time price reductions so they can be promoted in your advertising?		
COMPETITION AND PRICING When you set prices, you have to consider how your competitors might react to your prices. The starting place is learning as much as you can about their price structures. The following questions are designed to help you check out this phase of pricing.		
Do you use all the available channels of information to keep you up to date on your competitors' price policies? (Some useful sources of information are: things your customers tell you; the competitor's price list and catalogs, if he uses them; his advertising; reports from your suppliers; trade paper studies; and shoppers employed by you.)		
Should your policy be to try always to sell above or below competition or only to meet it?		
Is there a pattern to the way your competitors respond to your price cuts?		
Is the leader pricing of your competitors affecting your sales volume to such an extent that you must alter your pricing policy on individual items (or types of items) of merchandise?		
Do you realize that no two competitors have identical cost curves? (This difference in costs means that certain price levels may be profitable for you but unprofitable for your competitor or vice versa.)		

Practices that Can Help Offset Price Some small-business people take advantage of the fact that price is not always the determining factor in making a sale. They supply customer services and offer other inducements to offset the effect of competitors' lower prices. Delivery service is an example. A comfortable shopper's atmosphere is another. The following questions are designed to help you take a look at some of these practices.		
Do the items or services you sell have advantages for which customers are willing to pay a little more?		
From personal observation of customer behavior in your store, can you tell about how much more customers will pay for such advantages?		
Should you change your services so as to create an advantage for which your customers will be willing to pay?		
Does your advertising emphasize customer benefits rather price?		
Are you using the most common nonprice competitive tools? (For example, have you tried to alter your product or service to the existing market? Have you tried stamps, bonus purchase gifts, or other plans for building repeat business?)		
Should policies on returned goods be changed so as to impress your customers more favorably?		
If you sell repair services, have you checked out your guarantee policy?		
Should you alter assortments of merchandise to increase sales?		

*This worksheet is based on material that originated with Joseph D. O'Brien, then a professor of marketing at Boston College.

WORKSHEET 15
Developing Profiles of Target Markets

Note: Complete a separate profile for each market you intend to pursue. Check only those that apply.

PERSONAL DEMOGRAPHIC INFORMATION

1. Sex: male_____   female _____
2. Age: Under 6 _____ 6 to 11 _____ 12 to 17 _____ 18 to 24 _____ 25 to 34 _____
   35 to 44 _____ 45 to 54 _____ 55 to 64 _____ 65 & over _____
3. Martial Status: Married _____ Single (never married) _____ Widowed _____
   Divorced or separated _____
4. Education: Grade school or less (grades1-8) _____ Some high school (grades 9-12) _____
   Graduated from high school _____ Some college _____ Graduated from college _____
   Some postgraduate college work _____ Masters degree _____ Doctoral Degree _____
5. Principal Language Spoken at Home: English _____ Spanish _____ Other _____
6. Ethnicity: _____
7. Employment: Unemployed_____ Not employed, looking for work_____ Self-employed at
   home _____ Self-employed outside the home _____ Employed, working for someone
   else _____ Employed full time (30 hours per week or more) _____ Employed part time
   (less than 30 hours per week)_____
8. Occupation: Professional and technical _____ Managers, officials, and proprietors, except
   farm _____ Clerical _____ Sales _____ Craftsman _____ Foreman _____ Nonfarm laborers
   _____ Service workers _____ Private household workers _____ Farm managers _____
   Farm laborers _____ Farm foreman _____ Armed forces _____ Retired _____
   Student _____ Other _____
9. Geographic Region: Northeast _____ Metropolitan New York _____ Mid-Atlantic _____
   East Central _____ Metropolitan Chicago _____ West Central _____ Southeast _____
   Southwest _____ Metropolitan Los Angeles _____ Remaining Pacific Rim _____
10. Geographic Type: Central City _____ Urban Fringe (suburbs) _____ Town _____ Rural _____
11. Population of city or town: 25,000 or less _____ 50,000 to 25,001 _____
    100,000 to 50,001 _____ 250,000 to 100,001 _____ 500,000 to 250,001 _____
    1,000,000 to 500,001 _____ 5,000,000 to 1,000,001 _____ 5,000,001 or more _____

HOUSEHOLD DEMOGRAPHIC INFORMATION

12. Household Size: 1 member _____ 2 members _____ 3 members _____ 4 members _____
    5 members _____ 6 members _____ or more
13. Number of Children: None _____ One _____ Two _____ Three or more _____
14. Children in household by age : Under 2 years _____ 2 to 5 years _____ 6 to 10 years _____
    11 to 13 years _____ 14 to 18 years _____ 19 years or older _____
15. Other dependents in household by sex: males _____ females _____
16. Household income: Under $15,000 _____ $15,001 to $25,000 _____ $25,001 to $50,000 _____
    $50,001 to $100,000 _____ $100,000 or greater _____
17. Income Earners in the Family: Male _____ Female _____ Children _____ Other _____
18. Residence Ownership: Own _____ Rent _____
19. Dwelling Characteristics: House (unattached) _____ Attached home _____ Apartment _____
    Mobile home or trailer _____ Other _____
20. Type of work of primary wage earner: unskilled _____ blue-collar worker _____ self-employed
    business owner _____ self-employed professional _____ employed professional or
    manager _____ independently wealthy/unemployed _____ unemployed _____ other _____

PSYCHOGRAPHIC INFORMATION

21. Typical member of target market is: Very competitive _____ Usually follows others _____
    Wants things arranged, organized, secure, and predictable _____ Self-centered _____ Seeks
    independence _____. A joiner _____ Analyzes self and others _____ Seeks aid, help, and
    advice from others _____ Desires to control and/or lead others _____ Feels inferior _____
    Wants to help others _____ Is seeking new occupations _____ Sticks to a task and works hard to
    complete a job _____ Enjoys social activities _____ Ambitious _____ Self-confident _____
    Stressed _____

LIFE-STYLE PREFERENCES AND ATTITUDES

22. Leisure activities: Entertaining _____ Movies _____ Plays _____ Concerts _____ Opera
    _____ Dinner _____ Reading _____ Listening to music _____ Watching television _____
    Internet activities _____ Playing games _____ Watching sporting events _____ Cooking _____
    Other _____

23. About the Family: Thinks the man should be the boss and run the family _____ Thinks the woman should be the boss and run the family _____ Believes marriage should be a partnership with no bosses _____ Thinks children should be an important part of most family decisions _____

24. Regarding dress: Likes to wear casual, comfortable clothes most of the time _____ Wants to look fashionable and stylish most of the time _____ Is concerned about a professional appearance most of the time _____

25. Physical Condition and Health: Is concerned about health _____ Is unconcerned about health _____ Has a health problem _____ Has a weight problem _____ A frequent user of nonprescription drugs _____ A frequent user of vitamin, mineral, or herb supplements _____ Exercises regularly _____ Desires to exercise regularly, but does not do so _____

26. Finances: Is financially secure _____ Concerned about finances _____ Habitually in debt _____

27. Risk Preference: Conservative and does not take chances _____ Willing to take calculated risks _____ Frequently takes chances _____

28. Buying Less Expensive Products: Picks the same brand habitually in most cases _____ Looks for bargains, deals, premiums _____ Wants quality and will pay extra to get it _____ Rarely takes chances on unknown products or manufacturers _____ Likes to try new and different products and services _____ Plans shopping carefully with a list of needs and makes an excursion out of the trip _____ Analyzes ingredients, weight, and package size _____ Never reads the information on a package to find out what it contains _____ Relies heavily on the opinion of others prior to purchase _____ Relies heavily on advertisements for information _____

MEDIA USE

29. Primary Sources of Information on Products or Services: Word-of-mouth from friends _____ Newspaper ads _____ Radio ads _____ Television ads _____ Direct mail _____ Telephone solicitation _____ Ads on busses and transit vehicles _____ Billboards _____ E-mail _____ Internet _____ Other _____

30. Uses media at these times: 6 A.M. to 10:00 AM _____ 10:00 A.M. to 3:00 P.M. _____ 3:00 P.M. to 7:00 PM _____ 7:00 P.M. to midnight _____ Midnight to 6:00 A.M. _____ Pays particular attention to these types of stories or programs: Local news _____ National news _____ Weather _____ Sports _____ Business and finance _____ Editorials and interviews _____ Classified _____ Daytime serials _____ Comics or comedy shows _____ Crime news or programs _____ Adventure _____ Quizzes or game shows _____ Movies _____ Self-help stories _____ How-to-do-it _____ Theater arts and entertainment _____ Editorials _____ Interviews _____ Travel _____ Drama _____ Soap Operas _____ Reality shows _____ Dramas _____ Situation comedies _____ Science Fiction _____ Cooking and homemaking _____ Cartoons _____ Beauty contests _____ Documentaries _____ Other _____

WORKSHEET 16
Developing an Advertising and Publicity Budget

Project	Month		Year to Date	
	Budget	Actual Expenditure	Budget	Actual Expenditure
Media				
Newspapers				
Radio				
TV				
Internet				
Literature				
Direct Mail				
Other				
Promotions Associated with Advertising				
Exhibits				
Displays				
Contests				
Sweepstakes				
Premiums				
Discount Coupons				
Other				
Advertising Expense				
Salaries				
Supplies				
Stationery				
Travel				
Postage				
Subscriptions				
Entertainment				
Dues				
Other				
Totals				

WORKSHEET 17
Sales Interview Objective Assessments

Objectively rating potential sales personnel during job interviews is particularly challenging because sales-people are trained to sell–a product, service, and themselves. Therefore, the more objective we can be regarding rating potential new hires, the better. One way of doing this is to use the semantic differential scales provided in this worksheet. This allows a good assessment both of the individual potential hire as well as a comparison with other candidates who may interview at a later time. Just circle the number that best represents your impression and then add these numbers. If you have special criteria to consider, just add it to the list.

1. General appearance

poor   1   2   3   4   5   6   7   8   9   10   excellent

2. Dress

poor   1   2   3   4   5   6   7   8   9   10   excellent

3. Verbal communication

poor   1   2   3   4   5   6   7   8   9   10   excellent

4. Technical knowledge

poor   1   2   3   4   5   6   7   8   9   10   excellent

5. Persuasiveness

poor   1   2   3   4   5   6   7   8   9   10   excellent

6. Flexibility

poor   1   2   3   4   5   6   7   8   9   10   excellent

7. Attitude toward work

poor   1   2   3   4   5   6   7   8   9   10   excellent

8. Intelligence

poor   1   2   3   4   5   6   7   8   9   10   excellent

9. Ability to sell himself or herself

poor   1   2   3   4   5   6   7   8   9   10   excellent

10. Overall Impression

poor   1   2   3   4   5   6   7   8   9   10   excellent

Total Point Score _____ points

WORKSHEET 18
Determining Objectives and Resources for Trade Shows

To determine your objectives for going to a particular trade show in their order of importance, look at the list below. In the second column, rank each objective by its order of importance. In the third column, check off each objective as the resources have been allocated and you are fully prepared for the trade show. Work on the most important objectives, according to your ranking, first.

Objective	Your Ranking	Preparation Complete
To test market a new product		
To recruit new sales personnel or new sales representatives or dealers		
To develop new sales territories or new distribution channels		
To encourage your customers to bring their technical problems to you for solutions		
To introduce new products or new services or policies		
To make sales		
To demonstrate equipment that could not otherwise be shown easily to a customer		
To bring together your representatives, internal sales and marketing people, and other key executives for conferences during the trade show		
To expand your list of potential customers		
To check on your competition and what they are offering		
To increase the morale of your sales personnel and representatives and encourage them to work together		
To build your company's image in the industry		
To demonstrate your interest in and support of the sponsoring association		
Other		
Other		
Other		

WORKSHEET 19

Deciding on Which Trade Shows to Attend

It will not be possible for you to attend all trade shows, even if this were physically possible for you to do. It would cost too much money and take too much of your time and other resources. In order to make decisions about which shows to attend, use this worksheet. First look at each factor in column one. In column two, assign an importance percentage for each factor so that no matter how many factors you have listed, the total is exactly 100 percent. For example, if the number of people attending was very important to you, you might assign an importance percentage of 40 percent. Let's assume that the geographical area was of very little importance to you and you assigned an importance percentage of only 1 percent. What you are saying is that the number attending the trade show is 40 times as important as the geographical area that these people come from. Of course, for some, the opposite could be true, and the geographical area of the show attendees might be the most important factor. In column three, assign a numerical value to each factor from 1 to 5 according to how well each criterion is met. For example, if this show had very high attendance, you would want to assign a 5; if low attendance, assign only a 1. Now, multiply column two and column three and put the numerical result in column four. Total these up and repeat the process on a different sheet using the same system. By comparing the total values, you can differentiate the high value shows that you should attend from the lesser value shows, which you should skip.

Important Factors (Column 1)	Importance to You in Percent (Column 2)	How Well Criteria Are Met (Column 3)	Value of Each Factor (Column 2 × Column 3)
Who has attended in the past and who are the people that these shows attract?			
How many attend?			
The geographical areas from which the attendees come			
The industries and markets the attendees represent			
The job titles and responsibilities held by the attendees			
The topics of seminars, workshops, and events that may be offered at the show			
The physical location of various exhibit booths available and the location relative to other events going on, entrances, exits, and so forth			
Other services provided by the show sponsors			
	100%	Total Value ⟹	

WORKSHEET 20

Determining Size of Booth Requirements at a Trade Show

Calculate the number of prospects for your product or service likely to attend the show	**A.**
Divide this number by 2	**B.**
Number of hours the show will be open	**C.**
Divide B by C to get the number of visitors per hour	**D.**
Divide D by 15 prospects, the average number of prospects a salesperson sees in an hour	**E.**
Multiply E by 50 (square feet) to get the number of square feet necessary for the salespeople	**F.**
The square footage required for your display, furniture, and equipment	**G.**
Add F and G to get the total square footage required **Total Square Footage Required** ⟹	

WORKSHEET 21

Checklist for Developing a Web Site

Actions to Take	Done	Date to Complete
Pre-Setup		
Target market identified		
Purpose of Web site established		
Look at competitive Web sites		
Features needed on your Web site documented		
General layout of home page and others noted		
Name of site and desired URL chosen		
Frequency of site updating considered		
Duties and responsibilities of those running the site fixed		
Means and costs for promoting the site documented		
Consider potential links to other sites		
Setup		
Internet Service Provider (ISP) selected		
URL registered		
Software program for developing the site selected		
Site developed		
Site loaded online		
Check site for appearance, graphics, speed, navigation, use with different browsers		
Correct site where needed		
Post Setup		
Send link requests to other sites		
Begin search engine submittals and optimization		
Begin Web site marketing campaign		

WORKSHEET 22

Checklist for Getting a Web Site Listed in a Top Position with Search Engines

Actions to Take	Done	Date to Complete
Develop and register your domain name.		
Select and include keywords and phrases describing your product or service frequently and prominently in your Web site.		
Ensure that keywords and phrases are included in your ⟨title⟩ tag.		
Ensure that meta tags containing a more detailed description contain your keywords and phrases		
Ensure that the first paragraph of your Web page again repeats your keywords and phrases.		
Check repeats of major keywords and phrases. Unless crucial to your presentation, don't repeat more than five times in the title, headings, or first paragraph, and more than ten times per page.		
Start your campaign to link to other Web sites—popularity is demonstrated by number of links and frequency of clicks counts!		
Ensure that your site has one consistent theme. You can sell many products or services, but they should all relate to the one theme of your site throughout.		
Monitor your site frequently in rankings with major search engines and keep your site up to date.		

WORKSHEET 23

Checklist for Promoting a Web Site

Actions to Take	Done	Date to Complete
Think of your site as a sales document (it is!), and ensure that it is supporting your basic concept, theme, and what you are trying to accomplish.		
Check your site for grammatical and spelling errors. Seek perfection.		
Make certain that everything on your site works properly. Check it visually not only on your computer, but on other computers as well.		
Choose keywords and phrases that optimize your site for search engines.		
Submit your Web site to the major search engines.		
Start a campaign to promote an exchange of links to other Web sites.		
Consider the use of banners on other sites to link to your site.		
Write articles that appear in media read by your target audience and give your Web site.		
Develop a short speech of interest to individuals interested in your offering.		
Try to find a publicity "hook" that might interest media regarding what you do, and do a publicity release.		
Think of a way of linking your Web site to non-Internet advertising read by your target audience.		

WORKSHEET 24

Checklist for Obtaining a Patent

Task	In Process	Done
Maintain invention records and periodic review and signature by two witnesses if process not yet started.		
Obtain services of U.S. patent attorney if desired.		
Research material at U.S. Patent Office Web site to decide on type of patent required.		
Submit patent disclosure through U.S. Patent Office's Disclosure Program.		
Search for prior patents at Patent Office or Depository Libraries.		
Prepare patent application and submit.		
Include "patent applied for" on the copies of the invention you produce.		
Consider patenting in foreign countries and if so, obtain services of foreign attorney.		
Revise application and resubmit if required.		
Include the U.S. patent number on the copies of the invention once the patent has been awarded.		

WORKSHEET 25

Checklist for Obtaining a Copyright

Task	In Process	Done
Research material at U.S. copyright office Web site to decide on type of copyright needed.		
Decide on type of copyright indicia to be included with your publication.		
Put the copyright indicia on the publications you produce (remember that unlike patents, a copyright is automatic as soon as you create the publication—you're just registering it).		
Obtain copyright registration forms from the Copyright Office.		
Submit the completed form with fee and copy of your published material.		

WORKSHEET 26

Checklist for Obtaining a Trademark

Task	In Process	Done
Decide on the trademark you'd like to adopt.		
Research your desired trademark to ensure it hasn't been previously adopted.		
Put "TM" or "SM" on your material.		
Obtain the necessary forms from the Patent and Trademark Office to register your trademark.		
Once registration is complete, put the Registration mark ® on your material instead of "TM" or "SM."		

WORKSHEET 27

Forecasting Labor Requirements

Project/ Task	Type of Individual Required	HOURS OF WORK ESTIMATED BY MONTH											
		Jan	Feb	Mar	Apr	May	Jun	Jul	Aug	Sep	Oct	Nov	Dec
Monthly Labor Requirements by Title (1)													
Current Labor Resources on Hand (2)													
Additional Labor Required (1) – (2)													

APPENDIX

USEFUL WEB SITES THAT CAN HELP YOU DEVELOP A MARKETING PLAN

Business and Marketing Plans has a template and tools and a library of thousands of plans that can be searched.
URL: http://www.morebusiness.com/templates_worksheets/bplans/

How Marketing Plans Work has links to numerous important subareas including the executive summary, developing strategies, positioning, the SWOT analysis, and more.
URL: http://money.howstuffworks.com/marketing-plan.htm

How to Write a Marketing Plan is a short article that covers all the main topics and provides a good and quick overview of the process.
URL: http://www.infotoday.com/mls/jun99/how-to.htm

How to Write a Marketing Plan and Sample Marketing Plans is one of the most popular sections of The Marketing Virtual Library and part of *KnowThis.com.* It contains many of the basics plus links to a lot more, including sample plans.
URL: http://www.knowthis.com/general/marketplan.htm

How to Write a Marketing Plan by The Write Market has links to many subareas useful for developing a marketing plan and a lot of additional information not covered anywhere else.
URL: http://www.thewritemarket.com/marketing-plan.shtml

Marketing Plans, Programs, and Small Business Management Articles & Resources. This site contains many links that can help with marketing planning including: "10 Tips to Help Calm Marketing Plan Panic," "Internet Marketing Plan Success," "Developing a Website Marketing Plan," "When You Write a Marketing Plan," and sample marketing plans.
URL: http://www.websitemarketingplan.com/

Marketing Teacher offers a free newsletter and a description and links of different parts of the plan and their importance.
URL: http://www.marketingteacher.com/Lessons/lesson_marketing_plan.htm

MPlans.com has articles, sample plans, products, services, marketing calculators, software, and other materials.
URL: http://www.mplans.com/

Small Business Development Center National Information Clearing House contains sample plans and links to both a 13-part series on how to develop a marketing plan and the Small Business Administration's course on how to develop a marketing plan.
URL: http://sbdcnet.utsa.edu/SBIC/marketing.htm

Index